I read everything Chuck Colson writes. He is one of the most brilliant thinkers and cultural analysts of our time. Today many people make the mistake of thinking the good life is all about *looking good, feeling good,* and *having the goods*. But the true good life comes from being and doing good. Read this, and be changed!

RICK WARREN
Author of *The Purpose-Driven Life*

Life is under attack. As a quadriplegic, I especially feel it. Whether it s pulling a feeding tube from a brain-damaged woman or pulling apart a human embryo for its stem cells, life-value is plummeting at breakneck speed. Why? And what should we do about it? In *The Good Life,* Chuck Colson gives measured and reasoned arguments that help us find the line and dr aw it in the sand. It s absolute reading for those who are looking for the  absolutes  in our society.

JONI EARECKSON TADA
Author of *Heaven*

With a generation of pioneering Christian service behind him, Colson here deploys a strategic sprawl of stories, his own among them, to show by object lesson how, despite everything, a faithful relationship with the Savior-God of the gospel constitutes the good life. In the face of today s skepticism, nihilism, and quiet or noisy despair, he makes his point with the compelling and inspiriting force that we have come to expect from him. This is a great read for Christians and non-Christians alike.

J. I. PACKER
Author of *Knowing God*

A four-star recipe for human flourishing. Chuck Colson knows how to help people thrive, and his knowledge arises from great depths of intelligence, determination, and pain.

CORNELIUS PLANTINGA JR.
Author of *Not the Way It's Supposed to Be*

"Drawing on his own experience and that of others, Chuck Colson makes a compelling case for the good life in a way that will seize the attention of believers, nonbelievers, and readers who don't know what to believe."

RICHARD JOHN NEUHAUS
Author of *Death on a Friday*

*the* GOOD LIFE

# *the* GOOD LIFE

## CHARLES COLSON

## HAROLD FICKETT

TYNDALE HOUSE PUBLISHERS, INC. WHEATON, ILLINOIS

Visit Tyndale's exciting Web site at www.tyndale.com

*TYNDALE* is a registered trademark of Tyndale House Publishers, Inc.

Tyndale's quill logo is a trademark of Tyndale House Publishers, Inc.

*The Good Life*

Copyright © 2005 by Charles Colson. All rights reserved.

Charles Colson photo taken by Russ Busby. All rights reserved.

Harold Fickett photo courtesy of *The Wichita Eagle*.

Designed by Jessie McGrath

Edited by Lynn Vanderzalm

Unless otherwise indicated, all Scripture quotations are taken from the *Holy Bible*, New International Version®. NIV®. Copyright © 1973, 1978, 1984 by International Bible Society. Used by permission of Zondervan Publishing House. All rights reserved.

Scripture quotations marked KJV are taken from the *Holy Bible,* King James Version.

**Library of Congress Cataloging-in-Publication Data**

Colson, Charles W.
  The good life / Charles Colson, Harold Fickett.
    p. cm.
  Includes bibliographical references.
  ISBN-10: 0-8423-7749-2
  ISBN-13: 978-0-8423-7749-2
  1. Christian life.   2. Success—Religious aspects—Christianity.   I. Fickett, Harold.   II. Title.
  BV4501.3.C648 2005
  248.4—dc22                                                                    2005004943

Printed in the United States of America

11   10   09   08   07   06   05
7    6    5    4    3    2    1

DEDICATED TO
WENDELL
CHRISTIAN
AND
EMILY

*my three children, who have contributed so much
to making my life a good life.*

*This book is dedicated with the fervent prayer
that they will continue in relentless pursuit of the truth.*

*"The supreme function of reason is to show man that some things are beyond reason."*

BLAISE PASCAL, *PENSÉES*

# CONTENTS

*Introduction: The Good Life* . . . . . . . . . . . . . . . . . . . . . . . . . . . . . . . . . . xiii

SEARCHING FOR THE GOOD LIFE

The Unavoidable Question . . . . . . . . . . . . . . . . . . . . . . 3
A Shattered Life . . . . . . . . . . . . . . . . . . . . . . . . . . . . . 11
The Great Paradoxes . . . . . . . . . . . . . . . . . . . . . . . . 23
A Nice Party with a Lot of Nice People . . . . . . . . . . . . 35
Shopping for the Holy Grail . . . . . . . . . . . . . . . . . . 45
Laughing at Death . . . . . . . . . . . . . . . . . . . . . . . . . . 57
More Important Than Life Itself . . . . . . . . . . . . . . . 73
A Life of Significance . . . . . . . . . . . . . . . . . . . . . . . 83
A Silent Good-bye . . . . . . . . . . . . . . . . . . . . . . . . . . 93
My Happiness, Right or Wrong . . . . . . . . . . . . . . . . 103
Whose Life Is It? . . . . . . . . . . . . . . . . . . . . . . . . . . 113
A Very Rich Man . . . . . . . . . . . . . . . . . . . . . . . . . . 121

GIVING TO OTHERS

Living Legacies . . . . . . . . . . . . . . . . . . . . . . . . . . . 131
Greater Love Hath No Man Than This . . . . . . . . . . . 145
My Life for Yours—but to What End? . . . . . . . . . . . . 155

SEARCHING FOR THE TRUTH

Journey into Illusion . . . . . . . . . . . . . . . . . . . . . . . 161
Living within the Truth . . . . . . . . . . . . . . . . . . . . . 173
Can We Know the Truth? . . . . . . . . . . . . . . . . . . . . 187

*"The supreme function of reason is to show man that some things are beyond reason."*

Blaise Pascal, *Pensées*

# CONTENTS

*Introduction: The Good Life* . . . . . . . . . . . . . . . . . . . . . . . . . . . . . . . . . xiii

## SEARCHING FOR THE GOOD LIFE

The Unavoidable Question . . . . . . . . . . . . . . . . . . . . . 3

A Shattered Life . . . . . . . . . . . . . . . . . . . . . . . . . . . 11

The Great Paradoxes . . . . . . . . . . . . . . . . . . . . . . . 23

A Nice Party with a Lot of Nice People . . . . . . . . . . . 35

Shopping for the Holy Grail . . . . . . . . . . . . . . . . . . 45

Laughing at Death . . . . . . . . . . . . . . . . . . . . . . . . 57

More Important Than Life Itself . . . . . . . . . . . . . . . 73

A Life of Significance . . . . . . . . . . . . . . . . . . . . . . . 83

A Silent Good-bye . . . . . . . . . . . . . . . . . . . . . . . . . 93

My Happiness, Right or Wrong . . . . . . . . . . . . . . . . 103

Whose Life Is It? . . . . . . . . . . . . . . . . . . . . . . . . . . 113

A Very Rich Man . . . . . . . . . . . . . . . . . . . . . . . . . 121

## GIVING TO OTHERS

Living Legacies . . . . . . . . . . . . . . . . . . . . . . . . . . . 131

Greater Love Hath No Man Than This . . . . . . . . . . . 145

My Life for Yours—but to What End? . . . . . . . . . . . . 155

## SEARCHING FOR THE TRUTH

Journey into Illusion . . . . . . . . . . . . . . . . . . . . . . . 161

Living within the Truth . . . . . . . . . . . . . . . . . . . . . 173

Can We Know the Truth? . . . . . . . . . . . . . . . . . . . . 187

What Is Life Worth? . . . . . . . . . . . . . . . . . . . . . . . 197

God's ID . . . . . . . . . . . . . . . . . . . . . . . . . . . . . . 213

Morality and the Natural Order . . . . . . . . . . . . . . 229

The Gift of Knowing Right from Wrong . . . . . . . . . 247

Beauty: The Sign of God's Care . . . . . . . . . . . . . . 255

Written on the Heart . . . . . . . . . . . . . . . . . . . . . . 269

Postmodernists in Recovery . . . . . . . . . . . . . . . . . 275

Hope, Freedom, and Happiness . . . . . . . . . . . . . . . 291

The Bad News . . . . . . . . . . . . . . . . . . . . . . . . . . . 305

## LIVING THE GOOD LIFE

Providence . . . . . . . . . . . . . . . . . . . . . . . . . . . . 319

A Good Death . . . . . . . . . . . . . . . . . . . . . . . . . . 335

Infinite Truth and Love . . . . . . . . . . . . . . . . . . . . 347

Epilogue: Back to the Beginning . . . . . . . . . . . . . . . . . . . . . . 359

With Gratitude . . . . . . . . . . . . . . . . . . . . . . . . . . . . . . . . . 367

Notes . . . . . . . . . . . . . . . . . . . . . . . . . . . . . . . . . . . . . . . 371

Recommended Reading . . . . . . . . . . . . . . . . . . . . . . . . . . . 389

About the Authors . . . . . . . . . . . . . . . . . . . . . . . . . . . . . . 393

# THE GOOD LIFE

THIS IS A BOOK about the good life—not the good life touted in Budweiser commercials or on *Lifestyles of the Rich and Famous* or *MTV Cribs,* but the good life that you and I want to live when we reflect about what really matters.

What makes life worth living? Why am I here? What's my purpose? How can my life be meaningful? These are questions on everyone's mind, both at times of crisis and underneath the surface of daily events.

For most of us, life is messy and confusing, filled with paradoxes. We wake up in the night, worrying about our jobs, our kids, or the best laid plans, which suddenly unravel due to the pressures of living in our high-tech, fast-moving world. One day we seem to have things under control; the next day we get steamrollered by events. If you haven't experienced this, please write me; you would be the first person I know to have life all together.

As I was editing the final draft of this manuscript, I had an eye-opening experience that illustrates how this book may help us make sense out of life and cope with its frustrations. My daughter, Emily, and her son, Max, were home with Patty and me for Christmas. Emily is the single mother of a fourteen-year-old autistic son. Autistic kids can be loving and wonderful, but they demand special attention because of the problems they have communicating and cognitively processing information. They especially need order and certainty in their lives. When Max arrives at our house, he immediately checks the closet for his toys, scans the pictures on the wall, and tries the appliances. If anything has changed from his last visit, he is visibly distressed. Any unusual noises or changes in a day's schedule can provoke the kind of tantrums common to autistic kids. "Meltdowns," as Emily calls them, are serious events to be avoided. At age fourteen, Max's meltdowns can be cyclones.

I've watched Emily help Max through his struggles. One evening, we had an unexpected visitor, and Max began to frown and become agitated. Because autistic kids can process information better if they see it rather than just hear it, Emily often uses her artistic gifts to help Max see events through pictures. As she sensed Max's distress that evening, she immediately sat down with him and began sketching simple line drawings, one after another, each in its separate graphic box—like a comic strip. She was providing Max with an explanation for the changes he had witnessed. This man, the visitor, worked with Grandpa. He was also a friend who occasionally took Grandpa fishing. See the boat? See the sunshine? He just brought by a Christmas gift. See the box in its wrapping and the big bow?

Max calmed down. Emily's words and pictures helped him make sense of what he was seeing and experiencing, in the same way that an instruction manual can make sense of assembling a bike or inserting a graphics card into a computer. The more Max understands, the less prone he is to become confused and distressed.

As I watched Emily, I thought, *Of course. This is what we all need—a manual for how things work when our own cognitive abilities leave us bewildered and our coping skills have reached their limit.* All of us are like Max at times. We can't figure out what's happening to our world, why we're feeling tense and frustrated. So we throw our own kind of tantrum: We gossip or assert our superiority; we get drunk or have an affair; we go on a credit-card shopping spree; we irritate the boss until he's obliged to fire us. We thrash around in the face of a world that we can't understand and can't manage. The many ways people "act out" prove what a challenge life is.

Our difficulty in understanding how the world works and how we fit into it has been aggravated, I believe, by the false expectations our culture breeds. We are like people trying to go up the down escalator. We huff and puff and go nowhere. The problem is, the culture is pushing one way, and we haven't figured out it's the wrong direction. When we ask the basic questions about our purpose and meaning, we receive false answers. Our attempts to live by these misleading answers inevitably leave us angry and terrified. What we need is to seek the true picture of how the world really works and what we need to live well. I hope this book will help you do that, just as Emily's box-by-box drawings help Max understand his world.

In the following pages we will be probing deep questions, examining the experience of living. This is no abstract exercise. How we answer these questions determines how we will live and how we will die and whether our lives will count for something.

---

Almost thirty years ago, when I was just coming out of prison, I wrote a book entitled *Born Again,* which to my surprise sold millions of copies and was published in forty countries. I've done a lot of living since then. I've ministered to prisoners around the globe, met a host of fascinating people, been awarded prizes and honors, and been schooled by my autistic grandson and many others in what living is all about. In a way, *The Good Life* looks at what I wrote in *Born Again,* but with the benefit of seeing it through the rearview mirror. What have I learned from one tumultuous life?

In one sense this is a thematic memoir—the rest of the story after *Born Again.* It includes reflections on my own life, some joyful, some painful. It recounts some of the crucial moments in my life and the lessons I've learned from them. I hope it also reflects my personal pursuit of what we all want—to live a life that matters, a life of significance.

Please don't think that this book is a grand summing up by a senior statesman who means to impress you with his accumulated wisdom. No. This book is for seekers—seekers of any kind, of any or no religious faith. That may surprise you. Anyone who knows about me knows that I'm a Christian. I have deep and abiding convictions, and I can hardly claim to be a neutral observer. But I am a seeker too. My search led me into Christianity, and since then it has driven me to uncover more fully the truth that we are meant to know and live.

The search I'll be conducting here will be undertaken, as much as I'm able, without relying on any prior assumptions or sectarian convictions. This may unsettle my Christian friends, but I think it makes sense simply to follow where human reason and the human imagination lead until we can follow them no longer. In the end we'll see whether reason and the imagination demand that their scope be enlarged through faith. Perhaps what we might call merely human truth does not connect with faith, but then again, perhaps it does.

———•◆•———

Blaise Pascal, the great French philosopher and mathematician, once said that there are only two kinds of people in the world: seekers and nonseekers. Either we are pilgrims looking for answers in order to make sense of our world, or we are wanderers who have turned off onto byways of distraction or despair, alienating ourselves from *wonder*. If you are reading this book, you probably are a seeker. That's good. To be alive is to seek.

If you think you already have good answers to the great questions, read on anyway. This book will help you understand your convictions in an entirely new way and live them more fully.

The people for whom I feel the greatest compassion are those in Pascal's second category—the nonseekers. To turn away from the great questions and dilemmas of life is a tragedy, for the quest for meaning and truth makes life worth living.

Many people—particularly the young—have been persuaded that such a search is futile. They have been told from their preschool days on that one person's opinion is as good as another's, that each person can pick his or her own truth from a multicultural smorgasbord. If one choice proves unsavory, pick another, and so on, until, in a consumerist fashion, we pick the truth we like best. I think the despair of Generations X, Y, and now E comes from this fundamental notion that there's no such thing as reality or the capital-*T* truth.

Almost every new movie I see these days features a bright, good-looking, talented young man who is so downright sad, he can barely lift his head. I want to scream, "What's wrong with this guy?" Then I feel a profound compassion because his generation has been forbidden the one thing that makes life such a breathtaking challenge: truth.

Many boomers have shied away from their youthful enthusiasm for the search for quite a different reason. They've run up against reality once too often, discovering the promises of the sixties to be hollow. They have misgivings about the pragmatic accommodations they have reached with life, although they're careful not to acknowledge these compromises in front of their grown children.

Some people put such questions aside as they age, even disparaging any search for truth as the impractical fancy of youth. To me, the big questions are more relevant and pointed now than ever before. Advancing age brings with it the advantage of seeing how the answers to the great questions on which one bases one's life have worked out. As I get older, I find myself assessing my life critically: Have I lived up to my expectations? How well have I done? Have I used my gifts to their full potential? When there's not much time left, you'll be making some assessments too. I promise you.

But a word of caution: The search for truth and meaning is a lifelong process, and if you ever think you have all the answers, you can become insufferable and dangerous. That is why I still consider myself a seeker. I have passionate convictions, as I've said, but I'm still on a pilgrimage. I'm learning new things every day, as expressed in these great lines from T. S. Eliot:

> Old men ought to be explorers
> Here and there does not matter
> We must be still and still moving
> Into another intensity
> For a further union, a deeper communion[1]

So let me invite you to join a conversation about what makes life worth living. Together we'll look to find "another intensity" and "a deeper communion" with life—a way of living that makes life truly good.

In the first half of the book, we'll look at the lives of people searching for the good life. What drives them to the life choices they make? And do those choices work? In the second half of the book, we'll look more closely at the search for truth. Is truth knowable? What difference does it make for our daily lives? As we do this, keep in mind the little parable of Emily and Max. What she does for Max, drawing pictures that help him make sense of his world, is what I hope to do for you: draw word pictures that show the truth of how the world works and how we fit in.

In the end, however, even after the best explanations, we're faced with an additional challenge: Are we capable of living the good life? Where can we find the strength and courage we need? In the final chapters I'll provide the only answer I know to those questions, the only answer that has experiential proof to back it up.

The method for examining these crucial ideas will be stories— some from my own life, some from the lives of people we all know, others from movies, still others from people who have shaped history. Taken together, I hope this mosaic of stories—some colorful, some shadowy—will help you see your own story and the beliefs that drive your search for meaning, purpose, and truth.

The reason this book devotes so much attention to life stories is not merely because they provide entertaining reading but because human experiences help us engage life and grapple as closely as possible with life as it is lived. I'm not telling stories merely as illustrations of ideas; they are part and parcel of the grappling. Thinking and living are bound together: We think in order to know how to live, and we learn what's true through living. The good life demands a union of the two, an integrity of life and thought, the poet's "deeper communion."

*Thinking and living are bound together: We think in order to know how to live, and we learn what's true through living.*

Writing this book with my longtime and gifted colleague Harold Fickett turned into a real adventure, one in which I grasped ideas and reached conclusions I could never have imagined or arrived at otherwise. What I've found is exciting. See for yourself. It's the path to living the truly good life.

# SEARCHING
## *for the*
# GOOD LIFE

# CHAPTER 1

# THE UNAVOIDABLE QUESTION

AN OLD MAN walks down a wide path through a colonnade of evergreens. He has a full head of gray hair, combed from a wavy peak to one side. His eyebrows spike with a grandfatherly flourish toward his temples. He wears a light blue Windbreaker over a golf shirt with a horizontal stripe, Sansabelt slacks, and the crepe-soled shoes his doctor recommended. His gait is quick but stiff—stiff like someone who has just gotten himself up. He marches forward with great intent and purpose, as if he's hunting out something or someone.

Behind him trail his family. His wife is closest, his son and daughter-in-law a step or two farther behind, bracketing their children.

The man's eyes show that for the moment he's not thinking of his family, although he seems to be dragging them in his wake. His eyes are at once wide-open yet fixed, poached by what can only be dread. His mouth works in a way that shows his stomach is in his throat. Off to the left his family can see the curve of a long shore, hear the soughing of the waves, and nearly breathe in the scent of the brine. But the man looks neither to his right nor to his left. He keeps stumbling forward, his body tense yet determined.

When he finally turns to his right, he steps onto a vast lawn striped with thousands of white crosses that extend toward the horizon. Here and there a Jewish star adds to the procession of markers that contrast starkly against the green sward. The old man's pace speeds as he makes his way through this vast cemetery. His family struggles to keep up.

James Ryan's determined march finally halts in front of a particular cross. The rims of his eyes show red. He wipes at them with a shaking hand, sniffs hard, tries again to breathe. Here it is, his captain's cross, the name, the date: Captain John W. Miller, June 13, 1944.

He takes another sniff against his watering eyes, bites his lip. He's almost choking as he struggles to breathe in the heavy air. His knees give way, and he kneels before the cross, his shoulders heaving. His wife is suddenly at one shoulder, his son at the other. He's glad they are there, but they cannot help with what needs to be done.

He mumbles that he's all right, and they retreat several steps, leaving him to the thoughts that press so hard he can't bear the weight.

Not until this moment does he realize that what he has been looking forward to yet dreading is a transaction. An exchange of some kind. For him this visit to the Normandy American Cemetery is no sightseeing tour. It's a profound action. Even now he cannot say why he believes this to be the case. The emotion that's seized him declares it to be so, however.

Whatever must happen involves the question that's dogged him his whole life. The unspoken question that's brought him here. He feels its presence in every memory, and not only the good ones.

Now that he's looking at his captain's grave, Ryan has to ask the question.

Decades earlier, on June 6, 1944, Captain Miller and his men had landed at Omaha Beach, a horror James Ryan had been spared as part of the 101st Airborne. His unit had been dropped into Normandy the night before the sea assault. He later learned from the tales of his buddies and from seeing newsreel footage what D-day had been like. Although Germany had not been expecting the assault at the place Eisenhower chose, the air assault hadn't softened their positions one whit, and when the armored front of the Higgins boats opened onto the beach, the men were ducks on a pond to the enemy's machine guns. Many of those sitting forward in the landing craft never had a chance to move from their seats as the Germans opened fire. Those who jumped over the craft's sides to swim and crawl ashore could only cling to the Belgian gates and iron hedgehogs—the jack-shaped defensive works strewn in rows all along the shingle that prevented tanks from making the initial assault.

The army rangers humped forward in waves, men falling to the right and left every few feet. They were getting hit not only by machine-gun fire but by artillery as well. Bodies flew with the explosions. The wounded picked up their severed arms and stumbled a few more feet to their deaths. The waves washing onto the beaches ran red with blood, lapping at the dead, who lay scattered and senseless.

Captain Miller and a few of his company made it to the seawall. Although 50 percent of the men in the first waves to hit Omaha Beach were killed in action, the others broke the first line of German defenses.

Soon after the hell of D-Day, Captain Miller and a squad of seven men were assigned to find paratrooper James Ryan and bring him home—alive. The army's chief of staff, General George C. Marshall, had personally issued the order for Private James Ryan to be taken out of the war. Ryan's two older brothers had died in the great assault, and a third brother had been killed in action in New Guinea. Marshall thought that three sons were enough for any mother to contribute to the war.

Captain Miller and his squad found Ryan with remnants of the 506, Baker Company, which had orders to secure a bridge on the far side of a river. The company had been ordered to hold the bridge at all costs—or, as a final defense, to blow it up. When Captain Miller and his squad arrived to take Ryan home, Ryan refused to leave. Miller asked him what he was supposed to say to Ryan's mother when she got another folded American flag. Ryan replied, "You can tell her that when you found me, I was with the only brothers I had left. And that there was no way I was deserting them. I think she'd understand that."[1]

Captain Miller and his squad told Ryan angrily that they had already lost two men in the search to find him. Miller finally decided that they'd make Ryan's battle their own as well and save him in the process.

The Germans soon came at them—nearly a full company of men, two Panzer tanks, two Tigers. The Americans lured the Panzers down the village's main street, where they staged an effective ambush. The only thing Ryan had been allowed to do was pitch mortar shells like hand grenades. Captain Miller never let Ryan leave his side, protecting the private every step of the way.

Still, one tank blew their sharpshooter to eternity. Another soldier died in hand-to-hand combat with a knife to his heart. No matter their ingenuity, the squad couldn't hold off such an overpowering force, and the men made a strategic retreat to the other side of the bridge. In the retreat one of the sergeants was hit and collapsed.

Captain Miller took a shot beneath his ribs as he struggled to fix the wiring on a detonation device. Then an artillery blast knocked him nearly unconscious. All hope lost, Captain Miller began shooting at a tank coming straight at him.

Suddenly, Tankbuster aircraft shrieked down on them, blowing the enemy's tanks to smithereens and routing their foot soldiers. The Allies' own armored reinforcements rolled up minutes later.

Of the squad that had come to save Ryan, only two men escaped relatively unscathed. The others were dead or dying.

Captain Miller lay close by where he had been hit, his back slumped against the bridge's wall. Ryan, in anguish, was alone with his rescuer in the final moments before Miller died. Ryan watched as the captain struggled in his last moments, shot clean through one lung. The captain wouldn't take another breath, except to grunt, "James. Earn this . . . earn it."

Were these dying words a final order or charge?

Private Ryan has always taken it that way.

These memories rivet the aged James Ryan, who now finds himself staring at the grave marker and mumbling to his dead commander. He tells Captain Miller that his family is with him. He confesses that he wasn't sure how he would feel about coming to the cemetery today. He wants Captain Miller to know that every day of his life he's thought of their conversation at the bridge, of Miller's dying words. Ryan has tried to live a good life, and he hopes he has. At least in the captain's eyes, he hopes he's "earned it," that his life has been worthy of the sacrifice Captain Miller and the other men made of giving their lives for his.

As Ryan mutters these thoughts, he cannot help wondering how any life, however well lived, could be worthy of his friends' sacrifice. The old man stands up, but he doesn't feel released. The question remains unanswered.

His wife comes to his side again. He looks at her and pleads, "Tell me I've led a good life."

Confused by his request, she responds with a question: "What?"

He has to know the answer. He tries to articulate it again: "Tell me I'm a good man."

The request flusters her, but his earnestness makes her think better of putting it off. With great dignity, she says, "You *are.*"

His wife turns back to the other family members, whose stirring says they are ready to leave.

Before James Ryan joins them, he comes to attention and salutes his fallen comrade. What a gallant old soldier he is.

———◆◦◆———

Who of us can see this scene from Steven Spielberg's magnificent film *Saving Private Ryan* and not ask ourselves the same question: Have I lived a good life?

Does there exist an exact way of calculating the answer to this question? How do we define living a good life? What makes the good we do good *enough*? Is our life worthy of the sacrifice of others? The unavoidable question of whether we have lived a good life searches our hearts.

Not everyone experiences what Ryan did in such a dramatic way. Yet this question of the good life—and others like it—haunts every human being from the earliest years of our consciousness. Something stirs us at the very core of our being, demanding answers to so many questions: Is there some purpose in life? Are we alone in this universe, or does some force—call it fate, destiny, or providence—guide our lives?

These questions don't often occur to us so neatly of course. Usually the hardest questions hit us at the hardest times. In the midst of tragedy or serious illness, when confronting violence and injustice, or after seeing our personal hopes shattered, we cry out, "Why is the world such a mess? Is there anything I can do about it?"

There's a mystery at work in these perennial questions of human existence. I doubt anyone who has ever seen *Saving Private Ryan* or read great works of literature like Dostoyevsky's *The Brothers Karamazov* or Camus's *The Plague* has ever doubted the relevance of such questions. Neither does anyone who has ever marveled at the beauty of the Milky Way or sat weeping at the bedside of a dying loved one.

What distinguishes humans from all other creatures is our self-consciousness: We know we are alive and that we will die, and we cannot keep from asking ourselves questions about why life is the way it is and what it all means.

And isn't it odd that we all understand immediately why Private Ryan would feel compelled to live an honorable life? Does he believe that in doing so he can make his comrades' sacrifice worthwhile? Evidently, he does, and we sense the rightness of this. But why does he feel in their debt? Why does he feel that their actions have to be recompensed by his own, as if blind justice with a sword in one hand and balancing scales in the other really existed? And why should goodness be the means of repaying this debt? Why not revenge? Why should he not set about killing as many former Nazis as possible? Somehow that does not satisfy, though. If sacrifice can be repaid at all, it can be done only by sacrifice, not by slaughter. We *know* this. But *why* do we know this?

A broad answer lies in our humanity. Because we are human, we ask questions about meaning and purpose. We have an innate sense of justice and our own need to meet the demands of justice. Moral attitudes differ from culture to culture, but take people from a Stone Age culture in a remote village in Papua New Guinea, sit them down in front of *Saving Private Ryan,* and they will immediately understand the issues involved. They will understand Ryan's questions and his sense of gratitude.

The word *should* in the questions that arise from Private Ryan's life immediately grounds us in ethical considerations. It implies there must be a variety of answers to these questions. It suggests that some answers are better than others—some are right while others are wrong. So, where does this *should* come from? What does it mean that we possess an innate sense of these things?

At the very least it points to the notion that we all live in a moral universe, which is one of the reasons human beings, regardless of background or economics or place of birth, are irresistibly religious. If nothing else, we know there is someone or something to which we owe a debt for our existence.

Our questions also presume that we can choose our answers to these questions and act on these choices. The freedom of the human will, even if circumscribed, is built into the way the human mind works.

Commenting on life's questions, U.S. Supreme Court Justice Anthony M. Kennedy, in the case *Planned Parenthood v. Casey,* said, "At the heart of liberty is the right to define one's own concept of existence, of meaning, of the universe, and of the mystery of human life."[2]

Kennedy asserted that beliefs about these matters define the attributes of personhood. We are who we are, we are the type of creatures we are, because we are obliged to come to our own conclusions about the great questions. Although I disagree profoundly with the legal conclusion Justice Kennedy drew from this observation, I must admit his summary captures what makes us human.[3]

I can remember when I first began asking questions early in life. I have particularly vivid memories of the Sunday morning in December 1941 when our family was riveted to the radio, listening with growing anxiety to the reports of the Japanese attacks on Pearl Harbor. I was certain we'd be fighting Japanese soldiers or German SS officers in the streets of our sleepy Boston suburb. I remember asking my father, "Why does there have to be war and bloodshed and death?" He replied—mistakenly, as I now think—that it was all part of the natural process, like famines and plagues that prevented overpopulation.

During the war, I organized fund-raising campaigns in my school, even auctioned off my treasured model airplane collection to raise funds for the war effort. Instinctively I knew I was meant to do my part to protect our freedoms. I wanted my life—even at age twelve—to matter.

I also remember standing in our yard many nights, the world around me in darkness, blackout shades covering every window in the neighborhood, protecting us against the expected air raids. I would stare into the dazzling array of stars above me and wonder where the universe began, where it ended, and what I was doing here. As a student, I struggled to grasp the concept of infinity—what was beyond those stars.

I've continued to ask these kinds of questions, especially during times of stress. I've asked them in my life as a government official, as a husband and father, as a convicted felon, and then as a Christian leader. Many times in the inner recesses of my conscience I've asked Ryan's questions: *Have I been a good man? Have I lived a good life?* Sometimes I've been unsure; other times I've been sure that I have failed. But where do we go to answer these questions? Whom do we ask? Who can tell us the truth about the value of our lives?

While the quest to find answers to such questions can be arduous at times, even heartbreaking, the search for the truth about life is the one thing that makes life worthwhile, exhilarating. The ability to pursue such a search makes us human. Emmanuel Mounier, the founder of the French "personalist" philosophical movement, writes that human life is characterized by a "divine restlessness." The lack of peace within our hearts spurs us on a quest for the meaning of life—a command imprinted on "unextinguished souls."[4] Pope John Paul II sums up the matter elegantly: "One may define the human being, therefore, as *the one who seeks the truth.*"[5]

What will be the truth of our lives and our destinies? Most people want to arrive at Captain Miller's cemetery cross—or whatever judgment seat they envision—with some confidence that they have lived a good life.

But what is a good life? How does such a life incorporate answers to the great questions? How can such a life be lived?

Have I lived one?

Have you?

# CHAPTER 2

# A SHATTERED LIFE

ON SUNDAY, JUNE 13, 1971, the *New York Times* ran a quiet headline over what would become an explosive front-page story: "Vietnam Archive: Pentagon Study Traces 3 Decades of Growing U.S. Involvement." The story by Neil Sheehan, as well as an additional analysis by Hedrick Smith, reported that in 1967 former Secretary of Defense Robert S. McNamara had commissioned a highly classified Pentagon study of America's involvement in Vietnam going back to the Truman administration. The study, written by multiple authors, ran to three thousand pages, to which four thousand additional pages of official documents had been attached.

To the casual reader the study may have looked like no more than a dry historical recounting of events surrounding the immensely unpopular Vietnam War. I was at the time Special Counsel to President Nixon, and to those of us inside the president's inner circle, it was anything but dry history. The headline was horrifying, and a portent of a disaster to come that would shake the nation to its very roots and affect all of us in ways that none of us could then imagine.

The entire report, called the Pentagon Papers, provided an inside look at how America became embroiled in a war that would eventually rupture people's faith in government and lead to the politics of cynicism and recrimination we know today. Soon it became known that the highly classified document had been stolen from the Defense Department by one of its authors, Daniel Ellsberg, who gave it to the Senate Foreign Relations Committee in 1969 and then to the *New York Times,* the *Washington Post,* and seventeen other newspapers several months before the *Times* began publishing it.

With its first stories covering the study's findings, the *Times* began running extracts from the study's top secret attachments, beginning with McNamara's report to President Johnson on the situation in Saigon in 1963. The extracts confirmed Americans' worst suspicions: The government had known all along that its efforts were unlikely to succeed, that its South Vietnamese allies were unreliable and often corrupt, and that our government's own strategy lacked internal coherence.

This plainly contradicted the government's constant announcement of good news from the battlefront. The Johnson administration had told the Americans that we were winning the hearts and minds of the Vietnamese. Body counts indicated the enemy was sustaining evergreater casualties. Yet somehow we needed more and more soldiers, until half a million Americans were fighting in Vietnam.[1]

## THE ROOSEVELT ROOM, JUNE 14, 1971

On Monday morning, the day after the story broke in the *Times*, those of us on President Nixon's senior staff met as we did each day, at eight o'clock in the West Wing's Roosevelt Room. Nixon's authoritarian chief of staff, Bob Haldeman, chaired the meeting. His right-hand man on domestic policy, John Ehrlichman, attended, as did the unofficial head of American foreign policy, Henry Kissinger, who was the national security adviser. Press secretary Ron Ziegler looked frazzled from the bombardment he'd already taken that morning from the aggressive press corps. I was at the meeting, as were Bill Timmins, the legislative operator, and six others. One look at Haldeman's grim expression, and we knew that trouble was ahead.

The Roosevelt Room is at the epicenter of the White House. A cream-mantled fireplace dominates the room's east end and is flanked by two dark mahogany paneled doors inset into half-arches. The door to the right leads directly to the door of the Oval Office, across the hall. Two years earlier, President Nixon had redecorated this conference room, transforming what had been the "Fish Room" into the Roosevelt Room. On the north wall are bronzes of the two Roosevelts, Teddy and FDR. A painting of Theodore Roosevelt in his Rough Rider uniform, mounted on a horse, hangs above the mantel. Theodore Roosevelt's

Nobel Peace Prize, won in 1906 for his intervention in the Russian-Japanese dispute of 1905—the first Nobel Prize won by an American—sits on the mantel itself. The huge Chippendale conference table is surrounded by buttoned leather chairs that make long meetings a little more comfortable.

Because the Roosevelt Room occupies part of the West Wing's interior, the room lacks windows. Despite its fine appointments, the room can seem like a concrete bunker at times, especially when its occupants feel as embattled as we did that June morning.

The White House was a tense place in those days. Throngs of protesters kept it under siege as they marched outside the gates and carried signs declaring "Nixon Killers" and "Butchers of Pennsylvania Avenue." Often a mix of marijuana smoke and tear gas floated in the air when the police, sometimes with the help of the army, would have to clear a path for the White House workers. We were apprehensive about what would happen now that front-page articles announced secret documents confirming the people's worst fears.

Haldeman called the meeting to order, dispensed with the usual preliminaries, and got right to the real threat posed by the *Times* story. "The president wants our counsel," he said somberly. "This could have dire consequences."

"The first thing is to arrest the traitor who stole the documents," someone suggested.

"The Senate is ready to cut off funds for the war itself," Timmins said. "With this, the House may join them. The president may find himself compelled to drag us home with our tails between our legs."

"Or flout the Congress. Not that the prospect isn't tempting," someone added.

As the president's chief political adviser, I saw a ray of hope in the doomsday atmosphere. "Wait. Think for a minute. All of these things happened on the watch of Democratic presidents. At least for the most part. Johnson's the one who's really on the hot seat. We're just cleaning up his mess. Maybe we should get the Senate Foreign Relations Committee to hold hearings."

Kissinger had come in a minute or two late and was standing at the far end of the table. He dumped a stack of folders on the table with a thump. "None of you understands," he shouted. His face was so red that it was already bleaching white toward the temples. "You can't keep any secrets in this government, and this is a calamity, a catastrophe. This will ruin everything—I mean *everything*—we are trying to do. There can be no foreign policy in this government. These leaks will destroy us!"

I'd learned to read Henry, who often used hyperbole to make his point and command center stage. He acted as if he had the world in his hands, and the truth was, often he did. He had others on his side as well this time.

Kissinger whipped open the top folder, sending three sheets of paper spinning across the table. "Look at those. They are cables from Australia, Great Britain, and Canada, protesting the publication of this study. The Pentagon documents that are being published expose how they helped us out as back channels. They contain cable traffic that could even lead to the exposure of human assets [CIA and other intelligence agents]. This cannot stand. The president must do something to counteract this today. He has to go strong on this—as strong as possible."

Henry's anger became infectious. Everyone—myself included—began denouncing our enemies, foreign and domestic. The Nixon administration had long had a problem with information leaks. I had been assigned several times to track these down—and I knew the damage they caused. As the meeting continued, the president's men singed the walls with blasts against the enemy in our midst. Vindictiveness and recrimination ruled. The leaks had to be stopped!

Those of us gathered in the Roosevelt Room that morning came unstrung, in part because of a clash between our idealistic visions and what it would take to realize those ideals. President Nixon spoke of bringing about a "generation of peace." Despite what the administration's detractors claimed, he meant it. It was his sincerity about this goal that initially drew me to him when I first met him in the 1950s. Maybe it was his Quaker upbringing, but he really cared about peace, so we on his staff were doing everything in our power to make that vision happen. Nixon's hopes rested on a reconfiguration of the world's most powerful states—a new balance of power that would neutralize the overtly aggressive policies of the Soviets and to some extent the Chinese.

In retrospect, we know Nixon had many faults, but even his harshest critics agree that he was a geopolitical mastermind. He understood the chessboard of the world—how a diplomatic measure in Jakarta would have an effect in Addis Ababa. He wanted to bring the troops home from Vietnam but under conditions that would not make the United States and the Western world more vulnerable to the expansive ambitions of the Soviets and the Chinese.

At that time, Kissinger was conducting multiple negotiations so sensitive that they needed to be kept secret even from our own State Department. He had established many back-channel contacts, which simply means that a senior official of the government, usually someone who works directly with the head of state, will contact a senior official in another government, without the knowledge of the diplomatic corps of the two nations. Kissinger was also trying to advance negotiations on the Strategic Arms Limitations Treaty—the SALT agreement—which would eventually draw the world back from the brink of nuclear cataclysm, and at the same time he was engaged in secret negotiations with the North Vietnamese in Paris. Finally, Kissinger was negotiating the way for Nixon to make his historic trip to China. I learned about this inadvertently. The president, Kissinger, Haldeman, Ehrlichman, and I were out on the presidential yacht *Sequoia* one night, and after a couple of glasses of his favorite Bordeaux, Nixon started ribbing me for failing to get Congress to approve a supersonic transport so he could fly on it to China. Kissinger blanched because he was at the moment on the verge of going to Pakistan, from where he would be flown secretly into Beijing to meet with the Chinese leader Zhou Enlai.

The three negotiations were linked. If we could not win a satisfactory deal from the North Vietnamese, their patron state, the USSR, would be less likely to accept the terms of the proposed SALT agreement. If we could not demonstrate our ability to wring concessions from the Soviet Union, the Chinese would be less interested in opening their doors to the West. The Chinese had their own conflicts with the Soviet Union, chiefly border disputes that set the two at odds over many other things. The more we engaged the Soviets in bilateral relations, the more the Chinese would be forced to abandon their insular policies and open up to the West. We were delighted, in turn, to keep both governments off balance in order to prevent a Sino-Soviet alliance that could overpower the West.

So when Kissinger exploded, I knew much of what was at stake.

No government wants to have its unofficial diplomatic exchanges exposed. These discussions inevitably play in the media as policy and either force people's hands or restrain them unnecessarily.

That morning Kissinger avoided addressing a second and even more pressing cause of his anger: National Security Study Memorandum 1, which outlined how the Vietnam War might be quickly ended. NSSM 1 described all options, including the use of tactical nuclear weapons, which would be used to take out the river dikes and flood half of North Vietnam. Such action would have brought a quick end to the war, but the cost in lives would have been too great. Other options included mining the Haiphong harbor and bombing Hanoi and the Ho Chi Minh trail in the north (options later used).

The possible publication of NSSM 1 presented a host of problems. We did not want the North Vietnamese—or the Chinese or the Russians—to know the measures we might ultimately decide to employ. The memo's publication would also have hardened the attitudes of the North Vietnamese, making negotiations more difficult. Finally, the publication of NSSM 1 would have severely damaged Henry Kissinger's reputation.

Fortunately, no one ever published NSSM 1. The memo itself was delivered anonymously to Senator Charles "Mac" Mathias, a liberal Maryland Republican, and to the Russian Embassy. But both of them, though for different reasons, returned the material to the administration.

Reflecting on that June 14 meeting, I am still impressed with the enormity of the crisis, which I believe historians have radically underestimated. We had a real fear that the United States government would lose all credibility. If that had occurred no SALT agreement would ever have been signed, President Nixon would never have gone to China, and we might well be living in an even more dangerous world than the one we know today.

The meeting was pivotal not only in the fortunes of the Nixon presidency but in my life as well. Out of it came "the plumbers," a special White House unit so named because it was assigned to stop the administration's leaks. Out of the plumbers and the wild imaginations of Howard Hunt and Gordon Liddy came the bugging of the Democratic National Committee and the break-in to Daniel Ellsberg's psychiatrist's office. That Roosevelt Room meeting led directly to the political scandal known as Watergate, which brought down Richard Nixon's presidency.

As I thought about the Pentagon Papers' ramifications for Vietnam that day, I became increasingly troubled and angry. I wanted to see the Vietnam War end as much as any of the protesters in the streets. My two sons, Wendell and Chris, were nearing draft age. Bill Maloney, the friend who had inspired me to join the marines after college, was serving at that moment in Vietnam, flying rescue missions behind the lines, shot at day and night. John McCain, the son of my close personal friend Admiral Jack McCain, was a prisoner in the Hanoi Hilton. I wanted to see these men come home—alive and healthy.

The opponents of the Vietnam War thought the publication of the Pentagon Papers would make the war's end more likely. I believed that it would have the opposite effect—or inspire more such wars in which my sons and my friends would have to fight.

Dr. Daniel Ellsberg, the man who distributed the Pentagon Papers to the media, soon admitted publicly what he had done and became an instant hero of the antiwar movement. Until this crisis, I had never heard of Ellsberg. When I found out who he was, I had nothing but disdain and contempt for him. He was in my mind a traitor, taking secret documents in a time of war, leaking them to the media, and imperiling our military forces in combat.

In the days following June 14, the administration sued to have further publication of the Pentagon Papers stopped, which became a famous test case of "prior restraint"—attempts by officials to have material suppressed before publication. The legal points quickly became moot. Ellsberg had given so many newspapers copies of the Pentagon study that one paper after another began publishing, frustrating Attorney General John Mitchell's efforts to get restraining orders in the courts.

The president called me into the Oval Office one day after Ellsberg's role had been confirmed. Pacing in front of the doors to the Rose Garden, Nixon said, "I want Ellsberg exposed, Chuck. I want the truth about him known. I don't care how you do it, but get it done. We're going to let the country know what kind of 'hero' Mr. Ellsberg is."

"Yes, sir, it will be done," I said. I, the former marine officer, was so full of fire for the job, I could have saluted.

I wasn't sure how I would fulfill the order the president gave me, but I knew that I had to obtain information about Dr. Ellsberg. If I could find a way to prosecute him, I'd do that. If I could find a way to undermine his credibility, I would do that. This was not child's play or politics as usual. Too much was at stake. I wasn't blindly following orders. I was thinking about what was right and what was wrong.

I went to White House Counsel John Dean and asked him to get me Daniel Ellsberg's FBI file. The FBI compiles an encyclopedic background dossier for anyone who works in a government position as sensitive as Ellsberg's. The bureau interviews friends, enemies, wives, and ex-wives, and everything that's said in these interviews, true or not, is noted.

Ellsberg's file contained very derogatory personal material. It seemed to be the perfect means to fulfill the president's wishes. If we could show the nation that Daniel Ellsberg was far from a hero, then his action of releasing the Pentagon Papers would be viewed in an unfavorable light. He would appear to be the traitor I took him for rather than a champion of free speech and government openness.

I invited a reporter from the *Detroit News* into my office for information "on background"—meaning sensitive information he could use as long as he kept his source confidential. I showed him Dr. Ellsberg's FBI file. "Do you want to know who the guy is who is trying to bring down Nixon and our foreign policy?" I asked. "Just read this."

I was certain that Ellsberg's stealing the documents was wrong, but I never even stopped to question if my efforts to stop him were wrong. As I later realized, in handing that reporter Ellsberg's file, I committed a crime. Yet that never registered with me. The "still, small voice of conscience" that usually deters us from our worst actions seemed to be cheering me on. I felt totally righteous, even idealistic, in what I was doing. After all, I was serving the cause of peace and security.

I want to make it clear that I never did anything in the White House that I thought at the time was illegal. I would never have knowingly risked my law license that I'd worked so hard to earn. I would go right up to the line, but if I thought something was beyond the line— and there were many such occasions—I wouldn't touch it. I didn't think giving materials to the newspapers about somebody who'd stolen documents was illegal. (Indeed, it wasn't, until I pleaded guilty; the prosecutor said my case established the precedent.) But the reporter did not have the necessary government clearance to see the documents, a fact that I had purposely overlooked. It was also, as I later pleaded, an obstruction of justice to attempt to affect a defendant's rights in court.

What undid me, as I'll be discussing in greater detail later, was my blind self-righteousness. I thought I had built such a moral hedge around my actions that I *couldn't* commit a grave moral offense, much less a crime. My defense against moral and legal failure assured me that I couldn't be in the wrong even as I committed a felony. Once I had reflected, I knew at the deepest possible level that I had betrayed my own standards, but in the moment I disengaged whatever alarms my conscience might have triggered by the powerful presumption of my own innocence.

Ironically, the *Detroit News* reporter never printed the material I provided. The Copley Press did, however, when someone within the FBI delivered the same information.

At my urging, the president approved Ellsberg's prosecution, which had been recommended by the Justice Department. Ellsberg was indicted on June 28, 1971—two weeks after the first stories broke—for unlawful possession of secret government documents. The case was dismissed in April 1973 because of the government's misconduct against him, including my own.

The Ellsberg case, including the plumbers' breaking into his psychiatrist's office to seize records about him, was a central issue in the great scandal known as Watergate, which exploded in June 1972, when some of the same plumbers engineered the break-in at the Democratic National Committee headquarters. The FBI and the U.S. Attorney's office began an immediate investigation.

I had known nothing of the break-in, and the initial prosecutors in the case cleared me. But the real scandal of Watergate was the cover-up—the attempt to protect the president and his staff. It started with modest efforts to throw the prosecutors off the trail. In a matter of months it turned into a massive cover-up. In the spring of 1974, indictments came down against several of us who were senior assistants to the president.

In May 1974, although I had earlier declined offers of a lighter sentence in exchange for testimony against Nixon, I realized that I was, in fact, guilty of interfering in the Ellsberg case. After conferring with my closest friends, I decided to plead guilty to the single charge of obstruction of justice, for which I was given a sentence of three years.

I admitted that I had devised "a scheme to obtain derogatory information about Daniel Ellsberg, to defame and destroy Mr. Ellsberg's public image and credibility, . . . to influence, obstruct, and impede the conduct and outcome of the Ellsberg trial."

Through much soul-searching I had come to the conclusion that this was a just charge—one whose very words I composed myself. By attempting, if not accomplishing, the release of damaging information about Daniel Ellsberg's character, I had hoped to make it impossible for him to receive a fair trial. As a lawyer I should have known that smearing him in the press would prejudice the entire country and any possible pool of jurors. (I was being smeared daily by Woodward and Bernstein, so I knew how it felt.)

On July 8, 1974, my friend Graham Purcell drove me to a dingy Baltimore hotel, where four armed U.S. marshals picked me up and took me to prison. The meeting place had been arranged as a means of avoiding the press, but the media chased us from my home in McLean, Virginia, all the way to Baltimore. After giving my wife, Patty, a final kiss, I was put in the back of an unmarked car and taken to a prison on the army base in Fort Holabird.

Driving to prison at Fort Holabird, I felt almost emotionless. I was totally drained. My father was sick (he died a month later), and Patty was left with huge responsibilities she'd have to handle alone. I had been through the wringer in the national press. I did feel a measure of relief that part of the ordeal was finally over. And strangely, I felt no fear. In fact, on that ride to Baltimore, I remember wondering why I wasn't afraid, even knowing that high government officials often have their lives threatened by resentful prisoners. But the day of my arrival at Holabird, I felt some semblance of peace. I knew I had to do this, to get it behind me. I figured as a former marine, I could handle myself in prison. I hated being away from the family, of course, and I did feel disgraced. I couldn't imagine what the future held, but I was prepared to do prison one day at a time.

Fort Holabird reminded me of a ghost town. The windows of its redbrick buildings and soot-covered, green wooden shacks were boarded up. Rampant weeds clung to every wall. In the midst of the otherwise deserted base, a nine-foot chain-link fence topped by razor wire surrounded one of the wooden buildings. One thing about the barbed wire surprised me, however. It was tilted outward—as if it was more important to keep people out than to keep the inmates in. I soon discovered why.

Holabird was filled with high-profile witnesses, most of whom were in great danger because they were "government witnesses": mafiosi who had entered the federal witness-protection program and former drug kingpins who had copped pleas in exchange for testimony against their bosses and others. One of the inmates was a hit man who had killed twenty-eight people. Other inmates included men from the famous French Connection drug case and people who had turned state's evidence against judges. I learned that most men at Fort Holabird had a contract out on them, which explained why the guards were all heavily armed and why the barbed wire pointed outward. Odd to be more in danger from the people outside prison than from the people inside.

Holabird would also house all the major Watergate figures who would be testifying before grand juries. When I first arrived, only Herb Kalmbach, the president's personal attorney, was in residence. John Dean and Jeb Magruder had yet to arrive.

The prison building was a far cry from the regal surroundings of the White House. Paint was peeling from the grimy walls, and steam pipes ran down the long corridor through the center of the building, which was illuminated only by dim lightbulbs dangling every thirty feet.

The deputy marshal led me to the control room for fingerprints, Polaroid snapshots, inspection of my personal effects, a thorough shakedown for drugs and contraband, and the filling out of endless forms.

After I completed the processing, I was turned over to Joe, a swarthy inmate who spoke halting English. He showed me to my room, a nine-by-twelve cubicle tucked under the eaves on the second floor. The room was furnished with a maple bed, a battered dresser, and a small wooden desk. The desktop was etched with graffiti from the generations who had passed through this room—from young army lieutenants to federal prisoners. The temperature in the room was over a hundred degrees. Baltimore was in the grip of the worst heat wave of the year.

As I lay on my bed that night, trying not so much to sleep as to catch my breath in the oppressive heat, I wasn't afraid—at least not physically. I had been in the marines and had lived in just about every kind of circumstance. I'd always been resilient. I wasn't worried about the future or about making a living after prison. I was confident that I could get a good job in business or get my law license back, at least in some jurisdictions. The thought of having to live in these circumstances for the next three years was difficult, of course, but most painful was the separation from my family and my sense of helplessness.

But for me, the most shattering thing about prison was the thought that I would never again do anything significant with my life. I was always a patriot, which is why I volunteered for the marines. I had gone into politics motivated by idealism, believing I could make a difference for my country. When the president asked me to serve him, I readily gave up a six-figure income (a lot of money in the 1960s) because I thought it was my duty to serve, to make this a better world. Now my own government had thrown me in prison. That cloud would follow me for the rest of my life. I would forever be an ex-convict. I had known the heights of power, helping to shape the policies of the most powerful nation on earth. In the future I wouldn't even be able to vote, let alone go back into politics, which I loved. I could never fulfill my dreams.

> *The most shattering thing about prison was the thought that I would never again do anything significant with my life.*

The story I had been living had come apart, and I couldn't find the ghost of a theme that might continue. My future seemed imprisoned—for life. True, I had thought of success in material terms—power, money, fame, security. But I had also seen success as doing things that affected how people lived. How could I ever achieve this now? I would always be a marked man, an ex-convict, a disgraced public official.

# CHAPTER 3

# THE GREAT PARADOXES

PRISON TURNED OUT to be one of the best things that ever happened to me, which is why, on the *60 Minutes* program marking the twentieth anniversary of Watergate, I told a startled Mike Wallace, "I thank God for Watergate." Not only did prison radically transform my view of life, but the experience also gave me the one thing I thought I would never have again—an opportunity to serve others in significant ways. In my case that service has been a ministry to prisoners around the world.

My experience vividly illustrates that paradox lies at the very heart of life's mystery: What we strive for can often be what we least need. What we fear most can turn out to be our greatest blessing.

G. K. Chesterton defined a paradox as "truth standing on her head to get our attention."[1] You cannot search for the good life without stumbling over paradoxes: seeming contradictions that turn out to be true.

All of my early expectations in life were certainly turned on their heads before my life righted itself. In this way I discovered the first of life's great paradoxes: *Out of suffering and defeat often comes victory.*

The great nineteenth-century novelist Fyodor Dostoyevsky experienced this paradox in an unexpected and dramatic way. Enamored with French utopian socialism, the young Russian intellectual attended a meeting that the czar believed was subversive. For that, Dostoyevsky was condemned to eight years of hard labor. After he had been in custody for a time, he learned that his sentence had been changed to execution by firing squad.

On a bleak winter day, Dostoyevsky and his fellow prisoners were marched through the snow in front of the firing squad. As a military official shouted out the death sentences, a priest led each man to a platform, giving him an opportunity to kiss the cross the priest carried.

Three of the prisoners were then marched forward and tied to a stake. Dostoyevsky looked on, realizing he would be next in line. He watched the soldiers pull the men's caps down over their eyes. He felt revulsion in his stomach as the firing squad lifted their rifles, adjusted their aim, and stood ready to pull the triggers.

*Out of suffering and defeat often comes victory.*

Frozen in suspense, Dostoyevsky waited for what seemed like a lifetime. Then he heard the drums start up again. But they were beating retreat! He watched, stunned, as the firing squad lowered their rifles and the soldiers removed the prisoners' caps from their eyes. Their lives—and life would be spared.[2]

Immediately after this incident, Dostoyevsky wrote a letter to his brother about the change the experience had worked in him: "When I look back on my past and think how much time I wasted on nothing, how much time has been lost in futilities, errors, laziness, incapacity to live; how little I appreciated it, how many times I sinned against my heart and soul—then my heart bleeds. *Life is a gift.* . . . Now, in changing my life, I am reborn in a new form. Brother! I swear that I will not lose hope and will keep my soul and heart pure. I will be reborn for the better. That's all my hope, all my consolation!"[3]

Dostoyevsky's near execution and the eight dreary years in a Siberian prison gave him a unique gift: the ability to see life from its end. He understood what really mattered in a way most of us never do. And this perspective equipped him to write great novels filled with incredible insights into the human condition and into the battle between good and evil.

Dostoyevsky's novels helped keep the Christian faith alive during the seventy years of Soviet repression. Aleksandr Solzhenitsyn, the dissident whose Nobel Prize–winning books exposed the repression of the Soviet gulag, took many of his cues from Dostoyevsky. Through Solzhenitsyn and other dissidents who treasured Dostoyevsky's work, Dostoyevsky's suffering proved an indirect but powerful force in toppling the evil Soviet regime. Out of suffering and defeat comes victory.

This paradox was evident as well in the life of a twentieth-century

American on Wall Street. During the Roaring Twenties, William Wilson made a fortune as a stock analyst. He was one of the first to investigate companies personally, riding up and down the Eastern Seaboard on a motorcycle, his wife in a sidecar. Nearly broke, Wilson bought one or two shares in companies like General Electric and Alcoa, just enough to represent himself as a stockholder, someone whom the management had an obligation to entertain.[4] The famous stock speculators Frank Shaw and Joe Hirschhorn valued Wilson's reports and began paying handsomely for them. They lent him money so that he could buy for himself some of the stocks he recommended to them.

Soon Wilson and his wife bought two adjoining apartments in a Brooklyn brownstone, knocking out the common walls to produce a luxurious residence. However, Bill Wilson had a deadly habit: He drank too much. That habit soon cost him everything and sent him deeply into debt. A New York physician told Bill Wilson that if he did not stop drinking, he would soon be dead.

Thinking he knew better than the doctor, Bill Wilson did not stop drinking. He found himself in the hospital three more times before he finally called out for help. "If there be a God, let Him show Himself now!"[5]

The peace and relief that Bill Wilson suddenly experienced after calling out to God gave him the strength never to drink again. He and Dr. Robert Smith ("Dr. Bob") cofounded Alcoholics Anonymous, whose tenets include the paradox that "bottoming out" is the foundation of a new life. As a result of AA, millions of men and women around the world know that out of defeat and suffering comes victory. By this I don't mean to suggest an inverted value system, that we should indulge personal failings so that good will come out of it.

Many people go through transforming experiences that have nothing to do with self-destructive behavior. Before marrying former Beatle Paul McCartney, Heather Mills was one of Britain's supermodels. On a skiing trip to the former Yugoslavia, she witnessed the first onslaught of fighting in Croatia. She immediately organized a campaign to aid the war's victims. Later an accident with a police motorbike in London left her with an injury resulting in the amputation of her left leg below the knee. Rather than sulk in her misery and focus on what she had lost, she chose a different route. She told the press, "Something good is going to come out of this accident. It seems like fate's way of telling me there is something else in store."[6] Drawing on the same compassion that propelled her into responding to war victims, Heather dedicated her energy to acquiring artificial limbs for poor people. Then she, along with her husband, Paul McCartney, launched a campaign against land mines. Her difficult circumstances enabled her to identify with people in need. Out of defeat and suffering comes victory.

What do these experiences have in common? Do they teach us that overcoming a crisis somehow magically erases our weaknesses? Hardly. Dostoyevsky, for all of his vows to lead a sterling life after his near execution and imprisonment, became a compulsive gambler. Bill Wilson suffered from depression to the end of his life. Speaking personally, I'm far from the image people have of me from reading my books.

What's more, not everyone is affected in the same way. Countless people go to prison or suffer from addictions or witness war's atrocities and remain the same people—or become even more deeply flawed. No particular virtue comes from having undergone a trial. The outcome depends on how we choose to react to the crisis. It's not so much what happens in life that matters as how we react.

What these experiences do have in common is their power to open our eyes to *reality*. If you haven't had that moment and you're a person of prayer, pray that you will. Life, as I have discovered, is infinitely richer thereafter, for crises can show us who we truly are.

———·•·———

When I was in Australia a number of years ago, I was invited to speak at the National Press Club, which has a weekly luncheon in the capital, Canberra. The speech and questions were broadcast live across the country. I spoke for twenty minutes about my own experiences and took questions for the remaining thirty minutes. If I thought the American press corps was rough, that was only because I hadn't met the Australian press corps. It was a bruising session. Near the end, an Adelaide reporter stood, raised his hand, and said, "Mr. Colson, you're the only person alive who has lived two lives. Sum up for us what you have learned."

I looked at the clock and saw fewer than thirty seconds remaining. Searching for a quick answer, I simply repeated what Jesus once said,

"Whoever wants to save his life will lose it, but whoever loses his life for me will save it."

With that, the minute hand on the clock hit 2:00 p.m., and we were off the air. I imagined people all over Australia scratching their heads in bewilderment. What about those Yanks who come down under and speak in riddles, eh?

I've discovered in my own life the truth of a second great paradox: *We have to lose our lives to save them.* Losing our lives means getting ourselves out of the way. This is a profoundly radical message in today's popular culture, which has produced an entire industry devoted to teaching us how to "find ourselves." But the good life isn't about finding ourselves; it's about *losing* ourselves. Once self is subordinated, we can discover a new identity with others—and a new understanding of who we really are.

My experience in prison helped me see who I really was. When I was shipped from Fort Holabird to the federal prison camp at Maxwell Air Force Base in Montgomery, Alabama, I experienced some depressing moments. The place was dreary—a big, old, one-story dormitory building with cots lined up every few feet. Everything in the place was a beige fog. The dirty floors, the blankets, the lockers—everything was beige or a drab brown. When I was assigned my cot, I took the mattress outside, removed the cover, and shook it. Half a pound of dirt blew into the wind.

*We have to lose our lives to save them.*

My fellow prisoners were everything from small-time offenders like moonshiners, embezzlers, and drug dealers to heavy-duty murderers and armed robbers.

The third day I was at Maxwell, it rained, and the work detail to which I was first assigned, the groundskeepers, were excused from duty. I found an empty spot in the dayroom to do some quiet studying and I was reading the Bible when I came across a verse that struck me hard: Christ had become human so that He would not be ashamed to call us His brothers.[7]

That was a profound moment of insight for me, an epiphany. I suddenly saw life differently. The men around me weren't "murderers" and "robbers" and "drug dealers"; if Christ was not ashamed of them, they were brothers, human beings just like me. Some of them had done terrible things, sure. But so had I. I might have some talents that society rewarded more highly than it did the talents of these men, but those abilities had been given to me at birth. I had nurtured them, it's true, but I had also misused them time and again. I realized that anything that might distinguish me from these other men was a difference in degree, not kind. We were all gifted and flawed people, and I could no longer pretend that I was qualified to judge anyone. If Jesus was not ashamed of me, who was I to place myself apart? I became convinced—no, *convicted*—that in God's eyes, I was fortunate to be someone, like my fellow prisoners, of whom Jesus was not ashamed.

Dostoyevsky had a similar experience. In his Siberian prison he found himself the beneficiary of a peasant's unstinting friendship. One day in their dormitory the peasant looked at Dostoyevsky with tremendous brotherly love. Remembering the encounter, Dostoyevsky wrote, "When I got off the plank bed and gazed around, I suddenly felt that I could look on these unfortunates with quite different eyes, and suddenly, *as if by a miracle,* all hatred and rancor had vanished from my heart."[8] He later wrote in *Diary of a Writer* that he had discovered in his contacts with other inmates, "a brotherly merger with them in a common misfortune." He then said that he realized that he had been "made equal to them, and even to their lowest stratum."[9]

———•◦•———

I never truly understood people until I was crushed. Until I lost everything and ended up in prison, I was never genuinely empathetic. My defeat allowed me to experience a compassion that I had never known before. Through losing my life, I began to have more genuine relationships with those around me, and through them with life itself.

Hundreds of people have told me that when they first heard about my Christian conversion and my work in the prisons, they were suspicious, if not cynical. Many thought that I was trying to get back into the good graces of society; I was trying to prove that I was really a good guy, not the bad guy I had been painted in Watergate. Others believed that I was trying to work my way back into politics. I laughed when I realized half the world believed that. The other half probably thought I'd lost my mind.

The truth was, I really didn't care if people thought I was crazy or if they thought I was angling for public sympathy. I was no longer a prisoner to other people's expectations. I had decided to do what I believed was right. We have to lose our lives to save them. A bewildering paradox, but it is the most liberating experience imaginable.

This led me to the discovery of a third great paradox: *Freedom lies not in conforming to the world's expectations or even realizing what we take to be our deepest wishes; it lies in following the call on our lives.* Most of us think of freedom as the absence of restraint or the elimination of responsibility. But that's not it at all. Each of us is called to some work, and our ultimate joy and fulfillment—yes, freedom—will come in our obedience to that mission.

When I was released from prison on January 31, 1975, I expected to finish writing a book I had started in prison and then resume practicing law in Massachusetts. I also had some good business opportunities offered to me. Even former President Nixon offered to help. He called one day from his exile in California to welcome me home. After a few pleasantries he said, "I know you're involved now in this religious effort. I hope you're not thinking about that as a career." I told the president that I hadn't made a decision, that I needed some time to get adjusted to life after prison. He said, "Well, you know, boy, you have tremendous ability. You can go to the top in the business world and make millions. You just give me the word, and I'll call my friends. I know Bob Abplanalp or Jack Mulcahy or any number of others would love to have a guy like you. You just tell me."

*Freedom lies not in conforming to the world's expectations or even realizing what we take to be our deepest wishes; it lies in following the call on our lives.*

Nixon's was not the only call. I received others as well from onetime clients and friends. But through this period I found that none of the offers, tempting though they might once have been, seemed to have any appeal to me. I could not get out of my mind the men I had met in prison. Freedom, I was discovering, had less to do with being inside or outside of a prison than with not having to live up to false expectations.

One of the prison experiences that haunted me happened one night when I was in the common meeting area at the end of the dormitory, writing a letter to Patty. Many of the other inmates were crowded around a noisy television or playing cards. Previously I had noticed a tall, sometimes angry, African-American who was something of a leader. Archie was also a jailhouse lawyer. Suddenly—I don't know what prompted it—he stood up and said in a loud voice, "Hey, Colson! What are you going to do for us when you get out of prison?"

I was startled, thought for a moment, and then said, "Archie, I won't forget you guys when I leave here."

Archie took the deck of cards in his hands and threw them down. They scattered into fanning piles, some of them cartwheeling over the floor. "Ah, that's what all you big shots always say, but then you forget little guys like us."

In the months after I was released, I often thought about Archie's comments, and it gradually became clear to me that I had been in prison for a purpose. I had encountered people who had no hope, who had no one to care for them. Some of the men spent year after year in prison without a single visitor. They needed a champion.

It took a year and a half of wrestling through the decision, but in the summer of 1976 Patty and I realized that caring for prisoners was my calling. So out of my prison experience, paradoxically, came a challenge, which has turned out to be more fulfilling than anything I could have ever imagined. Freedom lies in obedience to our calling.

An even better example of this paradox at work is evident in my precious daughter's life, which you caught a glimpse of in the introduction. Emily was a wonderful child, even during those late-teen rebellious years. I have always been so proud of her. After college she married a man who had an excellent job. I could see my daughter's perfect life emerging—happy marriage, success in business, a family grounded in the church, and children.

But after the couple's autistic son, Max, was born, their lives changed. The strain on the family resulted in divorce.

When this happened, Emily was almost paralyzed with fear. And I was cast into deep depression, grieving for the turn her life had taken.

But Emily fought back—and continues to do so. She has battled every inch of the way to get additional educational funding for Max, who is in a special school. She has been through all the agonies that single moms face as she raises a child under particularly challenging circumstances.

What has happened to Emily in the process, however, is truly extra-ordinary. She is a radiant person, filled with joy and excitement—and with an iron-strong character. Her own personal faith has deepened, so that at times she puts me to shame. Although she is a gifted artist and writer, she invests almost all of her life in her son. In all of these years, I have never heard her complain; on the contrary, she constantly talks about the joy of raising Max, who is indeed a very loving kid. When she describes her life, she says she has been entrusted with a box with the Hope Diamond inside. The box doesn't look that attractive, but when you open it, you see the most dazzling beauty.

Emily's story isn't just another example of someone who overcomes adversity. She illustrates how a person can find real joy in her calling, even when that calling comes as the result of difficult circumstances. A calling doesn't have to be to get to the top of the corporate ladder or to be the most glamorous woman at the party. The call might involve changing an older child's diapers, serving someone who can do few things but share his love. Freedom comes in obedience to our calling.

The idea that our calling might be something that's initially unat-tractive and doesn't enjoy much status may cause us to flinch. The pur-suit of the good life, as we will discuss it in this book, often makes demands that are both counterintuitive and countercultural.

---

Which brings me to a fourth great paradox: *We have to understand the evil in ourselves before we can truly embrace the good in life.* Until we understand our propensity to do wrong, we never achieve the ability to do the right thing.

> *We have to understand the evil in ourselves before we can truly embrace the good in life.*

Even if we know what is right, some-thing in us, some stubborn force, resists do-ing it. This was captured in a powerful scene from the old movie made of Tolstoy's classic novel *War and Peace*. In the film we see much of the great Napoleonic wars through the eyes of one particularly hapless character, Pierre. For him, things go wrong much more than they go right. At one riveting point in the film, Pierre, realizing his own inadequacies, looks heavenward, shakes his fist, and says, "Why is it that I know what is right, but do what is wrong?"[10] And if my experience is any guide, he might have added "and when I do what is wrong, I never admit it."

This paradox raises what is for many people an offensive notion: that we are basically fallen beings, that original sin has disposed us to do the wrong thing. It is too early in our journey together to examine that proposition, but suffice it to say that it would take a willful disregard of reality to argue that there is no such thing as sin. We need only look around us at the parade of horrors that confront us daily in our morning headlines.

Why do we know what is right but do the wrong? Why do we have such difficulty seeing the good and acting on its behalf?

I've thought about that a lot in my own life. I was well educated and well trained as a lawyer. I worked hard at my profession and thought I had a sterling code of ethics. If you had asked me in 1969 if I knew right from wrong and had the willpower to do the right thing, I would have been insulted. Of course I did! My dad taught me serious lessons about truth and truth telling, about right and wrong.

And yet in my life's most crucial hour, knowing what was right, I did what was wrong. Then I spent two years trying to justify what I'd done. As hard as doing the right thing is, acknowledging our own responsibility is often harder.

Seeing who we really are may be the greatest gift we receive from a significant personal defeat. People who are coping with addictions or trying to rebuild their lives after prison know that they are not innocent; they are part of what's wrong with the world.

Believe it or not, we all are.

Sadly, many people do live in denial. One of the little-remarked-on phenomena of the Nixon White House, which I believe had a great deal to do with the Watergate scandal, is that many of Nixon's top advisers were Christian Scientists. The president's chief of staff, Bob Haldeman, and domestic adviser, John Ehrlichman, among them. I cast no aspersions on anyone's belief; as I said at the outset, we're all seekers. I have known people who live very decent, upright lives as Christian Scientists. Still, there's one big flaw in their belief system— that evil is an illusion, that there is no sin or evil, that evil simply isn't real unless we allow it to invade our minds.

The weakness of this belief was most evident in an interview one of the original plumbers gave to the *Christian Science Sentinel* thirty years after Watergate. Egil Krogh, after explaining the laws he broke and the crimes of which he was found guilty, said: "But the truth is, I was never really guilty. The human experience indicated that I went through this life experience: working for Mr. Nixon, going through all that stuff. . . . But the fundamental idea was that my innocence had never, ever been touched. To explain it clearly, honestly, and do the best I can within the human context, my innocence became clearer as I went through it. By understanding my innocence, I was able to take the steps necessary to take responsibility for my actions. . . . My spiritual nature never changed."[11]

Guilt is innocence? If we can't accept our own failure and sin, then we can never escape it. Paradoxically, we can find the good life only when we understand we aren't good. Denial of evil always produces tragedy, in our own lives and in the community at large. We have to understand the evil in ourselves before we can truly embrace the good in life.

---

Understanding life's paradoxes is a key to finding and living the good life. Without understanding the paradoxical nature of life, we'll be unprepared for its unexpected reversals. We'll let things and circumstances throw us off course. We will feel as if we are trying to go up the down escalator.

We have to learn how victory can emerge out of suffering and defeat, and how we lose our lives to save them. We have to be obedient to our calling in order to be free, and we need to acknowledge our own evil in order to embrace the good. These upside-down truths are counterintuitive, decidedly countercultural. They are also wise beyond knowing.

> *We can find the good life only when we understand we aren't good.*

# CHAPTER 4

# A NICE PARTY WITH A
# LOT OF NICE PEOPLE

ON OCTOBER 28, 2003, a jury of the state supreme court in Manhattan watched a homemade video of the fortieth birthday party that L. Dennis Kozlowski threw for his second wife, Karen. The party, held on the island of Sardinia off the Italian coast, cost more than $2.1 million—or $28,000 per guest. Assistant District Attorney Ken Chalifoux introduced the video into evidence as part of one of the biggest corporate scandal cases ever. Kozlowski, the former CEO of the conglomerate Tyco International, and Mark Swartz, Tyco's former CFO, were accused of grand larceny and enterprise corruption for allegedly stealing some $600 million from Tyco.[1]

The birthday celebration included nearly a week's worth of activities, highlighted by the final poolside bash at the Cali Di Volpe hotel. As the Kozlowskis and their guests gathered, young women in togas and bejeweled headdresses scattered rose petals at their feet. Male models dressed as soldiers and gladiators were also there to lend a hand—or a cheeky hug.

During the course of the evening, pop singer Jimmy Buffett performed at a cost of $250,000. While Buffett sang Van Morrison's hit "Brown Eyed Girl," Dennis Kozlowski danced his heart out. The culminating party included a laser light show in Karen's honor, a birthday cake with exploding breasts, and an ice-sculpture fountain, a replica of Michelangelo's *David,* that streamed Stolichnaya vodka.

A poolside ballet was the night's most lavish production. Water nymphs in gauzy dress appeared first. Then, to the accompaniment of drums, bodybuilders in winged centaur costumes rushed down upon the nymphs. They circled the pool, preening for the nymphs and audience alike. Then the male and female demigods joined in pas des deux, their dance celebrating youth, beauty, eroticism—their own divine powers.

---

The prosecutor introduced the video because he felt it represented one of the many excesses that Kozlowski allegedly engaged in while allegedly defrauding his own company and its stockholders. Kozlowski picked up half the tab for the party, but he charged the other half to Tyco, although no business had been conducted during the weeklong celebration. Kozlowski reasoned that since half the guests were Tyco employees, the company should bear half the party's costs. The government disagreed.

An alleged theft of $600 million dollars makes the Great Train Robbery look like a 7-Eleven stickup. The magnitude beggars the imagination, particularly when one considers that L. Dennis Kozlowski's *authorized* compensation over the ten years he served as Tyco's CEO added up to more than $500 million. How, according to the government, did Kozlowski and Swartz do it? And why?

Behind these two questions lies a more searching one, the question of identity: Who would do such a thing?

L. Dennis Kozlowski was raised in a poor section of Newark, New Jersey. His family never had enough money to buy a home; his father worked as a private investigator. During his college years, Dennis worked to put himself through nearby Seton Hall University. He majored in accounting, keeping a B average. His middling grades were more the product of time constraints and priorities than lack of ability. In addition to his studies and his off-campus work, he joined two fraternities.

In 1975, Kozlowski met Joseph Gaziano, the chairman and CEO of Tyco Laboratories of Exeter, New Hampshire, which had been founded in 1960 as a scientific research lab. Often confused with the Mattel plastic-toy-making subsidiary by the same name, Tyco International had already grown by the 1970s into a large conglomerate through mergers and acquisitions.

Gaziano, who specialized in hostile takeovers, was a huge man with matching appetites; he owned a jet, a helicopter, and three luxury apartments. Gaziano hired Kozlowski to work for Tyco as a restructuring specialist, transforming the companies that Gaziano acquired into lean-and-mean profit centers.

In the early 1980s, when Tyco began to founder, John F. Fort III replaced Gaziano, his polar opposite. Fort, a frugal and circumspect New Englander, did away with the corporate jet and flew coach class. Perquisites such as company cars and country club memberships became taboo. Fort told Wall Street, "The reason we were put on earth is to increase earnings per share."[2]

Kozlowski showed that he could combine Gaziano's bold moves with Fort's bottom-line mentality. He cut base salaries. Each manager could earn substantial bonuses, though, for meeting or exceeding projections—far more in total compensation than under the old system. He fired managers for poor performance and sometimes made spectacles of them. Kozlowski held a yearly banquet at which he presented awards to both the best warehouse manager and the worst. The booby prize Kozlowski gave out was an ordeal for everyone. "It was kind of embarrassing watching a guy go up," says R. Jerry Conklin, a former Grinnell executive. "It was like his death sentence."[3]

Kozlowski was promoted to Tyco's board in 1987 and was named president and chief operating officer (COO) two years later. John Fort stepped aside in 1992, when Kozlowski became CEO.

Kozlowski was already enjoying the fruits of his labors. Even before he became CEO, he had moved with his wife, Angie, and their two young daughters into a $900,000 home in posh North Hampton on the New Hampshire coast. They seemed to have the perfect family. But as soon as Kozlowski made it to the top, his marriage apparently began to falter. Early in the 1990s he met Karen Lee Mayo, a statuesque blonde, who was also married. Karen would eventually become his second wife, but this hardly slowed down Kozlowski's philandering, which is said to have included many more affairs.

When Kozlowski became CEO, he moved rapidly to address Tyco's greatest vulnerability. The conglomerate looked well diversified, but 80 percent of the company's business came from commercial real estate building, a highly cyclical business. When commercial building slowed down, Tyco's revenues could drop like a stone.

Kozlowski proposed that Tyco move into a field that people need in good times and bad: health care. He moved to acquire Kendall International, which made disposable medical supplies. The acquisition proved to be a huge winner. Kendall soon formed the heart of Tyco Healthcare Group, which grew through further acquisitions to become America's second-largest provider of health care devices, right behind Johnson & Johnson. In 1995, the acquisition doubled Tyco's revenues and sent its stock soaring. The board raised Kozlowski's salary to $2.1 million dollars and awarded him a big block of shares under a new restricted-stock-ownership plan.

A major component of Kozlowski's management style consisted in hiring and promoting people like himself. He looked for people who were smart, poor, and hungry to be rich. After the Kendall deal, Kozlowski made his head of mergers and acquisitions, Mark Swartz, Tyco's chief financial officer. Swartz had neither an Ivy League background nor an MBA, but he had turned around a key report on Kendall's financials in twenty-four hours.

In addition to promoting people with a lean and hungry look, Kozlowski also kept a small core of devoted people around him. Their loyalty protected Kozlowski against suspicion for a long, long time. To everyone who worked with him, Kozlowski made the same proposition: You can be rich beyond your wildest dreams, or you can be gone.

Kozlowski's success at building the company through mergers and acquisitions kept the board so pleased that they left him alone, and the CEO's management style kept everyone else loyal and silent. At mid-year in 1995, Kozlowski convinced the board that Tyco should move its executive offices from Exeter, New Hampshire, to Manhattan. Tyco leased palatial offices at 7 West 57th Street on the forty-third floor overlooking Central Park. Kozlowski's personal office included a private bathroom and a separate kitchen the size of a one-bedroom apartment.[4]

With the shift to New York, Kozlowski's extravagance began in earnest. When Tyco's board approved a relocation plan for its executives, Kozlowski and his human resources director came up with a far more generous relocation plan, which allegedly included renting a Fifth Avenue apartment for $264,000 per year from 1997 to 2001. He also purchased with interest-free loans a $7 million Park Avenue apartment. It's been reported that Kozlowski repaid $5,118,125 of the loan and then simply forgave himself the balance. He also purchased a second, even more extravagant apartment in 2001 for $16.8 million and spent $3 million in improvements and $11 million in furnishings.[5] Despite these sybaritic perks, Kozlowski felt that he should pay no taxes on these benefits, so he ordered that they be "grossed up"—that is, he granted himself additional compensation equal to his tax liability. He enjoyed it all tax-free.

In 1997, Kozlowski earned $8.8 million dollars. In July of that year he received 3.3 million stock options. This upped Kozlowski's pay in 1998 to $67 million. It reached $170 million in 1999, ranking him second in income among all CEOs.[6]

The CEO's legitimate earnings, as huge as they were, did not meet his cash requirements—or wants. So Kozlowski turned another Tyco program into an ATM. Tyco's key employee loan (KEL) program was designed to enable employees to hold on to their company stock. From 1997 to 2002, according to the Tyco suit, Kozlowski borrowed $274,205,452 in KEL loans, nearly a quarter of a *billion* dollars. He used more than $245 million of this for purposes other than his tax obligations. He bought his racing yacht *Endeavor* (at a cost of $30 million); he paid for construction and remodeling at his various residences; he purchased more than $15 million worth of art.

Once Kozlowski made the transition from family man in North Hampton to wheeler-dealer in New York, his wanderlust demanded an increasing number of encampments. Besides his apartments in New York, he acquired homes in Nantucket, Massachusetts, and Beaver, Colorado. He also wanted to have his mistresses close at hand. As testimony at the trial revealed, events planner Barbara Jacques and secretary Mary Murphy lived cost-free in Tyco apartments during the time of their affairs with the boss. Kozlowski eventually gave $1 million of Tyco funds to Barbara Jacques, and Mary Murphy earned $765,000 for her year of dalliance. Both women were granted loan payoffs and generous severance packages.[7]

———•◦•———

Kozlowski began to run into trouble at Tyco when he pressed the firm to acquire its own piggy bank: a financing company known as the CIT Group. Many conglomerates have nearly foundered running their own financing arms; Westinghouse, AT&T, ITT, and Textron are notable examples.

Nevertheless, Kozlowski was enthusiastic for the idea of acquiring the CIT Group. One of Tyco's board members, Frank Walsh, introduced Kozlowski to CIT's chairman and CEO, Albert R. Gamper. This meeting led to Tyco's acquiring the CIT Group in June 2001 at a cost of $9.2 billion.

Kozlowski was grateful to Walsh and agreed to pay him $20 million for serving as a liaison. According to Tyco, the two then pledged to conceal this payment from the rest of the board.

Flying high in the aftermath of the CIT Group deal, Kozlowski hired a public relations firm and began promoting his ultimate ambition—a desire for enduring fame. He began eulogizing himself as the twenty-first century's corporate superstar. He wanted to be remembered for "some combination of what Jack Welch put together at GE . . . and Warren Buffett's very practical ideas on how you go about creating return to shareholders."[8]

On January 9, 2002, the Tyco board learned of the payment to Walsh for his work on the CIT deal. When CFO Swartz mentioned the unauthorized bonus in a rough draft of a proxy statement, alarm bells finally went off. The board confronted Walsh, who refused to give the money back and left the board. (Tyco promptly sued Walsh to recover the money.)

Kozlowski defended himself to the board by admitting the payment to Walsh was a mistake. He protested that he had halved Walsh's initial request for $40 million. Tyco hired the law firm Boies, Shiller & Flexner to investigate the Walsh payment and any other improprieties related to compensation.

———◆•◆———

Trouble was gathering for Kozlowski in another, unsuspected place. Irwin Nack, an investigative counsel to the superintendent of the New York State Banking Department, began tracking a series of unusual bank transfers. Over a few days, a number of wire transfers in the millions were made to the bank account of Manhattan art dealer Alexander Apsis.[9]

Nack thought he might be looking at money laundering. One

$3.95 million transfer came from a Tyco bank account in Pittsburgh. He knew nothing about Tyco and investigated its status. Nack called a fellow attorney, who suggested that the transactions might be related to tax evasion.

After the district attorney's office subpoenaed bank and transfer records, it found that Tyco was paying for paintings. But according to the government's subsequent indictment of Kozlowski, Tyco *wasn't* paying for more than $1 million in sales tax due on the paintings. Purchases made in New York by out-of-state residents for out-of-state uses are not subject to sales tax. The government concluded that Kozlowski was misusing this loophole to defraud the state of New York by having paintings shipped to the Tyco corporate offices in New Hampshire and then promptly returned to his apartments in New York.

The CEO's apparent tax-evasion behavior caused the district attorney's office to look at the whole scope of Kozlowski's spending. The district attorney eventually found all the facts that led to Kozlowski and Swartz's indictment for $600 million worth of corporate corruption.[10]

As Kozlowski's tangled web began unraveling, the CEO devised an exit strategy. On January 16, 2002, he proposed to his board that Tyco be broken up into four parts and sold.

Wall Street was spooked by the hastily arranged break-up plan, however. Investors feared Tyco was running short of cash. The CIT Group was shut out of the commercial paper market—a lender's chief source of ready cash. Tyco had to borrow more than $13 billion to cover its immediate needs.

When the investigating law firm started asking questions about executive compensation, they came up with answers that opened new avenues of inquiry. Pandora's box soon split wide open. In early May, New York prosecutors subpoenaed Tyco records related to Kozlowski's art purchases and compensation.

As these events unfolded, Kozlowski began to wear the look of a hunted man. He must have realized that his exit strategy was fatally flawed. For the company to be broken up, independent auditing teams would have to be brought in to double-check the finances of all Tyco subsidiaries. Not only would the investigation uncover his compensation scheme but also the scavenging effect of his management style.[11]

In April, Kozlowski retracted the break-up plan, informing the public that only the CIT Group would be sold. He had to admit that the acquisition of the CIT Group had been a mistake.[12]

Kozlowski tried to rally, keeping up a brave front. During a chat with editors of *BusinessWeek* in early May, he insisted that he would never resign as CEO. A week later, he gave the commencement address at St. Anselm College, a small Catholic school in Manchester, New Hampshire. "As you go forward in life," Kozlowski told the graduates, "you will be confronted with questions every day that test your morals. The questions will get tougher, and the consequences will become more severe. Think carefully, and for your sake, do the right thing, not the easy thing."[13]

Had he compartmentalized his own thinking to such an extent that he could extol virtue while practicing larceny? Or when he said, "for your own sake," was he reflecting on the fall just ahead?

On Friday, May 31, Kozlowski finally informed his board that he was about to be indicted. Tyco's board requested his resignation that Sunday, and Kozlowski gave it without a word of protest. Two days later he took his televised "perp walk" into court to be arraigned on the tax-evasion charges.

---

Is Dennis Kozlowski just another monster of greed and appetite that defies understanding? Or is there something in his story to which we can all relate?

Kozlowski's appetites were certainly monstrous, but they originated in desires common to us all. Dennis Kozlowski was reaching for a destiny many pursue. He liked to say that money is how you keep score. It would be a mistake to conclude that money alone drove him, however. If it had, he might have been satisfied with the $500 million in legitimate compensation he gained during his tenure as Tyco's CEO.

Kozlowski was after far more than money. He wanted to be known, remember, as a combination of GE's Jack Welch and the famous investor Warren Buffett. He wanted to be the early twenty-first century's most celebrated superstar of business. He wanted to be revered as a cultural icon. Fortune was his pathway to fame.

Even fame was insufficient to satisfy his longings, however. To fame Kozlowski added the thrill of trespass. He wanted to make up his own rules and then cancel these out and start again whenever he wished—a characteristic of both his sexual affairs and his business relationships. He wanted to do what he wished in the way that he wished to do it. And he wanted to be applauded and even loved for doing so.

Who enjoys such privileges?

Only the gods.

The birthday party on Sardinia was much discussed for its erotic flourishes. Commentators remarked on the party as a Roman orgy. Its true inspiration, however, was not Roman but Greek, not the feasts of Caligula but the lustful Mount Olympus. Barbara Jacques—the former mistress who planned the birthday party—knew the man who had briefly been hers. She saw him as a drunken Dionysus, wine glass in hand, chasing after nymphs. He was Riot incarnate. His was the Budweiser good life rendered in its proper mythological context. "A nice party, with a lot of nice people," Kozlowski remarked on the event—and by way of extension, his life.

These days, the chants of "Par-teh! Par-teh! Par-teh!" ring out across the cultural spectrum, don't they? Who doesn't want what Kozlowski wanted?

Who does not have an inner voice that says, "I can do what I please, in my own way and time, and be loved for it in the bargain"?

Because I am . . . god. "Maybe not *the* god," as Bill Murray's character claimed in *Groundhog Day,* "but definitely *a* god."[14]

What we see in Dennis Kozlowski is simply the infernal majesty and horror of that voice within us *winning*.

CHAPTER 5

# SHOPPING FOR THE
# HOLY GRAIL

THE STORY OF DENNIS KOZLOWSKI is a real-life parable of the good life conceived as wine, women, and song, with the power to replenish supplies at the snap of one's fingers. While the dimensions of his appetites make the story grotesque, their outsized character makes it easier to see our common longings for what they are. Kozlowski wanted to be rich. He believed that wealth would lead to limitless pleasure and achievement would lead to fame. He became obsessed with gratifying his own desires, despite the consequences to others. He thus exemplifies the modern American desire for personal autonomy, defined as freedom from all restraints, with the added kick of flouting the law. His ultimate goal became to do just as he pleased—to be his own god.

There may be saints immune to these siren songs, but I am not among them, and I doubt that you are either. Bizarre though Kozlowski's story is, I can identify with him. We both came from modest backgrounds. My view of life was particularly influenced by having seen bread lines in the Depression, and I vowed never to let that happen to me.

We both had an enormous drive to succeed. I won a scholarship to college and from there was determined to make it big. One night in my senior year, a fraternity brother and I discussed our futures. With the Korean War at its height, both of us were heading into the military: I into the marines and my friend into the navy. When we talked about what we would do after our service, my friend said, "I want to go for broke. I'd rather shoot for the top and crash in flames than never take chances in life." I was adventuresome by nature and agreed enthusiastically. We shook hands on it and said, "We're both going to hit it big. We'll be earning $10,000 a year." In 1952 that was an enormous salary.

After I got out of the marines, I scrambled up the ladder, finishing law school at night while working for a U.S. senator. Then, when I was only thirty, I cofounded a law firm that would become very successful. Eight years later I was seated in the office next to the president of the United States. I kept my bargain with my fraternity brother.

Yet at the peak of my power, I found the so-called good life empty and meaningless.

I have an idea that at the peak of Kozlowski's wealth and fame, surrounded by scantily clad nymphs, wine and song flowing, he found his life just as empty and meaningless. What do you do when the party is over?

In our heart of hearts, all of us understand that there has to be something more to life than money and fame. We have to see these counterfeits for what they are—fool's gold, not the genuine desires of our humanity. But it is not easy to do this in a culture that exalts the consumer and lavish spending.

———•◦•———

In one generation, America has experienced a dramatic transformation from a producing society to a consuming society. Thirty years ago, we measured our economy by what we produced. Textile mills employed hundreds of thousands in the South, and the biggest problem of great industrial centers was pollution from the giant smokestacks. America was the engine of the world's economy. Today we measure our economy by what consumers spend. Watch how economists make their forecasts on confidence polls, how closely the market follows Christmas retail sales.

In the transformation to a purchasing instead of producing culture, we have completely reversed the Protestant work ethic, which fueled the great economic growth in this country in the nineteenth century. At the heart of the work ethic was a belief that one should work hard, be thrifty, save, and produce. Delayed gratification was a virtue.

Today the concept of delayed gratification is seen as a denial of some inherent natural right, even a constitutionally protected one in many people's minds. If you can't afford it, finance it. In 2004, total consumer debt reached an all-time high of $2.03 trillion. The credit-card debt of the average American family increased by 53 percent from 1989 to 2001. Personal bankruptcies rose by 125 percent.[1] In old-fashioned terms, that means a lot of people got used to spending more than they had.

Consumerism has had a powerfully transforming effect, not merely on the spending habits but also on the beliefs and values of Americans and Western Europeans. The poster girl for the consumer age might well be young Washington hairstylist Jamie Gavigan, who was profiled in the *Washington Post*.[2] Jamie works nine hours a day, five days a week in a cramped space at a chic hair salon. Her clients pay as much as $285 and wait as many as six weeks to have Jamie highlight their tresses. She earns a handsome six-figure income.

Her money goes into serious shopping. Every year she takes fall excursions to New York, where she hits Barney's, Gucci's, Louis Vuitton's, and her personal paradise, the Manolo Blahnik shoe boutique on West 54th Street. Manolo Blahnik shoes sell at $445 for suede pumps to more than $1,100 for boots. Jamie Gavigan has thirty-seven pairs of Manolo Blahniks, which cost her, conservatively, more than $20,000. On one recent shopping excursion, she paid $900 for a white fur evening bag and $1,700 for a shearling bomber jacket designed by Michael Kors. Jamie Gavigan drops thousands of dollars on every foray to the Big Apple.

The attitudes of supershoppers like Jamie are summed up by Christine Kelley Cimko, a fifty-one-year-old vice president at a public relations firm. Christine speaks of the sense of security she receives from filling her home with possessions. She has salespeople—a whole network of them from Neiman Marcus to Saks to Nordstrom—who make it a point to contact her. "You have this little world that grows up around you, of people who are almost taking care of you. They are meeting your needs, finding those shoes in your size or making sure that when the Chanel bag comes in in beige, you get the call."[3] Her favorite purchase is a gold quilted Chanel handbag. "This is my treasure. . . . It's my little Holy Grail."[4]

April Witt, the author of the article about Jamie Gavigan and other supershoppers, comments: "Consumerism was the triumphant

winner of the ideological wars of the 20th century, beating out both religion and politics as the path millions of Americans follow to find purpose, meaning, order, and transcendent exaltation in their lives."[5]

One theorist of the consumer society, James B. Twitchell, finds in
the "shopper's epiphany" a kind of salvation. "It's that feeling of, phew,
I found it, I am saved." He defends consumerism as a belief system.
"[Shopping] is a heck of a lot fairer than the old systems where rank was
a birthright and largely immutable. And competitive consumerism is a
lot less bloody than epic battles over whose God is greater."[6]

We have come to see money as the key to pleasure, and pleasure as
the key to happiness. This definition of happiness has become the *sum-
mum bonum,* the ultimate American virtue. As one writer put it, "If you
are not chasing money, what are you chasing? . . . Happiness is the new
bottom line."[7]

This belief is so much a part of American culture that even people
who should know better get confused. According to a recent study, over
half of evangelical Christians agree with the following statement: "The
purpose of life is enjoyment and personal fulfillment."[8]

------•◦•------

But does consumerism *work* as a belief system? Can being a rich corporate executive or a supershopper make you happy? I had this question,
in a slightly different form, posed to me at a gathering in Hobe Sound,
Florida, one of the watering holes of the superrich. A friend who has a
home there was throwing a party, and she asked me to share my life experiences with her guests.

When I arrived that evening, I discovered a huge white tent spread
over the grand lawn behind my friend's majestic shoreline home. It was
extraordinarily beautiful. At five o'clock people began sauntering in,
most dressed in their evening finery. Following cocktails and my short
speech, they would all depart for their respective clubs, dinners, and parties. I've frequently been around powerful and wealthy people. Many, including some in attendance at my friend's party, have the air of assuming
that God had created the world expressly for them and their kind.

As the sun was setting over the Sound, I made my remarks to an audience that, for the most part, maintained a rather studied indifference.

Most Hobe Sound parties do not include speeches like this, intruding on people's pleasure. And if people felt any interest in what I was saying, the last thing they would do was admit it to their fellow guests.

When I concluded my remarks, I was received with respectful but unenthusiastic applause. At the suggestion of my hostess, I asked if anyone had questions. A few people had questions about Watergate, Nixon, or politics. No one asked about my conversion or my experience in prison.

After a few minutes, the hostess came forward and mercifully announced, "One more question."

A man leaning casually against a tent pole at the back, a cocktail in his left hand, gestured toward the water and said, "Mr. Colson, as you can see, all of us here live a very good life." Hobe Sound was filled with large and elegant yachts. "None of us, of course, would have any experiences like yours, going from the White House to prison. What would you say to people like us, who have no problems in life?"

I stared for a moment at the man and then told him that I had yet to meet anyone who did not have problems and that if people at the party were without problems, I'd really like to talk to them afterward to find out how they managed it. I told him that I could see that the surroundings were indeed regal and that the guests obviously had all of the so-called good things in life. "But," I said, "I question your premise. For example, what are you going to think on your deathbed, when you're lying there knowing that all of this is about to go away?"

The man looked like a suddenly flattened bellows, his expression crumpled and pained. An awkward silence followed.

I was grateful when the hostess brought my presentation to an end, but I then spent the next hour listening to people's tales of woe—divorce, family squabbles, civil suits, drugs, wayward kids, the works. No one accepted my invitation to explain how life can become problem free. No one under the tent lived such a life. The attitude was pure facade.

Over the years, studies have confirmed the old adage that money can't buy happiness (something people say but don't really believe). Take, for example, lottery winners—ordinary people like factory workers, small-business owners, and students. Suddenly, they hit it big, beyond their wildest expectations; they are instant millionaires. All the world is theirs, lying at their feet. In case after case, investigative journalists have reported that the winners either become recluses, lose their money to scam artists, or end up in drunken despair.

A similar fate happened to many of the survivors and heroes of the celebrated 2002 mine disaster in Somerset, Pennsylvania. After nine miners were buried alive, the town and the nation waited anxiously as rescue efforts were organized. Bob Long, a thirty-seven-year-old surveyor, was picked to pinpoint the spots where the air holes would be drilled. Had he missed, the miners would have died. But using his satellite surveying instruments, Long found the exact spot. He was an instant hero when all nine men were rescued alive.

In the immediate aftermath of the rescue, church bells rang, and people prayed to God in gratitude. Things quickly turned sour, however. The national press camped out in town and turned ordinary people into overnight celebrities who were soon quibbling over airtime. Several of the miners, flush with the checks for the TV rights to their story and basking in the nation's adulation, quit their jobs.

For Bob Long, briefly the hero, there was a movie and TV contract, sealed with a check for $150,000—more money than Long had ever seen.

Soon others began to resent Long. Some of the rescued miners were experiencing depression, loss of memory, migraines, and sleeplessness. Bob Long's life had not been endangered. Why was he receiving so much attention?

Long's newfound wealth, celebrity status, and the community's anger and resentment sent him into a tailspin. One evening, when his wife arrived home, she discovered her husband asleep on the couch. When she woke him, he was angry that he couldn't find his socks. Before she was able to grasp what was happening, Long walked out to his Dodge pickup, took his 9mm semiautomatic Glock pistol, and put it to his head. His wife, who had followed him outside, screamed, "Please don't do this!" Long pulled the trigger and killed himself in plain sight of his horrified wife.

The same destructive spiral can happen to anyone who becomes obsessed with money. A few years ago I visited an old friend whom I'd not seen in ten years. David had started with nothing, came out of the military, and worked in a factory. Although uneducated, he had an uncanny sense of value. He began trading in property and soon amassed a fortune. He was often generous, giving to a variety of worthy enterprises. He was nearly eighty years old when I visited his beautiful oceanfront Florida home.

We drank coffee on his terrace, looking at the surging waves of the ocean—a spectacular scene. I asked David what he was doing with his time. "I work on my investments," he told me. I asked if he traveled, exercised, or had hobbies. He shook his head.

As I was getting ready to leave, he invited me to see his office. It was in the back of the house, in a mostly darkened room with only a small side window. In the center was a massive desk that had once adorned his skyscraper office, from which he had looked out over his Atlanta real-estate fiefdoms. Occupying the center of the desk was a simple computer monitor surrounded by pages of investments.

"You're here all day?" I asked.

"Yes," he said nodding, "as long as the markets are open."

I asked him why he spent all day in a dark office. He certainly had plenty to live on comfortably and enough to give away all he wanted. He said, "I have a goal. Before I die, I want to double my estate." He smiled for the first time in our conversation.

I was saddened by my friend's response, even when he explained that all his money would be given to charity when he died. Was this purpose? Was it happiness?

Paradoxically, striving for possessions and money, the things we think will bring us pleasure and happiness, actually strips the meaning from our lives. We become cynical and crass. Life becomes banal. Our greatest thoughts turn out to be inanities, as in the case of Jack Welch, the former General Electric CEO who achieved the iconic status Kozlowski coveted. Welch ran up GE stock for the benefit of his stockholders, and not incidentally, his own benefit, accumulating nearly half a billion dollars.

When Welch retired, GE gave him free use of the corporate plane, the corporate apartment in New York, and generous retirement benefits. He was in great demand as a speaker, lecturing at Harvard Business School and elsewhere. This was the perfect American success story, apparently marred only by two failed marriages.

Following Welch's open-heart surgery, a reporter asked him whether he had had any epiphany during the ordeal. "I didn't spend enough money" was Welch's reply.

As for an epiphany, Welch vowed he would never again let a bottle of wine costing less than $100 cross his lips.[9]

What a commentary on the emptiness of material success.

Money, of course, is not an evil. The Bible says the love of money is what contaminates it.[10] There's nothing wrong with working hard, earning a living, accumulating resources, improving life for our families, investing for the future, and contributing to the world around us at the same time. We all want to make things better for our kids than we had it ourselves. If we're successful and manage to get out of credit-card debt, put something aside for our retirement, make gifts to those in need, and still have money left over for disposable income, then we're unusually blessed.

I have many friends who have built businesses and accumulated vast wealth. I have noticed that the happiest of these people, however, are the ones not controlled by their wealth. One such man is Dois Rosser, a close friend and automobile dealer from Tidewater, Virginia. At age sixty-five, when most men retire, Dois started a ministry with his own funds, building churches around the world, from Cuba to Vietnam, from India to Africa. Nearly twenty years later, Dois is still jetting from continent to continent.

After one grueling trip, he decided it was time to discuss the future with his family, so he gathered his wife, his three daughters, and their husbands for a weekend. The first night Dois announced that he was reviewing his estate plans and told each of his daughters what they could expect to inherit, unless, that is, they decided they would rather have him leave everything to the foundation for the continuation of his ministry.

It took only one family meeting to reach a decision. The daughters and their spouses unanimously agreed that everything should be devoted to building churches.

No one could ever say that Dois was obsessed with money or that obsession controlled him. He enjoyed creating great wealth and took even greater pleasure in giving it to people in need. Wealth, power, and fame are means that can be put to either good use or ill. It is only when we see them as ends in themselves that they reduce our humanity.

Mounting evidence supports the proposition that materialism cannot produce genuine happiness. Americans today enjoy a prosperity like no other people in human history. So if money produces pleasure and pleasure produces happiness, we should be the happiest people ever assembled on this planet.

The fact is, we are not. How can this be?

This is the question *New Republic* editor Gregg Easterbrook addresses in his provocative book *The Progress Paradox: How Life Gets Better While People Feel Worse*. Easterbrook reviews the extraordinary progress made since the time of our great-great grandparents: Average life expectancy has increased dramatically; we are far healthier, without the threat of dreaded diseases like polio and smallpox; the typical American adult has twice the purchasing power his or her parents had in 1960, with the quality of life immeasurably improved.[11] We ought to be very happy, Easterbrook concludes.

Yet Americans rank number sixteen in a survey of the happiest people in the world. (Nigerians rank number one.)[12] Americans tell pollsters that the country is on the wrong course, that their parents had it better than they do, that people feel incredibly stressed out. More people are popping Prozac and Zoloft pills; the number of people clinically depressed has increased tenfold in the post–World War II era. Remember the paradoxes we talked about earlier? Well, here is another: Life is better, but we feel worse.

At the root of this paradox is our mistaken belief about what produces happiness, as some fascinating research shows. In 2003, Harvard psychology professor Daniel Gilbert and his fellow researchers—psychologist Tim Wilson of the University of Virginia, the economist George Loewenstein of Carnegie Mellon, and the psychologist and Nobel laureate in economics Daniel Kahneman of Princeton—conducted an academic study to explore what produces happiness. Their task was to examine the ways in which we make decisions to shape our well-being, to explore what we think will make us happy, and then to discover how people actually feel when they achieve their goals. In short, the question

> *Life is better, but we feel worse.*

was, How well do our decisions about life give us the emotional consequences that we expect?

Their findings, reported in a fascinating *New York Times Magazine* article, made them wonder "if everything you have ever thought about life choices, and about happiness, has been at the least somewhat naive and, at worst, greatly mistaken."[13] Gilbert and his associates discovered that human beings overestimate the intensity and duration of emotional reactions. The researchers offer the example of believing a BMW might make your life perfect. Such a purchase always turns out to be less exciting than you anticipate, and its excitement lasts for less time than you imagine it will. The problem, Gilbert says, is not that you can't always get what you want. Getting what you want often doesn't give you the thrill you anticipated. In addition, you "can't always *know* what you want," because your desires bear little relation to the things that truly lead to happiness.[14]

According to researchers, a growing body of data points to the conclusion that the amount of money accumulated above middle-class comfort level has no impact on our happiness. While material acquisitions do not produce happiness, the researchers found that social interaction and friendships do give lasting pleasure.

Can we conclude from this that our natures as humans are shaped in a certain way? The researchers would certainly seem to think so, arguing that behavior follows a predictable pattern. This is why it is so crucial for us to understand this pattern—what this book will refer to as the natural order of life.

We all recognize the battle within us: One part of our nature says life has a higher purpose, and the other part wants to indulge all our desires. We want instant gratification. These temptations pull hard on us in this consumerist era in which the good life is constantly portrayed in terms of possessions and goods.

The problem is, if we give in to our basic desires, we sink deeper and deeper into self-indulgence—and feel worse and worse about ourselves. It's like drinking salt water; the more you drink, the thirstier you get. And if you don't understand what sodium does to the human body, you won't be able to figure it out. You will keep drinking, believing that more liquid will satisfy your thirst, and instead, of course, it will eventually kill you. The more we have, the worse we feel.

The task in life is to subdue our lower nature and govern ourselves by what I would argue we intuitively know to be our higher nature. Then we need to redefine for ourselves and our culture what happiness really is. It is not hedonism or self-gratification. The pursuit of happiness, our Founders said in the Declaration of Independence, is a God-given right. But the word *happiness* as the Founders used it has been drained of its meaning in our commercialized culture. What the Founders had in mind was the classical meaning—what the Greeks called *eudaimonia,* the virtuous life. This could be achieved only by righteous living, decency, honor, doing good. This is the definition and understanding of happiness that needs to be restored in American life.

*The truth is that happiness demands far more and far less than the sum total of our possessions and pleasures.*

Think about it. Put yourself for a moment in the shoes of Kozlowski or the other corporate raiders who acquired lavish possessions. Do you really believe that stealing a hundred million dollars, living in palaces, and drinking expensive wine gave them peace? All this could satisfy the sensory gratification that the lower nature requires, but I don't believe they could ever bring a true sense of fulfillment and meaning and purpose.

The truth is that happiness demands far more and far less than the sum total of our possessions and pleasures. What we truly long for isn't boundless riches. What we desire is a sense of significance and value—of human dignity.

# CHAPTER 6

# LAUGHING AT DEATH

ON THE EVENING of August 30, 1966, Nien Cheng sat alone in her study, reading *The Rise and Fall of the Third Reich*. It was a damp, cool night in Shanghai. The perfume of the magnolia tree outside drifted through the open windows. The house was unusually still, as if holding itself in against a cataclysm. Except for her two servants, Nien was alone. Her daughter, Meiping, was still at work at the Shanghai Film Studio, where she had been obliged to attend indoctrination meetings.[1]

Toward midnight Nien heard a truck rumbling down her street. It stopped outside. She caught her breath and waited. The next moment she heard the doorbell ring repeatedly and people pounding on the outside gate and shouting revolutionary slogans.

The Red Guards had finally come.

After she called to her servant Lao-zhao to open the door, Nien snatched a copy of the Constitution of the People's Republic of China. Her heart was racing, although she knew that she must appear calm at all costs. She was going to be bullied, and fear only incites a bully.

A gang of thirty or forty Red Guards burst through Nien Cheng's front door. Most of the guards were young, ranging in age from fifteen to twenty; three older people, their teachers, stood by.

The leader of the Red Guards stepped up to Nien Cheng. "We are the Red Guards. We have come to take revolutionary action against you!"

Nien Cheng held up the copy of the Constitution and looked the leader in the eye. "It's against the Constitution to enter a private house without a search warrant."

The man grabbed the Constitution out of Nien's hand and threw it on the floor. "The Constitution is abolished. It was a document written by the Revisionists within the Communist Party. We recognize only the teachings of our Great Leader Chairman Mao."

One of the Red Guards took the stick he was carrying and smashed the mirror hanging over a wooden chest in the entryway. Another guard replaced the mirror with a blackboard that bore a quotation from Mao: "When the enemies with guns are annihilated, the enemies without guns still remain. We must not belittle these enemies."[2]

With that, the young guards tore through the house, smashing furniture, dumping shelves of books onto the floor, slashing priceless paintings by Lin Fengmian and Qi Baishi. On a rampage, the eager students looted the closets and drawers, tearing most of Nien Cheng's clothing and linens. They overturned the bed mattresses and hacked them to pieces. Then they smashed her music recordings. Pressing on, they found the food pantry and dumped flour, sugar, and canned goods onto the ravaged clothing. They broke several bottles of red wine, pouring it over the mess.

When the Red Guards reached the third floor, where Nien Cheng kept most of her antique porcelain collection, they were making such a racket that it sounded as if the house were being razed, not merely looted. She went up to see what was happening, arriving just in time to see the intruders taking pieces of her valuable porcelain collection out of their padded boxes. A young man had arranged a set of four Kangxi wine cups in a row. He began jumping up and down on the first one.

Nien dived at the young man's feet. The wine cups were three hundred years old! She caught his leg as he raised it to smash the next cup. They both fell in a heap. He scrambled up and kicked Nien hard in the chest. Her cry brought other Red Guards to see what was happening.

Nien tried to reason with the guards in a conciliatory way. "Your being in my house has already improved my socialist awareness. It was wrong of me to have kept all these beautiful and valuable things to myself. They rightly belong to the people. I beg you to take them to the Shanghai Museum."[3] The students, having been taught that nothing from the past had any value, thought that Nien Cheng was trying to trick them.

She was particularly concerned about a blanc de chine Goddess of

Mercy figure called Guanyin. It was the work of the famous seventeenth-century Ming sculptor Chen Wei. The creamy-white figure's face was so beautifully captured that it seemed to be alive.

Nien said, "One of your placards reads 'Long Live World Revolution.' If you are going to carry the red flag of our Great Leader Chairman Mao all over the world, you'll need money to do it."[4] Her antique porcelain collection, she said, was worth at least one million yuan—the better portion of a million dollars.

The magical number *one million* caused the teachers in the group to take counsel with their young charges. The Red Guards finally decided to put the porcelain pieces back into their boxes and let their masters decide the matter later.

The next day, while the Red Guards still occupied Nien Cheng's home, a representative from the Shanghai city administration appeared to explain the long-range consequences of the Red Guards' revolutionary action. He told Nien that she and her daughter would be allowed to live in two rooms of the house. The additional rooms would be given to other families. "You won't be allowed to maintain a standard of living above that of the average worker," he said. "It's not the purpose of the proletarian class to destroy your body. We want to save your soul by reforming your way of thinking."[5]

When the Red Guards finally left her home, Nien Cheng found that they had posted a door sign saying that a "foreign spy" lived there. Even though her living situation in China was unusual, she was anything but a spy.

Nien Cheng came from a wealthy, landowning family. She had met her husband in London, where both were studying. In 1939, they married and returned to Chongqing, China's wartime capital. Her husband became a diplomatic officer of Chiang Kai-shek's Kuomintang government. In 1949, when Mao came to power and the Kuomintang fled to Taiwan, Nien's husband was director of the Shanghai office of the Ministry of Foreign Affairs. The Chengs did not flee the country, hopeful that the Communists' policies would moderate. Nien's husband helped with the transition from one government to another, serving as the foreign affairs adviser to the new mayor of Shanghai.

The following year he was allowed to leave the government to become general manager of Shell International Petroleum Company's office in Shanghai. Mao needed Shell. It was the only major petroleum company willing to do business with China. As a result, the Chengs were treated well by Party officials.

When Nien's husband died of cancer in 1957, Shell brought in a British general manager to replace him. The new manager needed help with the nuances of dealing with Chinese officials, and the company asked Nien to work as an adviser to management. She served as management's liaison with the Shell Labor Union and its overseer for government filings. She worked in this capacity until the spring of 1966, when Shell closed its Shanghai office after the government nationalized Shell's holdings. Until the first days of the Cultural Revolution, Nien Cheng had worked for a capitalist firm with the blessing of the Chinese government.

The collective mind of the Chinese government was always in flux, first favoring one faction, then another. Mao's Cultural Revolution was meant to insure the absolute rule of his policies, especially over those of a moderate, Liu Shaoqi. During the Cultural Revolution, Party members scrambled to align themselves with Mao's policies or at least to sidestep the necessity of contradicting them. Party factions sought to enhance their own power by demonstrating that their rivals had associated themselves with anti-Mao policies. Their power plays combined divide-and-conquer tactics with guilt by association.

Powerful people were about to make Nien Cheng their favorite sacrificial lamb—or to die trying. They thought she could be used to discredit their opponents. The ransacking of her house had been only a first step.

---

Several weeks after the guards had seized her home, a Red Guard and an older Revolutionary took Nien Cheng to a school building for a "struggle meeting," which was really a kangaroo court, packed with Red Guards and older Revolutionaries. The prosecutor announced to the gathering that the woman had descended from a landholding family, had been educated in England, was the wife of a man who had been a Kuomintang official as well as a worker for Shell International Petroleum Company. The prosecutor claimed that her interests lay with the capitalists—everyone at Shell deferred to her—which made her the natural enemy of Mao's China and China's great Cultural Revolution. He further made the case that since Shell conducted intelligence gathering for the British, sending agents deep into China's interior under the pretext of selling kerosene to the peasants, this woman must be a master spy for the British.

"You have listened to the evidence against you," the prosecutor said. "Your crime against the Chinese people is extremely serious. You can only be reformed by giving a full confession, telling us how you conspired with the British imperialists in their scheme to undermine the People's Government. Are you going to confess?"

Nien found the question outrageous. "I have never done anything against the Chinese people and government," she declared. "The Shell office was here because the Chinese government wanted it to be here. The order to allow Shell to maintain its Shanghai office was issued by the State Council and signed by no less a person than Premier Zhou Enlai."

With that, everyone in the packed room began screaming, "Confess! Confess!"

"We will not allow a class enemy to argue!" the prosecutor screamed. The Red Guards crowded around her and shook their fists in her face. They pulled at her clothes and spat on her jacket. "Dirty spy," they yelled. "Dirty running dog. We will kill you."[6]

Nien said in as firm a voice as she could muster, "I'm not guilty! I have nothing to confess."[7]

———•◦•———

On September 27, 1966, Nien Cheng was taken to the No. 1 Detention House, where most of Shanghai's important political prisoners were kept. By this time she had been separated from her daughter for several weeks. Meiping had been confined to the Shanghai Film Studio's "cowshed"—house-arrest quarters for those who had been denounced as "class enemies."

Nien's first sight of the prison corridor was something she would never forget: the long line of doors with their heavy bolts and padlocks receding to an uncertain and shadowy end.

Her cell proved to be unimaginably filthy. The walls, once whitewashed, were yellowed with age and streaked with dust. A single naked bulb hung from the ceiling. The damp cement floor had black patches of mold, and in one corner stood an open concrete toilet. The only light came from a small window shielded by iron bars. When she succeeded in opening it, a shower of dust and peeling paint rained down. The room contained only three narrow beds of wooden planks, one against the wall and two in bunk-bed fashion. The door to the corridor was solid except for an iron shutter through which her food and other necessities would be passed.

She took the few scraps of toilet paper she was allowed and tried to dust her bed. She thought she would never be able to sleep in a place so filthy, so she went to ask for a broom.

"It's past 2 a.m.," the guard shouted back. "You just go to sleep."[8]

Nien tried, only to be attacked by a swarm of mosquitoes. She waited through the night until the bulb in her room was finally turned off near daybreak and the first light stole through her small window.

Nien's first prison meal was dished into a battered aluminum container. She found that she would have to live on watery rice porridge with a few strips of pickled vegetables.

Soon after her first meal, she asked to speak to a responsible person, someone who would be able to clarify her case. She insisted that a mistake had been made. She had never committed any crime.

The guard told her that she must be guilty. Why would the authorities bring an innocent person to the No. 1 Detention House?

Nien remained undaunted and turned her attention to more immediate matters. She had to do something about cleaning up her room. She asked again for a broom. The guard informed her that normally prisoners were allowed brooms only on Sundays, but since she had just arrived, she could use one.

Soon after Nien set to work with the broom, a guard passed a piece of paper through the iron shutter. It was a receipt for the four hundred yuan she had been carrying when she was arrested—money she had meant to give her gardener as a last payment for his services. She was told that the money had been banked for her and that she could buy essentials with it. She instantly requested a washbasin, two enameled mugs for eating and drinking, some sewing thread, needles, soap, towels, a toothbrush and toothpaste, and some toilet paper.

The midday meal turned out to be boiled rice and green cabbage. Using a little of the rice, she made a paste to glue toilet paper along the edge where her bed met the dusty wall. This barrier against the filth made her feel much better. She used some of her drinking water to clean the room as well. Normally any change in a prisoner's cell, however minor, was not allowed. To justify her action, she quoted Mao: "To be hygienic is glorious; to be unhygienic is a shame."[9] In this way Nien adapted herself physically to her surroundings.

Nien resolved never to make a false confession. She had seen many people, even seasoned Party members, make ritual confessions because they hoped in this way to lessen their immediate suffering. Her firm resolution in the face of what became ever-greater persecution presents both a marvel and a profound mystery.

"When I was taken to the detention house, I could not look into the future," Nien Cheng would write later. "I was not afraid. I believed in a just and merciful God, and I thought he would lead me out of the abyss."[10]

Nien Cheng's formal interrogations in the detention house began a few months later. She was led into a back area of the prison compound, where a large wooden board announced: "Lenient treatment to those who confess frankly. Severe punishment to those who remain stubborn. Reward to those who render meritorious service."[11]

At first two officials handled her case, a lead interrogator and a secretary who kept records of what was said. During the interrogation Nien also noticed a small, shuttered opening through which these officials were being watched by another—undoubtedly a superior.

The lead investigator announced, "This is the Number One Detention House, a prison for political prisoners. This is the place where counterrevolutionaries who have committed crimes against the People's Government are locked up and investigated."

"In that case," Nien said, "I should not have been brought here."

The interrogator pressed on. "You are locked up here precisely because you have committed a crime against the People's Government."

"There must have been some mistake," Nien said.

"The People's Government does not make mistakes."

Nien continued, "You are a government representative. You can't make wild accusations like that."

"It's not a wild accusation."

"You will have to provide some evidence to prove what you are saying."

"Of course we have the evidence," the interrogator lied.

"Produce it then," Nien said sarcastically. "I don't believe you could possibly have any evidence against me . . . because I don't think you, or anybody else for that matter, could have something that simply doesn't exist."[12]

---

Nien and various interrogators would debate for years whether the People's Government had evidence that she was a spy. Her interrogators asked her to write copy after copy of her autobiography, hoping to catch her in discrepancies. They cited her friendships with British diplomats and others whom they suspected of espionage, but they could never prove their charges.

Nien's position throughout her interrogations was based on one principle. "Am I not to expect justice from the People's Government?"

"Justice! What is justice?" her interrogator said, scoffing. "It's a mere word. It's an abstract word with no universal meaning. To different classes of people, justice means different things. The capitalist class considers it perfectly just to exploit the workers, while the workers consider it decidedly unjust to be so exploited. In any case, who are you to demand justice? When you sat in your well-heated house and there were other people shivering in the snow, did you think of justice?"

"You are confusing social justice with legal justice," Nien said, countering. "I can tell you that it was precisely because my late husband and I hoped that the People's Government would improve conditions in China that we remained here in 1949 rather than follow the Kuomintang to Taiwan."

"In any case," her interrogator said, "we are not concerned with the abstract concept of justice. The army, the police, and the court are instruments of repression used by one class against another. They have nothing to do with justice. The cell you now occupy was used to lock up members of the Communist Party during the days of the reactionary Kuomintang government. Now the Dictatorship of the Proletariat uses the same instruments of repression against its own enemies."[13]

Yet Nien was convinced that a thorough and honest investigation of her case would allow justice to be done. She was so sure of this that she laid down the gauntlet to her opponents. One day she handed her interrogator the following statement: "I am a patriotic Chinese and a law-abiding citizen. I've never done anything against the People's Government. If the investigators of the People's Government should ever find anybody in the whole of China from whom I have tried to obtain information of a confidential nature, I'm prepared to accept the death penalty. At the end of the investigation of my case, when I am found to be completely innocent, the People's Government must give me full rehabilitation, including an apology to be published in the newspaper."[14]

In March 1969, the Revolutionaries staged another struggle meeting in order to break Nien. They drove her from the detention house to the school where she had earlier been harassed. There, in front of an audience of former Shell employees, they dumped her on the floor in handcuffs. For the last two years the Shell group had been imprisoned in the school while they were "re-educated" in Mao Zedong Thought.

The hall where the meeting took place was lined with large banners denouncing Nien as a spy. One by one Nien's former colleagues were compelled to come forward to indict her as a British agent. Finally, the chief accountant of the firm, a man named Tao, "confessed" to having been recruited as a British spy by Nien's husband. He accused Nien of offering him a large bribe to keep the nefarious activities of the firm secret.

Overcome by the stupidity of the show trial, Nien raised her head and laughed uproariously. Her laughter resounded in the hall and then came back to her as a ripple of giggles from her former colleagues. Her jailers quickly snatched her up and took her back to No. 1 Detention House.

They immediately put her through another interrogation session, demanding to know how she could laugh at being accused of a capital offense. "If you put on a comic play, you must expect the audience to laugh. It's the natural response," she replied.[15]

The People's Government did not have truth—or evidence—on its side, but it possessed power in abundance over Nien Cheng's life. One day Nien was taken to an interrogation where five people swarmed around her. Male and female guards pushed her from one to another. "You are the running dog of the imperialists," they shouted. "You are a dirty exploiter of workers and peasants."[16]

A male guard then picked up Nien by the lapels of her jacket and threw her against the wall. Before she collapsed, he grabbed her once more and threw her even harder against the wall. He repeated this again and again.

Nien was finally allowed to collapse into a chair. The guards kept raining blows on her, slapping her face. They screamed, "Are you going to confess? Confess!"[17]

When Nien refused yet again, the guards slapped handcuffs on her. "These handcuffs are to punish you for your intransigence. You will wear them until you are ready to confess. Only then will we take them off. If you confess now, we will take them off now. If you confess tomorrow, we will take them off tomorrow. If you do not confess for a year, you will have to wear them for a year. If you never confess, you will have to wear them to your grave."[18]

Just before Nien was led out of the room, a female guard ratcheted the handcuffs several notches tighter. She then took Nien to a five-foot-by-five-foot windowless torture cell. There Nien spent a sleepless night as her manacled hands began to swell and burn furiously. Guards came at random intervals to ask her whether she was ready to confess.

After twenty-four hours in the torture cell, Nien underwent another round of interrogation, where her accusers confirmed that the hard-edged handcuffs she was wearing could do serious long-term damage to her hands. "You are worried about your hands. That's quite right," they said. "Hands are very important to everybody, but especially to an intellectual who must write. You should try to protect your hands and not let them be hurt. You can do that easily by just agreeing to confess."[19]

The guard took Nien back to her regular cell but kept the handcuffs on. Soon they began to wear through her skin toward the bone. She felt only a small measure of relief from the swelling and burning by propping her hands on a rolled blanket as she tried to sleep sitting up. In the morning the blanket was covered with pus and blood. She began to run a high fever.

The handcuffs all but prevented her from eating and drinking. She was able to take in only a little nourishment by spilling her cup of rice and cabbage out onto a towel, then eating the food like an animal.

The guards' attempts to exact a confession from her never ceased. Their commands grew more distant, however, as her strength ebbed.

One day she came back to consciousness after fainting to find a group of guards standing above her. "Get up! Get up!" a man shouted at her. "You are feigning death! You won't be allowed to get away with it."

Nien's head cleared a little, and she found that her hands, although still bent behind her back, were no longer handcuffed.

"Get up! Get up!" a female guard shouted.[20]

Nien had been manacled for eleven days.

———•◆•———

Twice the lack of heat in Nien's cell during the severe winter sent her to the hospital with a case of pneumonia that the doctors presumed would kill her. The poor diet caused severe gum disease and menstrual hemorrhaging.

Neither her illnesses nor the torture caused her as much pain, however, as her longing for her daughter. What had happened to Meiping? Nien kept expecting to receive some word via a gift; other prisoners occasionally received packages with toiletries and other necessities from their families. None came. For a long time Nien Cheng told herself that because she was being denounced as a foreign spy, her daughter could not risk her own safety by contacting her.

By November 1971, the clothing the guards had retrieved for Nien five years earlier had worn out. She requested new clothes. She especially needed a new padded jacket because nearly all the stuffing had fallen out of her old jacket. The authorities promised they would do something.

One day she finally received a large bundle. When she untied it, she found the padded jacket, the fleece-lined winter coat, the two sweaters, and the pair of woolen underpants that the Red Guards had allowed Meiping to keep when they first looted the Cheng's home. Meiping's winter quilt was wrapped up in the bundle too. Nien looked at the blue jacket lined with maroon silk. She had bought it for her daughter in 1966, and it still looked as new as the day it came off the shelf.

Nien began frantically examining each article. None could have been used for more than one season. Nien could not resist the idea that her daughter had suffered the full measure of the Cultural Revolution's violence. Why else would the clothes have hardly been worn?

Suddenly it hit her with full force: Her daughter was dead. The thought came on Nien so violently that she found her legs shaking uncontrollably. Had her captors used her need of clothing to inflict a crippling psychological blow? If so, they had succeeded.

She called the guards and asked what had become of Meiping. The guard acted as if nothing had happened.

Nien summoned the guard again, but this time she did not respond to Nien's standard call. Throughout the next days Nien continued to call out to one guard after another.

She asked if she could send a card to Meiping.

The guards refused.

She asked if Meiping could at least write her a card saying, "Long Live Chairman Mao."

The guard told her that prisoners were not allowed to receive messages from their families.

Nien Cheng's anxiety over her daughter's fate was so great that she began wasting away. She became delirious. She was sent to the hospital, and even though her will to live had given out, she survived. She returned to No. 1 Detention House just before Christmas.

Throughout her years in prison, Nien Cheng had devoted her time more and more to prayer. Although raised in a traditional Buddhist home, Nien Cheng had become a Christian during her teenage years. She couldn't let the guards see her praying, so she opened up her copy of Mao's quotations—Mao's writings were the only books she was allowed—and bent over the book while she turned her thoughts to God. In prayer she sought solace for her grief. Her prayers began to inspire memories of the love she and her daughter had shared and the happy events of their life together. "More and more I remembered the days of her living," Nien writes, "and less and less I dwelled on the tragedy of her dying."[21]

In February 1972, President Nixon's elaborate secret plan paid off, the Pentagon Papers and the *New York Times* notwithstanding. He visited Beijing, the first American president to do so. While the Maoists trumpeted Nixon's visit as a great victory for Mao Zedong and a great defeat for the Kuomintang in Taiwan, Nixon's visit had a moderating effect on Chinese politics, just as he had hoped. It strengthened the hand of those like Zhou Enlai and Deng Xiaoping, who preferred pragmatic solutions to China's problems over Mao Zedong Thought and continual anarchy.

Oddly enough, Nixon's visit affected the political rivalries that caused Nien Cheng to be arrested. The Cultural Revolution had been the means by which Mao Zedong sought to gain the upper hand over Liu Shaoqi, Zhou Enlai, and other political moderates. One of Mao's radicals was most likely behind Nien Cheng's arrest.[22] If she "confessed" to being a spy, then the policy of the Shanghai moderates in sanctioning Shell's presence could be proven folly. The radicals and their allies could then replace the officials who favored the moderate policies of Zhou Enlai with their own loyalists.

Nixon's visit helped to prove the point that diplomatic relations and trade with other nations was in China's interest. Since Mao and Zhou Enlai were now united in their belief in international trade, there was no advantage in proving that Shell's former presence in Shanghai had been a mistake. International diplomacy had rendered Nien Cheng useless as a pawn. In fact, her continued persecution was now an embarrassment.

On March 27, 1973, Nien was ordered by a guard to gather all her things and was taken to an official who told her that her case had been clarified. The People's Government had concluded that her arrest was justified because she had defended the traitor Liu Shaoqi and had once mentioned the unavailability of bread in Shanghai to people in England. During her six and a half years of imprisonment, her attitude had shown improvement, however. The People's Government had decided to show Nien "proletarian magnanimity" by refraining from pressing charges against her and allowing her to leave the detention house.

"Haven't you something to say?" he asked. "Aren't you grateful? Aren't you pleased that you can now leave as a free person?"

She was so angry that she trembled. "I can't accept your conclusion," she said.

The truth was so important to Nien Cheng that she demanded a full apology in the Shanghai and Beijing newspapers. Until these apologies were made, she would not leave the prison.

The interrogator stood up. "I have never seen a prisoner refusing to leave the detention house before. You must be out of your mind. In any case, when the government wants you to go, you have to go. Your family has been waiting for you since early this morning."[23]

Nien's anger suddenly disappeared with the hope that she might see her daughter. Was Meiping waiting outside? Nien was willing to forego the apology and leave the prison immediately for the sake of seeing Meiping.

At the second gate beyond the prison Nien saw a young woman waiting beside a blue taxi. But she was shorter than Meiping.

It was her goddaughter Hean.

———•·•———

As Hean helped Nien Cheng move into the two-room apartment the government had designated for her, the goddaughter reluctantly explained that according to officials. Meiping had "committed suicide" soon after Nien's imprisonment. The government claimed Meiping had jumped out of the ninth-floor window of the Shanghai Athletics Association building.

Once Nien Cheng knew for certain that her daughter had died, she wanted to leave China. She would not emigrate, however, before fully investigating the circumstances of Meiping's death and bringing justice to bear. She reasoned that nineteen-year-old girls full of vitality and an eagerness for life simply do not jump out of windows.

Nien also had to take some time to recover her health. Because of her severe gum disease, all of her teeth had to be extracted. Her diet and the stress of prison had caused the acute hormonal imbalance that had precipitated her hemorrhaging.

Nien investigated Meiping's death slowly and quietly, for she was still being watched by political enemies. She was able to confirm her suspicions, however. For one thing, the ninth-floor windows of the Shanghai Athletics Association building were simply too small for anyone to jump out of. In time, Nien learned that Meiping's interrogators had wanted her to denounce her mother, giving evidence that Nien was a spy. When Meiping refused to do so, her interrogators began torturing her. They were not supposed to kill her, but as in many cases, the torture eventually became lethal.

Nien petitioned the government for her own full rehabilitation—the equivalent within Communist China of an apology—and for a full investigation of Meiping's death. In November 1978, twelve years and two months after her arrest, Nien was officially rehabilitated and declared a victim of wrongful arrest and persecution.

A short time later the Shanghai Film Studio was allowed to conduct memorial services for its members who had died as a result of persecution. The memorial for Meiping was attended by more than two hundred of her friends and fellow artists.

Much later a young man was tried for and convicted of Meiping's death, but he was given a suspended sentence. Political opponents in China remained wary of running up new scores that might be settled later on them.

Relations between China and the United States played a role in Nien's final exodus. Mao died in 1976, and those most responsible for the Cultural Revolution were imprisoned. Deng Xiaoping gradually assumed the reins of government, and the United States began considering most-favored-nation trading status for China. Regulations governing this status stipulate that nations must let their citizens travel for the purpose of family reunions.

Nien Cheng, with her indomitable will and tenacity, argued successfully that she should be allowed to visit with her two sisters in the United States. It did not hurt her cause that when her antique porcelain collection was discovered among property looted during the Cultural Revolution, she made it a gift to the Shanghai Museum.

She could take nothing with her to America, anyway, except her profound sense of dignity and worth.

# CHAPTER 7

# MORE IMPORTANT THAN LIFE ITSELF

THE STORIES OF Nien Cheng and Dennis Kozlowski appear to be worlds apart. However, they share one important truth: Both experienced the consequences of a materialistic worldview. Kozlowski embraced materialism; as he was fond of saying, "Money is how you keep score." Nien Cheng's oppressors believed, just as fervently, that man *does* live by bread alone. The difference between Kozlowski and the Maoists was who gets what and how—not the importance of getting itself. For materialists, reality begins and ends with money and the power that money can buy. As we see from these two stories, materialism is a closed, mechanistic, and ultimately dehumanizing life view.

Materialists of all stripes believe that who we are is determined by what we possess. The class from which we come, our education, our value to the labor market—all these determine our value. The Kozlowskis of the world—and the Kozlowski inside all of us—believe that being rich and powerful makes us better than others—so much so that we come to believe we are above the law. Communists simplify the equation by simply stating that the powerful *are* the law.

Westerners commonly make a distinction between *status* and *value*. Wealth and power confer privileges others do not have, and may even make someone a celebrity. A person like that certainly has *status* in our society. But we do not like to think of him or her as *better*.

Or do we? The popular television show *American Idol* suggests we do. The inner-Kozlowski believes that possessing money, power, and fame reveals the person's *being* as superior—as someone almost fit to worship. Indeed, some people have suggested that the celebrities of our day are substitutes for the Greeks' gods. We might think our fascination with celebrities is all in fun, something we don't take seriously, but how many people gear their lives to the attainment of celebrity status, and how many envy those who succeed? We are more prone to equate human worth with societal status than we'd like to admit.

Marxist–Leninist–Mao Zedong Thought fully endorses the equation. It even claims that a person's position determines his or her experience of being human. That's why Nien Cheng's captors were so astounded at her ability to resist making a false confession. Here she was, the poster girl of the decadent capitalists. The revolutionaries were certain that someone who enjoyed her privileges would find confinement in a filthy cell unbearable. Her spirit would crumble once the material props of her old life were removed.

The measure of Nien Cheng's life was not found in what she owned, however. Nothing in Mao Zedong Thought prepared her captors to understand this. She possessed a gritty determination to preserve her human dignity—a dignity they were utterly incapable of understanding.

Nothing in Kozlowski Thought can enable us to understand Nien Cheng either. She's not an American idol. But our better selves recognize her as the person we would like to be.

Both the Nien Cheng and the Kozlowski stories depict worlds gone mad. Young revolutionaries are empowered by the government to show up at the door and trash a home? An approved compensation of $500 million over ten years isn't enough? *That's crazy,* we think.

Nien Cheng's tormentors used every means to force her to join the madness. One idea, though, kept her sane. It's the one idea that can save us from the Kozlowski madness as well. Nien Cheng believed in the truth. Through committing herself to the truth, she never lost her humanity. Her captors had the power to take everything else away, but they could never deprive her of what she knew to be right.

Because she held fast to the truth, Nien Cheng, in her essential humanity, remained unaffected by the appalling changes in her circumstances. Nien showed her captors that it is possible to react in perfect freedom to a radically different environment. Once again, we see the great paradoxical truth: Our character is determined not by our circumstances but by our reaction to those circumstances.

Nien's embrace of the truth also allowed her to envision that justice would prevail, and that good could thus come out of evil. She looked evil in the face and didn't blink or falter. She stayed steady at her post, indeed, shaking her fist and laughing at her tormentors. As is so clear in Nien Cheng's experience, adversity not only doesn't have to destroy us, it may actually strengthen us if countered with principle.

In this, Nien Cheng was greatly fortified by her Christian faith, which alone among the great religions of the world gives value and meaning to evil and suffering. British novelist Dorothy Sayers captured the essence of this: Christianity "affirms—not like Christian Science, that evil has no real existence, nor like Buddhism, that good consists in the refusal to experience evil—but that perfection is attained through the active and positive effort to wrench a real good out of a real evil."[1] This is the essence of what Christians call redemption, and it underscores the paradox we discovered earlier: We have to understand the evil in ourselves before we can truly embrace the good in life.

I first met Madam Cheng in 1987 at a dinner given in her honor at the Reston, Virginia, headquarters of Prison Fellowship, the ministry I founded after my release from prison. I had struck up a relationship with Madam Cheng when I wrote to her right after the publication of her remarkable book *Life and Death in Shanghai*, telling her how it inspired me. She wrote back to say that my autobiography, *Born Again*, was the first book given her by her sister when she was released from prison. We shared many common experiences by correspondence, which led to the memorable evening in Virginia.

Nien Cheng is a petite, delicate-looking woman, the scars on her wrists the only visible evidence of the brutality she experienced in prison. Her tormentors and the incredible hardships she faced did nothing to affect her grace and quiet dignity. One could easily imagine this lovely woman seated in her elegant Shanghai living room, surrounded by precious works of art, serving tea to visitors.

The gala in her honor was attended by a dozen or more senators, government officials, and sixty other friends of the ministry. After dinner, Madam Cheng recounted her experiences. She voiced her implacable opposition to Communism—which remains very much in power in China, despite its marketplace reforms. Near the end of her remarks, she smiled and told the audience that she was looking forward to the following week and what would be for her the most thrilling moment of her life—the day she had dreamed about in prison. Drawing herself up to her full five foot one, her eyes sparkling, she announced proudly that she had an appointment at the Federal District Court to take the oath as a citizen of the United States. For a moment she struggled to maintain her decorum, as the crowd of hardened Washington veterans rose in a sustained ovation, many drying their eyes.

As I listened to her remarks that night, my appreciation of Madam Cheng's character deepened. Remarkably, she was filled with an overwhelming sense of gratitude. First to God. She credited her faith for sustaining her in the face of seven years of prison brutality and the loss of her daughter. And second, gratitude to the United States for remaining a beacon of freedom. Through the darkest moments of her life, our nation's very existence gave her hope that someday she could be free. Her gratitude was key to her survival and her ability to live a full life after years of imprisonment and torture.

The good life, as we see in the life of Nien Cheng, is not conferred by lavish parties in Sardinia or other momentary pleasures. Just as important, it cannot be denied even in the midst of horrific adversity. In fact, we often find true meaning and purpose in deprivation, when all the distractions of modern life are stripped away. The good life is realized in our ability to hold fast to the truth and our human dignity that rests upon it.

———•◦•———

Possessions and status have so little to do with human worth that a lifetime of poverty cannot expunge our innate sense of dignity. Many of the most impressive people I've met live in abject poverty.

A few years ago, I realized that I had failed to give my own children an adequate education about life. Oh, I had taken them on trips, but we always stayed in good hotels. They had been to some of the most important places in the world, including the White House and Buckingham Palace. But it struck me that while they had seen how the privileged few live, they were totally unaware of how much of the world struggles in poverty.

So I invited them to accompany me on a trip to Lima, Peru, where

Prison Fellowship has an active ministry in some of the toughest prisons in the world and where my colleague Mike Timmis runs microenterprise projects for the poorest of the poor.

My three children did not know what to expect. Wendell and Chris were fairly relaxed, but Emily packed a clean pillowcase—not knowing where she would lay her head at night—and brought with her dozens of medications to protect her from the various bacteria that roam through the Third World.

It turned out to be one of the best weekends I've ever spent with my children. We visited four prisons, where I spoke and where Emily, Wendell, and Chris found themselves embraced by strangers who were clapping hands and waving Bibles. Even in some of the institutions where putrid odors poisoned the air, my grown-up kids seemed to catch the people's spiritual enthusiasm. Fear of the unknown was soon replaced by genuine joy.

*The good life is realized in our ability to hold fast to the truth and our human dignity that rests upon it.*

But the most memorable experience was our visit to one of the loan-credit projects. Like most major capitals in Latin America, Lima has been expanding rapidly as peasants come in from the countryside and build their homes on the outskirts of the city. On every square inch of available ground on the arid hillsides and plains surrounding Lima, thousands of squatters stake out their area and then start building. From a distance these barrios seem overwhelming and forbidding.

Close up, however, one discovers that the Peruvians are quite adept at building their cinder-block homes. One thing that struck my children was that most houses have no roofs. It hasn't rained in Lima in forty years, and the climate is temperate year-round. Why bother with a roof? Most of the neighborhoods have no plumbing or other water source, so the city delivers water to a cistern in front of each house. The homes are all in various states of continuous construction. Once the first floor is built and the owners have enough money, they build a second floor. Everyone paints his house a different color—mostly bright—to give the neighborhood variety.

My children and I drove through miles of dirt roads with these homemade structures piled like little blocks on both sides of the road. Mike took us to one community literally built on the top of a garbage dump—an area that had been filled in and that squatters immediately began to occupy. We spent time with a family that had received a hundred-dollar loan from the project's bank, and with it the father started a thriving recycling business. The man spent most of the day walking the streets of the barrio, collecting stray bottles and scraps of metal and paper, bringing it all back to his yard, where he separated it into piles. He then bundled it and once a week sold it for salvage. With that business, he was able to make a decent living, feed and clothe his family, and see that his children got to school.

Pulling up to his house, we had to make our way past mounds and mounds of garbage and trash that he was in the process of separating. The father greeted us, grabbing a rag to wipe his hands, but when he realized that he couldn't get them clean, he offered us his elbow, which we gladly shook.

We were also struck by the warmth with which we were received. Inside, the house was primitive—a dirt floor, no running water, simply a hole in the ground for a toilet. This small room was home not only for the man and his wife but also for his daughters and their husbands and children. They were certainly cramped, yet they were joyous, excited to have us visit them. Emily had a camera with her and started to take a picture of the family's adorable little girls. As Emily squinted through the lens, the mother stepped in between Emily and the children, put one finger up to signal that we should wait, and then took both the little girls to the cistern. She grabbed a ladle of precious water and washed both of their faces so they would be prepared for the picture. This small gesture was an unforgettable manifestation of her rightful pride in her daughters—a sign of their infinite value.

That day we did not see a slum. We didn't see struggling, poverty-stricken Peruvians of Indian ancestry. We saw a family that had a desire to present themselves well. They exhibited a sense of dignity and order even as they were living in circumstances most of us couldn't imagine. They were proud of their home, proud of their job, proud of their self-sufficiency, proud of their family. It was a striking lesson for the Colson clan.

———•—•—•———

Our modern consumerist age is deluded to think that life consists of meeting our animal needs: eating, drinking, money, power, sex, and leisure. Charles Malik, at one time undersecretary-general of the United Nations, saw how badly this missed the real human need. In arguing for the inclusion of freedom of conscience and religion in the U.N.'s original Commission on Human Rights, he said, "All those who stress the elemental economic rights and needs of man are for the most part impressed by his sheer animal existence. . . . This is materialism whatever else it may be called. But unless man's proper nature, unless his mind and spirit are brought out, set apart, protected and promoted, the struggle for human rights is a sham and a mockery."[2]

Malik saw clearly the great danger of materialism: It strips the individual of meaning, dignity, and worth, thereby denying any basis for the protection of human rights.

———•—•—•———

Something within tells us that humans do enjoy a unique status, a unique value. During the long, arduous hearings after President Reagan nominated Robert Bork to the Supreme Court, a debate arose over whether we are governed by any natural law or whether the written Constitution is our only guide. Bork strenuously argued that while there might be some natural law, judges are bound only by their interpretation of the Constitution.

At one point in the hearings, Joseph Biden, a moderately liberal senator from Delaware, challenged Bork. Usually conservatives more than modern liberals favor the argument for a natural order. But Biden, in his introductory remarks before questioning Bork, made an elegant statement as to the fundamental basis of human rights: "I believe my rights are not derived from the Constitution. My rights are not derived from any government. My rights are not derived from any majority. My rights are because I exist. They were given to me and each of my fellow citizens by our Creator, and they represent the essence of human dignity."[3]

Just because we exist, we have meaning and purpose. Our very understanding of what it means to be human involves dignity and rights. This truth is written on our hearts, as we will discuss later.

If we think about it hard enough, we realize that under some circumstances our human dignity and self-respect are not only more important than pleasure and status but more valuable than life itself. This point was powerfully made in *The Tenth Man,* a story written by Graham Greene and later made into a movie.

The scene is a Nazi prison in France during World War II. The French Resistance in the local town has killed three people: a military aide, a sergeant, and a young girl. A young German officer comes into the prisoners' dormitory to announce that one prisoner of war is to be shot for each of the local casualties. The prisoners themselves are to choose three from their company to be executed.

After much debate, the prisoners agree to draw lots, scraps of paper made from an old letter. Crosses are drawn on three of the scraps, and whoever draws those scraps will be executed. The papers are then put into an old shoe.

The prisoners draw according to their last names, in reverse alphabetical order from *Z* to *A.* Tension mounts as the first two crosses are drawn. People begin to calculate their odds of getting the third cross. Finally the shoe comes to Monsieur Jean-Louis Chavel, a wealthy lawyer. Three pieces of paper remain. He grabs one, returns it without looking at it, grabs another—only to find the paper contains the last deadly cross.

In a panic, Monsieur Chavel offers a hundred thousand francs to anyone willing to take his place. When no one accepts his offer, he ups it. He finally offers everything he has—money, land, a grand house at St. Jean de Brinac. The other prisoners are embarrassed by his cowardice and urge him to accept his fate with good grace.

But the offer has been made, and finally a young man named Michel Mangeot accepts. He is disappointed to hear that the house at St. Jean de Brinac is not more modern, but he is pleased that he will be leaving a legacy to his mother and sister. His death will count for something. Chavel and Mangeot spend much of the young man's remaining time arranging for the assets to be transferred to Mangeot's family after he is executed.

The next morning, Mangeot and the two other condemned men

are led outside to the courtyard. As the firing squad's shots ring out, Monsieur Chavel sits in the dormitory, wondering what his life has become.

After the war, Chavel becomes distraught. He cannot bear to live with the guilt of his murderous cowardice, so he decides to commit suicide. But before he does so, he visits Mangeot's family at his old home in St. Jean de Brinac. Chavel poses as Jean-Louis Charlot, someone who knew Michel and the scoundrel Chavel in the German prison camp. He enters his old home as a beggar, looking for a meal.

Unexpectedly, Mangeot's young sister takes pity on Monsieur Chavel and invites him to stay as the family's servant. Her compassion is two-edged, though, as the coward discovers that he has not only taken the life of her brother but also stolen her joy. Although the sister now lives in wealth, she suffers from an implacable hatred for this Monsieur Chavel. How could her brother have been so foolish as to believe she and her family would not have infinitely preferred his presence over their ruinous wealth?

Monsieur Chavel finds living so intolerable that when another imposter tries to win the sister's hand, Chavel finally admits to the truth of what he's done, at the cost of his own life. In a final chaotic scene, Monsieur Chavel lets the second imposter shoot him rather than let the man exploit the family once more. He will not have Mangeot's sister preyed on as he once took advantage of her brother. Monsieur Chavel thus makes the ultimate sacrifice—redeeming himself finally—based on what he should have known all along: that no price, however large, can be placed on a life because any price whatsoever demeans its infinite value.

---

The purpose of *The Good Life,* as we explained earlier, is to seek answers to the questions that plague us all. How do we make sense out of life? What gives it meaning? What is the truly good life?

Simply satisfying our physical instincts, indulging our animal appetites falls far short. What affirms our innate dignity and value as human beings is far more important. More important, indeed, than life itself, as Monsieur Chavel discovered.

How does human dignity express itself then? In what does it find its fulfillment and satisfaction? Where does that dignity want to take us?

# CHAPTER 8

# A LIFE OF
# SIGNIFICANCE

I CONFESSED EARLIER that when I was in prison, my greatest fear was that I would never be able to live a life of significance again. I've always been idealistic. What drew me to politics was not just power but the chance to fulfill my lifelong idealism.

As a schoolboy during World War II, I organized a fund-raising effort that raised enough money to buy a Jeep for the army. I started in politics as a volunteer even before I could vote. In college I studied political philosophy and steeped myself in the writings of Burke and Locke. I joined the marines because I wanted to do something worthwhile for my country. My job at the White House represented not just personal gratification but a chance to make people's lives better.

My anxiety in prison, I see now, stemmed from confusing power and fame with significance. Living a life of significance does not depend on the prerogatives that belong to high position; it depends even less on others' esteem and praise. Living a meaningful life consists simply in embracing the responsibilities and work given to us, whatever they are. The nature of work itself connects us with the moral order (and the God who created it, a point we will later discuss). The workbench, the kitchen counter, the computer station, or any

*Living a meaningful life consists simply in embracing the responsibilities and work given to us, whatever they are.*

other workspace is an altar. There is intrinsic meaning to work well done—and when we fail to grasp this, we become hollow persons.

I had to deal with this in prison, when I had nothing to do but the most menial tasks I was assigned. Before I went to prison, a friend had given me Dietrich Bonhoeffer's book *Letters and Papers from Prison*. Bonhoeffer was a German pastor and theologian who courageously resisted Hitler, spent several years in prison, and then was martyred, executed by the Nazis. He feared that the desultory prison life would begin to affect his habits, discipline, and mind. For three years in Berlin's Tegel prison, Bonhoeffer followed a strict regimen. He forced himself to get up every morning at five o'clock to pray and read the Bible. He deliberately took a bracing cold shower to wake himself up. Then he organized his day into various projects: reading, writing, and prayer.

When I arrived in prison, my caseworker told me, "Just settle in, accept it. This is where you live now. Don't think about your home." Reading Bonhoeffer convinced me to do just the opposite. I was facing three years in prison. I, as the caseworker said, didn't want to "adjust" to prison. So following Bonhoeffer's example, I drove myself to work as hard as I could. My entire day was consumed with writing, studying, doing my job in the prison laundry, exercising, and helping other inmates. I seldom allowed myself any recreation. More than anything, I feared doing nothing.

In the prison laundry room, I ran the washing machine, and next to me the former chairman of the board of the American Medical Association ran the dryer. Our work consisted of putting clothes in, taking them out, and then putting them in bins for inmates to pick up at the end of the day. The hardest part of the job was simply that it wasn't hard enough; we were busy with the laundry itself for only one hour out of every eight. The rest of the time might have been taken up with watching the machines go round, except that I used the time to read and think about how I might begin to live again. Ironically, what I came to learn through my reading confirmed the importance of my experience right there in the laundry—that any type of work can be significant and satisfying.

I could see that the empty hours sucked the life out of many inmates. They allowed the areas around their bunks to become dirty and unkempt; they ignored even simple hygiene like keeping their toothbrush and shaving equipment in a neat container. If they were on a work project, they hung around talking, usually about their resentments against betrayers and other personal enemies and "the system." Those who didn't have work assignments would spend most of their days on their bunks, half-dazed, trying to escape into the emptiness of their thoughts. They were sleeping their lives away, literally.

I came to understand what a severe punishment prison is. While society's ultimate punishment is taking a person's life, a prison sentence is taking a piece of one's life.

It wasn't until after I was released from prison, when Patty and I took some vacation time together, that I realized the real toll Watergate and prison had taken on my life. I would find myself being uncharacteristically harsh with Patty, often snapping at her for no reason at all. I was physically and emotionally exhausted. When I reflected on my state of mind, I realized my problem wasn't so much Watergate. I had thrived on political combat, even when I was the one in everyone's crosshairs. But the effort to remain usefully engaged—working—despite the lethargic atmosphere in prison had exhausted me. What was most fatiguing about prison was the forced inactivity and the anxiety it bred about my family and friends. That's such an unnatural state that it's overwhelmingly stressful. I had kept myself so wound up in prison that the first unwinding was more like an unraveling.

Still, it is possible to transcend even extreme circumstances in prison, as Nien Cheng teaches us, and as I saw in the life of a remarkably "successful" man one Easter Sunday morning in the Mississippi State Penitentiary at Parchman. After I spoke to the general prison population, I visited death row, as is my practice. I like to go from cell to cell, speaking with those who want to talk. The inmates on death row are the untouchables, who have no regular life in the prison and can attend none of the events. These inmates are desperately alone, suspended in time as they wait for their appeals to be exhausted and an execution date set.

As I approached one cell this Easter day, I noticed a tall African-American sitting at a desk piled with Bibles and books. He was peering at a book through his half-glasses, but when he saw me approach, he bounded up, came over to the bars, and with a huge grin, greeted me. He introduced himself as Sam and told me excitedly that he had read all of my books and had been so encouraged by my ministry.

I learned that Sam, who was a strong Christian believer, was using his time on death row to study theology. "When I get out of here," he said, grinning and pausing for a moment, "that is, if I get out of here . . . I'm going to preach. I want to be like you. I want to be a minister."

Sam may have been on death row, may have been confined to one lonely six-by-nine cell, and may have gotten out of that cell only one hour a day for exercise and a shower, but he was as industrious as anyone I've known. He was like a trial lawyer preparing for a big argument in court. He knew exactly what he wanted to accomplish in life, and he was diligently pursuing it.

I looked around Sam's cell and realized that, unlike every other inmate on death row, he had no television. I knew that inmates were allowed to purchase TVs from the commissary. I said to him, "I notice you don't have a TV. I'd be happy to arrange to get one for you from the commissary."

"No thanks, Chuck," he said. "I'm really grateful for that, but you know, I'd rather not have one. You can waste a lot of time with those things."

Death row, counting down the hours before you die, but wanting to use every hour productively? As we walked away, my associate said to me, "He was crazy not to take you up on that offer."

I turned to my friend. "No, he's the one who is sane. We're the ones who are crazy." Sam was fulfilling his desire for significance—even as judges were deciding when to put him to death.

You may be glad to know that Sam's appeal was successful. He was released from death row and returned to the general population, where he put his theological reading to good use, telling others of his convictions. He died of natural causes in 2000. Even behind bars, Sam lived a life of meaning and significance.

———•◦•———

We don't often hear people talk about the fulfillment of the great American dream in terms of work and responsibility—just the opposite, in fact. When I was growing up, I thought the goal was to rise from my modest beginnings, earn good money, and put enough away to retire. When that magic sixty-fifth birthday arrived, I'd abandon work responsibilities to nest in a sunny paradise, endlessly playing golf or fishing.

The life of leisure is not just a dream. Most people in the rich Western world consider it a right. Employment contracts generally guarantee European workers six weeks of holiday along with nine to twelve additional days off. Europe shuts down in August; vacation is the high moment of the year. The number of hours that the Germans, French, and British work has steadily declined. Even though America has maintained a stronger work ethic than most of Europe, Americans increasingly talk about free time and leisure when identifying quality-of-life issues.[1]

Living as I do in a beautiful Florida retirement community, I have watched a steady parade of retired executives buy condos and tile-roofed villas, leaving behind the hubbub and pressures of business, grabbing their golf bags, and heading for the course. I've seen in very short order how long that initial burst of joy and freedom lasts. At best, six months.

Boredom soon sets in. As one disillusioned former executive asked a friend, "Do I have to play golf *every day?*" Retirees begin to be nostalgic for the day when they were doing something important, when others looked up to them.

I have seen how debilitating the lack of stimulating work can be. One friend, a person of some accomplishment, stopped practicing law early in life so that he could enjoy traveling with his wife and visiting their four homes. He had everything the American dream tells us we should live for, but he had nothing significant to do. Over a ten-year period I watched him deteriorate mentally, emotionally, and physically. I really believe the stress of trying to appear normal in a circumstance where he had nothing to give, nothing to fulfill his desire for significance, became draining to the point of destruction. When people are idle, they lack purpose and begin to corrode like an unused piece of equipment.

I have visited enough elderly people in retirement centers—some people call them "Leisure World"—to realize that while these facilities are often necessary, they are anything but paradise. Some senior citizens have discovered that the goal of life is not leisure but to keep working, sometimes into their seventies, eighties, and nineties. Correspondent

Morley Safer of *60 Minutes* took his camera crew to the Vita Needle Company in Needham, Massachusetts, where thirty-five senior citizens are employed in a small manufacturing plant.[2] One of them is ninety-year-old Rosa Finnigan, who still works thirty-seven hours a week. Safer asked her why.

"Because I would be bored to death sitting and doing nothing," said Rosa. "Besides that, I'd be all stiffened up; my fingers would be all stiff. No way. I tried it and I did not like it."

Bill Frison arrives at his workbench at six o'clock in the morning, five days a week. Frison once retired when he was sixty-nine, but he found retirement wasn't for him—or his wife. "My wife wasn't used to having me home another eight hours a day. Well, I couldn't find enough to do. . . ." Frison, who is now eighty-three, has been working at the company for fourteen years.

The owner of the company discovered that older employees are extremely productive, allowing the company to remain unusually competitive.

Safer then took his crew around the country, pursuing the same story. He found a ninety-seven-year-old barber in Manning, South Carolina; an eighty-seven-year-old mayor in Potsdam, New York; and a scientist, Ray Crist, still on the job nine hours a day, five days week, at age one hundred and two. "How can this be work?" the scientist asked. "This is so interesting. Look, look, I'm finding out what's going on."

One of Safer's interviewees summed it up. "People are living longer and longer and longer. And increasingly people are realizing that just because you've reached your 60th or 65th birthday doesn't mean you're kind of in the last inning. . . . Last year the average retiree watched forty-three hours of television a week, and for many people, it's become sort of a wasteland."

If given the choice, many people would choose life at the Vita Needle Company over a retirement home any day. What the people featured in Safer's program had discovered is that work fulfills their very nature. It reinforces their self-respect and sense of accomplishment. Work enables them to conform their lives to the demands of human nature.

Our consumer society teaches that buying and enjoying goods will bring happiness. Yet the facts about our very nature establish an entirely contrary proposition. Day in and day out we are taught that work is a

necessary evil and that leisure—the freedom from labor and productiv-
ity—is the great goal of the consumerist society. But inside we know
that leisure in itself simply doesn't satisfy.

If our nature desires dignity and self-respect, those needs can be
satisfied only when we discover our purpose, which will embrace our
work and our responsibilities. We need to use our gifts and creativity,
whether on the job or taking care of our families (which is a *big* job).
We are indeed "hardwired" for work, and we inevitably find great satisfaction in it.

You may be saying, "That's fine for you—writers are by nature
creative, and their work can be fascinating. But what about ordinary
people whose work can be menial, most of it drudgery?"

Businessman Howard Butt Jr. tells the delightful story of a friend
who stopped by a garage to have a tire repaired. He watched the mechanic pop the hubcap off with a tire iron, spin loose the bolts with his
wrench, and mount the wheel on his tire changer. With the mechanic's guidance the machine soon worked the old tire off and the
new one on. In ten minutes or less, the mechanic had tightened down
the last bolt on the restored tire. Then he said, not to his customer,
but as if speaking to the new tire, "There, another good job done by
me." Butt said of the mechanic, "Changing tires didn't define him,
but doing a good job did."[3]

Anyone who has not had a similar experience, doing a concrete
task well, with the pleasure that brings, has had a poor life indeed. The
mechanic's simple phrase, "Another good job done by me," expresses
the connection we all feel to the truly good things in life through work.

I've known the pleasure of work in routine chores. Loving auto-
mobiles as I do, for me a good Saturday pastime is to wash and wax my
car. I clean the body thoroughly with soap and water, rinse it off, and
dry it with a chamois. Then I often apply wax, rubbing hard until I have
a sparkling gloss. When I finish one section, I often back up, look at it
and admire it, then do another section and repeat the process. It takes a
lot of muscle power to wax an entire car, but I find it unusually satisfying, every bit as fulfilling as writing a good chapter in a book. When I
finish my work, I often go into the house, get Patty, and bring her out
so she can admire it as well. I'll walk around the car and look at it from
different angles to see the beauty of the car as it glistens in the sun.

In recent years, I've had less time for projects around the house and so often get someone else to clean and polish the car. I like having the car clean, but when another person does it, I don't walk around the car and examine it from every angle. I don't call my wife out to look at it. I take no particular personal satisfaction in the sparkle.

Aren't we all like that? Don't we really enjoy doing something well, whatever it is? Not all of us are composers of great music or architects of beautiful buildings, but we are all craftsmen or artisans. All of us appreciate doing our work well.

*True happiness . . . is found in fulfilling our higher nature, shaping our lives and our circumstances to reflect the way we are hardwired.*

The English novelist Dorothy Sayers wrote often about work, particularly in its relation to Christian theology. She said that work is "the natural exercise and function of man—the creature who is made in the image of his Creator."[4] She summed it up in this pithy expression: "Work is not, primarily, a thing one does to live, but the thing one lives to do."[5] Work, Sayers argued, is the measure of one's life, and the real satisfaction is not so much in the work as in the fulfillment of one's own nature and in contemplation of the perfection of his or her work.

I submit that one of the chief causes of unhappiness is when society tells us one thing but our true nature dictates something else. In these instances we are, in the fullest sense of the word, dysfunctional. The important thing, as we will discuss later, is to find the natural order, not just in our work but in every area of life. Then, taking no thought for society's myths, conform our lives to that order.

* * *

So what have we learned so far about the good life? Is it eat, drink, and be merry, living as if there is no tomorrow? Does it consist in leisure, pleasure, and the satisfaction of every sensory desire? No, true happiness is achieved not through material comforts and satiating our appetites. It is found in fulfilling our higher nature, shaping our lives and our circumstances to reflect the way we are hardwired.

This can never be accomplished in a vacuum, as solitary individuals apart from others. Here we encounter another great myth of our society, the idea that we can live life for and by ourselves. But the truth, as I discovered from a poignant encounter with one of the tragic Watergate figures, is that life can never be lived alone or for ourselves only. We live in community, and we live for others, despite what our culture tells us. We are not, as many like to think, our own gods.

# CHAPTER 9

# A SILENT GOOD-BYE

WE LIVE IN the age of personal autonomy, which defines our lives by our own choices. The role of society, our culture believes—and courts have agreed—is to do nothing to limit our choices. As one pundit put it, we live in the "republic of the imperial self," in which we are free from all unnecessary restraints in order to pursue whatever we believe will bring us happiness.

The premises on which men and women base their lives are often revealed by how their lives end. So what does a life lived for personal happiness and power look like at its end, and what does this tell us about the ideal of running our own lives for our own purposes? I had a poignant encounter with a former White House colleague that answered this in a dramatic way.

Politics may be the perfect world in which to observe individualism as the be-all and end-all. Politicians never know whom they might be running against during the next election, so they cannot confide in anyone. They find it increasingly necessary to keep their own counsel, which can bring about a disorienting isolation. Politicians' staffs jockey for position as well, fighting for access to power and perks—better salaries, more spacious offices, and chauffeured limousines. No one ever lets down his or her guard in this "Who's on top?" world.

When I arrived at the White House, Bryce Harlow, the friend who had recommended me to President Nixon, gave me the following advice: "Chuck, you're coming into the most powerful office in the world. But everybody is a prima donna, so the first thing you need to remember is that you really can't trust anybody. So as you walk through these corridors, keep your back to the wall."

In the Nixon White House the name of the game was getting close to the president (and the theme song was musical offices, getting as close as possible to the president's). Harlow's advice was everyone's watchword: None of us trusted the others, which reflected in part the president's own personality, in part just politics.

The general atmosphere of distrust in the Nixon administration did not keep me from admiring many of the people I worked with. One of those was John Ehrlichman, Nixon's right-hand man on domestic policy. The players in a competitive environment know their rivals' strengths, and John had formidable gifts.

When I think of John Ehrlichman, I see him in his spacious White House office, which was right above the Oval Office. The windows behind John's desk looked out over the south lawn to the Washington Monument. When I walked in for a meeting with him, I felt a certain awe. John had a powerful personal presence, distinguished and reflective. Peering over his half-glasses, his eyes were dark and penetrating. He spoke with authority. He was tough and decisive, a brilliant lawyer.

John Ehrlichman seemed at home in his role as assistant to the president, made for the part, in fact. He and his wife, Jean, an intelligent and poised woman, had three children, Peter, Jody, and Jan. John and Jean liked going out on the social circuit, to the opening of plays, movies, and galas, where John relished being announced to the crowd's applause.

John, along with Bob Haldeman and Henry Kissinger, formed a powerful triumvirate that guarded the gate to the Oval Office. Ehrlichman had a wonkish streak and was often the lone voice of reason on the Nixon staff. While others were ready to make quick judgments, John often saw the wisdom in soliciting opinions from a wide variety of people. He always managed to stay calm and think clearly during crises.

I found John one of the easier people to work with in the administration. He was collegial and gracious. The lawyer in both of us clicked.

John proved to be blind, however, to the trouble the plumbers unit would cause. The president put Ehrlichman and Kissinger in charge of the plumbers to stop leaks of government documents. They, in turn, delegated this responsibility to two deputies, Egil "Bud" Krogh and David Young. One of the great disservices history has done is to blame Ehrlichman exclusively for what happened with the plumbers; the truth is, others shared the responsibility.

John did make a series of unaccountably bad decisions in regard to Watergate. During the entire scandal the only written memo ever found authorizing illegal action—the break-in of Ellsberg's psychiatrist's office—had John's signature on it.

John had a resolute will, determination, and influence. But I do not think he ever saw that the same attributes that made him a great man could also precipitate his downfall. As a devout Christian Scientist, he believed, like Krogh, whom we discussed earlier, that reality consists in how we think about it and that we can avoid negative consequences by changing our thinking. The president's chief of staff, Bob Haldeman, shared John's belief system. These men did not believe in the reality of evil—not as a destructive force within every human heart. I think this may have led them to believe a cover-up would work. Reality would be what they chose to make it.

In the Watergate hearings, Ehrlichman staunchly defended the Nixon administration, challenging his questioners on the Ervin committee investigating Watergate. He came off as critical and defensive, which was a total departure from his usual manner. Oddly, Bob Haldeman, whose style was pure Doberman pinscher at the White House, tried to conciliate the committee.

When the day came that President Nixon had to fire John Ehrlichman, John asked a most poignant and revealing question: "Mr. President, just one favor. I want to know what I can tell my kids." I knew exactly what was troubling Ehrlichman. He had been a successful politician and could never explain to his family that he had been fired. He was deeply hurt. From that moment I think he determined someday to clear his own name.

During the time John Ehrlichman was being tried for his role in Watergate, his life began to unravel. He had an affair, well publicized at the time, which led to the breakup of what had appeared to be his storybook marriage to Jean. The affair was so out of character for John that I concluded he was cracking under the enormous pressure of Watergate.

Both Ehrlichman and Haldeman were convicted for their Watergate activities, and John was also found guilty for his role in the Ellsberg case. John went to prison, serving eighteen months of his four- to eight-year sentence at Swift Trail Camp, a minimum-security federal prison south of Safford, Arizona.

---

I liked John and wanted to maintain contact with him. I wrote to him in prison and even after he was released, but I sensed a bitter edge in his replies. I had never testified directly against John, but in the course of my testimony about Watergate, I was honest about what I knew of his role. I had also recommended the hiring of Howard Hunt—one of the men who later broke in at the Watergate—to John. I'm not sure he ever forgave me for that.

After Ehrlichman left prison, he wrote several books: *Witness to Power: The Nixon Years* and two novels, good ones, *The Whole Truth* and *The China Card*. I wrote him letters congratulating him on these works, and he'd send back a note. These were friendly enough, but in his public comments about me, the bitterness remained. I had to wonder whether it was because I had become a Christian and was moving on with my new life, while he seemed tethered to the past.

Eventually John remarried and moved to New Mexico, where Patty and I visited him in 1984. He lived on a mountainside in a beautiful Spanish-style house with grand stone patios overlooking the hills below. He had grown a beard and dressed very casually, even Bohemian. The button-down political operative had become the endearingly spacey writer. We met his young wife, with whom he'd had a son, Michael. He loved this child dearly, later describing him as his soul mate. It appeared that John had his world put back together. His old commanding personality certainly asserted itself during our visit.

I had just published my third book, *Loving God,* and gave him a copy.

He commented, "*Loving God,* huh? That's what we need, a loving God."

"No. It means the other way around—our loving God, not God's loving us."

The look he gave me signaled that despite his new life, he still had raw, open wounds from the past.

I lost track of John for a short time; then in the mid-1990s I heard that he had moved to Atlanta and that his second marriage had broken up. At that point he was getting remarried again, this time to a woman who owned a restaurant.[1] Soon after I learned of John's whereabouts, I read an interview in which he seemed to lay much of the blame for Watergate on me. "No one at that meeting did anything about Brookings. Nixon finally found someone who saluted first and exercised judgment later—Charles Colson."[2]

Soon after, the producer of a film project about Watergate called to ask whether I would consent to be interviewed for the film, which John was putting together. I turned the interview down because I wanted to leave Watergate in the past. Then John called personally. This must have been a difficult thing for him to do because he had to hope that the statement he had made in the interview hadn't angered me too much. When we talked, I could hear how much the project meant to him. He saw the film as a definitive statement about Watergate, and it seemed to have become the most important thing in his life. I realize now that he meant it to serve as his vindication and legacy. John promised to treat me fairly, not to be unnecessarily critical. He really went to great lengths to get me to be part of the film. In an attempt to rebuild my relationship with him, I agreed to the interview.

I flew to Atlanta for the taping. The man financing the film met me at the airport and took me to International University, where I did over two hours of taping. After the interview, Ehrlichman and I spent time visiting. He was upbeat about his life. He believed he had found his true love in his third wife, Karen. He took great pleasure in her restaurant. They had just come back from the Baja Peninsula, where they had watched the whales on their yearly migration. "It was an experience like I've never had in my life," he said. "I can only describe it as a spiritual experience, watching those whales."

I tried to speak to his spiritual hunger. "Nature can be a marvelous thing," I said. "The heavens declare the glory of God. But it's God, John, who is the source of true spirituality. There's a God-shaped vacuum in every heart. . . ." I went on to tell him of my Christian faith and the difference it has made in my life.

"We'll have to get together again," he said. "I really would like to discuss this." Even though he was putting me off, I also felt he was listening.

In the end the film suffered from John's exculpatory motives. It was his *apologia,* and it wasn't entirely credible for this reason. John kept trying to undo what had already been done, and the forgiveness that he may have been looking for wasn't to be found in the public's response to the film. In some ways the film project was an exercise in pride—in John's drive to reshape his tarnished reputation. If human dignity comes from embracing the truth, the value of art comes from embodying it. Any attempt to manipulate the truth for false purposes always produces flaws.

———•◦•———

In the summer of 1998, I received a frantic phone call from Patricia Talmadge, a friend of John's. "John Ehrlichman is seriously ill. He doesn't have many friends, and his family is not here," she said. "I'm trying to look out for him. Could you come see him?" Patricia had taken an interest in John after they had met at a party. John didn't hold it against her that her former father-in-law, Senator Herman Talmadge, had been one of his inquisitors on the Ervin committee investigating Watergate. It was then I learned that John's third wife had left him. I also knew that his children lived on the West Coast.

I traveled to Atlanta to visit John in his nursing home, noting how different this institutional setting was from his palatial home on the mountainside in New Mexico. Patricia met me and went to John's room to prepare him for my visit. He was suffering from renal failure caused by diabetes.

When I walked into John's room, I saw this once-powerful, imposing, distinguished man sitting in a wheelchair, wearing a cardigan, a blanket over his lap. He was only in his early seventies, but his health had been decimated. He had lost fifty or more pounds, and the skin of his face hung in limp folds. His beard was unkempt.

I felt a sudden rush of compassion for John. Nixon had betrayed him. He'd lost his power. He'd been disgraced and had gone to prison. The women who had loved him were no longer by his side. Even his kids were not around. This man who had once been sought out by the most powerful people in the world, whose wishes commanded hundreds around him, found himself desperately ill and virtually deserted. His world had contracted from his office above the president's to a lonely nursing home.

We had a long conversation. I asked about his children, avoiding the subject of his third wife. I told him about my own activities. As I did, I spoke of what motivates me and gives my life meaning, my faith.

He looked at me with the same pensive expression I'd seen so many times before. Then his eyes narrowed, and the light went out of them. All at once, he said, "The doctor says that with a little shot of morphine, he can put me out of things. There'll be no pain. I'll just go to sleep. Nobody cares about me anyway. Why should I stay alive? Tell me. Why should I stay alive?" His words came across slowly and listlessly, as if he were resigned to his fate.

Cold chills raced up and down my back. He was serious, and I wanted to give him the best answer I could muster. I struggled to choose my words carefully. A life was in the balance.

I told John that his life was not his own, that it was a gift from God. I assured him that his life was created in God's own image, which gave him an innate dignity, a dignity unaffected by circumstances. I reminded him that he owed it to his children to care for his own life. He would be setting a terrible example for them if he ended his life. I told him that he could know his creator intimately in the time that remained to him, that he could have a relationship with God and even experience joy, despite his suffering.

I don't know exactly what effect my words had, but he did not ask for an overdose of morphine. Patricia Talmadge told me later that my argument about the poor example he would be setting for his children had a real effect.

I visited with John one more time before hearing from Patricia that he was dying.

At the beginning of 1999, John decided to discontinue his dialysis. His children were coming to his bedside to say good-bye. Patricia called to ask if I would come and pray with him before he died. I was just then recovering from a serious attack of the flu, and my doctor ordered me to stay put. I also didn't want to infect John, so I asked one of my close friends and board members, Pat MacMillan, to visit John and give whatever help he could.

Pat told John of Christ's love once more and prayed with him. John said nothing except to stare and nod. I hope and trust that he was praying too.

John Ehrlichman died on Valentine's Day 1999. For the man who once held enormous power, there was no funeral. No one came to mourn. John had told Patricia that he wanted a "silent good-bye." He was cremated, and his ashes were shipped to his son Peter.

———————•◦•———————

John Ehrlichman's last years present a parable of how personal autonomy turns into a nightmare. If we live for ourselves, our happiness our only concern, then why should anyone care when our happiness turns to sickness and sorrow? And why should we go on caring about our lives in these circumstances? The logic of individualism, of living a life devoted to self-perfection and personal vindication, is finally—and paradoxically—suicidal. If we belong only to ourselves, then nonexistence is the only solution when we find life too great a burden.

> *The logic of individualism, of living a life devoted to self-perfection and personal vindication, is finally—and paradoxically—suicidal.*

But something tells us this is wrong. Very wrong. So the logic of the self-perfecting, self-directed, self-consumed life must be wrong as well.

What does the Ehrlichman story teach us? John was raised in a religious tradition that believes sin and evil do not exist; they are merely illusions of our minds. He lived his life blissfully in this belief system until he confronted evil within himself and had to reckon with it. But his way of thinking provided no means of making such a reckoning. How can one reckon with an illusion? The only way is to try to prove that what others believe to be reality isn't reality at all. I believe that's why John tried so hard to vindicate himself through his writings and his film project. He could try, but he simply couldn't prove what isn't so. He only got caught up in an endless cycle of self-obsession and tragic self-destruction. John's story brings to mind a prayer generally attributed to St. Augustine, "Lord, spare me from the lust of self-vindication."

John Ehrlichman not only couldn't find forgiveness for himself but also couldn't forgive others, which meant that he had to carry other people's sins to his grave. His belief system reinforced at every turn the pride that we all suffer from—the will to be our own gods. The turn of the final screw in John's life shows that when we try to create our own lives and our own realities, we put ourselves at disadvantaged odds with reality itself. Everyone knew that Ehrlichman had

> *Living a good life begins with exposing the great lies of modern life.*

messed up. Everyone knew that others had contributed to the mess. John couldn't get right with his own failures, and he couldn't let the failures of others go. So he was left, finally, with nothing but his own illusions.

My assessment may sound harsh, and it may seem self-righteous of me to say it. After all, I managed to survive Watergate, and Ehrlichman in one sense didn't. But I will be very quick to say that I was no different from John. I was filled with all of the same desires for self-vindication that eventually consumed him. In fact, during the first two years after Watergate, I assembled a massive file of information, attempting to establish that the CIA had been involved in the fall of the Nixon presidency. I had come to realize that some of the things I had done were wrong, and I desperately wanted to recover my good name.

The crucial difference between John Ehrlichman and me was not that I was a better person than John. I wasn't. I am not today. The only difference is God's grace. Pure and simple. It was God's intervention that enabled me to find forgiveness and peace. Here we confront two of the great paradoxes again: We have to understand the evil in ourselves before we can truly embrace the good in life, and we have to lose our lives to save them.

Hyperindividualism—whether embraced in the public's glaring spotlight or in the shadows of more private lives—leads to loneliness, isolation, and despair. Personal autonomy looks appealing at the outset, but it doesn't come with a warning label listing its consequences. Living a good life begins with exposing the great lies of modern life. Personal autonomy, which is so revered in our time, is at the top of the list.

# CHAPTER 10

# MY HAPPINESS,
# RIGHT OR WRONG

ALBERT CAMUS, the French existentialist philosopher whose writings were all the rage on American campuses in the sixties, called suicide the first philosophical question. Initially, that sounds just like the kind of thing a French philosopher would say. It's a real-life question, though; it's the question, after all, that John Ehrlichman asked me. Another way of putting the question might be, What good is life? If we can no longer find any good in it, why shouldn't we end it?

Before we can find the good life, we have to find what's good about life itself. Why do most of us embrace life, especially in light of the world's evil and suffering. That's a question that every seeker after truth must face. The way in which we confront that question depends on our assumptions.

The reason John Ehrlichman asked that question in such a despairing frame of mind was, I'm convinced, because he saw his life first and last as *his*. It was his to make of it what he would. He thought he had an absolute right to define himself. So he devoted himself to becoming a great man, and in many ways, he achieved that goal.

However, when people set out to become great, reality has a harsh way of revealing their limitations. Greatness demands that the world concur with their opinion. When popular sentiment turns against great men and women, their pride demands vindication. Those who unrelentingly

> *Before we can find the good life, we have to find what's good about life itself.*

persist in this course will eventually alienate not only their enemies but also their friends and even their family members.

That was the tragedy of John Ehrlichman. He became an exile on the island of his own self-determination.

The idea of defining one's own life—of choosing to live on one's own terms—is rarely presented in this negative light. In fact, postmodern society tells us that the ultimate goal of life is personal autonomy—to be free from all restraints, free to pursue our own happiness. As a result, pleasure and personal gratification rule the day. Our culture tells us that we *alone* are capable of making ourselves happy, that life is all about finding out what we really want and then letting nothing get in the way of achieving our hearts' desires.

The Oscar-winning film *The Hours* presents exactly this point of view. Based on Michael Cunningham's Pulitzer prize–winning novel, the multilayered film pulls back the curtain on the intersection of the lives of three women in three different eras. The film shows Virginia Woolf (played by Nicole Kidman) in 1923, as she begins to write *Mrs. Dalloway*. We also see Laura Brown (Julianne Moore), a pregnant Los Angeles housewife in the 1950s, reading *Mrs. Dalloway* while she bakes a cake for her husband's birthday. In contemporary Manhattan, fifty-year-old Clarissa Vaughan (Meryl Streep) throws a party for the gay poet Richard Brown (Ed Harris), a former lover who nicknamed her Mrs. Dalloway during their brief affair in college.

Each of the women confronts the question, What's the good in living?

Because Virginia Woolf suffers from delusions and crushing depression, her husband, Leonard Woolf, moves her from London to a suburb, Richmond, believing a quieter life would be good for her emotional state. As Virginia begins writing *Mrs. Dalloway,* she finds the quiet difficult to bear. In a panic she escapes the house, runs to the train station, and flees to London for distraction. When her husband discovers her missing, he dashes to the station to find her, fearing she'll become overstimulated in the city and do something foolish. She's already attempted suicide twice.

When Leonard finds his wife at the train station, he pleads with her, urging her to return home. She resists, voicing her despair. "My life has been stolen from me," she says, referring to her illness and the changes it has brought. "I'm living in a town I have no wish to live in. I'm living a life I have no wish to live."[1] She confesses that she desperately wants to move back to London. "This is my right; it is the right of every human being. . . . The meanest patient, yes, even the very lowest is allowed some say in the matter of her own prescription. Thereby she defines her humanity. . . . But if it is a choice between Richmond and death, I choose death."

The film sees all its characters in a similar predicament: Each one must choose what will make him or her happy, despite the consequences. When Clarissa Vaughan tries to tell her daughter what it means to live, she explains that when she's with Richard, she feels that she's living. Otherwise, life seems trivial and silly.

The mother quickly realizes that her comment has trivialized her relationships with her daughter and with her lesbian partner, so she tries to cover up the faux pas. What she means to say, she begins again, is that her happiest moment, the moment filled with the greatest possibility, occurred during her college affair with Richard. She wistfully recounts how decades earlier she had walked out of an old house on Cape Cod onto the beach. Richard caught up to her, kissed her on the shoulder, and said, "Good morning, Mrs. Dalloway."

"And I remember thinking to myself," Clarissa says, "so, *this* is the beginning of happiness. This is where it starts. And, of course, there will always be more. It never occurred to me it wasn't the beginning. It *was* happiness. It was the moment—right then."

Like Virginia Woolf, Clarissa defines her life through her choices, and these choices are driven by her need to cultivate "perfect moments." These moments give her life value. Even Clarissa suspects that her times of great happiness are over, however, and that she is left with only remnants through the care she extends to Richard, who is dying of AIDS.

Clarissa and Richard have the talk I had with John Ehrlichman. (This scene between two fine actors, Meryl Streep and Ed Harris, is the movie's high point.) While Clarissa is busy during the day, preparing for the party she's giving in Richard's honor, Richard himself is assessing whether he wants to continue living. When Clarissa arrives in the afternoon to help him get dressed, Richard is thrashing about, clearing away furniture that impedes his access to a window. As he opens the window and seats himself on the sill, he tells Clarissa that he thinks he's stayed alive only to satisfy her. He asks her if she'd be angry if he died.

She reminds him that the doctors have told him he can live for years. She begs him to live. "That is what people do. They stay alive for each other. You do have good days still. . . . You know you do."

He protests. "Not really. I mean it, it's kind of you to say so, but it's not really true." Then he asks Clarissa to tell him a story from her day.

Desperate to keep him from jumping, she recounts how fresh the morning had been. He instantly connects her reflection with the moment they both were happy together—that perfect moment on the beach at Cape Cod. "I was nineteen years old, and I'd never seen anything so beautiful. You coming out of a glass door in the early morning, still sleepy. Isn't it strange? The most ordinary morning in anybody's life."

Remembering the extraordinary beauty of that ordinary morning isn't enough, however, to persuade Richard to face the many difficult hours that his illness will force him to endure. He turns to Clarissa and says, "You've been so good to me, Mrs. Dalloway. I love you. I don't think two people could have been happier than we've been."

Then he jumps out the window. The happiness of the perfect moment was not enough.

When Clarissa arranges for Richard's funeral, she calls his mother, who comes to New York. His mother, it turns out, is Laura Brown, the Los Angeles housewife.

Laura, we learn, has also confronted the question of whether life is worth living. The film shows her locked up in a hotel room with *Mrs. Dalloway* and a lethal dose of sleeping pills. She feels suffocated by her life. In the end she decides not to commit suicide. Instead, she abandons her family, leaving without a word of explanation. The lesbian kiss she gives one of her neighbors in front of her little boy, Richard, is meant to explain her unhappiness.

Clarissa Vaughan knows that Laura Brown's decision to abandon her family had profoundly damaged Richard, who regarded his mother as a monster. As a result, Clarissa receives Laura into her home rather coldly, suspiciously. After Laura admits that she abandoned her family, she says, "I left both my children. They say it's the worst thing a mother can do." With these words, she becomes tearful, caught between justifying her behavior and wanting to undo it. "What does it mean to regret when you have no choice? It's what you can bear. And there it is. No one is going to forgive me. It was death. I chose life."

The film suggests that Laura is forgiven or at least accepted when

Clarissa's daughter, Julia, gives Laura a good-night hug. The film knows no other moral imperative but seeking one's own personal happiness, and if that meant abandoning her family, Laura was not only right to do so, she proved her *nobility* in the effort. The film suggests that Richard had simply misunderstood his mother. She had really done nothing wrong.

In reviewing the film, feminist Gloria Steinem comments on Virginia Woolf's death, shown dramatically in the film's prologue. Steinem refers to Woolf's suicide as a "radical act of self-deliverance."[2] Many people would classify Richard Brown's suicide and Laura Brown's desertion of her family in the same way—radical acts of self-deliverance.

———•◦•———

"It's what you can bear. And there it is," Laura Brown said. Another way of putting it might be: My happiness, right or wrong. The film's message (and our culture's message, perhaps) is that we live to fulfill our happiness, but if it is no longer attainable, we are free to end our lives. This, after all, is the ultimate expression of personal autonomy. It's *my life* to do with as I see fit.

People who hold this point of view would say that I gave John Ehrlichman the wrong advice. They would say not only should I not have encouraged him to live his life to its natural end, but I should have—as a moral obligation—done my best to see that his doctor administered the overdose of morphine as quickly as possible. If you think I'm pushing things too far, think about how many movies and television shows depict a brave and noble nurse or other caregiver who assists a terminal patient in committing suicide. Are any of these characters ever scripted as anything less than heroic?

The strength of *The Hours* lies in its unflinching adherence to its point of view: Finding one's own happiness is all there is in life. But the artists involved in making *The Hours* are too good, as artists, to force reality to conform entirely to that vision. They express too much of reality in the film, and in doing so, they radically undercut their own point of view. Ironically, *no one* is happy in *The Hours*. Despite praise from many critics, the film was only a mild winner at the box office because it is an invitation to depression. Only if you are fond of brain-crushing sadness would you want to sit through it.

So the question becomes, Why is living for oneself a certain prescription for becoming depressed and possibly suicidal?

Reality provides us with two indicators that personal happiness must never become the final goal in life. First is the simple matter of our own emotions. I've had many "perfect moments" in my life. You probably have too. But I've had far more ordinary moments, and I've endured the hours of deep discouragement and depression that we all have. We live in a very stressful world. Just watching the evening news can make us depressed. We face all kinds of pressures and fears—terrorists and crazies who kidnap children off the streets. Stress can affect us emotionally as well as physically. We get cranky. We get depressed. We develop stress-related illnesses. So, if life has value only when we are happy, only when the hours are marked by "perfect moments," we are headed for deep disappointment, or *The Hours* mentality.

Second, something tells us that it's wrong to purchase our happiness at the expense of others. Cultural forces and our own selfishness are so strong in teaching us to forget about everyone else, however, that we've become oblivious, on principle, to our effect on others.

I found this out one night at a party given in a luxurious home on a Gulf lot in Naples, Florida. The guests assembled just before sunset and stood behind massive windows looking out at the ocean. Everybody was waiting for the "green flash," the moment at which just a sliver of light is visible above the waterline and it suddenly turns a bright green. The green flash is visible only once every few months, at best. We all stood around waiting for the phenomenon, engaging in the usual chitchat.

Our host had recently retired as president of a major corporation. He and his wife were well-traveled, interesting people. Their new home displayed art from around the world.

That night our hostess was regally dressed, her hands sparkling with sizable diamonds. She was the picture of refinement. At dinner I ended up seated to her right, and she told me she had just come back from a fascinating weekend at an "est" seminar. The Erhard Seminars Training was a fad back in the seventies and eighties.

I was intrigued to find out what she had learned at the seminar. She explained that "est" taught people how to release their inhibitions

so that one's true self emerged. She said it had been hugely successful; she had gotten rid of a lot of feelings that were oppressing her.

Curious, I asked her how this came about.

She said, "Well, you walk around in a social time and say to people exactly what's on your mind. You don't think about what's politically correct or what's nice or appropriate. You just say whatever comes into your mind."

She continued, "I walked up to this one guy and screamed in his ear, 'You are a stupid——!'" She released a string of expletives, which seemed thoroughly out of place coming from this dignified woman.

Somewhat incredulous, I asked her, "How did this make you feel?"

She closed her eyes and tilted her head back. "Wonderful! It released all of the tensions inside of me."

Even more curious, I asked, "How did it make the guy feel?"

She looked at me as if I had said something totally impolite and rude, as if to say, "Why would that matter?" She didn't respond. She merely chuckled and turned to talk to the person on her left.

The hostess never realized that the whole episode revealed her inner contempt and her total disregard for others. All she did when she got in touch with her inner self was discover how miserable and wretched she really was. She may have felt good for a bit. But I suspect that if she were to really think about what she had done, her euphoria would fade.

How in the world did we ever arrive at this sorry state, where the unrestrained right to shout expletives in a stranger's ear is considered to be a good thing? What have we come to if we feel *obliged* to satisfy the unrestrained self with no regard for the feelings of others?

---

Today's belief that we truly can seek our own happiness at any cost is the result of fundamental changes in the way people view the world and humanity's place in it. Before the eighteenth century's Enlightenment and the scientific revolution, Westerners believed that we are God's creatures living in a world an all-powerful, intelligent, personal God designed and created. Finding the good life was a matter of correctly understanding and responding to the Designer's "operating instructions" for humanity. These instructions were known through the faculties of reason and imagination, through the "book of nature," and as the scope of reason and the imagination were enlarged through the revelation of God in the Bible.

As the Enlightenment took root in the nineteenth century, many came to believe that the universe is not God's creation at all but is a type of machine that came into being on its own and operates by its own laws or by chance. Others continued to believe that the universe was designed, but they conceived of God's role as being like a clockmaker's: God wound up the world and then left it to run on its own.

Either proposition eliminates any role for God in determining human affairs. A mechanistic universe has nothing to say about human aspirations, including a person's desire to lead a happy or meaningful life. But then how do people make sense of life? What could living a good life mean?

After World War II a group of philosophers known as the existentialists offered an answer: Since people are "condemned to freedom," as they were fond of saying, people don't find the good life, they create it. And in making it up, they "invent themselves" because they define for themselves how they want to live: their values, their goals, the criteria by which their lives might be evaluated. People began to be infatuated with the notion that we are self-invented creatures.

As Virginia Woolf might have said, "Every patient *defines* her humanity by having some say in her own prescription," in making life-and-death decisions for herself in perfect freedom.

The change in Western attitudes was announced in 1966, when *Time* published an issue whose cover shouted, "Is God Dead?" The issue asked whether religion was still viable in American life, whether Friedrich Nietzsche's pronouncement "God is dead" had come true. Whether Nietzsche was correct or not, Americans—and in an even more aggressive way, Europeans—began to behave as if God were indeed dead. The driving force was to overcome the nothingness by our own heroic efforts and to find our own meaning and our own humanity. Thus, the 1970s became the "me" decade, and in the 1980s the self-help industry sprang up, devoted to helping us invent ourselves. The once avant-garde idea had become mainstream.

Popular culture always picks and chooses from the cafeteria of the philosophers' recommendations. Pure existentialism proved too bleak for most people because it insisted that we are truly without any guides at all as to how to live. So, popular culture found a more congenial alternative. This idea had its most influential formation in the work of nineteenth-century German philosopher Hegel and in the pantheism of Eastern religion. Hegel's idea was that God is synonymous with the universe itself. The universe is an unfolding process that rises to self-awareness in humankind. Humans are therefore the crowning achievement of the god-as-world process, and we are God's self-consciousness. Therefore, if we want to know who we are and how to live the good life, we need only look within to discover God and the direction in which God is evolving. This eventually gave birth to the New Age religious fad.

How many times have you heard the suggestion that you have to make your own happiness, find the true self within, discover the god within? That's the self-help industry's prescription for attaining the satisfying life that seems perpetually just out of reach.

I can tell you that when I truly looked within myself, I was shocked and then disgusted. I found a self-righteous, self-satisfied guy who thought of himself as incorruptible because he had been taught ethics by his parents and had been highly educated. My self-righteousness had led to a failed first marriage, for which I bore the responsibility. It led me to play it as close to the line as possible when it came to dirty tricks in political campaigns. It utterly blinded me to the fact that I was committing a crime when I showed FBI files to a reporter. It told me I was a good guy, a caring person, when I did nice things for people. When I took a good hard look at all this, I didn't find "the god within." I found my corruption and even more devastating, *my will to remain corrupt.* Except for the troubling pain my failures were causing me, I enjoyed the way I was and I wasn't sure I wanted to change. For two years after Watergate, I was proud, defiant, blind, and as intent on self-vindication as John Ehrlichman was.

If we truly examine our own lives, we encounter the agonizing distance between what we should be and who we really are. For all the talk about honesty these days, why are we never honest about this? The only people who don't experience this disturbing tension between the good we want to do and the evil we practice are sociopaths. It is precisely the lack of a guilty conscience that enables sociopaths to indulge their appetites for rape, torture, and murder. These dark appetites exist within us all. Think about your response the last time someone betrayed you or cheated you or verbally abused you. If you are like most people, you wanted to hurt the person who hurt you, and that's the symbolic equivalent of what the sociopath practices.

The only ways to escape that darkness lie in denial (we really didn't do that), rationalization (we're no worse than the next person), killing our consciences (we practice vice so often we become habituated to it), or declaring our innocence through appointing ourselves god.

In his recent book *The Prophets: Who They Were, What They Are,* Norman Podhoretz argues that when the ancient Jewish prophets faulted Israel for idolatry, they meant that people were indulging in self-deification—replacing the will of God with their own wills. Podhoretz claims this is exactly what's happening more and more in America today. Anyone's infatuation with the self always leads in this direction, as we saw in Dennis Kozlowski's birthday party for his wife. They were so rich, so powerful, so immune to common moral standards that the trappings of their party suggested that they dwelt on Olympus as gods.

For most people in humbler circumstances, it's not nearly so easy pretending to be god, which is why the look-within movement spawned the huge self-help industry. Self-help guru Tony Robbins will teach us to *Awaken the Giant Within: How to Take Immediate Control of Your Mental, Emotional, Physical, and Financial Destiny!* and provide the secrets to *Unlimited Power.* Because we live in the tension between who we are and who we should be, self-help gurus can forever sell us the lie that we can close this gap ourselves. It's a mighty attractive offer. It's just not true.

As the Catholic philosopher and novelist Walker Percy said in *Lost in the Cosmos: The Last Self-Help Book,* the self *cannot help itself.* This is the bad news, humanity's common denominator, and the defining element of modern tragedy. Those who try to save their own lives will lose them—that persistent paradox. Any worldview that cannot reckon with this tragedy can neither be real nor provide hope. Those who persist in believing that the self can indeed help itself must ultimately despair because they are buying illusions.

Recognizing this enables us to get beyond self-obsession and helps us see the crucial importance of relationships. To live the good life, we have to understand how much our lives belong to others and what a good thing that is.

# CHAPTER 11

# WHOSE LIFE IS IT?

LET ME ASK a question: Who says, "It's *my* life"? Where have you heard that phrase before? With teenagers, of course, as they are struggling to establish their adult lives. Yet increasingly, we hear adults say essentially the same thing: "No one can tell me what to do with *my* life."

Such a claim is pure folly. Just take a good look at the way the world actually works. None of us is independent from others. We need each other, whether or not we want to admit it.

Reality sometimes has to force its way past our pride, even knock us down, before we are willing to pay attention. Roberto Rivera, one of my young colleagues, suffered a fall before he was able to see how much he needed other people.

Roberto is a gifted man with an extraordinary range of interests and talents—from Greek philosophy to ACC basketball, from gourmet cooking to classic blues artists. He's also a single father who takes care of an autistic son. If anyone has a right to be proud of himself, it's Roberto. His pride led him to make a fetish of self-sufficiency, however, resisting the help of friends and family.

Then while visiting his sister in New Jersey one Christmas, Roberto fell down a flight of steps and tore the quadriceps muscle of his left leg. His youngest brother and brother-in-law took him to the emergency room, where he spent the night. After he was released, his family continued to care for him, getting him out of bed in the morning, taking him to the bathroom, and helping him get dressed. A few weeks after the accident, Roberto learned that he needed surgery that would result in four weeks in a cast and six weeks in physical therapy.

When Roberto returned to Washington, a close friend picked him up at the train station, took him grocery shopping, and made sure he had everything he needed. Over the next several weeks, as Roberto recovered and tried to take care of his autistic son, friends brought them food and enabled them to keep going in a host of ways.

The experience shattered Roberto's illusions of self-sufficiency and dealt a blow to his ego. As he said later, "Pride is impossible to maintain when someone has seen you undressed." Through his experience of utter dependency, Roberto saw the flaws in his own thinking about personal autonomy and self-sufficiency.

Believing we are independent is simply a fiction—an increasingly unhelpful one. We all live in a vast network of friends, family, coworkers, and the incredibly complex associations that make up a culture. Infants are dependent on their parents. Students are dependent on their professors as well as their parents, who help pay the bills. It's hard to find any truly solitary profession in the marketplace. We are dependent on service providers, salespeople, purchasing agents, accountants, advisers, and lawyers, to name a few. Even the last of the Alaskan fur trappers depend to some extent on the outside world and quite extensively on the harmonious workings of the natural order. However, our pride often blinds us from acknowledging our interdependence.

This pride bleeds into many areas in our cultural lives, including the whole issue of "death with dignity." The advocates for euthanasia are most concerned about the supposed indignity that comes with people's being dependent on others. They don't want their illusion of total independence taken from them by being cared for. But a world where aging parents are considered to be a burden to their children is a cruel and sad world, filled with people dying alone, uncared for, unloved, unmourned. A world like that can't work because mutual dependence is built into the natural order. We are meant for community.

I've seen the reality of this in prison, sometimes to excess. A number of years ago when I visited the federal prison camp for women in Alderson, West Virginia, virtually the entire population filled the gymnasium for my talk. The women were warm, excited, and very receptive. They also sat together in pairs, many holding hands and showing obvious affection for one another. Somehow I was able to keep my composure and give a biblical message, even as the women were openly defying biblical teaching.

I've discovered the same thing in other prisons. Prison officials say it's natural. When women arrive in prison, after they're checked in, searched, and have their possessions taken away, they experience a desperate desire to regain some sense of belonging. A woman's nesting instinct quickly leads her to attach herself to another woman, and usually two to three to four such "couples" compose a mini-society of their own. Inmates in male institutions tend to form "macho" gangs, less intimate but no less binding.

I've also seen how prisons use enforced and unnatural isolation as punishment. Recalcitrant inmates are thrown into "the hole," which in prison talk means solitary confinement. In some prisons around the world, I've encountered extreme cases where extended solitary confinement progressed from punishment to mental torture to physical barbarism. I've seen holes where the inmate has to crouch down to get into the space, where light can be shut out for months. A person who stays in solitary confinement too long may suffer permanent mental and emotional damage.

The stories that came from North Vietnam's main prison where the American prisoners of war were kept—dubbed the Hanoi Hilton by the POWs—underscore the human need for community. Most inmates were kept in solitary cells, but they developed their own system of communication, using Morse code. The coded messages tapped on the walls from one cell to another kept many men sane and alive. The brief moments prisoners found themselves together, even for the brutal interrogation and brainwashing sessions, became occasions to be savored.

In her isolation, Nien Cheng relished looking through the slot in the cell's iron door to see the face of the Labor Reform worker who sometimes brought her meals. The worker was one of the few people who smiled at Nien Cheng during those years, and the brief glimpse of a smile carried sustaining power.

---

Empirical research supports the conclusion that people need each other. Thirty-three research scientists investigated the relationship between human development and community, reporting their findings in a 2003 report, *Hardwired to Connect.*[1] The report argues that all children need authoritative communities devoted to transmitting a model of the moral life. Without loving connections—to people and institutions that give children moral and spiritual guidance—children become more prone to psychiatric disorders that develop in late adolescence. The complex interaction between children and their families and community actually seems to affect the way in which their genetic makeup develops. The report says that we are biologically primed to find meaning through attachment to others.

The report goes on to state that the search for moral meaning and the quest for a transcendent reality arises from "our basic biology and how our brains develop." Whether this came about through providential design or chance, I leave for now as an open question, but the report gives clear empirical evidence that the desire for truth and meaning is rooted in our biological makeup.

Most of us understand the importance of relationships without needing a scientific study to prove it. Times of crisis quickly bring this truth to light. When terrorists attacked the World Trade Center and the Pentagon on September 11, 2001, I was in Florida moving books into a new home Patty and I had just purchased in our attempt to downsize. Neither our television nor radios were connected yet, so I was oblivious to what was happening. One of the movers came running into the house, shouting, "They've attacked the World Trade Center and the Pentagon!" When I asked who attacked, he just shrugged his shoulders—and ran out. At that point all I knew was that an enormous catastrophe had occurred. The first thing I did was grab my cell phone and call Patty and our three children. Only after I was assured that everyone in the family was all right did I attempt to find out the full story.

Over the last few years I've asked people what they did when they heard about the terrorist attacks. The overwhelming majority did exactly what I did. And, of course, many of the people who were tragically affected by the attacks did the same thing. They made calls from the airplanes and the Twin Towers, scribbled notes, and sent last frantic e-mails. Trendy philosophies come and go, but in the depths of our very being, we *know* we need each other. Living a community life with diverse individuals is how we find our security, learn to help neighbors, and form vibrant cultures. Contemporary scholar Ken Boa writes, "We cannot become authentic selves without being embedded in community."[2]

The historic notions of community have been badly shaken in America, however, as we have become a highly mobile society. A few decades ago, if people went to college at all, it was near their homes. Mostly they then worked in their own hometowns. Today we think nothing of moving across the country—or the world, for that matter—leaving our families and roots behind forever. Some people amass fortunes, build mansions in the Hamptons or Palm Springs, and completely forget the communities in which they were reared.

——•◦•——

Some places in America, however, still reflect formative communities in which people reinvest the fruits of their success to sustain that community. These are communities where tradition, history, and culture mean something. Such a place is Grand Rapids, Michigan, a community full of people who have benefited from their largely Dutch Reformed culture and have then reinvested themselves and their resources in it.

A few years ago I was in Grand Rapids to help dedicate the Rich and Helen DeVos Center for Arts and Worship at the Grand Rapids Christian High School—an outstanding institution from which Rich, one of America's great entrepreneurs and motivational speakers, graduated. He went on to build an international business based in Grand Rapids, a hugely successful venture now known as Alticor, Inc. (formerly Amway).

Unlike a lot of executives who create a company, earn a lot of money, then take their profits and move to a soaring skyscraper condo somewhere in the world, the DeVoses have remained residents of Grand Rapids. They've lived in the same house, in fact, for most of their lives. Rich has never lost his love for his community, expressing that love through generous philanthropy.

He's not alone. As I drove through Grand Rapids and neighboring Dutch communities, I saw countless buildings named after the families who had settled the area: the Van Andel Institute for Medical Research, the Prince Conference Center at Calvin College, as well as the DeWitt

Center and the DePree Art Center and Cook Hall at Hope College. These founding families have remained committed to their community through generations. Many began very successful businesses, but they didn't look at their corporations as a chance to pump their own stock. The founders of these companies, people like Herman Miller, limited executive pay to a reasonable multiple of the going wage for a factory worker. They looked at business as an instrument to serve the community and produce things of value for the customer—the classic economist Adam Smith's ideal.

Commitment to community through generations helps us know who we are—and that keeps us from pretending to be who we aren't. Commitment to community also means that we have a realistic appreciation of those who have gone before us. The late Russell Kirk, one of the great scholars of modern times, not only wrote about the importance of roots and tradition, but he also lived it. I visited Kirk at his home in Mecosta, Michigan, a short time before he died in 1994. He lived in an old Victorian home that looked as if it could be inhabited by ghosts—and it was, in a sense, because six generations of his family had lived in his hometown, and the house, a frequent topic in his essays, was filled with their collective memory. The town of Mecosta isn't much more than a truck stop in the central Michigan countryside, and that presented inconveniences to Kirk's frequent, global travels. But he remained there because he understood the value of community and belonging.

"It's the performance of our duties in community," Kirk writes, "that teaches us prudence and efficiency and charity."[3] Kirk believed in "custom, convention, and continuity." This isn't a head-in-the-sand approach. Rather, he realized that the wisdom of the ages and the experiences of those who have gone before us are far more reliable guides to living than the utopian schemes of coffeehouse dreamers. Kirk understood the enduring moral order, which "is made for man and man is made for it: human nature is a constant and moral truths are permanent."[4] Community is essential to this order—to the good life—because without it, we're lonely and lose the capacity to transmit values, develop character, and inform conscience.

This sense of responsibility to community—civic duty—was once regarded as a cardinal virtue. Alexis de Tocqueville, often quoted as one of the keenest observers of the American scene, wrote that the human person cannot exist "entirely within the solitude of his own heart."[5] He also remarked that in all of France he could not find ten people who did what Americans did every day as a matter of course—raising barns, feeding the hungry, looking after orphans.

I grew up seeing rich community life in action. Some of my earliest childhood memories were of my mother taking meals to neighbors who were out of work during the Great Depression of the 1930s. Often my parents didn't even know the neighbors very well, but it was enough that they lived in our community and had needs. So my mother responded.

This sense of obligation to the people around us is what fuels genuine patriotism, which is not the mindless nationalism that presumes America is the world's greatest country. Rather, true patriotism arises from a desire to pay back the community in which we live.

That's why I went into the marines at the height of the Korean War. I felt a debt to those who had given themselves to establish the freest nation on earth. That's also why Saint Thomas Aquinas, in his *Summa Theologica,* included the just-war doctrine under the heading of "Christian Love." People willing to sacrifice themselves for the protection and defense of their neighbors offer a supreme act of love, which is why the military and the fire and police departments are considered the noblest of callings.

> The good life is found only in loving relationships and community.

Patriotism and the vitality of community recently came together in a stunning story. In the recent Iraqi conflict, Staff Sergeant Dustin Tuller was shot four times, and field medics doubted he would live. After losing both legs, Tuller was eventually able to return home to Milton, Florida. The father of four, Dustin Tuller would have to learn to live with computer-assisted titanium legs.

Sergeant Tuller's community wanted to show their appreciation for his sacrifice. One hundred twenty volunteers donated materials and built Dustin a handicap-accessible new home. One of the volunteers remarked, "A fellow has gotten himself hurt trying to defend what our nation is about. And if we can't do something about it, something is wrong."[6] The man who initiated the effort lived in a Florida city called—ironically enough—Bagdad.

What impressed me most about these events was the spirit shown by both Sergeant Tuller and his community. The sergeant retained a positive attitude, even his sense of humor, concentrating on his family and the life before him. His neighbors, in turn, thought that what they were doing was what *anybody* should do.

C. S. Lewis remarked that we cannot love the whole world, but we certainly can love our neighbors. We innately understand this duty because it's part of what makes us human. Sergeant Tuller and his neighbors in Milton, Florida, demonstrate this at its best.

— • —

The myth of personal autonomy—of "my point of view, right or wrong," of "my happiness, right or wrong"—is a mere counterfeit of what you and I really want. It substitutes an illusion of self-sufficiency for the sustaining reality of nurturing relationships within a community. The good life? We do not experience it in the loneliness of today's fads of self-expression and self-gratification. The good life is found only in loving relationships and community.

But even this, important as it is, doesn't get us to the good life. There's more to it, a matter of the heart, as we see in the life of someone who could be any of us.

# CHAPTER 12

# A VERY RICH MAN

THE GOOD LIFE is made possible when we expose some of the lies of modern culture—the belief that money and things give us happiness, the seductive notion that we can design our own lives and enjoy unrestrained autonomy. Even when we realize that it is dignity, not riches, that constitutes the good life, when we have our family and community life together and are usefully engaged, we can still find our lives incomplete. Something more is needed, something that shakes us out of the comfortable routine of life—a moment of awakening when we question what gives us our significance.

This is the point raised in the movie *About Schmidt,* which opens at the moment the proverbial carrot is taken away. The movie begins with Warren Schmidt's retirement from Woodmen of the World Life Insurance Society in Omaha, Nebraska. The rest of the movie sees him examining what significance, if any, his life possesses.[1] (The part is brilliantly played by Jack Nicholson, who should have won an Oscar.) This same moment of crisis comes to many people in a variety of ways: job loss, the death of a child, divorce, or a terminal illness. I experienced that moment when I resigned from my position at the White House. Once I stopped running after what I thought I had always wanted, I had to ask myself: What was my life truly all about?

At Warren Schmidt's retirement dinner, his friend Ray, already retired, tries to sum up the meaning of Warren's life, proclaiming him a "very rich man." More than fifty of his coworkers and their spouses are gathered around circular tables while Schmidt occupies the place of honor at the dais. They've been enjoying a steak dinner in the function room of Johnny's Café.

Ray knows about retirement, he says. The dinner, the presents, even the monthly checks from social security and the company pension—these things don't mean a thing. The only thing that has value is devoting your life to something meaningful. Doing your job and doing it well. Taking care of your family. Earning the respect of your peers and the greater community. That's the only way to make lasting friendships.

In Ray's opinion, Warren has done all of this. He has gained for himself the only things that really matter in life. That's why Warren is a very rich man.

While the guests applaud, raising their glasses in a toast, Warren himself is not so sure. He excuses himself and retreats to the restaurant's bar, where he orders a stiff drink.

One by one Warren questions the ideas guiding his life. He visits the younger man who has taken his place at the insurance company, only to find that Warren's help is the last thing the man wants. On Schmidt's way out of the building, he sees that the files he developed over a lifetime have been summarily deposited next to the Dumpster for disposal. His work has literally become trash.

The morning after his retirement, his wife, Helen, leads him by the hand out to their new Winnebago Adventurer. The RV is so big, it barely fits in their driveway and dwarfs the house itself. Helen has prepared a surprise breakfast that's all laid out on the galley's table, with eggs, bacon, sliced melon, the works.

"Isn't this fun, Warren?" she asks. She raises her orange juice glass. "Here's to a whole new chapter."

The truth is, Warren has almost no interest in a life of leisure, particularly if it means spending more time with Helen. He finds himself irritated by everything about his wife. Helen throws out perfectly good food simply because the expiration date has come and gone. Yet she refuses to replace her old down-at-the-heel slippers. She has to try every new restaurant, and she keeps buying those blasted Hummel figurines. When Warren wakes up in the middle of the night and looks over at her plump figure, he can only ask himself, *Who is this woman?*

Warren finds some release from his frustrations through an entirely unexpected source. On a whim, he decides to become the foster parent of a poor African boy, Ndugu Umbo, through a charity called Childreach. The organization suggests that with his monthly check he might want to send a letter. The children appreciate learning about the person who is helping them.

Warren begins his first letter to Ndugu awkwardly, noting that he's sixty-six years old and recently retired from the Woodmen of the World Life Insurance Society. As he writes, the words begin to come more easily, then they flood. He finds that he can tell Ndugu what he can say to no one else. The truth is, he's enraged at having been turned out of his company. He can't stand his wife, Helen. He loves his grown-up daughter, Jeannie, but she's about to marry a conniving fool. Warren never thought life would be this way. When he left college, he believed he would become one of the people who made things happen in the world. He felt somehow singled out and that a certain light shone on him.

His outpouring of emotion to Ndugu shocks him. Before he sends the letter, he crosses out much of the passion, but he continues to support Ndugu and to send him updates on what's happening in his life.

Within a few short weeks of Warren's retirement, his wife dies. He finds her lying in the kitchen, the vacuum cleaner still running by her side, its nozzle sucking the air furiously.

A month or two later, Schmidt faces the task of going through her things. He has to pack up his wife's clothes, box her toiletries, figure out what to do with her jewelry. As he begins sorting, we hear the letter he is composing in his mind to Ndugu. Warren may have given Ndugu the wrong impression about Helen, he writes. He was fortunate to have had such a good wife. He takes a whiff of Helen's perfume. He longs so much to have her with him again that he applies her cold cream to his own face.

After he cleans himself up, washing away the cold cream and at least some of his emotion, he goes into her closet, where he fingers the polka-dot dress he gave her. He reaches for the boxes of shoes on the upper shelves and several stacks fall in a heap. One box spills out a packet of letters.

He sees from the postmarks that they date back to the early years of their marriage. They are addressed to "Dear Helen." "My Dearest Helen." "My Love." They are not in Warren's handwriting. He looks

quickly to see who wrote them. Ray. His best friend, Ray! The cuck-
olding snake in the grass who had so recently proclaimed him a very
rich man!

Warren's rage at the emptiness of his life sends him on an uncertain quest. One night, unable to sleep or find any other type of rest, he
boards his new Adventurer RV and begins traveling toward Denver to
see his daughter, Jeannie. He tells her that he would like to stay with her
for a while and help out with the wedding preparations, despite his dislike of her fiancé, Randall. Jeannie doesn't really want him there until a
day or so before the wedding, so she deflects her father's plan.

Schmidt writes Ndugu that he's decided to use the time to visit
old haunts. Warren journeys back to his hometown, Holdrege, Nebraska, only to find that a tire store now occupies 12 Locust Avenue,
where his boyhood home once stood. Next he travels to his alma mater, the University of Kansas, where he sees himself in a pledge-class
photo. Was he that thin, dark-haired, energetic young man? "With all
the world before me . . ."

One night during his wanderings, Schmidt parks the Adventurer by
a river. As darkness falls, he has a strange urge to climb atop the roof of
the RV and sit under the night sky. There Schmidt arranges a few votive
candles and the new assortment of Hummel figurines he's unaccountably
acquired. Huddled in a blanket, he sits before this makeshift altar and
looks up into the night sky, swarming with stars.

His travels have softened his heart. He asks his wife, Helen, "Was I
really the man you wanted to be with? Was I? Or were you disappointed
and too nice to show it? I forgive you for Ray. I forgive you. That was a
long time ago, and I know I wasn't always the king of kings. I let you
down. I'm sorry, Helen. Can you forgive me? Can you forgive me?"

Just then, a star shoots across the sky. A sign of forgiveness? His
right hand emerges from the folds of his blanket, and he hurriedly
crosses himself.

The next morning, Schmidt feels transformed. It's time for him to
push on to Denver, and he feels ready now. He writes to Ndugu that his
trip has become a mission. Nothing is going to stop him ever again
from doing what he must do—from living boldly. The guiding myths
of romance and career that both supported and failed him have now
been supplanted by a whole new idea: being absolutely and completely

true to himself, doing what he thinks is right, whatever the consequences. He's going to tell Jeannie exactly what he thinks of her impending marriage.

When he arrives in Denver, he drives to the home of his hostess for the week, Jeannie's future mother-in-law, Roberta. It's a small, weathered, wood-framed house in a lower-middle-class neighborhood.

When the door opens, Roberta, an aging hippie in a tent dress, welcomes him. The walls of her gimcrack house are covered with tacky modern art—the kind where everyone has either one eye or three—and macramé wall hangings so dusty that they are interlaced with spiderwebs.

The woman's a nightmare. She immediately launches into a conversation about her hysterectomy. She tells Warren she breast-fed his future son-in-law until he was five.

As soon as Jeannie arrives at the house—with Randall, of course, who asks, "How's it hangin', Dad?"—Schmidt tells her that he needs to talk to her. Alone.

She barely pays attention to what he's saying, brushing past him with the half promise, "Maybe after dinner."

Dinner at Roberta's house is attended by Randall's father, Larry, and his Chinese second wife, Saundra, as well as Randall's brother, Duncan. No one exhibits any manners. The drippy-eyed, twenty-something Duncan stuffs his face as if obeying a posthypnotic suggestion. Roberta gnaws on her chicken bones, then sucks at them.

The feed fest is interrupted only by Roberta, who with much profanity dresses down Larry as he makes a toast. Her harangue is like two fists banging down on a piano. This brings the meal to a finish, as discord echoes into plangent silence.

Schmidt finally gets Jeannie alone on Roberta's front porch. "Jeannie," he says, "you should think about this. The wedding, your future. You're making a big mistake. Don't do it."

Jeannie takes a step back, crosses her arms, and gives him a cold, stony look. "All of a sudden you are taking an interest in what I do? You have an opinion about my life *now?*"

What does she mean? He doesn't know what to say.

Jeannie continues, "Okay, you listen to me. I am getting married the day after tomorrow, and you are going to come to my wedding, and you are going to sit there and enjoy it and support me or else you can just turn right around right now and go back to Omaha."

She flounces past him, back into the house, back to Randall's side.

Schmidt's still on the porch when Randall and Jeannie walk out to her car. His daughter slams the door on her run-down Saturn, and the hole in the muffler rips out the evening's valedictory.

Schmidt has a hard time stomaching the wedding. He's nearly gagging when it comes time for him to toast the happy couple at their reception. He stands to one side of the main table to make whatever speech he can muster. He looks down at the cordless microphone, taking quick breaths through his nose. His anger at Jeannie threatens to rise to a scorching boil.

"What I really want to say," Schmidt begins, his cheeks bulging with suppressed venom. "What I really want to say . . ." He takes a breath and brings to mind the civility he's been taught, ". . . is how pleased my late wife, Helen, was that Jeannie found Randall. That she would have someone to be her partner in life."

Schmidt goes on to thank Randall's family for their warm hospitality, making complimentary remarks about each member. He goes so far as to say that Duncan, the idiotic brother, seems a very thoughtful person.

When Warren ends by saying that he is very pleased, the groom's father says, "Hear, hear," and everyone applauds.

Only Jeannie seems to notice the labor of her father's words.

Schmidt walks away from the gathering to take refuge in the bathroom. He's sweating, breathing hard, and presses his forehead against the cold tile. He stands in a hunched position, the burden not lifting.

On the way back to Omaha, Schmidt visits Kearney, Nebraska, where an arch over Interstate 80 contains a museum that honors the pioneers. He writes to Ndugu about its impressive displays. The people who came before the Warren Schmidts of the world, the pioneers who traveled west in their Conestoga wagons and made the country what it is, faced incomparable difficulties. Their fate makes him think how small he is in the big scheme of things. He asks, "What in the world is better because of me?"

Schmidt thought he had found a new way of living when he set out for Denver to tell Jeannie she was making a big mistake. But his new faith in self-assertion came to nothing. Jeannie married the nincompoop anyway.

As Schmidt opens the door of his home in Omaha, he's still writing a mental letter to Ndugu. "I am weak," he confesses, "and I am a failure. Relatively soon, I will die. Maybe in twenty years, maybe tomorrow, it doesn't matter. Once I am dead and everyone who knew me dies too, it will be as though I never existed. What difference has my life made to anyone? None that I can think of. None at all."

Schmidt gathers up the mail that's fallen through the slot and takes it into his home office. Among the bills and junk mail he finds an unusual envelope with red striping around the edges.

It's a letter from Sister Nadine Gautier, who is writing on behalf of six-year-old Ndugu, who cannot yet read or write. The boy wants his foster father to know how much he appreciates his help. Awhile ago Ndugu had an eye infection, but with the extra money that Schmidt has supplied, he was able to purchase medicine and is doing fine now. Ndugu painted a picture to express his appreciation. He hopes that his foster father will enjoy this picture.

Schmidt opens the attached folded sheet. It's a crayon drawing of a larger figure and a smaller one holding hands under a beaming sun. Both figures are smiling, but the child's smile is especially wide.

The paper trembles in Schmidt's hands. His head falls back, and his eyes clamp shut as the anguish and joy of this lone and almost-too-casual act of mercy registers. He's done one thing right, it seems. One thing. At least this one thing. The realization brings with it a shaking sweat. His gaping mouth is so drawn by pain and the first tentative fingers of relief that Schmidt's quiet passion breaks into full view. He doesn't know if his heart is breaking or mending. Finally, a dark joy wins out. A smile, even a look of satisfaction, replaces the tears. His life has counted for something, after all.

# GIVING

*to*

# OTHERS

# CHAPTER 13

# LIVING LEGACIES

THE STORY OF Warren Schmidt may strike you as an odd one for me to be telling, yet Schmidt is an Everyman for whom family, community, work, and even faith have become perverted. The kind of desperation and panic he experiences at the emptiness of his life is something many of us feel. We have only to think of how many times we've stared vacantly at our desks or how excruciating the Thanksgiving and Christmas holidays can be for many families. Suicide rates spike at this "most wonderful time of the year."

*About Schmidt* reveals the withering selfishness that often turns a very good thing—family—into a source of woe and oppression. Spouses neglect each other or, worse, cheat on each other. Dads can be so distracted by their work, as Schmidt was, that they do not notice what is really going on in their children's lives until it's too late. Where there is great potential for the good life, there is also the possibility of devastation. It hurts to have our deepest longings betrayed. Schmidt is like many of us who get caught up in the self-centered, mundane pursuits of life and fail to see any higher purpose or goal.

With all its ambiguities, *About Schmidt* is ultimately a story of quiet redemption. Schmidt's last-gasp redemption comes out of the purity of his giving to Ndugu—an act of pure graciousness. He's not looking *for* anything from Ndugu when he begins extending him financial support. But the picture the child finally paints for Schmidt is a gift of incalculable worth; it illumines his dark life with the sheer joy of having done something for another person for no other reason than that it was the right thing to do. It's the one moment in which Schmidt is absolutely certain that he's done the right thing and knows he's made a positive difference in another's life. One pure act of kindness, charity, and love gives his life significance. It is his first real experience of the good life.

Life does not depend, as Schmidt finds out, on any great revelation about living boldly and being absolutely committed to going one's own way, whatever the consequences. One of the great paradoxes I've discovered is that every element of the good life depends on pure and often sacrificial giving, on losing one's self. Giving yourself to others and living for others may feel like a radical idea in our times. But all of us who are part of healthy families know this is what makes them work.

Patty has been an incredibly dedicated partner in ministry. I know I could never have done what I have without her unfailing support. I've always been able to take her into my confidence about anything and know that she will do nothing to violate that confidence. She has been a true soul mate.

And don't we enjoy seeing our children do better than we do, and our grandchildren in turn do better yet? Seeing my kids go beyond what I've done is a source of indescribable joy. Both of my sons have become very successful in their businesses and are great dads and husbands— better than I was. My daughter, Emily, is a spiritual giant; the way she cares for her son and lives her life is an inspiration to me. These things make me rightfully proud. Like every grandparent, I'm quick to pull out the latest pictures of my grandchildren.

My children have also formed me as much as I have formed them. I never made major career decisions without talking them through with the kids. When I was trying to decide whether or not to go to the White House, they gave me very helpful advice. Wendell told me to do it because if I didn't, I'd always regret it. (Good advice from a fifteen-year-old.) Both Emily and Chris gave me excellent advice when I was deciding about pleading guilty during Watergate. And throughout the time I was attacked so brutally in the press, my three children and Patty constantly affirmed and supported me. I need my family and their support as much as I need food and water.

As we give to our families, we are sustained in return. The family is often described as a "school of charity," in the sense that it's the easiest place to learn how to give ourselves to others.

Sometimes we have to extend ourselves as we would never do otherwise. My co-writer, Harold, is a middle-aged man with an older son and two little kids. Recently his nine-year-old son, Will, begged to attend a Boy Scout campout called "Dad and Lad." The overnight was to take place at Camp Pirtle, which is located deep in the Piney Woods of East Texas. At that time of the year the Piney Woods were about as hot and sticky as a tropical rain forest.

Harold is not the camping type. His idea of a dream vacation is to check into a resort on a Northern California beach, sit on a private balcony, read a good book, and look out over the water. He had not been camping for forty years—since he was Will's age. He had never pitched a tent, and by his own reckoning is one of the least "handy" people on earth.

Still, Will desperately wanted to go on the campout. He also wanted to extend the enjoyment of the experience by making long lists of needed supplies months before the actual event. At bedtime, he talked frequently with his father about all the fun they were going to have: the campfire, the s'mores, the ghost stories, the starry, starry night!

The prospect would normally have grizzled my co-writer's gills, but the longing in his son was so powerful that he agreed to the campout and even enjoyed discussing its prospects with his son, although he never paid enough attention to the supply list.

As the event neared, the weather report said that the campout weekend would be plagued with powerful lightning storms. The weather report was not wrong.

Harold and his son arrived at Camp Pirtle on Friday evening and managed to pitch their tent. It was a small tent—a one-and-a-half-person tent, at most. Other fathers unfurled great canvas condos and unpacked Coleman lanterns, portable televisions, cooking stoves, and deck chairs. Harold had packed all of his son's and his supplies in one of those rolling airline bags that goes in the overhead bin. The other fathers and their sons looked at Harold's airline bag and pathetically small tent with great pity and amused scorn. One of the other dads suggested that if Will and his father wanted to sleep in his ample tent, they were welcome.

As it happened, Will and his dad were comfortable and cozy in their small tent, even when it began to rain—hard. Then, in the middle of the night, about three o'clock, the predicted storm cells hit Camp Pirtle. When the lightning began flashing, their tent seemed to vanish entirely, becoming merely a sheath of white light. The lightning came on ferociously, striking every other minute. The whole world seemed not merely to rumble but to *bounce* with the thunder. The high trees about the camp sang out a whistling, clattering lament.

Will became frightened. "Dad! We're going to die!" he screamed. "We're going to die, Dad! We're going to die!"

Harold wondered what had led him on this disaster. He was in the forsaken East Texas woods at a place called Camp Pirtle—of all things—in order to . . . what? Scare his son to death and, as an added bonus, risk their lives? *Oh, this is terrific,* he thought.

But what Harold said was, "We're fine, Will. I wouldn't have brought us here if we weren't. We're fine. Here, let me hold you."

Whether they were indeed "fine," Harold really didn't know. But for hours he comforted his frightened child and counted the seconds between lightning flashes and the thunderclaps, trying to gauge whether the storm cells were right on top of them. Several times he counted only to one before he heard an earsplitting crack.

In the morning, when the lightning had abated (but not the rain), Harold spoke with another dad, who worked for the forest service, asking him how dangerous the previous night had been. "Oh, any closer and we might have taken some casualties," the man said.

Casualties? For the sake of a Boy Scout campout?

Of course, the weekend worked wonders for the relationship between Harold and his son. They had been through danger together and survived! Will came to believe that his father was a man of tremendous courage. Only Harold, of course, knew just how frightened he himself had been. But because his son needed him to remain calm, he had.

We sometimes do extraordinary things for the sake of our spouses and children. And in this process of learning the lessons of charity, we may find that living for others makes life worthwhile. We may also discover unexpected capacities in ourselves.

As a man who has always put his work first, I was deeply moved when J. Robertson McQuilkin gave up his career as a seminary president. He was at his peak, writing books, lecturing, running a great institution, when his wife was diagnosed with Alzheimer's. Most of Robertson's colleagues expected him to get Muriel nursing care or put her in a good care facility. But McQuilkin decided to care for his wife personally. His commitment was first to his wife; his career came second. When he announced that he was retiring early, he gave an emotional speech in which he said that Muriel had taken care of him for more than forty years, and now it was his turn to take care of her. Long past the days when Muriel even knew who he was, this loving husband cared for his wife until the day of her death. McQuilkin knew the joy of living for others.[1]

Even in our egocentric culture, many of us have experienced greater joy in the success of others than in our own triumphs. Some of the happiest experiences of my life have been in mentoring my coworkers or simply seeing people bloom within the organization I had a hand in starting.

I have been unusually blessed to work with hundreds of ex-cons whose lives have been turned around. Mary Kay Beard spent eight years in prison after being a gun moll on the FBI's Ten Most Wanted Fugitives list. When she got out of prison, I hired her to work with us in Alabama.

Struck by the needs of three hundred children who belonged to women incarcerated at the Julia Tutwiler Prison for Women, Mary Kay began a program called Angel Tree. She asked families in churches to "adopt" a child and provide gifts at Christmas.

A program that started in just a few churches and one shopping mall now operates in fifty countries around the world. During the past twenty years in America alone, six million kids whose parents are in prison have received Christmas gifts and visits from church members during the holidays. More than six hundred thousand are helped each year.

> *Living for others makes life worthwhile.*

Now many of these kids are going to Christian camps and being mentored themselves, as their lives are redirected from gangs, drugs, and violence into life-giving pursuits.[2]

My experience has not been limited to people coming out of prison. Through the years I've also kept my eye out for young people with writing talent. In 1986 I was looking for a research assistant who could help me draft editorials and commentaries. A friend sent me an article written by a Wheaton College student named Michael Gerson. His article about Mother Teresa was beautifully written, well reasoned, very original, and fresh. It made a great impression on me—so great that I can remember the article to this day.

I had one of my staff call Wheaton College and ask about Gerson. I discovered that he was a senior who would be graduating that summer. I then asked if he would be willing to meet with me when I was next in Chicago.

A few months later I had a layover in Chicago and met young Mike Gerson at the airport. Dressed in a dark three-piece suit, a silk necktie, and starched French cuffs with black onyx cuff links, he seemed to have stepped out of the Victorian era. I thought, *Who is this? Where was the usual student garb?*

We spent twenty minutes talking together, and I immediately recognized that Mike had unusual gifts. He was remarkably bright, deep, and very well-read. So I asked him straight-out if he'd like to come work for me. He told me he had been accepted at Fuller Theological Seminary for academic study in theology.

I said to him, "No. You're ready to get into the big leagues and join the fight to defend truth. I need you to come to Washington and write with me."

He was startled at my forwardness, of course, and said he would think and pray about it. A short time later he accepted my offer.

Mike was a treasure. When he first arrived in Washington, he didn't quite fit in with the culture of Prison Fellowship. He was more formal, more proper. I don't think any of us ever saw Mike working in shirtsleeves. What we did see, however, was a prolific writer and prodigious mind at work. After four months, Mike was writing stuff that I barely had to edit. He was incredibly gifted. He had a deep understanding of theology and the Bible, and he loved the Lord. We had a great two and a half years together. He exerted a substantial influence on me by encouraging me to reread Russell Kirk, Edmund Burke, and the other great writers of classical conservatism.

Mike called me one day after Dan Quayle was elected vice president in 1988 and said he needed to talk with me about the four-year commitment he had made to work for me. He asked my permission to be released from that commitment so that he could apply to work for Dan Coats, the congressman and also a Wheaton alumnus who had just been appointed to fill Quayle's vacant senate seat. Very characteristically, Mike said that if I had any objection, he would fulfill his commitment to me. I found his loyalty amazing—and rare, especially since I hadn't even asked him to make that commitment. Since Dan Coats and I were good friends, I went Mike one better and told him I'd call Dan and do what I could to see that he was hired. After working very successfully for Dan Coats, Mike worked for Jack Kemp. Eventually, this able young man took a job as a reporter for *U.S. News & World Report*.

I watched with joy as Mike married a Korean-American young woman and became the father of two beautiful boys. Throughout his time in Washington, Mike maintained a consistent witness to his Christian faith.

When then-Governor George W. Bush called and asked Mike to write speeches for him, Mike came to me and asked, "Should I do it?" I told him to grab the opportunity.

Mike wrote George W. Bush's major convention acceptance speeches and eventually the president-elect's inaugural address. The young writer went on to become one of President Bush's senior advisers and his chief speechwriter. He penned the crucial speech Bush gave to Congress after 9/11—the one that did so much to bring the country together.

As President Bush delivered the speech Mike had written, Mike sat in his living room and waited until it was over. The tension was too much for him to witness the event in person.

When President Bush arrived back at the White House, the first call he made was to Mike, thanking him for the speech. Mike felt emboldened to say, "Mr. President, I think God has put you in this position for this time."

The president's reply to him was, "Mike, God has put *us* in this position for this time."

Thirty years ago I went into the White House to have an impact on how people lived and on the great events of our times. I fell short because of the Watergate scandal. But Mike Gerson went on to do so much of what I had hoped to accomplish for our country—yet he has done it better, much better, because he is grounded in faith. He's written some of the greatest speeches any president has ever given. Mike is also creating a legacy of political thinking on many moral and other issues—particularly bioethics. Through Mike Gerson's life I'm seeing many of my own hopes and dreams fulfilled. And all it took was giving a highly talented young man a start, knowing when to let him go, and putting his ultimate welfare ahead of the benefits he brought to my organization. When we give to others, we discover this enduring truth: In giving we often receive more than we give.

———·•·———

The people we influence in a positive way constitute the real and lasting monuments of our lives. I learned this lesson twenty years ago when I was in England giving lectures.

One of the historical figures I deeply admire is the eighteenth-century British parliamentarian William Wilberforce, who began a crusade against the slave trade. He was joined by three or four other Christian politicians and businessmen who committed their lives to one another and to redressing this great evil. They moved into adjacent homes in the Clapham community outside of London and eventually became known as the Clapham Sect.

For twenty years these abolitionists waged the battle. Parliament would vote them down one year, and they'd be right back the next. They'd make a small gain in the vote count, then suffer two years of setbacks. Slavery was enormously profitable to the British Empire—five hundred sailing ships out of Liverpool plied the trade in human bodies, running from Africa to the West Indies to America. A good chunk of the thousands of pounds sterling earned by the slave traders found its way into the pockets of parliamentarians. That's where the English term *rotten borough system* came from. Against almost superhuman odds, Wilberforce and his band of friends persisted. Every day they met for three hours to pray and study the Bible. They circulated pamphlets and brochures throughout England. They stood on the floor of the House of Commons night after night, arguing for justice and righteousness.

> *In giving we often receive more than we give.*

Finally, in 1807, after two decades of struggle, the slave trade was abolished by a vote of Parliament. In 1833, as Wilberforce lay on his deathbed, slavery itself was abolished in the empire.

When I was in England that year, knowing that I would have time one evening following my day's lectures, I asked my host if he could arrange a visit to Clapham. I wanted to see the houses that the Clapham Sect had lived in, the church they had worshiped in, and any monuments that had been erected to honor their incredible campaign.

An English friend drove Patty and me to Clapham, which has been swallowed up by urban sprawl, one neighborhood among many on the fringes of London. When we arrived at dusk, a mist settled over the dark, cramped streets. The road twisted and turned up a hill, and my host said, "We're getting close to where the Clapham Sect lived."

All I could see were dreary, whitewashed row houses. "Where's the Thornton farmhouse?" I asked, alluding to one of the Clapham Sect's principal residences.

"Oh, I forgot to tell you," he said. "All those farms were leveled in the period of industrial expansion and turned into city homes."

That was disappointing, but not as disappointing as what followed. We drove down to the Anglican church on the green in Clapham. The mist had turned into a drizzle, and it was now almost completely dark. When we knocked on the church door, the rector appeared and greeted us.

"I want to see where Wilberforce preached," I told him, "and any monuments you have to Wilberforce and his group. He's my great hero," I explained.

The rector, who had been told we were coming, said, "Of course, of course. Come right this way."

We walked into the church, over stone floors, past the worn wooden pews to a place behind the altar. The rector proudly pointed to a stained-glass window in the apse. "There it is," he said.

The church was rather dark, so I squinted to see what he was pointing at.

The rector could tell I was having trouble. "Don't you see? There, in the center. The profile of Wilberforce." The famous man's portrait occupied a small square in the center of one stained-glass window not more than eight or ten inches wide. Below the stained-glass window was a shelf with some brochures and a sign over it saying, "Clapham Sect Information, 50 p."

I tried to hide my disappointment, thanking the rector and paying the few pence for a couple of the brochures, but I was crestfallen. Wilberforce had changed the course of Western civilization. Through sheer perseverance and holy determination, he had fought the most detestable villainy of his age. This great man had brought the slave trade to an end, and only one pane of stained glass existed as a memorial? I couldn't believe it.

We thanked the rector and left. Escorted by my friend, Patty and I walked across the village green to where we had parked our car. I asked to stop for a moment in the middle of the green to collect my thoughts. As I did, I had a powerful moment of insight. In my mind's eye I saw a long line of slaves in tattered loincloths, walking across the green with their chains falling off. *Of course,* I thought to myself, *Of course—that's it. Wilberforce's legacy is not in monuments or churches or stained-glass windows. It's in lives set free. The black men and women who are no longer subject to slavery are the living monuments of William Wilberforce and his work. Generations of people can thank Wilberforce for changing their destinies.*

---

I recently thought about what accomplishments in my life mean the most to me—the events that may comfort me when I'm lying on my deathbed. One episode helped clarify the matter.

In 1993, I learned that I had won the annual Templeton Prize for Progress in Religion. Other recipients of this award include Billy Graham, Mother Teresa, and Aleksandr Solzhenitsyn—distinguished company, indeed. When I first heard about it, I was startled and excited. Never in my wildest dreams did I envision winning such an award. I realized immediately that the Templeton Prize meant worldwide recognition for our ministry and would help us tremendously. The prize carries with it a one-million-dollar award, which I never had a second thought about donating to Prison Fellowship. The award was being given to me personally, but the Templeton Prize honored all those who have made the work of Prison Fellowship possible.

I traveled to Buckingham Palace in London to receive the prize from Prince Philip. Patty joined me for the ceremony, as did both Chris and Wendell. The ceremony was in May, and Buckingham Palace was surrounded by tourists eight or ten deep, looking through the fence at the changing of the Queen's Guard.

Policemen parted the crowd as our caravan of limousines made its way through the gates, guards snapping salutes. The day's tourists, not knowing who we might be, peered into the car, waving excitedly.

Our driver told us to wave back. That made me cringe. Some people love playing to the crowd and know how to reward people who appreciate their work with a certain air of greatness. I'm not a good politician anymore. I can't do it because I'm always aware that I'm far from the person they imagine.

Inside the palace, escorted by aides and police on all sides, we walked through a labyrinth of corridors until we reached the China Room, a spacious and ornate reception room at the front of the palace. Our party included more than fifty people: members of the House of Lords, government officials, previous winners, and dignitaries from church, business, and commerce. We were all lined up according to protocol. I stood at the beginning of the line, where Prince Philip would come and shake hands, and then he'd walk down the line, meeting each of the people to my right.

The protocol officer advised me that as an American citizen I did not need to bow before royalty, but some sign of respect was appropriate. He then told me not to say anything to His Royal Highness, not until the prince spoke first, and under no circumstances was I to approach Prince Philip. The prince would escort me to the center of the floor to receive the prize. The protocol officer repeated twice, "We never approach royalty. They approach us." I nodded in agreement.

We waited a few minutes, and then suddenly the conversation stopped. Through the huge, gilded doors walked Prince Philip and his escort of aides. He came right over to me, as expected, shook hands, and then went down the line, amiably greeting each of the visitors.

Prince Philip then walked to the center of the room and nodded to me—to approach him, it seemed. Behind Prince Philip stood the protocol officer, his back ramrod straight, shaking his head no. I assumed

Prince Philip was trying to tell me to come to the center of the floor, but the protocol officer was vetoing it.

Prince Philip looked at me and nodded once more. I looked at the protocol officer, who shook his head once more. It got awkward. Finally, I decided this was absurd and walked toward the center of the floor.

I had been told I had two minutes to speak in accepting the award, which I did. But Prince Philip immediately started asking questions about our work and was particularly interested in our programs for juveniles. It turned out to be a wonderful occasion, with a lively discussion. In the back of my mind, I had the persistent thought: *I'm standing here because thousands of inmates whose lives Prison Fellowship has been able to touch are counting on me.*

When I returned to my office at Prison Fellowship, the Templeton Prize medal sat on my desk, and I began to think about what to do with it. I called in Nancy Niemeyer, my longtime assistant, and discussed where we might put it. Once the big occasion at Buckingham Palace was over, the medal seemed like a useless bauble. What was I supposed to do? Stare at it every day and tell myself, "I'm a Templeton Prize winner"? For a few moments, I held the medal in my hand, flipped it over, looked at both sides. It was beautifully designed and crafted in a modern theme, but it was still only a piece of metal. I handed it to Nancy and said, "Find an appropriate place for this, okay?"

When she left with the medal, I opened a drawer and pulled out a letter I had received three years earlier from some inmates in a Siberian prison. The prison was full of dissidents still incarcerated in those last years before the collapse of the Soviet Union. A missionary had smuggled out their letter from the prison located in the city of Magadan—a remote place in Siberia, a place of nearly everlasting cold, drabness, and soul-destroying neglect.

I knew exactly what that prison looked like and what those men were experiencing because in 1990 I had the rare opportunity—one of the first granted to anybody from the West—to visit Perm Camp 35, a notorious prison for political dissidents. Located in the foothills of the Ural Mountains, a thousand miles east of Moscow, Perm Camp 35 was one of the most desolate places I had ever seen. Its cells were cold, dank, concrete holes. To get to the place, we had to drive through piles of snow so tall, we felt we were in a massive ice crater. For more than four hours we drove over potholes awash with melting snow and never saw any signs of life before we arrived at the prison.

I thought of those prison conditions as I held the letter the missionary had received. The inmates had written in response to my book *Loving God*, which had been translated into Russian, then sent through channels, and was finally released for the inmates to read. The prisoners wrote

12 June 1990

You sent your book *Loving God* to us, but for a whole month the prison authorities would not release it to us. When we found out about its existence, we complained to Moscow, and finally we were allowed to read this book.

In our camp there are about 3,000 prisoners, and everyone has read your book. In actuality, every evening someone would read aloud while 15 to 20 others listened. It's good that you wrote about the author, Colson. When we learned that he too had been in prison, we understood that he knew the meaning of freedom. In other words, we who hated, and thought that such feelings were experienced by all people, learned that it was possible to learn to love God and other people.

Please send greetings to Chuck Colson. We wish all Soviet people could read this book. It would be helpful for everyone. Chuck, please write to us, and Mr. Morgulis will translate into Russian. Or if possible, visit us! We need someone like you here. It would be great if more of your books could be sent here.

*Semyon Gorokhov*
*Valentin Sukonin*
*and the other 3,000 prisoners*

As I read this letter, I experienced an overwhelming sense of gratitude that I had been allowed to contribute something to the men's lives. I could see them, gathering in groups of fifteen to twenty, listening to

*Loving God* being read aloud—probably by candlelight—in the midst of the Siberian cold and dark. Through the book they had felt God's embrace, hope for their futures, and an awakening of forgiveness and love for their persecutors.

When I was writing *Loving God,* I never could have imagined that God would use it to touch people in this way. And there, of course, is the paradox again: During my years in the White House, I tried to affect the Cold War—with very limited success—but a book of mine found its way into a Soviet prison and gave three thousand men hope.

The Templeton Prize—a metal medallion—or the letter from Semyon and Valentin and their three thousand fellow prisoners. Which would mean more to you? All I can say is, I'm not even sure where the Templeton medal is hanging at this moment. But I keep the prisoners' letter in my briefcase, and when I'm overly tired, depressed, or discouraged, I take it out and read it again. If I'm allowed a period of reflection before death, I'm sure I'll keep that letter on my bedside table.

———•◦•———

Giving to others brings the greatest satisfaction. It's one thing to write a check, but sometimes we have to give *ourselves.* I mean, totally, including life itself. When we do, there's no limit to the way others' lives can be changed and our culture transformed.

We see this in the story of men caught up in one of history's greatest tragedies, men who nevertheless found the strength to value all that's truly good about life. It's the story of personal sacrifices that turned a whole community on the verge of death toward the good life.

# CHAPTER 14

# GREATER LOVE HATH NO MAN THAN THIS

AT THE BEGINNING of World War II, the Japanese enjoyed spectacular success in the Pacific theater. On December 7, 1941, the same day the Japanese decimated the United States naval fleet at Pearl Harbor, Japanese planes struck airfields in the Philippines. Within two days, the Japanese air force had taken out more than 50 percent of America's Pacific-based aircraft as well as the Cavite Naval Yard in the Philippines.[1]

The Japanese strategy was to wage a 150-day campaign, securing a defensive perimeter stretching from Burma in the west to the southern rim of the Dutch East Indies (now Malaysia) to the Gilbert Islands and Marshall Islands in the northeast. They believed they could defend this territorial arc against any counteroffensives and the Allies would sue for peace, granting Japan a new empire that spanned the western Pacific and included Southeast Asia and eventually all of China as well.

Japanese bombers destroyed the British air force at Hong Kong on December 8 and forced its British and Canadian defenders to surrender on Christmas Day. Guam fell on December 10. The Japanese overwhelmed the Australian and Indian forces defending Malaya and, by January 1942, had taken command of the entire country, except for the island of Singapore.

By mid-January, the Allies put together a unified command of American, British, Dutch, and Australian troops (ABDACOM) responsible for holding Malaya, Sumatra, Java, and approaches to Australia.

Three Japanese divisions landed on Singapore Island, however, and by February 25, ABDACOM ceased to function.

Although I was a boy at the time, I remember the feeling of panic these events inspired in America because the enemy was clearly winning. Thousands of the best British and American troops had either been captured or were scurrying in defeat to safety.

At that moment in history, the spring of 1942, the _Setia Berganti_ was bobbing westward in the vast expanse of the Indian Ocean. This tubby ketch carried a crew of ten British officers, a brave if ragtag band gathered from the forces driven from Singapore by the Japanese. The crew had sailed a fair part of their twelve-hundred-mile route from Sumatra to Ceylon (now Sri Lanka), thinking the island was their best chance for survival.

Among these men was Ernest Gordon, called "Rosie" by his shipmates because he was the picture of health—two hundred pounds of muscle on a six-foot-two-inch frame. A former student at the University of St. Andrews, Gordon had become a champion sailor on the Firth of Clyde, and he relished life at sea.

Gordon was still so much unaffected by the war that he thought when the war was over, he would return to Southeast Asia to serve as a military adviser to foreign powers, combining high adventure with earning a fortune. Foreseeing that most of the region's nations, including former British colonies, would someday become independent states, he imagined a future as a broker in power politics.

Then three dark smudges appeared on the horizon—the smoke of Japanese tankers. When the Japanese took the crew of the _Setia Berganti_ aboard, they told the men they would be executed as spies.

In the end, the Japanese preferred to dole out a slower form of death through forced labor. In violation of international conventions, Gordon and the other crewmembers were pressed into service as workers on what became known as the infamous Railroad of Death. The men were eventually transported to a prisoner-of-war camp called Chungkai in northern Thailand. Ernest Gordon tells the story in his remarkable book _To End All Wars._*

---

*Ernest Gordon, _To End All Wars_ (Grand Rapids: Zondervan, 2002). I highly recommend both the book and the film based on it. The story is truly a classic that will be remembered for generations to come.

The Japanese wanted to invade India, but their existing supply line by sea was vulnerable to submarine attack. So they decided to build a rail supply line by joining two already established lines, one from Singapore to Bangkok and the other in Burma from Rangoon to Ye. The gap between the two lines was hundreds of miles long, winding through the rain forests and mountains of Thailand.

The task of joining the rail lines would normally take five to six years. However, the Japanese drove their captives to complete the job in less than a year. They beat them with bamboo staves, fed them a couple bowls of rice a day, and worked them until they dropped.

Torture was widely practiced. The Japanese crushed some prisoners' hands in vises; they suspended others from trees by their thumbs or buried them alive in the ground.[2] At any sign of rebellion, the Japanese soldiers reacted with fury. Twenty-seven percent of the POWs died in their prison camps.

Shovelful by heavy shovelful, the men dug the railroad path out of the jungle. The way through the mountains had to be blasted with dynamite, which was so carelessly used that many men died in needless accidents. When the railroad crossed the River Kwai, the prisoners built bridges (as seen in the movie *The Bridge on the River Kwai*, a highly romanticized account). Prisoners chopped the pilings for these bridges out of the jungle, floated them out to the bridge locations, and then pounded them into the riverbed with hand-operated pile drivers. In this crude way, the prisoners built bridges that were five stories high. They tried their best to sabotage the construction even as they performed it. Doing heavy labor for twelve hours a day, on a starvation diet and in heat that often reached 120 degrees, quickly reduced the men to walking skeletons.

The gruesome conditions were compounded by the prisoners' despair. Everyone was obsessed with self-preservation. The prisoners dedicated themselves to "The Ladder Club"—scrambling over others to stay alive. It was a microcosm of Darwin's theory in practice: Survival of the fittest—or of the clever, the devious, and the outright malicious— became the order of the day. Those who fell ill were thrown into a hospital hut called the Death House, where they were quickly forgotten. The only interest the prisoners took in the dying, it seemed, was to scavenge their bodies for money, a wristwatch, a cigarette lighter. Such articles could be discreetly traded with the Thais outside the camp's wall for food. Extra calories meant the difference between life and death.

The prisoners stole from their living comrades as well. A friend of Gordon's, Iain Stewart, had his pack snatched from underneath his head as he slept. He lost his fiancée's photograph, his penknife, a notebook—things he had hung on to with fierce tenacity as the Japanese robbed him of his freedom and everything else. But when his fellow soldiers robbed him, he felt an abuse far worse than his treatment by the enemy.

Prisoners rushed the food pails that their Japanese captors put out every night after their own dinners. Gordon saw a man emerge from the scrum clutching a mess of rice and stew, bits of gravy dripping from it. The man trotted past him like a dog, cringing from others' view as he retreated to a private spot for his feast.

Within six weeks of capture, Ernest Gordon, the "Rosie" lad, found himself wasting away in the Death House, a long hut built at the low end of the camp, nearest the river. When the monsoon rains came, its floor became awash with mud. The latrines overflowed. The men lay close together in rows, head to feet. Tropical ulcers ate into their flesh and bone. The stench in the unventilated hut was unimaginable. Millions of bedbugs swarmed over the patients, feasting on the little flesh they had left.

Gordon suffered from recurrent attacks of malaria, amoebic dysentery, the aftereffects of a surgery for appendicitis, and a case of diphtheria that had already paralyzed his legs, lacing them with ulcers. He was also starving because the Japanese did not give rations for the sick. Reason told him that he would soon be dead, falling victim to his illnesses just like the other men around him, who were dying by the score daily.

Then, almost unaccountably, Gordon was among the first recipients of sacrificial acts of kindness that eventually transformed the camp's entire culture. Two of his friends from the *Setia Berganti* came to visit him one day. The skipper, Edward Hooper, and another crewmate, Joe Allen, came to see how Gordon was doing. At first, they passed by his bunk without recognizing him. Gordon could hardly speak because of a collapsed palate, but he managed to attract his friends' attention. When Hooper came to Gordon's bedside, Gordon plucked at his wrist. Hooper bent over the sick man, still wondering who it could be. When the skipper drew close, Gordon muttered his own name.

Hooper could not believe his eyes. "Good God!" Hooper exclaimed. "You can't be Rosie!"

Spurred to action by Hooper and Allen's report, Gordon's friends built him a hut that attached to their own. They stole the hut's materials an armful at a time until they had enough to build a room segregated enough not to endanger their own health but clean and quiet enough for Gordon's last days. On one side of the hut they installed a door through which he could look out onto the life of the camp. The view and the smell of freshly cut bamboo and palm immediately refreshed Gordon's spirits.

Two men assumed most of the responsibility for Gordon's care: "Dusty" Miller and "Dinty" Moore. Even in a loincloth, Dinty, one of Gordon's old schoolmates, was a dapper figure, with his neat mustache and carefully brushed hair. Dusty Miller, a former gardener from the north of England, was soft-spoken and caring. Both were men of faith: Dinty a Catholic, and Dusty a Methodist. Dinty helped Gordon in the night, when the long workday ended. Dusty, who was still recovering from diphtheria himself, took care of Gordon during the day.

Dusty Miller gave Gordon the first washing he'd had in six weeks. Gordon could not believe how good it felt to be halfway clean again. Dusty cleaned the ulcers on Gordon's legs and feet and then began massaging his legs, fighting the crippling effects of the diphtheria by encouraging the blood flow.

Dusty and Dinty joined forces in collecting extra food to improve Gordon's diet. On May 31, 1943, Gordon's twenty-sixth birthday, they were able to produce a cake—made from boiled rice, limes, bananas, and palm sugar.

Slowly, with Dusty and Dinty's aid, Gordon began to regain sensation in his legs. Finally able to sit up on the side of his cot, he began exercising by using his hands to pick up one leg and then the other. He could do this only a time or two at first. But Dusty's massage and the exercise had a good effect. Gordon soon was able to swing his legs from the knee, and his muscle tone returned with the increase of blood circulation. Before long, he was hobbling about with the aid of a bamboo crutch.

Gordon soon realized that the distressed prisoners around him were gradually feeling more hopeful. The kindness Gordon's friends showed to him was one of the quieter instances of sacrificial giving that began to displace the dog-eat-dog mentality. The stories of other more spectacular deeds quickly spread among the men, to amazing effect.

Every soldier in Gordon's regiment found a "mucker"—a buddy who would "muck in" with him, each watching out for the other's welfare. Angus McGillivray's mucker became extremely ill. Everyone thought the man would die, but Angus began giving all of his rations to his friend. He covered him with the only blanket he had against the chills of the monsoon nights. Angus risked his life, slipping out of camp at night to trade with the Thais for duck eggs and medicine for his friend. As a result, Angus's mucker got better. Unfortunately, starvation took Angus himself. One day the big, formerly robust man simply pitched on his face and died.

When Dusty heard the story of Angus's sacrifice, Dusty recalled a verse from the Gospel of John: "This is my commandment, that ye love one another as I have loved you. Greater love hath no man than this, that a man lay down his life for his friends."[3]

Angus's story inspired the entire camp. One evening as a work party was about to return to camp, their Japanese guard counted the shovels assigned to the men. One shovel appeared to be missing. Confident that one of the men had stolen it to sell to the Thais, the guard demanded to know who had taken the shovel. He kept up his accusations, working himself into a lather. Fury forged resolution. He would have that shovel no matter what it took. He demanded yet again that the thief confess. When no one stepped forward, the guard raised his rifle and pointed it at the first man in line.

"All die! All die!" he screamed. He was going to shoot the entire party, one by one, if no one confessed.

As his horrific threat sent the chill of panic through the company, one brave British soldier stepped forward and said, "I did it."

The guard flew at the man, kicking him, beating him with his fists until blood began pouring from the man's face. The prisoner's calm resolution provoked even greater wrath from his torturer. With a howl, the guard lifted his rifle over his head and brought the rifle butt down on the man's head, killing him instantly. As the prisoner lay dead on the ground, the guard continued to beat and kick him, not stopping until his rage finally waned.

The man's fellow soldiers took up his body and marched back to camp, handing in their shovels at the guardhouse. When the guards counted the shovels again, no shovel was missing. Rather than incite the men to resent the brutal guard even more, the man's sacrificial death inspired them.

Sometime later an Aussie private was caught trying to buy medicine for a sick friend. The private was quickly tried and sentenced to death. On the morning he was marched out to be executed, all the Japanese guards turned out to observe the scene. Every prisoner watched as well.

The condemned man's commanding officer and a chaplain attended him as witnesses. The prisoners noticed how casual and unafraid the man seemed as he walked to the spot of his execution. When the party was ordered to a stop, the commanding officer and chaplain were directed to one side. Alone, with only his sword-wielding executioner close by, the Aussie took out a small copy of the New Testament from his threadbare khaki shorts. He read a passage to himself, his lips moving but not making any sound. When he finished reading, he put the New Testament back into his pocket. Seeing the troubled look on his chaplain's face, the condemned man called out to him, "Cheer up, Padre, it isn't as bad as all that. I'll be all right."

The Aussie signaled to his executioner and bent his head forward, exposing his neck. The samurai sword whistled down.

Incidents like these convinced the men that their "ladder" ethic—or the "law of the jungle," a commitment to survival at all costs—was not the law for men. Life simply wasn't worth living if men weren't ready to die for something even greater than life itself.

The outstanding acts of sacrifice among the men motivated the other prisoners to do what they could for their fellows. The British officers voted to devote a portion of their meager pay to buying extra food and medicine for the sick.

Gordon's miraculous recovery impressed everyone with the benefits of massage and simple physical therapy. Squads of men devoted themselves to massaging their ailing comrades' legs.

The most vulnerable of the sick were often prisoners who had undergone amputations. Their inability to move about the camp severely limited their chances of survival. Two engineers designed and built an artificial leg out of available materials: Using strips of iron from old cans, they attached a foot, made from a block of wood, to a bamboo leg and a leather-and-canvas stump.[4] This artificial leg even had a joint that allowed the wearer to bend his knee. Once the prototype was designed, the engineers began teaching the amputees how to make their own. Soon they developed a cottage industry that enabled formerly immobile prisoners to troop around the grounds.

Scientists among the group, including botanists and chemists as well as medical doctors, began examining the flora in the area, gathering plants and fruits that had analgesic and anesthetizing properties. The homegrown medicines helped treat dysentery, vitamin-deficiency illnesses such as beriberi, and other ailments. The Death House began to function much more like a real hospital.

As a measure of physical health returned to more prisoners, their spirits began to revive as well. This expressed itself in a desire for learning. Many of the men had kept books secreted among their few possessions. They pooled the books and began both a lending library and a university without walls, pleading with experts among them to teach. Eventually, men taught courses in history, philosophy, economics, mathematics, the natural sciences, and at least nine languages, including Latin, Greek, Russian, and Sanskrit. The faculty for these courses often wrote out their own textbooks from memory. Language instructors composed new grammars on scraps of paper.

A virtual artistic Renaissance emerged as musicians put together their own orchestra, actors and directors produced plays, and the artists assembled exhibitions in which dozens participated. One man drew his children as he imagined they looked after his three-year absence.

As these renewing events gained momentum, the men became interested in whether a loving God might exist after all. A group of men who wanted to study the Bible approached Ernest Gordon. Did the Christian faith have any relevance to their current situation? If they found it had none, they would reject it outright. But they wanted to take an honest look at it first.

Gordon hesitated because he had no faith to speak of. He had been approached simply because he had been to university. So he began his teaching by confessing his doubts and his dislike of the sectarianism and class prejudice that often plagued the church.

Reading the accounts of Jesus' life in the Gospels, however, changed Gordon's mind and his life. He came to know a Jesus who had "no place to lay his head," who was often hungry, and was never favored by the privileged. Jesus had known in full measure the hardness of sheer labor, rejection, disappointment, and premeditated persecution. This Jesus had experienced nearly everything that the POWs knew as their daily lot.

"We understood," Gordon writes, "that the love expressed so supremely in Jesus was God's love—the same love that we were experiencing for ourselves—the love that is passionate kindness, other-centered rather than self-centered, greater than all the laws of men. . . . The Crucifixion was seen as being completely relevant to our situation. A God who remained indifferent to the suffering of His creatures was not a God whom we could accept. The Crucifixion, however, told us that God was in our midst, suffering with us."[5]

The ultimate sacrifices of a few prisoners, followed by the everyday sacrifices of the many, transformed Chungkai prison camp into a vital community. With the least means imaginable, the prisoners drew together to produce the identifying marks of civilization: care for the sick, scientific research, broad education, and the arts. In the end they saw everything that they did and accomplished as originating in faith and returning to faith.

"I was beginning to see," Gordon writes, "that life was infinitely more complex, and at the same time more wonderful, than I had ever imagined. True, there was hatred. But there was also love. There was death. But there was also life. God had not left us. He was with us, calling us *to live the divine life in fellowship.*"[6]

———————•◦•———————

Ernest Gordon survived World War II, but he didn't return to Southeast Asia to work as a broker in power politics. He didn't base his life on earning a fortune. Instead, he married his sweetheart, went through seminary, migrated to America, and became dean of the chapel at Princeton University.

Though in a less dramatic way, Gordon built another faithful community on the Princeton campus. In 1977, Harold Hughes, former liberal Democratic senator from Iowa, and I, the conservative Republican—an unlikely combination but now as close as brothers by virtue of our faith—gave a dialogue lecture at the grand cathedral at Princeton. This was in the aftermath of the sixties, when secularism reigned on major university campuses. But the Princeton chapel was full that day. In Bible studies and chapel activities, Hughes and I met with hundreds of students who were serious about integrating their faith and learning. I saw firsthand the enormous influence Ernest Gordon brought to the Princeton campus. And that influence continued throughout the chaplain's life as he taught students the true meaning of life and community.

> *As we give away our lives in service—as we lose our lives in order to save them—we discover the true meaning of our lives in the midst of fellowship and community.*

---

As we give away our lives in service—as we lose our lives in order to save them—we discover the true meaning of our lives in the midst of fellowship and community. None of this is possible, however, without sacrificial giving—the basis of culture and meaning in life as well.

Ernest Gordon did not have to ask, "Have I been a good man?" He embodied the good life.

# CHAPTER 15

# MY LIFE FOR YOURS—
## BUT TO WHAT END?

WE HAVE LOOKED at two alternative visions of the good life. One envisions it in terms of self-perfection. Its commitments are to pleasure, power, and personal autonomy. It believes in the limitless exercise of its own will. The good life in this—I would argue, counterfeit—form, might be summarized: *My way, right or wrong.* We've seen, however, that a total commitment to our own will leads to a life that is wretched and unlivable.

The other vision says the goal of life is not the vindication or satisfaction of the imperial self; it is the surrender of the self in service to others. The power of this vision can be seen in its transformative effects. Even in the extreme circumstances that Ernest Gordon knew on the Railroad of Death, this vision transformed the worst of prison camps into a mini-civilization. The Ernest Gordon story summarizes this second vision as: *My life for yours.*

As you review the stories we've told, I hope you'll recognize that the people who have discovered something of the truly good life have embraced the principle of my life for yours. I found life to be meaningful when I resolved to become an advocate for prisoners. Mary Kay Beard found the good life through taking care of prisoners' children. Wilberforce found it in fighting slavery.

But is giving ourselves, even sacrificially, the ultimate goal? Is this in itself the good life? Our world is filled with terrorists who are only too willing to give themselves sacrificially. The men who piloted the planes on 9/11 believed in self-sacrifice, and they also believed in what they were doing. Yet, they gave themselves sacrificially in the service of evil.

Remember Private Ryan's question: "Have I been a good man?" What distinguishes truly good men and women from terrorists? Must we in the end conclude that we all make our individual choices and that history finally assigns a value to our actions on the basis of its ultimate winners and losers? Do the *good* and the *true* have a transcendent meaning, or are they values assigned by one culture to terrorists and by another culture to the New York Fire Department?

Nien Cheng's captors believed the *good* and the *true* are simply instruments of the powerful. The Revolutionaries had no transcendent concept of justice—of an ultimate right and wrong, of a good life that could be known apart from who was winning or losing the political struggles.

Nien Cheng believed, however, that truth is knowable and that justice can be determined apart from human power structures. She believed in a transcendent truth and in the power of living according to that truth. Her life is obviously a more legitimate answer to Ryan's question than the lives of the Chinese oppressors or today's terrorists.

So sacrificing ourselves for others gets us only part of the way. The most important question is whether what we sacrifice for is the truth. Therefore, we need to ask ourselves, Is there such a thing as truth, and can we know it? Also, if we can know truth, can we be faithful to it, as Nien Cheng was? Where will we find the power to choose the right when our own times of testing come?

By *truth* I don't mean one of many possible ways of thinking about things. I mean *reality*—the way things truly are. I have said that this book is for seekers, for people looking for truth. A better way of saying it might be, this book is for seekers after reality. We are all too inclined to think of truth as negotiable. Many people believe that each person has his or her own idea of truth: You have your truth; I have mine.

> *Is there such a thing as truth, and can we know it?*

Stephen Covey, the author of *The Seven Habits of Highly Effective People* and a renowned corporate lecturer, tries to disabuse business leaders of the notion that truth is one thing for me, another for you. With twenty people sitting at desks or tables, he says, "There is truth—an absolute you can stake your life on." Then he acknowledges that many people have come into that room believing that truth is subjective, that we make up our own definitions of what is truth and what isn't.

Covey asks his lecture groups to put their heads down, close their eyes, and then raise their hands in the direction of true north. Everybody points in a different direction, of course. Then he tells them to open their eyes, and they see hands going every which way. He asks them whether or not there is one true north. Is north where the people pointed, or is north where north is? The participants see that there's a definite answer to that question. Covey then encourages them to see that there are definite, trustworthy answers to the big questions as well.

Truth is an absolute. Truth is what conforms to reality. That is truth's simplest and most elegant definition.

We need to get the picture right. Remember my daughter's drawing pictures for her autistic son, Max? If Emily doesn't get the pictures right, Max remains lost and throws a tantrum. Our lives will come unstrung as well if we don't get the pciture right.

We need to be seekers after reality, the reality we all share—the way life and the world really work—the singular direction in which true north lies. In a sense, then, this is not a spiritual book. It's not a religious book either. I don't know of any reason someone should care about either spirituality or religion if these two experiences do not grapple with reality. That's what I'm interested in, and I hope you are too.

*If we are going to sacrifice ourselves, we want to give our lives for a cause that is true.*

Can we find a way, then, to know the real truth and to live it? Because if we are going to sacrifice ourselves, we want to give our lives for a cause that is true. Worthy endeavors, I'll be arguing, must conform to reality—to the way things actually are. If we give ourselves to a lie, we give ourselves to nothing—or, worse, to destruction.

Many of us avoid this hard issue by compartmentalizing our lives. We place our religious life in one compartment, and we take care of that on Sunday mornings. We allocate our life of leisure to another compartment, and we live for the weekend. Over here is our business world, and we rarely think about truth in that compartment. And late at night, when the family has gone to bed, we flip on a porn film or go to a pornographic

Internet site, but nobody needs to know about that. We are good spouses and parents, although when we're on business trips, we allow ourselves a little flirtation. Once or twice we may have gotten carried away, but what happens in Las Vegas stays in Las Vegas, right?

When we divide our lives into compartments, however, they inevitably disintegrate. As the district attorney's office understood when it began investigating Dennis Kozlowski's art purchase, the person who cheats in one thing usually ends up cheating in many.

*Living the whole truth, living with integrity, means that we do not compartmentalize our lives but live each facet from a truthful center.*

The true good life means living in conformity with the truth—the whole truth. Living the whole truth, living with integrity, means that we do not compartmentalize our lives but live each facet from a truthful center. This is key to living a good life as Private James Ryan meant it. This is key to living a life of virtue, without which we and our society cannot flourish.

# SEARCHING

*for the*

# TRUTH

# CHAPTER 16

# JOURNEY INTO ILLUSION

IN NOVEMBER 1954, Albert Speer, not quite fifty years old, decided to take a walking tour. He first mapped out the route from Berlin to Heidelberg. In order to maximize the trek's educational value, he read everything the local library could supply on the area and its points of interest. Going further in his research, he ordered guidebooks and worked on the area's cultural history. As he walked, he kept a diary of his findings and observations.

He decided not to stop at Heidelberg but to travel on to Munich. Then he really ventured out, heading for the Balkans, Istanbul, and through Afghanistan to India. Once he had seen Asia, he crossed back through China to Siberia and from there leapfrogged to North America. Walking south from Los Angeles, he crossed into Mexico, recording in his diary: "Merciless sun on dusty roads. . . . My soles burned on the hot ground . . . where milestones mark my doleful passage."[1]

The seas and oceans presented no obstacle to Speer's global trek because during his journey, you see, he never actually left Spandau Prison, where he was serving twenty years for crimes against humanity. Speer began as Hitler's chief architect and ended, by some reckonings, as the number two man in the Nazi regime. The former armaments minister made his epic journey to distant countries by walking around and around the prison garden. He kept fanatically accurate measurements of the number of laps he walked every day and correlated the miles with his imaginary routes. The guidebooks and the works of cultural history he read spurred his imagination of the places he would have been visiting, and his diary notes capped his illusory sightseeing. He pushed himself so hard on this journey that once his right leg swelled to twice its normal size, and he had to be hospitalized for a pulmonary infarction.

In the end, although he managed to keep his brilliant mind engaged, Speer's imaginary journey provided little satisfaction. He asked himself whether his walking tour was but "an expression of the madness I was trying to escape? I always looked down on my fellow prisoners, who were unable to occupy themselves or set themselves goals. But what goals did I really have? Isn't the sight of a man marching obstinately in a circle for decades far more absurd and weird?"[2]

Albert Speer started out in life as the son of privilege, reared by his well-to-do architect father and his socialite mother in Mannheim, Germany. He was a gifted mathematician but was deflected from an academic career by his father, who said he would earn little fame or money as a professor. Speer took his father's advice and followed him into architecture.

The generation to which Speer belonged remained under the spell of Hegel and Nietzsche. Hegel's philosophy of the world as a divine, evolving process directed people's religious feelings toward the latest cultural achievements. They viewed the literary work of Goethe and Schiller, the music of Wagner, and the writings of Julius Langbehn and Paul de Lagarde as a new revelation. Great works of culture became their bible.

This may be hard to grasp as we now see culture almost exclusively in terms of mass entertainment. The religious attachment to culture still exists, however—if in a highly secularized form—among people who often identify themselves as "progressives." Progressives believe that their political, ethical, and cultural attitudes ought to be informed by whatever advances emerge from the worlds of academia, the arts, and politics—from culture. The phrase "we now know" is their credo. "People used to think that God created the world, but *we now know. . . .*" "People once presumed that every civilization functioned by the same rules, but *we now know. . . .*" The progressives among us are Hegel's sons and daughters, and they worship what they take to be the world's evolving process—the latest and greatest thing.

Like today's progressives, Albert Speer and his generation championed the latest thinking of "culture" versus the outmoded ways of "civili-zation." They had a particular disdain for industrialization and sought to identify themselves with what they took to be the purity of nature. Like the hippies, they were "crunchy"—the original granola-and-sandals crowd. "We were always dreaming," Speer wrote, "of solitude, of drives through quiet river valleys, of hiking to some high mountain pasture."[3]

Not far beneath the surface in this generation lurked the same hypernationalism that drove World War I. Because Speer's generation presumed that German culture stood at the forefront of world history, they saw embracing this culture as a means of identifying with the world's progressive revelation. The worship of culture and nature con-stituted their progressive faith.

Speer's generation was also still very much under the sway of Nietzsche and his emphasis on transcending common morality for the sake of great achievement. This had a particular appeal for artists. Speer later commented that he had always been certain that he would achieve greatness. Toward the end of his life he said that he would have ex-changed all his power for the fame of designing one truly great building. The English poet John Milton said that fame is the "last infirmity of [a] noble mind."[4] Similarly, the masterpiece that will redeem all the artist's personal mistakes is his debility.

Speer never imagined politics would play a role in his future. In fact, he scorned politics. Germany's defeat in World War I led many Germans to make a sharp distinction between their culture—which re-mained unparalleled—and their civilization, whose weaknesses had been painfully exposed. Assuming an apolitical stance became a way for Germans to maintain their pride even as the Weimar Republic—the government that ruled Germany between the end of World War I and Hitler's rise—found itself incapable of coping with runaway inflation and economic depression. When many students of Speer's time began to embrace National Socialism—fascism—Speer felt himself to be above mere politics. He never dreamed that he would find Hitler and his vision appealing.

Civilization included the workaday worlds of government and busi-ness as well as all the complexities that industrialization had brought to both. Culture rebelled against these by invoking the communal ideals of an agrarian past and a state of innocence that supposedly predated civilization itself. That's why so much of the art the Nazis loved is filled with scenes of strangely asexual nymphs dancing in sylvan glades. Speer's generation wanted to "green" their dirty, complicated world. This split between the generation's ideals and the living reality all about them resulted first in an angry apoliticism. The youth of Speer's time were simply too good to engage in the hard business of making their government and economy function effectively. So they pointed out all its failings and refused to engage in what they saw as its corruption.

The split between the Germans' pride in their culture and their despair about government also contributed to widespread compartmentalized thinking. Both Speer's generation and their parents saw no connection between the working world and their personal, ethical standards. Ethics were for the home; pragmatism ruled in the workplace. In this way Germans like Speer and his family continued to give free rein to their ambitious natures with little concern for the state of the nation.

In 1930, Speer lived in Berlin, where he worked as a well-paid assistant to the architect Heinrich Tessenow. By this time Speer was married and beginning a family that would eventually include six children. Despite his apoliticism, he agreed to attend a meeting at which Adolf Hitler would be speaking. Speer later said that from this first time he heard Hitler, the man took hold of him and never let him go. Speer was enchanted.

In the midst of the despairing Weimar Republic, Hitler mapped out a grand vision for the German people—the culmination of the world's enduring battle of good versus evil. This future demanded the absolute sacrifice of every German toward its realization. It demanded that obstructionist forces be identified and eliminated from influence. Joined in one will, Germany could defeat the forces of Communism and economic distress that threatened to keep Germany the world's whipping boy. The ideals Germans treasured would be realized in a new state in which the petty class divisions of the past and the rule of unwarranted privileges were eliminated. The darkness of the hour simply meant that Germany must rise to fulfill its historical destiny.

Years later, when Speer was being interrogated by the Allies in May 1945, Captain Burt Klein cut off Speer's endless recitation of the Nazi regime's insane history. "Mr. Speer, I don't understand you," Captain Klein said. "You are telling us you knew years ago that the war was lost for Germany. For years, you say, you have been watching the horrible in-play among these gangsters who surrounded Hitler—and surrounded you. Their personal ambitions were those of hyenas, their methods those of murderers, their morals those of the gutter. You knew all this. And yet you stayed, not only stayed, but worked, planned with, and supported them to the hilt. How can you explain it? How can you justify it? How can you stand living with yourself?"[5]

Speer took his time to answer. He said that the good captain understood nothing about life in a dictatorship, nothing of its fear and the dangerous games that went with it. Most of all, the captain understood nothing about Hitler's irresistible charisma.[6]

Hitler's charisma began to operate on Speer even more powerfully after the young man experienced business setbacks. Speer gave up his post with Tessenow in 1932, when salaries suffered from Germany's ever-worsening economy. He moved to Heidelberg and worked his father's contacts for building commissions. Few if any commissions turned up, and Speer was reduced to managing his father's real estate holdings.

His fortunes began to improve through his contacts with the National Socialist German Workers Party (NSDAP), Hitler's political party, which Speer had joined in 1931. He was asked to renovate a broken-down Grunewald villa that the party had rented for a headquarters. Then they asked him to renovate another one in Voss-strasse. After that he worked on Joseph Goebbels's new propaganda ministry in Berlin.

What really brought Speer to Nazi officials' attention was his staging of the 1933 May Day celebration at Tempelhofer Field. With this design, Speer began to perfect the look and liturgy of Hitler's mass rallies. It was Speer's idea to position Hitler on a high wooden platform flanked by countless swastika banners. Speer staged the rally at night, with Hitler illumined by a spotlight suggesting the leader's power to turn political night into day. This staging was so effective that after witnessing a mass rally, the French ambassador, Robert Colondre, confessed that the mixture of "military magic, mystique, and exaltation had, for a moment, converted him to National Socialism."[7]

Hitler met Speer for the first time following the renovation of Goebbels's official residence, which the architect completed, to everyone's astonishment, within two months. Speer was invited to meet with Hitler to review the proposals for the first Nuremberg party rally after the führer's seizure of power. On this occasion, Hitler paid Speer little notice, merely glancing up from cleaning a pistol to look at the plans, pronouncing that he agreed with them, then returning to his gun.

Later Hitler asked Speer to supervise the restoration of his residence in Berlin. The führer, who had once aspired to be an artist and architect himself, came on-site almost every day to review the work's progress. Speer and Hitler began having many conversations, which eventually led to a lunch invitation.

When Speer arrived fresh from the worksite, his jacket was splotched with wet mortar. Not wanting the architect to be embarrassed, Hitler loaned the young man one of his own jackets. When Speer entered the dining room, Goebbels noticed that his jacket bore the golden party eagle that was reserved for Hitler alone. Hitler shushed Goebbels's protests and invited Speer to sit at his right hand. In very little time, Hitler appointed Speer his chief architect and gave him increasing power to override local and party officials alike.

Hitler and Speer developed a close and unusual relationship. Speer continued to think of himself as an artist—someone "above" politics. He once confessed at a dinner table, in Hitler's presence, that fascist ideas were "humbug." At the same time, his devotion to Hitler knew few bounds. Hitler promised Speer that he would be designing buildings such as had not been built since ancient Greece and Rome. Both Hitler and Speer became obsessed with turning Berlin into Germania—a totally reconstructed capital city that would outstrip contemporary Paris and ancient Rome. Hitler's relationship with Speer appears to have been influenced by the führer's delight in becoming the master of someone with a wealthy and cultured background. Speer lent Hitler a touch of class. Hitler also probably harbored homosexual feelings for Speer, which allowed Speer latitude in dissenting from Hitler's party line.

In Hitler, Speer found someone who released his own considerable powers. On his own, Speer tended to flounder. In league with Hitler's terrible force, he flourished.

Hitler and Speer's plans for the new Berlin envisioned a grand avenue with a gigantic domed hall at one end and a triumphal arch at the other. In between would be cultural buildings, an opera house, a philharmonic hall, a playhouse, a cinema seating six thousand, a variety theater, and several public baths. The domed Great Assembly Hall would be so big that the famous Brandenburg Gate, an august and regal structure, would become in comparative size a doghouse. The plans suffered from what has been described as "gigantomania." The incredible size of the proposed main buildings was meant to impress people with the Third Reich's total power and total dominion. The models of these designs—for nothing but a new chancellery building ever came into being—are uniformly sepulchral. Whatever their intended function, they look like gigantic tombs—dead, cold, and utterly inhumane.

Before Hitler and Speer could build the new Berlin, they had to raze the old city center, relocating the people living in the many buildings there. To facilitate this, Speer created a Central Department for Resettlement. Many of the buildings housed Jews, who initially were moved to share housing with other Jews. This was called the "de-tenanting" of Jews and their "boxing up" in existing Jewish housing.[8] Other Jews were boxed up because their apartments were assigned to non-Jews. This redistribution of the population made Goebbels's "cleansing" of Jews from Berlin more convenient. Speer's department came to work hand in glove with Goebbels's in what came to be described as the "evacuation" of Jews from Berlin. Instead of being forced into new quarters, the Jews were shoved into cattle cars and sent off to concentration camps. Urban redevelopment quickly turned into the Holocaust.

Later, despite Speer's own department's chronicle of how "de-tenanting" led to "evacuation," he claimed to know little about the Holocaust, apart from unsubstantiated rumor. This claim was given a certain plausibility by Hitler's divide-and-conquer management style. The Third Reich was anything but a highly rationalized bureaucracy. Clear lines of responsibility were nonexistent, and Hitler often gave the same or conflicting responsibilities to multiple officials. In this way Hitler deliberately set them plotting against one another. He wanted them to be so worried about their standing that they would never think of rebelling against him directly. This made Nazi officials highly secretive, of course, as they protected their power by shielding what they knew. In Speer's own case, he soon found his status as the regime's chief architect compromised by Hitler's promotion of a rival architect, Hermann Giesler. When Speer eventually rose to be armaments minister in 1942, it wasn't long before Hitler provocatively called on Speer's own deputy, Karl Saur, to perform certain functions when he wanted to take Speer down a peg or two.

As armaments minister, Speer had to struggle against Hermann Göring, who was in charge of the "four-year plan"—a blueprint for rebuilding Germany's economy. Göring, however, had little if any control over the raw materials and products that make an economy run. Speer invented a Central Planning Committee, to which he appointed himself and two others, in order to control enough of the economy's basic goods to supply his factories that were manufacturing guns, bullets, and bombs. Speer eventually succeeded in wresting most of Göring's power over Germany's economy away from him because Göring was a lazy drunk. Speer had a harder time with Heinrich Himmler, who remained in charge of the Luftwaffe and all the armaments required to run it. Himmler and Speer continued to steal supplies and workers from each other.

Speer's factories were consistently deprived of Jewish workers and technicians and other "undesirable elements." The factories' need for workers was supposed to be supplied by Fritz Sauckel, who rounded up Poles, Hungarians, and others in the occupied territories and pressed them into forced labor. Even so, Sauckel was unable to fulfill his promises, and Speer resorted to restarting factories in France and elsewhere, decreeing that those who were working for Germany's war machine must not be touched. The extension of the war industry from Germany to the conquered territories effectively deprived Sauckel of his power, since fewer people needed to be enslaved. Through this tactic and many others like it, Speer garnered more and more power within the regime.

In fact, Speer, the artist, was phenomenally successful as the armaments minister. He miraculously increased production of war materials during the very years when the Allies began bombing German targets at will. Speer's mathematical gifts made him by far the best manager within the Third Reich. Numbers became his solace and his refuge. Long after he realized the war was lost, Speer shut out reality by burying himself in his work.

During the last days of the regime, however, as Hitler began his retreat to the chancellery bunker where he would end his life, Speer finally rebelled against Hitler's demonic enchantment. As the Allied armies closed in on Germany, Hitler instituted a scorched-earth policy. He demanded that local officials burn every city and town, every village and farm that stood between the Allies and Berlin. If Hitler was going to die, Germany and the German people would die with him.

Speer spent many of the regime's last days flying from one place to another, countermanding Hitler's orders. Nazi officials maintained the dream that after Hitler was gone, the Allies would negotiate Germany's surrender with them. They anticipated remaining in power. Since Speer was among those who might succeed Hitler, many people obeyed Speer's orders, not wanting to risk alienating him. Hitler was clearly on the way out.

Still, in many places Hitler's scorched-earth commands were obeyed, even by Germans who had come to loathe the Third Reich. A destructive frenzy seized the country as cities and towns were put to the torch and millions of Germans began wandering the roads as refugees. Hitler knew what Speer was doing, and yet, unlike many others whom Hitler promptly shot for disobeying his directive, he let Speer live.

---

Albert Speer was among the twenty-two principal Nazi war criminals tried at Nuremberg in 1946. Unlike the rest of his fellow defendants, Speer confessed to his guilt in bringing about the catastrophe of the Nazi regime. He even owned up to general responsibility for the Nazis' crimes against humanity, including the Holocaust, while insisting that he could not be held directly responsible since he had no sure knowledge of the concentration camps.

Two moments during the trial clearly shook Speer. American general William Donovan showed the court a documentary that revealed what American troops found when they entered the concentration camps: decimated bodies strewn over the ground or hung on barbed-wire fences, smoke rising from crematoria. Speer's confession of "general responsibility" was revealed as a last stand of his self-righteousness.

What Speer saw shattered him. If he hadn't known before, he finally realized the full meaning of how de-tenanting had become Holocaust. Of course, only by an extreme and implacable compartmentalization of his thinking could Speer conceivably have been unaware of the "final solution."

Speer's feigned contrition also suffered when Sir Hartley Shawcross argued that the defendants had created Hitler; he never would have been able to run the horror factory of the Third Reich without them. Shawcross called them "perfectly ordinary murderers." He read a report from a German engineer who had witnessed a mass execution of five thousand Jews in the Ukraine:

> The people descending from the trucks, men, women, and children of every age, were made, on the order of an SS man with a horse-whip or dog-whip, to undress and put down their clothes in separate places, according to shoes, outer- and undergarments. I saw a pile of approximately eight hundred to a thousand pairs of shoes, and huge stacks of underwear and clothes. Without shouting or weeping, these people undressed, standing together in family groups, kissing each other good-bye and awaiting the orders of another SS man. . . . An old woman with snow-white hair was holding a child of twelve months in her arms, singing to it and tickling it. The child squealed with pleasure. The couple watched with tears in their eyes. The father was holding a boy of about ten by the hand, talking to him softly. The boy was fighting back his tears. His father pointed his finger at the sky, stroked his head and seemed to explain something to him. At that moment the SS man by the ditch called. . . . I walked around the mound of earth and was facing an enormous grave. The people were lying in it pressed together so tightly that only their heads were visible. From nearly all the heads blood was running over the shoulders.[9]

Instead of being hanged, Albert Speer was sentenced to twenty years in prison. The court found his effort against Hitler's scorched-earth policy to be a mitigating circumstance.

During Albert Speer's years in prison, he tried to find spiritual comfort. He read all nine thousand pages of Karl Barth's *Church Dogmatics*. He became a close friend to the prison chaplain, George Casalis. When Speer left prison in 1966, he regularly went to the Benedictine Abbey Maria Laach, where he found a religious adviser. But none of the people whom Speer consulted was able to help him find God or forgiveness or even true repentance. Speer said that if he had his life to live over again, given the circumstances, he did not know how he could have avoided making the same choices.

The claim that Speer never truly repented may be questionable since through his books *Inside the Third Reich* and *Spandau: The Secret Diaries* and the hundreds of interviews in which he freely confessed to the Nazi regime's horrors, he became known as a "titan of penitence." But there's a difference between confessing to the truth of historical fact and being able to comprehend and identify personally with true moral guilt. Joachim Fest, one of Speer's biographers, remarks:

> It was like a blind spot. He worked hard on the humble gestures that belonged to his role as a sinner, and he gravely repeated the formulas that the indulgence imposed on him. But at times it seemed as if he was like a puppet on a string and that, indeed, he was not without pride in the historic significance confirmed by the raised voices of his accusers. He had only a superficial understanding of the fundamental norms against which he had offended, why he had incurred guilt, and how he could have emerged from those years differently and unblemished. . . .
>
> This shortcoming was ultimately due to the fact that the whole spiritual dimension of life was alien to him. . . . He would have been unable to say why he should obey any moral commandments or regard them as universal law. In that respect he really was an "incomplete person" who, with all his outstanding gifts, lacked the one element that makes a human being a person.[10]

---

The path that Albert Speer traced in the Spandau Prison garden and the circles in which he ran as a principal of the Nazi regime were one and the same—a hellish alienation from reality, which is grounded not only in physical laws but moral ones as well.

Speer paid no attention to this reality, and according to biographer Joachim Fest, Speer was virtually incapable of doing so. He did have enough of a conscience, however, to recognize the terror documented at his trial and to resist Hitler's scorched-earth policy. The reality of the moral law seems to have been on a horizon that Speer could sense but never quite reach. So to the end he continued his imaginary journey—one that took him ever further into pure illusion.

# CHAPTER 17

# LIVING WITHIN THE TRUTH

FEW OF YOU will immediately relate to Albert Speer, an artist and organizer caught up in the most tumultuous events of the twentieth century.

But, as painful as it is to admit, I can.

Like Speer, when I was young, I dreamed of doing something great. From the time I was in prep school, I ate, drank, lived, and breathed politics. I worked as a campaign volunteer before I could vote. In college I majored in political philosophy and loved debating with a brilliant, liberal professor, Guy Dodge. The weaknesses I saw in his positions encouraged my conservatism. I have to say that he was extremely fair-minded and enjoyed my piping up with contrary views. He would sometimes end classes by saying, "We haven't heard from Mr. Colson in this hour. Why don't we let him give us the opposite side?"

My education gave me a good grounding in political philosophy. It emboldened the flag-waving patriotism that sent me into the U.S. Marine Corps and from there to serve as an administrative assistant in the U.S. Senate.

Then, at age thirty-eight, I occupied the office next to the president of the United States. Imagine what heady stuff that was! I wasn't promised the chance to redesign Berlin, but I was offered the prospect of helping to create a generation of global peace—a no less intoxicating offer.

During the first year of my working at the White House, I wasn't part of the inner circle. But I quickly joined it, coming to play a similar role for President Nixon that Karl Rove has played for President Bush.

Nixon and I developed a close working relationship. Various writers have said that I brought out his worst instincts and he brought out mine, that we played to each other's darker sides. We thought alike. As Nixon's strategist I was in a position to implement my ideas on a national scale. I could actually do what I had been talking about since high school. I went to work on cutting back government excesses, thereby restoring more freedom to people's lives. I worked to strengthen the military and tried to reduce the national deficit.

The time I enjoyed the most came during the 1972 presidential campaign. The three *A's* in our campaign were acid, amnesty, and abortion, as we began to define the conservative response to what has become known as the culture war. We were tough against busing—not because we didn't believe in equal rights and integration, but because running social experiments with little kids was no way to accomplish these goals, which moms and dads knew. We won over socially conservative Democrats by the hundreds of thousands.

The question I've asked myself is whether I had any early warning signs of the trouble brewing. Did my conscience tell me anything was amiss? I came to realize in the ensuing years that the Nixon White House was poisoned by a will for revenge that originated with Nixon himself and to which I contributed. But this toxic moral atmosphere did not come about overnight. And I didn't see it coming.

My first warning signal should have come through the White House's double standard on spending. Two or three times when I walked into the West Wing of the White House, I was taken aback by the sight of carpenters moving walls. Elaborate renovations became commonplace. I often heard the joke that you had to be sure you didn't fall asleep in your office because you might get walled in. Bob Haldeman spent lavishly on redecorating offices, and it bothered me to see him use taxpayers' money that way.

Then, I confess, I began to enjoy it. When I was moved into a larger office, I wanted new wall hangings. I called the White House staff decorator, who quickly ordered spectacular paintings from different museums and hung them in my office. I didn't like the old government-issue desk I had. "I wish you had those Knoll tables," I said to the decorator, and voilà I had a beautiful, oval, rosewood Knoll table. Then came Knoll credenzas. The drapes looked a little tired, so we ordered bright yellow drapes to go with my navy blue carpet. I—the puritanical New Englander—succumbed to the lure.

The selfish use of taxpayers' funds was a harbinger of things to come. I was in the president's office one night with Haldeman when we got word that copies of some of the Pentagon Papers documents had been kept at the Brookings Institution by a former National Security Council staff member. We knew this man to be very liberal and against the Vietnam War. Nixon erupted in anger, as he sometimes did. He slammed his fist on the desk and turned the air blue with profanity. "Bob, I've told you before I want a team of men who can go get those documents back. I don't care what they have to do. Break in. I need a team around here that can do those kinds of things for me."

Honestly, sitting in the Oval Office with the president that night, I was shocked. I had never heard him talk so bluntly about such things. Earlier, I had suspected that Nixon might want such activities conducted, but I never thought he would say so. At the same time, my conscience didn't exactly scream in protest.

My conscience remained undisturbed in part because the government did behave that way in some circumstances. I had a lot of dealings with the FBI and CIA, where government agents made unauthorized entries—"black bag jobs"—to get classified documents back. The government did this in extraordinary circumstances to protect itself against foreign powers. The Pentagon Papers put our relationships with other countries at risk; we felt our national security was at stake—or so I reasoned.

But espionage against hostile nations is one thing, and breaking into a domestic institutions quite another. It's a finer line than might be thought because foreign and domestic matters can't always be neatly separated, as the 9-11 Commission found out in 2004. But it was a line that we crossed that night, and my conscience was mute. No red flags went up. I was so focused on stopping the leak of classified government documents that could undermine national security that I never gave a thought to the fact that this might be wrong.[1]

In the fall of 1971, I learned that Howard Hunt and some of his men had broken into Daniel Ellsberg's office and stolen his records. At that moment my conscience did kick in. I was appalled by the thought that the White House was party to a burglary. These tactics were beneath us. I realized that burglaries are against the law and that Hunt and his gang were not CIA or FBI or anything like it—they were *our* agents. This was not a good thing, and I didn't want any part of it.

When Howard Hunt came and wanted to show me pictures of the files, I told him I didn't want to see them, hear about them, know about them, or for that matter know about anything remotely involved in the whole operation. After that I kept him at arm's length. He made me nervous.

After the Watergate break-in and the 1972 campaign, I took a phone call from Howard Hunt one day. I knew I should have nothing to do with Hunt, but I took this call because his wife had died, killed in a plane crash while traveling to Chicago.[2] I had previously known Howard socially and felt responsible for recommending him to John Ehrlichman. I was very sorry I'd ever gotten him involved in the White House shenanigans. So I took the call.

During that phone call Hunt made what anyone who listens to the transcript of the conversation—I recorded it—can detect as extortion threats. He was asking for more hush money. I was so determined that he not tell me anything—which I said about ten times—that I wasn't even thinking of the seriousness of what he was saying.

After I made the recording of the phone call, I asked my secretary to type up a transcript. I sent the transcript to White House Counsel John Dean with a cover note that simply said, "Now what the hell do I do?"

That was good for many laughs and was widely reported all during Watergate. In sending the note and the attached transcript to Dean, I never thought I was furthering a criminal conspiracy; I didn't know there was a conspiracy. I thought Dean was on the level. Although later, that one act resulted in my being included in the Watergate conspiracy. In retrospect, I should have known better. When you have to make continual efforts to avoid knowing what's going on, you are in big trouble.

By January 1973, when Hunt's lawyer came to me and made some pretty heavy-handed demands, I knew this thing had gone off the rails. I went to Nixon and told him so, which the presidential tapes show. But it took a lot before my conscience was really aroused. I liked my position. I liked my power. I didn't necessarily want that life to end.

I had become much too comfortable, seduced by the decor, by the guards' saluting, by the limousine at my disposal, and the waiting jet at

Andrews Air Force Base. That's a very heady business for anybody, especially for a thirtysomething who came from humble beginnings.

My dad had imparted to me a latter-day Puritanism: Never lie. Always tell the truth, no matter what the cost. Work hard at any task you are given. Give people a fair day's work for a fair day's pay. I learned so much about truth telling and integrity from him. What I hadn't learned was that by presuming I lived by his strict moral code, I would become blind to the ways I failed it. My self-righteousness enabled me to compartmentalize: to believe I was doing the right thing while simultaneously going along with the wrong thing.

As soon as you say, "Don't tell me. I don't want to know," you're done.

My failure was different in degree from Albert Speer's but identical in kind. How many times must Albert Speer have said, "I don't want to know." How many times did the German people say the same thing as the Jews were arrested amd carted off, and as the ashes began floating in the breeze from Dachau and Buchenwald? In his *Spandau* diaries Speer himself said that shunning knowledge was "criminal."

Speer lived to the end of his life as a tortured soul. The universal witness of conscience convicted him of his wrongdoing, yet conscience alone was not enough to keep him from aiding Hitler's evil. Perhaps the most pathetic thing about Speer's life was that he lacked criteria by which to discern Hitler's errors—even after these had been committed. At the end of Speer's life, he knew he had gone wrong, but he couldn't think how or why he could have avoided his fate. "Yes, of course, mea culpa," Speer said, "but the whole point is that I *didn't* feel this, and why didn't I? Was it Hitler, only Hitler, because of whom I didn't understand? Or was it a deficiency in *me*? Or was it both?"[3] He concluded, "I will never be rid of that sin," partly, one suspects, because he had no fundamental understanding of evil itself.[4] He remained unable to connect with reality's spiritual dimension.

*What I hadn't learned was that by presuming I lived by his strict moral code, I would become blind to the ways I failed it.*

One of the reasons I've chosen to tell Speer's story comes from seeing what proved to be his last public appearance on ABC's *Good*

*Morning America* in 1981. The interviewer, David Hartman, asked him, "You have said the guilt can never be forgiven, or shouldn't be. Do you still feel that way?"

I will never forget the look of pathos on Speer's face as he responded: "I served a sentence of twenty years, and I could say 'I'm a free man, my conscience has been cleared by serving the whole time as punishment.' But I can't do that. I still carry the burden of what happened to millions of people during Hitler's lifetime, and I can't get rid of it."[5] The heart of Speer's tragedy was that he could find no redemption, no forgiveness, for what he had done.

At the beginning, Speer should have questioned Hitler's understanding of the world. In Speer's writings, he admitted that he had never looked at Hitler's program critically, never evaluated the Nazi ideology. He should have questioned whether Hitler's promises could possibly come true—whether they were grounded in the way the world works.[6]

*Some people would argue that the truth doesn't matter. But they are wrong. The truth is the only thing that matters when it comes to evaluating how we are going to pour out our lives in service.*

In a similar way, I should have seen the machinations within the Nixon administration in a broader context than the ability of the president to be reelected or even than national security issues. I should have understood what was at stake: truthfulness and respect for the law.

Some people would argue that the truth doesn't matter. But they are wrong. The truth is the *only* thing that matters when it comes to evaluating how we are going to pour out our lives in service.

As we said earlier, truth is what conforms to reality. We all stake our lives on the choices we make, but often we fail to see if these choices are based on what is true and right. And failing to choose is itself a choice, going along with the crowd another, and believing that truth is subjective establishes one's own truth as life's single, if flexible—or flakey—absolute. If, like Speer, you choose a falsehood pretending to be the truth, your life will come to destruction. If you choose the truth—which is to say, if you choose to live in conformity with the way the world is supposed to be— and if you pour out your life in service to truth and justice, you will have a rewarding and meaningful and significant life, even in the most difficult circumstances that Ernest Gordon and Nien Cheng demonstrated.

Being faithful to what is true and right is the very definition of integrity, as I was reminded one day when I was speaking to two thousand marines at Camp Lejeune, where I had served as a platoon commander in the midfifties. In the question period, a grizzled marine sergeant wanted to know, "Which is more important, Mr. Colson, loyalty or integrity?" He was asking whether the truth had to be put aside at times for the sake of human allegiances, human relationships.

The marine's question jolted me. The motto of the Marine Corps, *semper fidelis,* means "always faithful." Marines tend to preach loyalty first, last, and always.

The question stirred difficult memories. In January 1974, the special Watergate prosecutor, Leon Jaworski, offered—in exchange for testimony against Nixon—to let me plead to a misdemeanor—meaning I would serve no jail time and would save my law license. If I had not been loyally committed to Richard Nixon, I would have taken Jaworski's offer, even though I disagreed with its terms. But Nixon still had my unconditional loyalty, and what Jaworski wanted me to say wasn't true.

I had been warned that Nixon would hardly be as loyal to me. In the middle of the 1972 campaign, when Nixon was riding high and we were soaring to victory, Haldeman and I had what seemed at the time an idle conversation that has haunted me ever since. He said to me, "Chuck, I don't want you to be disillusioned. Let me tell you something about Richard Nixon. He's a person who will use you, and when you have served your purpose, he'll throw you away like a used Kleenex." I was flabbergasted. I could not for the life of me understand why Haldeman would say that. It was brutal and cynical—far more so than Haldeman normally was. He made the remark without a smile, chuckle, or laugh. He was dead serious.

I could never buy that. I loved Richard Nixon, as a man and as a president. I highly respected him because of his extraordinary leadership, particularly in foreign policy. When I went to the White House, I considered what might happen if my interests and the president's were in conflict. I realized that I would be the knight on the chessboard, not the king. In a crisis, I'd have to take the fall for him. I served with that feeling in mind, much of it conditioned by my own military experience.

I later realized that Haldeman and Ehrlichman were conspiring to throw me over the side immediately after the election so that I'd deflect all the Watergate attention from the White House. Haldeman was making a decent gesture, I think, trying to soften my fall by giving me fair warning. He was trying to prepare me for the fact that after the election, instead of being the glorious hero, I was going to be made the goat. That's clear from the tapes.

Haldeman and Ehrlichman failed, of course. They really thought they could lay it all on me because the press had laid it all on me. They assumed that if I left, Watergate would be out of the White House. They only brought themselves down in the process.

I'll never forget the moment I was deeply disappointed by President Nixon. I was watching his resignation on a little black-and-white television in prison. I realized that he was taking himself off the field of battle and leaving his wounded aides behind without making any provision for them. This diminished him in my eyes.

Nonetheless, I remained loyal. In the trials I did not testify against him. In public I continued to call him my friend and said that I wasn't going to blame him for what I did, even though he ordered the specific offense I had committed. I just didn't think it was appropriate to blame him for what I had done. So I didn't. But inside, as I watched him leave without regard for the people who were in prison or about to go to prison because we had served him, our bond was loosened.

So, when the Camp Lejeune marine asked whether loyalty or integrity was more important, I could ruefully reflect on how the truth is so far more important than loyalty. Get that wrong, and your world collapses. I told the marine that the answer was integrity and that I wished I had thought of that long ago when I was part of the Nixon administration.

---

Integrity and seeking the truth inform some of the most joyous events of recent history. The 1989 Velvet Revolution in Eastern Europe raises our sights to the positive potential of such a quest. It demonstrates that we are not talking about academic questions; we are seeking to incorporate into our lives the most powerful force in human affairs.

In the late 1970s the Czech playwright Václav Havel wrote the essay "The Power of the Powerless" as part of a joint Polish and Czecho-slovak effort that resulted in a famous declaration of human rights known as Charter 77.[7] Havel's essay was distributed first via an underground network as *samizdat*—copies, often made one at a time on carbon paper, that passed from hand to hand as people yearned for the truth that could be garnered in the Soviet bloc only from unofficial channels. For this essay and his other activities, Havel was imprisoned for four months in 1977 and again in 1979 until early 1983.

In "The Power of the Powerless" Havel opposes Communism with no grand counter-ideology. Rather, he uses a common example of how Communism perpetuated itself and how it might be defeated. Take a greengrocer, he writes, who is asked by government officials to post in his shop window a placard declaring "Workers of the world unite!" In the former Eastern European Communist bloc, signs like this were posted everywhere—in the factories, the shops, and the billboards on the roadways.

When asked to post the sign, the greengrocer had to decide: Would he comply? He no longer believed the ideology expressed in the slogan "Workers of the world unite!" He did not believe that human beings are the product of their economic environment and that a heaven on earth could be brought in through changing social conditions. After forty years of Soviet hegemony in Eastern Europe, society had indeed changed, but only for the worse. People found themselves compromised by continuing to support what they knew was a lie.

In the government's view, fear that the people might discover that the Communist ideology was a lie was precisely why it was so important that the greengrocer post the placard. The placard kept him bound to the lie, and he became complicit in Communism's oppression. By participating in the lie, the greengrocer denied his own human dignity and made himself the servant of a false and imprisoning ideology. He also became the government's instrument of oppression against others because his example implied that it was too risky to contradict the authorities. After each lying action, the greengrocer became ever more easily manipulated.

In his essay, Havel shows that the big lie of Communism could be maintained only by the millions of small lies elicited from greengrocers. The Soviet Union and its satellites became a vast world of appearance devoid of reality. Everyone who helped the system run had to act *as if*—

as if economics determined destiny, as if the government protected the interests of workers, as if the rule of law were maintained, as if human rights were respected, as if freedom of religion were practiced. An elaborate system of ritual gestures—including the posting of placards in shop windows—had sprung up to enable the state's enablers to pretend to themselves and to others that Communism made life worth living.

For most people, this demanded an extreme compartmentalization—a public face and a radically different private face. In public, they acted as if they believed the lie, while in private they knew the truth. Greengrocers posted Communist placards because if they did not, they might lose their place as the shop's manager, have their wages cut, see their children barred from higher education, or face imprisonment. So most people in the Soviet bloc chose to live within the big lie.

Havel proposed that the most revolutionary action was *living within the truth*. The dignity of the human person consists in the ability to know the truth *and to live it*. Living within the truth would restore one's innate human dignity and make life again worth living—because the truth matters more than life itself. Havel writes,

> Under the orderly surface of the life of lies, therefore, there slumbers the hidden sphere of life in its real aims, of its hidden openness to truth.
>
> The singular, explosive, incalculable power of living within the truth resides in the fact that living openly within the truth has an ally, invisible to be sure, but omnipresent: the hidden sphere [of openness to truth]. It is from this sphere that life lived openly in the truth grows. . . . But this place is hidden and therefore, from the perspective of power, very dangerous. The complex ferment that takes place within it goes on in semi-darkness, and by the time it finally surfaces into the light of day as an assortment of shocking surprises to the system, it is usually too late to cover them up in the usual fashion.[8]

For Havel, living within the truth meant simply living with integrity: recognizing reality and then being faithful to reality in one's actions. Again, he called for no grand political scheme. Living within the truth meant "anything from a letter by intellectuals to a workers' strike, from a rock concert to a student demonstration, from refusing to vote in the farcical elections, to making an open speech at some official congress."[9]

By 1989, countless people across Eastern Europe had committed themselves to Havel's challenge to live within the truth. These included the other signatories of Charter 77 as well as Lech Walesa and the Solidarity movement in Poland, Pastor Laszlo Tokes and his followers in Romania, and the Hungarians who forced their government to hold free elections. As the result of the brave actions of many people, there did indeed occur a "shocking surprise to the system."

*The dignity of the human person consists in the ability to know the truth and to live it.*

These dissidents eventually inspired hundreds of thousands to spill out into the streets from churches in East Germany. The East German demonstrations began from Leipzig's St. Nikolai Church, where people had met for peace services since 1982. After the service on September 4, 1989, fifteen hundred people staged a demonstration, walking through the streets of Leipzig, holding candles. Even though the Hungarian government had recently opened its border to Austria, allowing thousands of East Germans to migrate to the West for the first time since World War II, the people who gathered at St. Nikolai were not satisfied with the right of free movement; they wanted to see real freedom in their own land. On September 4, they began chanting, "We are staying!"

By September 25 the marchers' numbers had swelled to eight thousand. Ten thousand turned out on October 2. Then, despite the government's threat of a Tiananmen Square–style massacre if the demonstrations continued, fifty thousand people marched on October 9. That's when the East German government utterly lost control of the population. In the next weeks street demonstrations swelled across East Germany as protesters held candles and marched in every city. A revolution by candlelight—expressing the deepest prayers of the people—was being staged. The Church of the Good Samaritan became a rallying point in East Berlin—not far from where Speer had practiced his "de-tenanting and evacuation," his cooperation with the Holocaust.

On November 9, 1989, as a result of some miscommunication within the government, word got out that free travel to West Berlin would be allowed. By midnight, hundreds of thousands of people were swarming back and forth through the Brandenburg Gate, celebrating their new freedom and what would soon be the reunification of Berlin and all of East and West Germany. The first sledgehammers started knocking down the Berlin Wall.

What remains one of the greatest positive events of my lifetime came about because brave people acknowledged that they knew the truth and pledged to live within the truth. In the very nation where Speer lived out a life of compartmentalized horror, hundreds of thousands forsook compartmentalized ethics. In 1989, heeding Havel's advice and that of others like him, they decided not to differentiate between their public and private faces but to live their beliefs no matter what it cost them. What an inspiration!

*Integrity and seeking the truth go hand in hand.*

We see in the negative example of Albert Speer and the positive example of Václav Havel the crucial lessons of life: In order to live with significance, we need to discover truth, to discover reality; and once we've discovered it, we must live in fidelity to it. Integrity and seeking the truth go hand in hand. It wasn't enough for Eastern Europeans to know the truth; they had to live it.

The experience of those who lived under Communism teaches that we are all not only truth-seekers but also truth-avoiders, when our appetites and desires and survival instincts make the truth inconvenient or threatening. One of Poland's dissident martyrs, Jerzy Popieluszko, said, "If truth becomes for us a value worthy of suffering and risk, then we shall overcome fear—the direct reason for our enslavement."[10]

Integrity is vital because any breach of our integrity pits us against reality, and that's a war no person has ever won. You can stave off reality only so long before it crushes you, which is what happened to both Nazi Germany and Communist East Germany.

These principles are so evident to deep thinkers that long before the Iron Curtain fell, Pope John Paul II foresaw that Communism was doomed. He understood that a system that was so radically untrue to human nature and the natural order simply could not endure.

———————•◦•———————

The big lie of Communism has all but vanished. But we live with another in its place. Tragically, in our times we are all greengrocers who
have placed in our shop windows placards declaring, "There is no such
thing as truth!" "Tolerance is god!" "Diversity must rule at all costs!"

The big lie of the West is that there are no absolutes—only subjective truths that compete with one another. As benign as this proposition
may appear, this big lie destroys what Havel called the "true aims of
life," or the good life, as we shall see.

# CHAPTER 18

# CAN WE KNOW
# THE TRUTH?

HAVEL'S BELIEF IN knowing the truth and living it goes to the very heart of what it means to live a good life. It raises the most urgent and controversial question in today's culture: Can we know the truth? Strident voices in our culture answer that question with a resounding no.

The principal reason for this is found in an extraordinary cultural revolution in the West. In the period after World War II, as we noted earlier, existential philosophers, mostly Frenchmen, took seriously Nietzsche's formulation that God was dead and that life has no transcendent purpose. The human challenge was therefore to overcome life's inherent lack of meaning through personal experience. This gave birth to the generation of the sixties, to Woodstock, to seeking meaning through protest, free love, and drugs. Existentialism was soon accompanied by deconstructionism in literary and cultural studies. This held that societies live in "the prison house of language," meaning that we can never escape our culture's prejudices; every claim about the way the world works can only be the expression of biased groupthink.[1] It doesn't take a philosopher to see that these two streams of thought undermine any authority structure.

Truth became whatever one person believes. So you have your truth, and I have mine. This is the essence of the postmodernist era.

But if all propositions are equally true, in the end none is true. Postmodernism has radically departed from Western civilization's historic tradition that we can know the truth through reason and the imagination. Historic Christianity further added that revelation enhances reason's power and completes its understanding, providing answers to the perennial human questions of purpose and meaning.

Sadly, postmodernism has not been simply the idle teaching of modern intellectuals and philosophers. It has infected all of American and Western European life. Polls show that 64 percent of the American people believe there is no such thing as moral truth. Even more alarming, 83 percent of teenagers see moral truth as a pretense.[2] The clear majority of Westerners believe we can make up our own rules for living. The result, as we will discuss later, is chaos in much of life. (Are we really surprised that cheating and stealing are commonplace in our classrooms? Or that the business community has produced a generation of Dennis Kozlowskis?)

> *The present generation horizon is limited to accommodation to the way things are. They live within the evil enchantment of believing that finding truth is utterly impossible, on principle.*

Just think what this has done to Gen X and Gen Y. Convinced that truth is relative, many twentysomethings and thirtysomethings have drifted into a culture of despair. Whatever else is said about the sixties, aging boomers who have confronted reality (particularly in the lives of their children) have begun to recognize that there may be such a thing as truth, although many have no clue how to find it. The present generation's horizon is limited to accommodation to the way things are. They live within the evil enchantment of believing that finding truth is utterly impossible. This is why many young people are confused, feeling as if they are trying to go up the down escalator.

---

My friend Phillip Johnson, the Berkeley law professor, tells the story of a distinguished professor at a politically correct university. The man's son arrived home one day and, to the surprise of his parents, announced that he was transgendered. The young man was involved in a trendy movement on American campuses: selecting one's own gender, irrespective of biology. He had absorbed large amounts of gender-bending literature.

Many parents are used to having their offspring come home with strange habits: young women with tattoos or, as was the case with one of my grandsons, young men with rings through their eyebrows. But a transgendered son shocked even this family.

Johnson reports the conversation that took place around the family table.[3]

"What does this mean?" the parents asked.

"It means I'm a girl," the son answered. "I want to wear dresses and makeup, and challenge the whole patriarchal, bourgeois idea of gender."

The parents were shaken. That very night they were expecting as dinner guests two of the most famous postmodern academics in America, Dr. and Mrs. Stanley Fish. Fish is a leader of the deconstructionist school of literature, the belief that art and literature have no objective meaning. The young man's parents were afraid that even Stanley Fish might feel uncomfortable. The father described his fears: "I imagined my son swirling down the stairs, arriving at dinner like Loretta Young, in flowing chiffon. How exactly would I explain such a phenomenon to my guests over hors d'oeuvres?"

The boy's parents told him he would have to remain a boy for the evening. Their son complied, resisting the temptation to tell them what hypocrites they were.

When the evening was over, the son explained that he had learned about transgendering from theorists like Michel Foucault and Judith Butler—from the very textbooks that his father assigned to students. In the eyes of many postmodernists, gender has no relationship to biology. It is simply an arbitrary designation; we can choose as we wish. This young man was not bucking the family philosophy; he was trying to follow it.

No wonder many young people are sexually confused and succumb to despair. They're being taught this by professors, teachers, the intellectual elite—even their own parents.

But the postmodern denial of simple common sense isn't limited to gender identity.

---

The debate between traditional Western beliefs and the postmodernist point of view came into stark focus in the wake of 9/11. After the attacks, President George W. Bush announced that America must "rid the world of [such] evil."[4] The word *evil* came immediately to the president's mind at the thought of the thousands of innocent men and women who died in the terrorist attack. Some commentators even suggested that 9/11 would undermine the whole postmodernist argument that there is no right and wrong, no objective good or evil.

Not so, however. Stanley Fish denounced the president's statement, calling his characterization of 9/11 "inaccurate and unhelpful" because it relied on "false universals." Even if there is truth, it is not knowable, Fish believes. Ideas about what is good and what is evil are useless concepts, invented simply as a means for one group to impose its will on another.[5] (The very point of view of Nien Cheng's interrogators.)

Fish was not alone in his objections. Many academics went so far as to say that labeling Al Qaeda's suicidal hijackers "terrorists" was far too judgmental. They argued that one person's terrorist is another person's freedom fighter. Students at universities in North Carolina and elsewhere were instructed not to judge the motives of the terrorists and were required to study the Koran.

But freedom fighters must actually be fighting for freedom, not the tyrannical rule of an Islamic elite who are intent on "purifying" their societies of their ideological opponents. That's fascism, even if it's wrapped in a theological package. Freedom fighters also engage their enemies directly, not the innocent civilians who are targeted by terrorists.

Richard Dawkins, the Oxford scholar who is a leading popularizer of Darwinism, said that if anything was to blame for 9/11, it was "religious fanaticism." He said, "To fill a world with the religion or religions of the Abrahamic kind, is like littering the streets with loaded guns. Do not be surprised if they are used."[6] So the "fanatic" label sticks not just on Islamic fundamentalists but on all of those intolerant absolutists who believe in the Judeo-Christian tradition.

Statements like these reflect a particularly hard-boiled postmodernist rejection of truth and commitment to moral relativism. They also reflect the belief that there are no absolute values except one—tolerance. This point was made by UN Secretary-General Kofi Annan, when he said, "Unquestionably very evil things happen in the world." Then he added that the difficulty, however, "is to know where to draw the line. . . . If we are intent on naming evil, . . . then let us name it as intolerance."[7]

So intolerance, judging the terrorists, is a greater evil than the evil committed by the terrorists? Tolerance once meant that we could use our reason to discern good and evil in open debate. Today tolerance has been used to call good evil and evil good.

———•◦•———

Surprisingly, intelligent people often reserve their outrage almost exclusively for what they see as judgmental attitudes—the one evil they are willing to indict with impunity. I discovered this at a friend's house one night when I sat across the dinner table from a very well-educated businessman who embarked somewhat pompously on a lecture about diversity, arguing that all cultures are morally equivalent. They are at various stages of development, he argued. I asked him whether he thought it was the same thing morally for a grieving widow to be comforted in America or to be hurled on a funeral pyre in India with her dead husband. He smiled, laughed knowingly, and said, "Well, we live in diverse cultures; some are progressing at different rates."

*Today tolerance has been used to call good evil and evil good.*

That's hard to say without choking on the words. It's asserting that tolerance is more important than truth and life itself. That's dead wrong.

The deeply entrenched ideas of postmodernism have made the New Age the fastest growing religion in America today. The New Age allows us to construct our own religion and makes no truth claims on anyone. It provides no genuine moral direction, for if god is in everything, god is in both good and evil.

New Agers and postmodernists have created a deity out of tolerance, and people have become greengrocers displaying placards saying, "There is no such thing as truth! Tolerance is god!" The only cardinal rule of American life is that we must respect everybody's opinions as morally equivalent.

Dorothy Sayers, the great English wit and writer, had a description for this state of affairs. "In the world it calls itself *Tolerance,* but in

Hell it is called *Despair*. It is the accomplice of the other sins and their worst punishment. It is the sin which believes nothing, cares for nothing, seeks to know nothing, interferes with nothing, enjoys nothing, loves nothing, hates nothing, finds purpose in nothing, lives for nothing, and only remains alive because there is nothing it would die for."[8]

This idea that it's intolerant to object to anyone else's position, however, is a complete perversion of the historic understanding of tolerance, which was that one had to have the respect to listen to anyone else's point of view, even one with which one might profoundly disagree. Tolerance did not reject truth claims; it respected them.

As a result of our distorted idea of tolerance, we are losing our right to free speech. These days, before we speak, we must consider every word in the light of increasingly restrictive speech codes. Coercion has become a substitute for the power of truth, because we no longer believe in the truth, only the importance of people's feelings. This has already worked itself out in the law. A 1992 Supreme Court case held that an innocuous to-whom-it-may-concern prayer of a rabbi at a Virginia junior high school commencement was unconstitutional because it infringed on a fifteen-year-old's right not to have to listen respectfully to the religious expression with which she disagreed. What once would have been considered a mark of civility and maturity—learning how to listen to another's points of view—now gives rise to a constitutional suit.[9]

Equally troubling is that, according to the courts, tolerance demands that we can no longer voice in compulsory public forums any religious expression that proclaims a "shared conviction that there is an ethic and morality which transcends human invention."[10] So if someone merely says in a public setting that standards exist beyond those of the private individual, the speaker has violated separation of church and state.

Postmodernism and its dogmatic tolerance can lead only to despair, as Sayers wrote and as we witness in the lives of so many today. Despair in turn leads to slothfulness, and slothfulness to boredom. In spite of our great technological advances and the highest level of education and material advances any society has ever achieved, we have managed to suck all of the meaning out of life, to destroy any basis for human dignity or human rights, to undermine moral and rational discourse—to leave ourselves adrift in the cosmos.

While postmodernism undermines belief in science because science depends on belief in the natural order, most postmodernists virtually worship science, which, of course, is completely illogical. But then, logic has been dispensed with. The discovery of logic four centuries before Christ was one of the unique accomplishments of the ancients. It encouraged extraordinary breakthroughs in the process of civilization because it enabled humans to think about what is true and not true. But postmodernism is no longer bothered with logic's rigorous demands that we find truth or seek consistency in the way we think or believe. In abandoning the religious "superstitions" of the past, knowledge itself has become nothing more than superstition—that's postmodernism in a nutshell.

This escape from reason makes intelligent discourse impossible. Occasionally, however, even determined postmodernists have to recognize the quandary their own beliefs put them in.

Some years ago during the high-tech bubble, I visited the Silicon Valley, then a place of rising real estate values, rising stock values, rising dreams and expectations. It was a place that promised its good life would never end. A close friend, Mark, arranged a private lunch meeting in one of the valley's tonier restaurants for several of his closest friends and members of his personal Bible study. On the way to the restaurant, Mark warned me that one person at the lunch would not be sympathetic to my point of view. The man was an extremely influential person, a nationally known futurist who could predict what kind of underwear people would be wearing twenty years from then. His newsletter was highly valued by manufacturers, marketers, and the investment community.

Our group was escorted into a private room and situated at a large square table, three or four men on each side of the square. Like everything in Silicon Valley, the surroundings were casual. After a brief time of small talk, my host introduced me, and I spent the next twenty minutes talking about prisons, the ministry, cultural issues, and the like.

I had hardly finished speaking when the famed futurist, sitting to my immediate left, looked at me with something of a scowl and said, "This is what I don't like about you Christians. You think you have all the answers—that only you know the way to heaven."

I was startled by his hostility and tried gently to explain what Christians believe. I told him that "No one comes to the Father except through me," were Jesus' words, not mine.[11] I reminded him that Jesus made that particular truth claim.

The futurist waved dismissively and said, "No, no, that's absurd. We know that all religions are alike and everybody's going to the same place."

I responded that all religions have exclusive claims. Jews believe they have an exclusive claim to truth: To be received by God, one must be among the circumcised, the covenant people. Muslims have an exclusive claim to truth: No one can live in paradise without pleasing Allah. Buddhists have an exclusive claim to truth: Our desires cause nothing but suffering and must be renounced. Like every other religion, Christians embrace a given set of beliefs—of claims about reality.

"No, no," the futurist countered once more, smiling as if to suggest that he had a more enlightened way of looking at these things. Sounding like Stanley Fish, he said, "They really aren't truth claims, simply the preferences or beliefs of these groups. They're all the same." Then he shrugged his shoulders, as if indicating what this mixed bag of preferences was finally worth.

"But they can't be," I said. "One set of claims excludes the other."

He was now shaking his head.

So I took out my pen and dropped it on the table. "Notice it falls," I told him. I dropped the pen again and again and again. "You'll notice it drops every time. There's never a time when it doesn't drop. Don't we call that the *law* of gravity?" I asked him.

"Oh, but that's not really dropping," he said, laughing. "I know enough about quantum mechanics to realize that particles are in constant motion, faster than the speed of light, and those particles simply are passing through one another."

I had a short one-word reply to that. "Bull. What you see," I explained, "is a pen dropping, mass hitting mass. If particles are passing through particles, so be it. You're still seeing a mass strike a mass. So there is truth, you see," I said.

Now my lunch companion's face flushed with a pinkish hint of anger.

I pressed on. "One claim to truth excludes another claim to truth. Both can be wrong, but both can't be right. All roads can't lead to heaven. Otherwise we'd have to suspend the law of noncontradiction. I'm sure you've read your Aristotle. He comes along in the syllabus a good deal before quantum mechanics."

Now my companion, red in the neck, looked very angry and flustered. He turned back to concentrate on his coffee, as if seeking solace. "Well, religious claims are extranatural," he sputtered.

People of faith are regarded by today's elites as irrational? The truth is, much of postmodernism has abandoned reason and in the process left its adherents with "both feet planted firmly in midair."

———•◦•———

It's so important to understand this so that you're not unconsciously sucked in to the irrationality of postmodernism, hanging the "Tolerance is god" placard in the window of your mind. You cannot keep solid footing unless you see through the big lie of postmodernism.

Carrying placards that deny truth is knowable may be what the cultural powers and elites impose on us, but we need to rise up and speak out for what is obvious—there is truth, and it's knowable. Ultimately this matters far more than the issues of gender identity or social tolerance or public discourse. It matters because it's literally about life and death.

*You cannot keep solid footing unless you see through the big lie of postmodernism.*

And this has become, for me at least, deeply personal.

# CHAPTER 19

# WHAT IS LIFE WORTH?

MY WIFE, PATTY, and I had a disturbing reminder of why the truth matters when we visited our autistic grandson's special-needs school one afternoon. The school is housed in a two-story, clay-red brick building, located at the intersection of two main arteries, about twenty miles from Boston. The building has a central, reflective-glass atrium tower. The brick wings on either side of the tower are totally unadorned, except for two rows of small and widely spaced windows. It's the kind of closed-in, airless building out of which factories operate and indeed, it has a machine shop in the basement. Max's school is on the first floor, where school officials have managed to rent enough space to take care of eighty special-needs children, most of them seriously autistic. The surroundings are pure industrial park. The only green in sight comes from the signs on the interstate.

Patty and I arrived just as school was letting out. Most of the children in Max's school live in group homes. Max is one of the fortunate few who can be kept at home—in part because Emily does an effective job managing him. As we opened the front door, one of the staff took us quickly by the arm and moved us to the side. "Stand over here," she said. "When the kids start coming out, they're likely to trample you." Within seconds the rumble began as the students, most of them in early or mid-adolescence, headed for the doorway. At first I thought the staff member's advice was overly cautious, but then I remembered that when Max wants to go from point A to point B, he never detours around anyone or anything. (Autistic children have little sense of their own physical presence. They can step on your foot without even knowing it.) The students headed pell-mell to their various marked school buses, bound for their suburban group homes. Patty and I called out hello, but few replied. Almost no one seemed to see us. The staff member was right to get us out of the way!

Autism is not the same thing as Down syndrome or congenital birth defects that result in physical deformity. Most autistic kids are as normal looking as their peers. Some do have a vacant, distant stare; others walk with an awkward gait from motor damage. Several of the kids carried computerized speaking pads that allow them to answer questions. These children have suffered so much neurological damage that they would be effectively mute if not for these devices.

The stampede nearly over, we saw Max at its tail end. When he saw us, he broke into a big smile and started skipping with arms wide, looking for a hug. He's a very loving kid, and we were glad to shower him with affection. He then grabbed both Patty's hand and mine and started to pull us into the school, excited at the prospect of showing us where he studied and eager for us to meet his teachers.

I was more than impressed with his teachers, who labor with him patiently hour after hour, day after day. They are paid a modest wage and work long hours under intense conditions. Autistic kids are demanding. Max, who is so gregarious, wants constant attention. He needs to be touched and held and loved. Many autistic kids, even in their adolescent years, do not have control of their bowels and must have their diapers changed.

At the end of each school day, when the students are dismissed at three o'clock, the workday is far from over. The faculty members gather to discuss the behavior of each student, meticulously planning the next day's activities. The student-faculty ratio is high: four teachers staff Max's class of seven. The job requires great physical stamina. The kids can be aggressive at times and must be gently restrained. Gentleness in this situation often demands as much force as several people can muster. Max weighs 130 pounds, and sometimes, when he doesn't know how to make his needs or dissatisfactions clear, he'll flop down over his desk or onto the floor and refuse to move. The physical demands Max makes on his teachers are mild compared to many of his classmates' demands.

The mostly female faculty members were all remarkably cheerful.

In fact, they radiated joy. *Where do they get people like this to work in these schools?* I wondered. A survey of teacher satisfaction revealed that helping the children was the teachers' primary motivation; altruism is alive and well in this profession.[1]

I understood their joy. I also have felt it as I've learned to love through taking care of Max. My grandson has taught me a lot more than I have taught him; he's schooled me in being a grandfather. When my kids were growing up, I was gone most of the time—too busy trying to save the world. I didn't enjoy the fun of rolling around with kids in the grass, not nearly often enough. Now, when Max is visiting or we're visiting him, my life focuses solely on him. There's no leaving him in front of the television while I go to my desk. At night, I can't just read him a book, say a prayer, pat him on the head, and tell him to go to sleep. In order to help him get to sleep, I play repetitive games with him, sometimes for hours. When Max visits, my schedule is Max's schedule.

The Max schedule makes me examine my priorities. It makes me think about the time I devote to *doing*—a lot of it simply indulging in distraction—versus how much time I give to *being*.

The day of our visit to his school, Max brought us through the cramped, gray-linoleum corridors to his classroom. It didn't have the profusion of "Bookworms," ABC charts, subject murals, Student of the Week posters, and the clustering of equipment into study centers common in most of today's elementary schools. His classroom was stark. Autistic kids find the world too stimulating; part of the condition means they are less able to process sensory stimuli. So Max's classroom had only seven metal-framed desks with wooden tops. A calendar at the front of the classroom showed the day's highly routinized activities—autistic kids find security in structure. Each child also had a job chart headlined with a picture of the child. At the back of the classroom was a break area with a hooked rug and close by it a bookcase and storage bins for toys. At the time of my visit, Max was working on being able to read by himself for five minutes. Reading itself is not the problem; working independently is Max's great challenge. The teacher's goal was for Max to work independently for as long as twenty minutes.

A lot of care had gone into making this room as comfortable and

welcoming to these kids as possible. This kindness would never be re-
ciprocated, at least not in the way we normally understand. Not only do
autistic kids find the world's jumble of stimuli confusing and fearful,
but they are even less able to express the information they can process.

As I was standing in the classroom, alone for a moment, an un-
welcome thought came to mind. A question really. Why do we as a society take such trouble with these kids? Why does the school system
spend as much as $65,000 per year to tend kids like Max? Max is never
going to graduate and go to college and get a productive job. He has
made huge progress, but there's a serious question about whether he'll
ever be able to take care of himself. Very likely, he will always be dependent on his family and the state. Simply to keep him busy, enter-
tained, and comfortable creates a huge financial drain. Even if he
weren't in school, institutionalization alone would run more than
$50,000 per year.

I couldn't help but think of Peter Singer, the Princeton ethicist
who argues that the governing philosophy for a society ought to be creating the maximum happiness or pleasure for the greatest number of
creatures, human and animal alike. Singer has been described by the
*New Yorker* as the most influential philosopher alive.[2] Think about how
much pleasure or happiness we could create for tens of thousands of
starving African children with the $65,000 it costs to keep Max in this
school. A chill came over me as I realized how powerful—how natural—Singer's argument sounds.

Singer's moral philosophy is a form of utilitarianism, which in its
modern form evolved from the nineteenth-century writings of John
Stuart Mill. Mill has profoundly affected modern liberal thought,
which views freedom as the absence of constraints. Morality, as one
sympathetic writer described Singer's view, doesn't come from heaven
or the stars; it comes from giving as many as possible what they want
and need.[3] Most atheists and the majority of people in the post-
religious societies of Europe accept this as the most reasonable way to
serve the social needs of society; if pleasure and happiness are the purpose or true end of life, morality must consist in rationally apportion-
ing pleasure and happiness to those most able to experience them.
Even many Christians have embraced this proposition because it
sounds so reasonable.

Peter Singer characterizes his philosophy as ethics catching up with the inevitable conclusions of Darwinism, and he carries his thinking to its logical, if controversial, conclusions. For example, he advocates infanticide for children born with defects.[4] Singer minces no words: "All I say about severely disabled babies is that when life is so miserable that it's not worth living, then it is permissible to give it a lethal injection." He asks rhetorically, "Why limit the killing to the womb?" As if to answer his own question, he says, "Infanticide . . . should not be ruled out any more than abortion."[5]

Singer's view is entirely logical, although most would find it intuitively repugnant—at least for now. Singer dismisses objections to his philosophy as mere sentimentality.

What do you do, though, with kids like Max and all of his schoolmates who somehow survived abortionists' forceps or the doctors' lethal injections? Max, after all, is a human being, a teenager, a beautiful bouncing kid who loves life and other people. Surely you would not eliminate him.

But think again about what you could do with that $65,000 a year, every year, not just for starving kids in Africa, but for American inner-city kids who need better public schools. What about medical care for indigents? Just think about how that money could be used in the Medicaid system, which is always starved for cash.

Those who think that humanity would never take severely disabled persons, particularly kids, and get rid of them are simply unaware of the history of Western civilization in the enlightened twentieth century. For example, take Germany in the 1930s, even before Hitler's regime took hold. The brightest and best-educated people in Europe were openly advocating eugenics—selective human reproduction and elimination of the disabled. Doctors and educators and cultural leaders discussed how to rid Germany of the "traditional compassionate nineteenth-century attitudes toward the chronically ill,"[6] as one doctor put it. The sterilization and euthanasia of persons with chronic medical illnesses became a topic of great interest in German medical journals. A propaganda campaign began to encourage the German people to adopt a utilitarian point of view.

The campaign led to a 1941 film *I Accuse,* which depicted a multiple sclerosis sufferer whose physician husband helped her to commit suicide. As the woman was dying, the husband's sympathetic colleague played a classical piece on the piano in an adjoining room. (How many similar "loving" acts of euthanasia have been the subject of television programs in this country?)

Children were not immune from the campaign. A high school text entitled *Mathematics in the Service of National Political Education* contained math problems dealing with the care of the chronically sick and crippled. The very question that so troubled me that day in Max's classroom was asked of these impressionable students: "How much money would be available for marriage allowance loans and to help newly-wedded couples if the state could save the money on the 'crippled, the criminal, and the insane'?"[7] In 1939, with the culture conditioned and dissent virtually stifled, Hitler issued a direct order for euthanasia. Medical institutions were required to report on patients who had been ill for more than five years and were unable to work. The questionnaires received about these patients were then reviewed by expert consultants, most of whom were professors of psychiatry in prominent institutions. Between November 14 and December 1, 1940, for example, the committee evaluated 2,109 questionnaires. This was the official start of what became a massive campaign of extermination of unwanted people.[8]

No sooner had euthanasia been established in Germany than an organization devoted exclusively to the killing of children was created, the Realms Committee for Scientific Approach to Severe Illness Due to Heredity and Constitution. Soon an elaborate system was established to transfer the socially unfit from their hometowns or institutions to trains and buses that would take them to facilities known as "liquidation institutions." Children were stripped to the skin, dressed in paper shirts, and led into a gas chamber. Once dead, their bodies were then carted to combustion chambers and incinerated. According to one German jurist, the smoke was visible over the town of Hadamar every day. The workers in the facility spent their nights in local barrooms, drinking heavily and talking freely about their daily chores. People feared that homes for the aged were being cleaned out and elderly people liquidated.[9]

But Hitler, you say, was a demonic exception to all historical norms. Not so. His directives were carried out by highly educated, intelligent, and otherwise moral and decent Germans. German doctors of that era were considered among the best in the world. They were people like Albert Speer, the nature lover, the father of six children. What is most shocking about great evil is how often it comes in the guise of the good, done for what seems a noble end.

Speaking of the eugenics practiced in Germany or the infanticide and sex-selection abortion in China or India today—and speculating about what might happen here—lets us off the hook too easily. Peter Singer's utilitarian point of view already rules our own health care system in significant respects.

What I'm about to say may well strike very close to home. In fact, it will resonate disturbingly in millions of homes across America and Europe. Nearly every young couple having a baby today receives information about the potential health care needs of their unborn child. Ultrasound, amniocentesis, and other tests are informing parents of a growing list of medical conditions—some 450 at this writing—in their unborn children. Doctors are afraid not to perform such tests lest they face suits for not fully informing parents of an unborn child's medical problems while the unborn child may still be aborted.

Think of the practical dilemma faced by a pregnant woman and her husband after they arrive home from a doctor's appointment. They have just been informed that their child may have neurological damage, which could display itself in a number of ways, including autism. The doctor has asked them whether they want to abort their unborn child.

What would you do? How would you reason about the decision? Would it make any difference if your health insurance provider informed you that it would not pay for treatment of complications discovered in the testing? According to some reports, 90 percent of the couples confronted with this dilemma abort their unborn children.[10]

*What is most shocking about great evil is how often it comes in the guise of the good, done for what seems a noble end.*

Would you bring a child like Max into the world? If not, why not? And if you found out about your child's severely impaired future a day or two after the birth and if the doctor offered you the option of infanticide, what would you do then? As laudable as places like Max's school may seem, why should such efforts continue if it's in our power to make them unnecessary? That's the utilitarian voice that's constantly whispering in our ear these days.

The person who says yes to Max now and in the future can reason only on the basis of something completely other than a cost-benefit analysis.

Tragically, the cold calculus of dollars and cents already determines many life-and-death choices being made in America and Western Europe today. Recently, for example, Amy Richards, who was carrying triplets, panicked at the thought of changing her lifestyle. "When I found out about the triplets, I felt like: It's not the back of a pickup at 16, but now I'm going to have to move [from the East Village in Manhattan] to Staten Island. I'll never leave my house because I'll have to care for these children. I'll have to start shopping only at Costco and buying big jars of mayonnaise."[11] Because these indignities overwhelmed her, Amy Richards decided to abort two of the children and keep the third.

In March 2004, many people in England were horrified to learn that an unborn child who was more than twenty-four weeks old—at the point of viability outside the womb—was aborted for "severe disability" because the child had a cleft palate. This case brought to Parliament's attention that since 1990 there has been an inexorable rise in the number of viable unborn children aborted because they had "severe disabilities." Since *severe disability* isn't defined in the United Kingdom's laws, this means that any child with a medical condition, even a treatable one such as cleft palate, may be aborted at any point in a pregnancy.[12] Of course, prochoice purists question why we would even make such distinctions about the fetus's condition. Why not abort anyone we choose? This debate is currently under way.[13]

> The cold calculus of dollars and cents already determines many life-and-death choices being made in America and Western Europe today.

———•◦•———

These aren't just intellectual issues. They're deeply personal and anguishing decisions that we're forced to contend with in the course of life. As I looked around Max's classroom and ran my hands over the scarred wooden desk that he sits at each day, my thoughts turned quickly to another logical extension of Singer's thoughts: Why keep people alive when they're miserable? Why not give them the opportunity to be an organ donor and give someone else life? If we get to the point where we agree with that, then why would we not just destroy the miserable person?

That's really at the heart of the issue in the raging global debate over embryonic stem cell research. An embryo, after all, is a life. If we can take a life that isn't worth living, then why shouldn't we use those embryos to find cures to the most feared diseases Americans experience? But if it's okay to take the embryo, why should we not use the body parts of a disabled infant who would otherwise be killed? Why waste them? Wouldn't we be contributing to the greatest happiness for the greatest number of people, maximizing human pleasure by helping people to achieve a better quality of life? The logic is precisely the same.

Where do we draw the line? Maybe places like Max's school will become a thing of the past, but who will be next? Prisoners convicted of capital crimes? Why should they sit on death row at our expense while appeals are processed? Obviously, we don't want mentally defective people forever panhandling on our street corners, if we can help it. Or do we?

I'm seventy-three years old. Like John Ehrlichman, I could wake up one morning and be told that I have renal failure. A kind, loving doctor could look at me and say, "Mr. Colson, do you really want to spend every morning hooking yourself up to one of these contraptions? People who use home machines often get devastating infections. You could come to the medical center for the same treatment, of course, but that means three days a week, three hours at a time. Your quality of life, Mr. Colson, will rapidly deteriorate. I just want you to know that we can handle the problem another way if you like. It's really only an extension of pain management—just a little extra morphine at some point, and you'll gently go to sleep."

Think of the huge social pressures that are coming to bear on the medical profession, on families, on individuals. The cost of medical care is skyrocketing because of extraordinary technological inventions. With a combination of machines, we can soon, if not already, keep people alive under almost any circumstances. What about the cost? Families can't pay this. The Medicare system will be broke in a few decades, sustainable only if taxes on workers are greatly increased. The demographic shifts in America are so dramatic that while at the moment 4 workers are paying to support one person on Medicare, by 2030 it will be 2.3 workers. Should we expect hardworking, middle-class Americans to be paying an ever-increasing share of their earnings to keep me alive while my "quality of life"—watch that term—deteriorates?[14]

Those pressures are already here, not only in countries such as Holland and states such as Oregon, where assisted suicides are legal, but in the everyday business of administering health care in hospitals throughout America and the Western democracies. An emerging doctrine called "futile care" provides a euphemistic cover for euthanasia.

For example, a friend of mine was severely ill for many years with deteriorating lungs and his life was becoming increasingly difficult. Although at times he recovered his vitality and felt his old energy and zest for life, the occasions when he had to resort to oxygen became more frequent. I was with him a number of times during this period and was called when he was hospitalized with a particularly difficult attack. His loving wife was at his side, reading the Bible to him.

A few days after I heard he was hospitalized, I received a call that he had died peacefully in his sleep. It wasn't until later that I learned he had what family and friends called a "beautiful death." After his loved ones gathered at his bedside to say good-bye, a doctor administered an extra dose of morphine. My friend got his wish. Was his death "beautiful"? Was it euthanasia? Was it murder? Who's to say?

Of course, that's the critical question: Who's to say? If you've been around the bedside of someone severely ill, you know the pressures on the family, the agony, the continuous vigil. In the back of some people's minds are questions about the cost: *How are we going to pay for all of this?* Friends and relatives are grief stricken over the pain their loved one endures. They're tired, exhausted. A doctor appears in a white coat, bigger than life—a professional, committed to helping and curing the sick. We're ready for him or her to tell us what to do in this terrible, agonizing moment.

Life and death become judgment calls, subject in some cases to ethics committees' determinations and hospital guidelines. But who decides what our ethics will be? If there is no truth, there are no true ethics, only prudential standards that reasonable people try to apply. So the best-intentioned doctors in the world have to make judgment calls, ever aware of the costs involved for the hospital in which they are staff members. Aware of the patient's suffering, pressured to handle as many cases as possible, embroiled in a quality-of-life matrix, the white-coated doctor becomes god, with nothing like God's judgment.

What the doctor has at the back of his or her mind may resemble Peter Singer's views. "If an individual hasn't stipulated while they're alive what they would like to be done," Singer says, "then it should be up to the family and an ethics committee. If a family wants the life of a severely mentally disabled or old person to end, and a physician confirms that there is *virtually no quality of life for that person and no chance of recovery, I think a lethal injection would be justified.*"[15]

Thus speaks the man whom many regard as the leading philosopher in America.

*Life and death become judgment calls, subject in some cases to ethics committees' determinations and hospital guidelines.*

Most of us find ideas like these—the use of a child's body parts, euthanasia—utterly repugnant. We refuse to think we are really measuring life on the basis of cost. We don't like utilitarian reasoning when we're forced to face it. There is something deeply, deeply wrong about this whole mind-set, in which so many of us are already profoundly implicated. But there's that terrible voice in the back of our minds that says: *I know what the right answer should be, but I'm sure glad that if I were in that situation, I'd have an out. If I had Alzheimer's and I could be cured, who cares about how the research was done?* That voice, like the greengrocer's placard saying "Workers of the world unite," keeps the whole deadly system going.

———•◦•———

So how does one answer Singer's seductive logic? The disabilities-rights activist Harriet McBryde Johnson made a valiant attempt to do so. Peter Singer invited the gifted Ms. Johnson to speak at one of his classes at Princeton and to debate him in an open forum, which she later described in a moving *New York Times Magazine* piece.[16]

Ms. Johnson, a lawyer, suffers from a muscle-wasting disease and describes herself as a "jumble of bones in a floppy bag of skin." In her forties, paralyzed in most of her body, Johnson weighs about seventy pounds. Her spine is a tightly reversing S curve. She sits up in her chair by letting her ribs fall on her lap, with her elbows planted on her knees. This position has become natural to her, and she suffers no discomfort from it. Her life entails other restrictions, though. She can eat only purees, soft bread, and easily chewable fruit like grapes. She needs help getting dressed, using a bedpan, bathing, and doing the morning exercises that keep her limbs limber.

The Sunday trip from her home in South Carolina to New Jersey did not go easily; it's not a small matter to move a wheelchair-bound body from one point to another. Her power wheelchair was torn up by the airlines. With makeshift arrangements she was transported late to her hotel in Princeton and got only a few hours of sleep. Her caregiver helped her through the two-hour morning routine, and with the help of a borrowed wheelchair, she arrived at an old gothic building on the beautiful Princeton campus.

There she was confronted with a new dilemma: how to get to a basement lecture hall. Politically correct Princeton had apparently overlooked the needs of people with disabilities in this building. She rode unceremoniously in a broom-closet-style elevator to the basement before being placed at the front of the lecture hall. She felt some apprehension as students began filing in.

Johnson spoke first, building her case on the grounds that as a person with disabilities, she is a member of a discriminated-against minority and that the presence or absence of a disability does not define the quality of life. She described how much she enjoys riding in her wheelchair—the exhilaration of feeling the breeze blow through her hair.

Singer was, she observed, "surprisingly soft in his response." He reframed the issues almost clinically before opening the discussion to students. From time to time, Singer interjected his views. He asked if an "individual is totally unconscious and . . . we can know absolutely that the individual will never regain consciousness . . . assuming all that, don't you think continuing to take care of that individual would be a bit—weird?"

Johnson responded that caregiving can be a beautiful thing. She could not specify exactly why this should be the case, though, and her assertion left Singer blank. The nobility of caregiving could not survive

Singer's argument that happiness is based on preference, and despite the powerful argument of Ms. Johnson's presence, Singer's arguments clearly won over the students.

The eerie thing about the whole encounter for Johnson was that she did not find Singer the neo-Nazi devil that her disabled friends had painted him to be on the basis of his writing. The classroom exchanges and those that followed at dinner with the faculty were, by Johnson's account, amazingly civil. She found Singer's verbal facility dazzling; he was so "respectful, so free of condescension, so focused on the argument, that by the time the show is over, I'm not exactly angry with him."

Despite herself, Johnson came away from their encounter with enormous respect for Singer. She writes that he is "a man of unusual gifts, reaching for the heights." She virtually applauds his "trying to create a system of ethics derived from fact and reason that largely throws off the perspectives of religion, place, family, tribe, community, and maybe even species." She sees him as taking "the point of view of the universe," concluding that his is a "grand heroic undertaking." His weakness, she argues, is his unexamined assumption that disabled people are inherently "worse off," which she described as prejudice.

In essence, Ms. Johnson did not disagree with Singer's fundamental premise, only with what constitutes a good life and whose preferences must be respected. Once she agreed that the issue is quality of life—that there is no objective standard, only subjective judgment about what constitutes a life worthy to be lived—she forfeited any chance of winning the debate.

The enchantment that Singer's benevolent-sounding reason worked on Harriet McBryde Johnson is a clear example of how we have fallen under the sway of the well-spoken, highly intelligent enemies of truth. If there truly is such a thing as evil, do you think it would present itself in its true character, as vicious and destructive? No. Most of the time, evil comes to us as the hand on the shoulder and the kind voice that says, "Let me help you."

Without a view of God, or at the very least a transcendent natural order, there is no intrinsic significance to life. Which is why Singer was so curious as to how someone like Ms. Johnson, who is as good an atheist as he is, could disagree with his entirely reasonable views. No one, no matter how skilled a lawyer, is going to be able to win an argument with

Singer without questioning his Darwinian premise that life came about by chance. This is precisely what makes Peter Singer and his kind so very dangerous in the postmodern age.

———•◦•———

When it was about time to leave Max's school, Max showed me one of his drawings. It reminded me once again how important making art together has become for my daughter and Max. It plays a pivotal role in their communication, providing a bridge to Max's otherwise unknown thoughts, emotions, and memories.

Every parent experiences anxiety about what a child may be thinking and feeling. Does my little boy's sudden dislike of kickball stem from a bad experience on the playground? Are my daughter's new friends the result of an unhappy rivalry among the old friends? Will my child ever tell me? With autistic kids, this universal problem is much, much worse. Max will often become suddenly uncooperative for absolutely mysterious reasons. He'll throw himself around the room, exhibiting an agony about which he's absolutely powerless to speak; he can't express in words what he's thinking and feeling.

Emily has discovered, as I mentioned in the introduction, that if she draws for Max, supplying images that serve as bridges to his inner world, he is able to make sense of what's happening around him. She's able to connect Max's throwing himself around the room with his having a headache or being unhappy with an unexpected rearrangement of his clothing.

Through her drawings Emily has had phenomenal success in helping Max understand things that happened to him when he was two and three years old, events that frightened him because he was unable to interpret their significance. Through the drawing he's able to ask Emily what these events were about and whether he needs to be afraid of them any longer. Emily takes a brush or crayon and adds a flourish to Max's picture, giving the piece a happy look. Max doesn't need to be haunted by the episode any longer. The two draw together in tears, celebrating their discovery and the new freedom it has brought into Max's life.

In a utilitarian accounting, such an experience is meaningless because Max's life is meaningless. Why, then, does Emily feel profound joy when she is drawing and talking with Max, reaching him at a deep level? Why can I say that Max has taught me ever so much more than I have taught him, as if Max is a gift to me? I don't want to be misunderstood here. Max's autism is not a good thing—it's part of the world's brokenness. Yet that brokenness has been used to enlarge my capacity to love. That's a very great gift. Paradoxically, Max has introduced joy into the lives of his teachers, his mother, his grandparents, and many others because of these costs, these sacrifices. How should one account for that?

How should Max account for himself, and why should he have to? Max is more than happy to be alive, thank you very much. Max knows a joy and wonder that puts me to shame. Why is that?

Let me just suggest at this point it's because the good life is not about the sum total of what we contribute to the world. It's about loving. Utilitarianism knows nothing of love. Love is the beginning and the end of the good life, however, and it's in love that our lives must be centered.

Truth matters because without truth, love is unreal. It's just another sentimentality. But we know in our hearts that within us is a love that calls out to the Love that we believe formed the universe. Otherwise, we're lost. It is failing to acknowledge this love beyond self that caused the gifted Harriet McBryde Johnson to lose her debate with Singer, just as anyone would.

> *The good life is not about the sum total of what we contribute to the world. It's about loving.*

---

I've read and reread Johnson's article and corresponded with her. Her story, I believe, contains the hidden pathos of a woman who intuitively knows more than her philosophy acknowledges. In the final paragraphs of her piece, she retreats from her minority-rights argument to other grounds, even if these have no formal place in her thinking.

> My goal isn't to shed the perspective that comes from my particular experience, but to give voice to it. . . . As a shield from the terrible purity of Singer's vision, I'll look to the corruption that comes from interconnectedness. To justify my

hopes that Singer's theoretical world—and its entirely logical extensions—won't become real, I'll invoke the muck and mess and undeniable reality of disabled lives well lived. That's the best I can do.[17]

How tragic. The corruption of interconnectedness Johnson speaks of is only a corruption of her avowed atheism. She knows too much of her own life and the lives of her disabled friends to agree with Singer, although her lack of belief in a created order keeps her from being able to argue that to put a price tag on humanity is to become inhuman. Her story is a powerful metaphor for the dilemma we face.

——•◦•——

The issue that has to be decided is clear if we're willing to see it. If we are here as the result of a random, chance process, then Singer is right; his ethics are, as he says, but a logical extension of Darwinism. If, on the other hand, we are creatures made in the image of God, then life has an ultimate value that cannot be understood within the context of a cost-benefit analysis. How much is a human life worth? Is it priceless, or is it determined by the preferences of the powerful? It all depends on how human life comes about, which, as we shall see in the next chapter, has given rise to a raging debate in our society.

# CHAPTER 20

# GOD'S ID

So WHERE DID we come from? This is the most crucial question humans can raise, because the answer not only determines what it means to be human and why we are here, but it also affects every area of human endeavor. There is a raging debate among scientists and philosophers over this question, whether life began by chance or by design. So focus carefully on where the evidence leads you, for the question is not just about science; it's about *you*—whether *your* life began by chance or by design. Your answer to this question directly determines how you live your life and what choices you will make. You cannot know and live the truth, as Havel put it, or experience the good life unless you get the answer to this question right.

Nien Cheng answered this question in a way many of us do. During her imprisonment, when the leadenness of her days exerted its full weight, she often sat on her bed longing for her daughter. At times she felt as if she couldn't breathe; her stomach was so often in her throat that her appetite failed. At one point she almost starved to death from grief.

Then she found an unexpected companion. Late one afternoon she looked up to her cell's iron-barred window, where she saw a tiny spider, no bigger than a dime. It crawled to the top of one iron bar. There, the spider paused, then swung out on its own silken thread to the closest bar. With the two ends of the silken thread secure, the spider became a tightrope walker, making its way back up the thread to its original starting position. It then leapt out across the chasm again, this time landing a little lower on the neighboring bar. Back the spider crawled to its launch point. Out it swung once more.

After framing the outer dimensions of its new web, the spider began plying the intricacies of its gossamer weave. The spaces it left between threads were amazingly uniform, the whole of the web perfectly symmetrical.

When its web was complete, the spider crawled to the center, where it waited vigilantly.

Nien realized she had just witnessed "an architectural feat by an extremely skilled artist."[1] She wondered at the size of the spider's brain. Had the spider acted purely on instinct? What did "instinct" mean, exactly? Had the spider come by its skill through evolution, or had God endowed the spider with its gifts?

As she wondered about the origins of the spider's gifts, she found its web-building virtuosity had a tonic effect on her spirits. She found the spider's web extraordinarily uplifting and beautiful.

Later that afternoon, the spider's web caught the elongating rays of the setting sun, turning the web into a bright, rainbow-colored disc. Nien's loneliness and sense of oppression began lifting. The loudspeaker across the street at the high school might still be blaring denunciations of the state's enemies, but the spider and its web, as fragile as they were, caused her to believe that God, not Mao, was ultimately in charge of the universe. "Mao Zedong and his Revolutionaries," she wrote, "seemed much less menacing." Paradoxically, the spider's ephemeral web had a permanence that the Cultural Revolution never would. Its dazzling display of craftsmanship moved Nien Cheng to thank God for the spider and all creation. It gave her a "renewal of hope and confidence."

Nien Cheng vowed that if she were ever released from prison, she would consult an entomologist about the spider. If she carried through on this promise, she would have discovered something quite remarkable. According to German scientist Werner Gitt, "Every spider is a versatile genius: It plans its web like an architect and then carries out this plan like the proficient weaver it is. It is also a chemist who can synthesize silk employing a computer-controlled manufacturing process, and then use the silk for spinning.

"The spider," Gitt continues, "is so proficient that it seems to have completed courses in structural engineering, chemistry, architecture, and information science." But we know that spiders don't go to college, so how does it know what it's doing? Gitt answers: genetic information. He then goes on to explain the anatomy of tiny *Uroctea* spiders. "The female has 1,500 spinnerets. . . . Silk having the required tensile strength is produced in the factories located directly below the spinnerets. All of these complex processes are computer-controlled, and all the required equipment is highly miniaturized." He explains that this complex, minutely detailed manufacturing process can be carried on without mishap because the system contains a "controlling program which has all the required processing information." In his textbook, Gitt diagrams the extraordinary complexity of a simple, tiny spider, and the extraordinary work of art that it weaves in its web.[2] Truly a wonder of nature's design.

It's not surprising that Nien Cheng would thank God. She was moved not only by her faith but also by the self-evident revelation that nature acting in some random process could not have produced a complex system capable of creating such remarkable beauty.

Most of us have had similar experiences. We look up on a starlit night, the Milky Way sheathing the indigo heavens, and we know that there has to be an intelligence that hung the earth upon nothing. Remember the Apollo 8 astronauts, who looked from outer space at our earth and saw a bright, vivid sphere, filled with life and beauty, against the backdrop of a barren, desolate universe. Their reaction was that only God could have made this possible. And when we look at the biological intricacies that produce architectural structures of grandeur like the spider's web, all in perfect and purposeful harmony, they cry out to us "intelligence and design."

Contrast Nien Cheng's discovery with Peter Singer's philosophy, which is rooted in the belief that the universe has no design or purpose, that we arose by chance. Despite the superficial appeal of his arguments, they cannot result in a life of innate dignity. Whether we believe that life is a result of design and intelligence or that we arose by chance is crucial to how we live. This great debate pops up in the headlines almost daily and has become the battleground in schools today.

---

The "intelligence and design" side of the debate, however, is not being taught in our schools. Much of modern science and virtually the entire educational establishment today tell us that the universe arose by chance, that the cosmos is all there is or ever will be, as the astronomer Carl Sagan said in his popular PBS series *Cosmos.* The spectacular multimedia presentation at Disney World's Epcot Center tells visitors that life began through a cosmic explosion that brought the matter of the universe into being, and then life, in the form of tiny single-celled plants, emerged out of the seas, capturing the energy of the sun. We are led to believe that something came from nothing, merely by chance.

Biology texts offer a variety of explanations of this process, but all are predicated on chance. They claim that through eons and eons of random mutations and natural selection, the complex system of nature and the even more astonishing complexity of human life have evolved. Life is the result, we are told by the National Association of Biology Teachers, of "an unsupervised, impersonal, unpredictable and natural process."[3] This view allows no room for the possibility of an intelligent force. The Darwinian view is about science, we are told, and science rules out faith.

I discovered how this monopoly works and the soft ground on which it rests when my granddaughter Caroline, a beautiful and bright young woman, called me in anguish one day from college. Caroline had believed in God in a vague way since childhood; then she became a Christian at a Billy Graham crusade, and her faith was later strengthened in Young Life Bible studies. At the time of the call, Caroline was enrolled in a freshman seminar on evolution, in which, as she ruefully described it, the professor dismissed Christianity as superstition, thoroughly discredited by modern science. She wanted to know how she could reconcile the professor's view with her own faith.

Caroline's dilemma is all too common. Hundreds of thousands of students face it in college, if not in high school. Those who do not lose their faith in the process often come to an accommodation of sorts, believing in God but also in chance-driven, Darwinian evolution. You can do that only if you are willing to hold two contradictory thoughts in your mind at the same time, not an altogether difficult thing in this age in which we compartmentalize so much. Some people believe in theistic evolution, for which a case can be made, but the difficulty is that it fails to satisfy the Darwinian scientific establishment, which rejects theistic evolution's central premise.[4]

In Caroline's case, I gave her a series of questions that expose glaring holes in her professor's theories of evolution. She asked these questions in subsequent classes until he caught on and stopped recognizing her. What's clear to me is that the debate between Darwinism and "intelligence and design" today has become less about truth and more about power. It's become a battle over who controls the way society looks at this issue and what is allowed to be taught in schools.

It's a sad thing when the scientific establishment, presumably advocating scientific inquiry, won't answer a student's questions about science.

———•·•———

The Darwinian establishment argues that there is no serious scientific investigation challenging Darwinism. This is simply untrue.

The fact is that many intelligent and highly educated people are challenging the truth claims of Darwinism, and they're challenging them on the basis of science. Many are beginning to ask questions that Darwinians, like Caroline's professor, often cannot answer. More and more scientists are exposing weaknesses in Darwinian theory and proposing positive scientific arguments for an intelligently designed universe. The scientific debate on the question of origins is being reopened for the first time in a century.

The first crack in the solid Darwinian phalanx appeared in the mid-1980s in the form of the book *Evolution: A Theory in Crisis,* written by Michael Denton, a relatively unknown agnostic Australian scientist. Denton was particularly skeptical of the Darwinian claim that the accumulation of slow, gradual changes within a species—accounted for mostly by gene duplication and mutation—could account for the development of complex biological systems. He pointed to the lack of transitional forms in the fossil record and to the complexity of biochemical changes that would have had to precede any anatomical changes.

The book created a small dustup among some skeptics of Darwin. It also attracted the attention of an unlikely observer—not a scientist but a tweedy, bookish University of California at Berkeley law professor named Phillip Johnson. While on a holiday in England, Johnson was rummaging through a bookstore and came upon Denton's book. His lawyer's mind began asking hard questions, and simply as an intellectual exercise, Johnson decided to reread Darwin. Quickly he became absorbed; his legal training told him that Darwin's arguments, at least about the origin of life, could be handily rebutted. He consulted an outstanding chemical physicist at Berkeley, Fritz Schaefer, who shared his doubts. Johnson began writing about Darwinism, taking it apart, and in 1991 he published *Darwin on Trial*.

The book caused tremendous controversy, and Johnson began debating Darwinists, who found, to their dismay, that the brilliant law professor could not be bullied by their credentials and authoritative manner. They had to engage his arguments, and when they did, they usually lost.

Johnson has devoted his life to building a school of students and disciples among younger scientists, people such as the author of *The Design Inference*, William Dembski, who holds Ph.D.s in both mathematics and philosophy.[5]

One of Johnson's early recruits was a Lehigh University professor named Michael Behe. With wisps of gray hair growing in all directions and a straggly gray beard, Dr. Behe, often dressed in overalls with suspenders over a flannel shirt, looks for all the world like a throwback to the 1960s. Behe, who grew up in Harrisburg, Pennsylvania, was always fascinated by how things work. He found his vocation in high school chemistry class. "This is fun," he said, "mixing things together, watching them blow up."[6]

After studying chemistry as an undergraduate, Behe earned a Ph.D. in biochemistry at the University of Pennsylvania and did postdoctoral studies at the National Institutes of Health. While at the NIH, he dated a Christian woman who had doubts about Darwinism. Michael made fun of her. His Catholic family taught him to believe that God could have chosen evolution as the process through which creation came into being. As a working scientist, he found no reason to challenge that comfortable assumption. Everything in his chemical and biochemical studies reinforced Darwinism as the first pillar of a true scientist's worldview.

Behe joined the faculty of Lehigh University in 1985 and shortly thereafter read Denton's book. He was startled to discover how clear and compelling its arguments were, and he wondered why he had never heard such objections in his doctoral and postdoctoral studies or in his life as an academician and a working scientist. The book had a strange effect on him; it made him angry. He felt like a fool—to have studied chemistry and biochemistry all this time and never thought of these things, never studied them. He felt misled. He began muttering to himself, then talking to his graduate students and colleagues. But no one wanted to engage Denton's arguments.

Then one day in 1991, Behe was walking down the hall of his department when he saw a copy of *Science* magazine lying on a table. It contained a news story on Phillip Johnson's *Darwin on Trial*. When Behe read the article, he became angry again—there's a lot of Irish in him, he says. The *Science* story completely avoided addressing Johnson's arguments. Rather, it printed a series of damning quotes from Eugenie Scott of the National Center for Science Education—an organization devoted to policing science texts to ensure their Darwinian orthodoxy. Behe fired off a letter to the editor, demanding that *Science* deal with the critics' arguments rather than simply attack them.

As a biochemist, Behe's specialty is the cell. He understands that each cell is a miniature world in itself, filled with highly complex and extraordinarily successful systems and micromachines that have to function in strict coordination with one another in order for the cell to live. With this background, Behe later found himself fascinated with another book about the origins of life, *Of Pandas and People*.[7] In that text he saw a picture of a message scrawled in the sand: "John loves Mary." The book pointed out that in everyday life, we know intelligence is involved when we see independent parts (in this case, letters) ordered in a way that gives a message that the parts alone cannot give. Behe said, "That sounds right. We see that all the time in biochemistry, too, that different parts are ordered together to form a system that does something that the parts by themselves don't."

The more scientists like Behe discover about the role of information in determining life, the more evident is the case for a Designer. Information isn't self-organizing; it doesn't happen by chance. Have you ever walked on a beach and seen a statement as simple as "John loves Mary" created by the wind in the sand? And "John loves Mary" is baby talk compared to the millions of genetic messages contained in a single strand of DNA.

Reading *Of Pandas and People* convinced Behe to write his own book. In *Darwin's Black Box* he argues for a concept he calls *irreducible complexity:* Many biological systems consist of parts that depend absolutely on one another for the system to operate. Evolution would be an impossible explanation because the component parts can't work on their own; if one part evolves, it would be useless without the others. The whole system has to evolve all at once, impossible in Darwin's theory of gradualism.

Behe compared these biological systems to a mousetrap. In order for a mousetrap to work, it must have a base, a spring, a catch, and a release bar with enough strength to trap its intended victim. None of the individual parts isolated from one another can do anything like catching a mouse. The base alone is useless for the purpose; the spring, the catch, the release bar—in isolation, the parts of the mechanism are nothing but junk. In the same way, many structures within the cell depend on proteins and amino acids that are essentially useless without one another. They work only by being ordered into a particular design. Often these designs are remarkably complex. Once again, they make the "John loves Mary" statement look like child's play. The system's irreducible complexity—the uselessness of its parts without the design that makes it function—is evidence that the system couldn't come about through a long, slow, chance process; rather the evidence clearly points to an Intelligent Designer.[8]

But it was Behe's work in studying the blood-clotting mechanism in humans that finally flushed out the Darwinian establishment, forcing them to pay attention. Our blood is able to clot—not too much but just enough—because of a series of ten steps that involve about twenty different molecular components.[9] If our blood did not clot (as it doesn't in the case of people who suffer from hemophilia), the least pinprick would be lethal. If it continued to clot after accomplishing the closing of a wound, we would all turn into bloody Jell-O.

The regulation of the blood-clotting mechanism is key. To create a perfectly balanced blood-clotting system, clusters of protein components have to be inserted all at once. Behe describes it as a cascading process. It is much like the domino effect. When you line up dominoes in a row, spacing them a short distance apart, and touch the first domino, it hits the second one, which touches the third one, which moves the fourth one, which strikes the fifth one, and so on. All the dominoes have to be in place at once for the process to work. Similarly, Behe concludes, blood clotting in humans is an example of irreducible complexity that rules out a gradualistic Darwinian approach and that fits the hypothesis of an Intelligent Designer.[10]

———•◦•———

At the same time that respectable and serious scientists like Behe have begun to challenge Darwinian theory on scientific grounds, they've also begun to discover that Darwinists often aren't as careful about the facts as they've let on. Apparently Darwinian science is not always true science.

The issue took on new dimensions when Behe was challenged by world-renowned Dr. Russell Doolittle, University of California at San Diego biochemist and member of the prestigious National Academy of Sciences. Doolittle spent forty years studying the blood-clotting mechanism in humans. In "A Delicate Balance," an essay published in MIT's *Boston Review,* he cited a study from the journal *Cell,* establishing that the blood-clotting mechanism was created as a result of a natural evolutionary process.[11] At the end of his analysis, Doolittle wrote, "The entire ensemble of proteins is *not* needed. Music and harmony can arise from a smaller orchestra." With that illustration, Doolittle seemed to dismiss Behe's argument.[12]

Behe took the challenge seriously. But when he read the study Doolittle cited, he was astonished. Although Russell Doolittle had extensively studied the blood-clotting mechanism, he proved to be a less than careful reader—or one too inclined to presume experiments must confirm the theories he held. For he had misread the study reported in *Cell.* The study was actually evidence in support of Behe's argument: Take away one of its parts, and the whole mechanism begins to malfunction—with lethal effects.

Behe e-mailed Doolittle, suggesting that he might want to read the experimental paper and its results more closely. Doolittle sent a reply, in which he admitted that he had misread the paper but insisted that the other theoretical arguments in his article were sufficient to counter Behe's contention. He never retracted what he had published.

Besides being careless in reviewing serious research, some Darwinists resort to name-calling and intimidation to avoid dealing with the truth.

One of Darwinism's chief defenders, Oxford professor Richard Dawkins, responded to a journalist's inquiries about Behe's theories this way: "Imagine that . . . there is a well-organized and well-financed group of nutters implacably convinced that the Roman Empire never existed. Hadrian's Wall, Verulamium, Pompeii—Rome itself—all are planted fakes. The Latin language, for all its rich literature and its Romance language grandchildren, is a Victorian fabrication. The Rome deniers are, no doubt, harmless wingnuts, more harmless than the Holocaust deniers whom they resemble. Smile and be tolerant, just as we smile at the Flat Earth Society. But your tolerance might wear thin if you happen to be a lifelong scholar and teacher of Roman history, language and literature."[13]

Being compared to Holocaust deniers and called "wingnuts" may be no fun, but Behe knows that such desperate rhetoric exposes his critics' inability to counter his arguments. He takes satisfaction in the realization that nearly ten years after the publication of *Darwin's Black Box,* no one has successfully challenged his arguments.[14]

Propose to any school board that the flaws in Darwinism or the theories of Intelligent Design should be discussed in the classroom, and you most likely will not only be turned down, but you may be vilified, accused of subverting the Constitution, and labeled a know-nothing fundamentalist. You may even be compared to the Taliban. Just look at the impassioned controversies, covered sensationally in the national press, that have erupted in Kansas, Ohio, and elsewhere across the country. Honest argument, including scientific evidence, is simply not tolerated.

But why not? Why not look at both sides? Isn't that what science is about—questioning assumptions, seeking truth?

Rodney Stark, a Baylor sociology professor, formerly of the University of Washington and University of California at Berkeley, offers a plausible explanation. Stark, who says he is neither an evolutionist nor an advocate of Intelligent Design, just a scholar pursuing historical evidence, did an in-depth study of Darwinian defenders. The study, published by Princeton University Press, is entitled *For the Glory of God.*

Stark concluded that the battle over evolution is not a case of "heroic" scientists fighting off the persecution of religious "fanatics." Stark writes that from the very start, "It has primarily been an attack on religion by militant atheists who wrap themselves in the mantle of science in an effort to refute all religious claims concerning a Creator—an effort that has also often attempted to suppress all *scientific* criticism of Darwin's work."[15]

For example, Thomas Henry Huxley, known as Darwin's "bulldog," adopted the tactic of presenting only two choices: Darwin or biblical literalism. The intellectuals of his day feared nothing more than being labeled biblical literalists. Huxley ridiculed his opponents' stories about species that sprang into existence without biological predecessors, despite knowing that with the Cambrian era explosion of new life forms, this seemed, in fact, to have been exactly what happened. As Stark points out, after 150 years of rigid Darwinian orthodoxy in the scientific establishment, Darwinians cannot fill in the blanks between life forms.

The misrepresentations of the Huxley family continued through the generations. As late as 1958, Julian Huxley, grandson of Thomas Huxley, boldly asserted that "[Darwin] rendered evolution inescapable as a fact."[16] Stark argues that Julian Huxley knew better but that he believed "his lie served the greater good of 'enlightenment.'"[17]

The pattern of deliberate deception persists to this day. Richard Dawkins, who attacked Behe so viciously, for example, says, "Even if there were no actual evidence in favor of Darwinian theory . . . we should still be justified in preferring it over all rival theories."[18] Really? No evidence?

As Stark points out, Darwin himself acknowledged significant deficiencies in, and questions about, his own theory. He could never establish that natural selection worked from one species to the next; all of his breeding experiments fell short. So he could never answer the question of where species come from. As well, he recognized that his principle of gradualism in nature was critical to his theory, yet evidence for it was missing. The evidence is still missing in the fossil record—all these years and vast numbers of archaeological digs later. Darwin acknowledged that if life forms did appear spontaneously, that would "enter into the realms of miracle."[19]

After carefully examining the Darwinian arguments, Stark concludes, "Darwinian theory does rest on truly miraculous assumptions."[20]

Stark says that while Darwinians haven't made their case, the mythology remains. The reason, he argues, is that Darwinians use intimidation to put down their critics—just as Michael Behe found. For example, when the great philosopher of science Karl Popper argued that the evolutionary theory falls short of being science and is instead an untestable tautology, he was vigorously condemned and subjected to much personal abuse.[21]

One cannot read Stark's analysis—at least I can't—without concluding that Darwinists have been less than fully forthcoming over the years; that failing to defend gaping holes in evolutionary theory, they have simply resorted to *ad hominem* attacks against their critics.

------

But why? There's one compelling reason, and that is Darwinism's dirty little secret. While Darwinians argue their position as science, it is, in fact, a worldview. What they oppose is any inquiry that might open the question of whether there is a God who created the universe and sustains it. This is the real doomsday scenario for post-Enlightenment thinkers. Stark goes to lengths not to impugn the motives of Darwinians, but he could not help but point out what Richard Dawkins has confided: "Darwin made it possible to be an intellectually fulfilled atheist."[22]

The historical record, Stark reports, suggests this ulterior motive of many Darwinists. The earliest proponents of Darwinism made up a virtual who's who of socialism. The pamphlet "Why I'm a Socialist," distributed at the time, gave the answer "Because I'm a believer in Evolution."[23] When Karl Marx read Darwin's *The Origin of Species,* Marx wrote to Engels that Darwin had provided the necessary biological basis for socialism.[24]

*While Darwinians argue their position as science, it is, in fact, a worldview.*

"Atheism," Stark concludes, "was central to the agenda of the Darwinians."[25] To abandon Darwin is to abandon materialism, not just in science, but in political and social philosophy as well.

Do people get a vested interest in a theory and then defend it even when they find holes in it? You need only look at the case of Albert Speer. Humans have an infinite capacity for self-justification, as I know all too well from my own experiences in the White House.

The question posed in this chapter, however, is, Who has the better case? The only way to answer that is to look honestly at the evidence. Forget the vested interest of advocates of either Intelligent Design or evolution. The task of science, after all, is to search for truth wherever it leads.

To do this, we must also put the controversy in perspective: The issue is not faith or religion against science; it is faith against faith and science against science. Clearly it takes faith to believe that God spoke the universe into being; but it takes just as much faith to believe that the universe has always existed, that there is no beginning or end, or that it came into being by exploding itself (which violates the law of noncontradiction). Just as it takes faith to believe we are made in God's image, it takes faith to fill in the acknowledged gaps in the fossil record—faith that a process called natural selection can be extrapolated back to the beginning of time and produce the order evident in the universe. No one was present at the beginning of time with a video camera, so these have to be faith arguments, which should be isolated and examined one against the other.

> *The issue is not faith or religion against science; it is faith against faith and science against science.*

Competing scientific claims should be examined on their merits. I do not believe Darwin is completely wrong. There is clear evidence of evolution *within* species, which is often called adaptation. Within species we see wide variations: Poodles and Saint Bernards are both dogs. But that is different from one species' transforming itself into another, for which there is no evidence at the moment. How well has the Darwinian notion of gradualism—that there should be no sudden emergence of new species in the fossil record—been validated by archaeological discoveries? It hasn't been. The Cambrian explosion contradicts it. All the Intelligent Design movement is asking is that the right questions be asked and honestly pursued. No one is trying to impose religion on anyone or substitute faith for science.

In the same way, unbelieving scientists should not use the prestige of science to promote their atheistic beliefs.

It's becoming clear that increasing numbers of scientists are leaning to the Intelligent Design argument—which is striking terror into the hearts of Darwinians. A recent poll showed that 55 to 60 percent of professors in mathematics, statistics, and physical science disciplines are religious.[26] One of those professors, Nobel Prize–winning Charles Townes, said that science cannot answer the question of origin and that there is "a need for some religious or metaphysical explanation. I believe in the concept of God and in His existence."[27]

Philosophers as well are being persuaded by the Intelligent Design arguments. In 2004, one of the world's most noted philosophers of atheism, eighty-one-year-old Antony Flew, had a change of mind and was courageous enough to announce it.[28] As a young man, Flew debated C. S. Lewis over the existence of God—Lewis himself being an atheist-turned-Christian. Behe's arguments played a significant role in Flew's change of mind. Darwinian evolution, Flew confessed, could not account for the origins of life and phenomena like information-packed DNA. Flew indicated that biologists' investigation of DNA "has shown, by the almost unbelievable complexity of the arrangements which are needed to produce [life], that intelligence must have been involved."[29] Most of Flew's colleagues who have worked with him through all these years at Oxford remain in stunned silence after his announcement.

What if Behe and the others like Antony Flew are right?

———•·•———

The question of where life comes from is the most important one you must answer to live the good life. Get it wrong, and life becomes dysfunctional or worse, expendable. The stakes are huge.

Remember, philosopher Peter Singer acknowledges that his ethical calculus assumes an atheistic universe. If the universe and life are purposefully designed, it means there is an authority higher than the sum total of human happiness. It means that Peter Singer's utilitarianism—his case against Max and people like him—collapses, and it means that humans are invested with innate dignity and the inalienable right to life. They cannot be manipulated or engineered or priced out by the utopian thinkers.

Contrast utilitarianism with the notion that design and purpose are evident in the universe—that what Nien Cheng saw in the spider and what you and I see in the starry heavens is reality, that there is a natural physical and biological order. If it is designed, then the Designer must have a *purpose,* a word that raises moral questions that influence every area of life. If the world is a product of Intelligent Design, it means there is a God or supreme power of some sort.

It should now be clear how the difference between these two views becomes a difference in the way a life is lived—in the way *your* life might be lived. If you hold to the first view, it doesn't much matter how you live your life. If you hold to the second view, then your next questions relate to the meaning and purpose of the natural order that the Designer has put into place.

# CHAPTER 21

# MORALITY AND THE NATURAL ORDER

LIFE HAS A demonstrable, natural order, which Behe and others argue is designed with a purpose. Sometimes in our utopian dreams we forget this. When we do, it can bring the roof down on our heads—literally, as the World Health Organization discovered.

In the early 1950s, a malaria outbreak occurred among Borneo's Dayak people. The World Health Organization responded by spraying the people's thatch-roofed huts with the pesticide DDT, which killed the mosquitoes but also killed a parasitic wasp that kept thatch-eating caterpillars under control. At nightfall the buzz of the malarial, bloodsucking mosquitoes was stilled, but sharp cracks and then wild screaming followed—as people's roofs caved in.

This was hardly the end of the problem. The geckos stuffed themselves on the toxic mosquitoes, which definitely took the spring out of their step; these lizards can usually race over water for yards at a time. They reeled like drunks on a DDT Saturday night. The neighborhood cats, after they had batted the disoriented geckos around to their satisfaction, gorged on them.

Then the cats died.

Thus was the Year of the Rat inaugurated in the life of the Dayak people. Rats were everywhere, streaming over and through the Dayak's roofless dwellings. The rodents were a greater threat than a mere skin-crawling, toe-biting nuisance. The rats threatened the people with bubonic plague—a condition far more serious than malaria, as bad as that is.

What was the World Health Organization to do? What unexpected additional disasters might occur if it poisoned the rats? Events were spinning out of control, and the brains at the WHO were performing pirouettes of rationalization. They had only been trying to help, after all.

Someone finally had the bright idea that what was needed was to reintroduce part of the natural order that had collapsed. Specifically, cats. They needed cats. New cats. They needed *a lot* of new cats to eat the rats ("who ate the geckos, who ate the mosquitoes, who ate the spider she swallowed inside her"). But how could the WHO transport thousands of cats into a remote section of Borneo?

One morning as the Dayak people awoke and came out of their dwellings, they heard the droning of a slow-flying aircraft. Soon the sky was littered with parachuting pussycats. Operation Cat Drop rained 14,000 felines down on Borneo. As soon as the cats hit the ground— undoubtedly, on all fours—their ears went up, and they raced to an undisclosed location (for reasons known only to cats—or the aliens who control them). Before too long, the cats got around to the business of mousing, or in this case, ratting, and the Dayaks were saved from mosquitoes, rats, and the World Heath Organization.[1]

---

The natural order provides direction not only for ecosystems but also for human behavior, which must cooperate with it. Stephen Covey, in his seminars, often makes this point about the natural order in what he calls the "Law of the Farm." He points out that certain cycles of nature are unchanging and that everyone respects a variety of realities in planting crops. No one, for example, puts a tomato plant in a dark closet and expects it to grow. No one plants corn in the same flooded fields that grow rice. Harvesting always comes after sowing. Anyone who has lived on a farm knows the importance of respecting certain laws of the farm; ignore them or make up your own laws, and you fail as a farmer.[2] You won't eat.

In the same manner, the natural order prompts our behavior in many areas of life, causing us to behave in one way rather than another. We call this the moral order, and it begins, in a sense, with trying to understand that human behavior is first a response to the natural order.

I can best explain what I mean by telling how one of the navy's most famous admirals used the physical law of gravity to influence people's behavior.

When I was a very young man starting in Washington, I worked in the Navy Department as a junior aide to one of the assistant secretaries. I had occasional contact with Admiral Hyman Rickover, the legendary developer of nuclear power for vessels. Rickover was a genius—but an eccentric one. When I visited him in his office, he invited me to take the chair across from his desk. The first time I sat down, I nearly slid out of the chair; Rickover had sawed off two inches of that chair's front legs. Throughout my conversation with him, I found myself sliding forward, bracing myself to keep from slipping to my knees. Needless to say, the pitched-forward chair was a good way to keep visits brief and young aides humble. (The sense that I was begging for his help became irresistible.) Rickover used gravity, the natural order, to encourage visitors to behave as he wished.

> *The moral order is first a response to the natural order.*

Let's assume the physical order has an Intelligent Designer, as Behe and others contend—God, if you will. Isn't it reasonable that this God would teach us, as Rickover did in a small way, to behave in a way that conforms to the created order? Morality, remember, is choosing to cooperate with nature's directions.

As we have already seen, ignoring nature's purposes, acting irrationally, brings many hazards. This is the case not only with ecosystems but also with the most intimate aspects of our own lives. It's one thing to advocate understanding the complexities of a given ecology and learning to cooperate with it. That's a fashionable position that nearly everyone can buy into. It's another thing to acknowledge that our sexual lives should take their cues from the natural order. In fact, this is *the* place where disregard of the natural order has become most acute in our culture. Sexually, we want to act just as we please.

I've thought long and hard about choosing to tell the following story of a man beset by same-sex attraction—a man who in the midst of living the gay lifestyle came to see the inherently disordered nature of the condition and chose to recover. It's a difficult story to tell and one that contains so much brokenness that it may be challenging for some readers. I've decided it's an important story to tell, however, precisely because this is the place where our culture's blindness to the natural order has become the most willful. It's not a story you'll find being told in today's mass media. To the media, people like Randy Thomas do not exist—or shouldn't. But they do. Thousands of them. And if the placards our culture is plastering in our minds are to change and if the lies are to lose their power over us, then I must tell this story.

———•◦•———

In 1981, when Randy Thomas was thirteen years old, he found a booklet on human sexuality in his middle school library in Nashville. The booklet said that if a person is attracted to members of the same sex, the person is probably a homosexual. The booklet concluded that homosexuality is a naturally occurring variant in sexual orientation. There is nothing wrong with it. A homosexual should embrace his or her sexual orientation and find fulfillment in it.

*So that's it,* Randy thought. As long as he could remember, his classmates had teased him about his effeminate manner, calling him "sissy" and "queer" and "fag." He had wondered why he had a singsong voice and gestured the way he did, but he lived in a household dominated by women—his mother, his grandmother, and his aunts—and he thought he had merely mimicked their mannerisms.

Randy knew—or thought he did—how his attraction to men started. When he was in fifth grade, he spent late afternoons watching exciting new television shows such as *The Dukes of Hazzard* and *CHiPs.* The male stars struck him as strong and powerful, dependable and good. He began to daydream about accompanying them on their adventures. Perhaps he'd save the day himself, and one of the stars would ruffle his hair in appreciation or put his arm around him. Randy fantasized about crawling into the star's lap and receiving a hug.

Then, as his body began to change in early adolescence and he discovered sexual pleasure, his daydreams about the men he idolized acquired an erotic dimension. He wanted to be held and feel the new-found pleasure.

The booklet convinced Randy that their feelings would never change. He was a homosexual. He was gay.

Randy was glad to know he was *something*, because at the time he changed identities almost daily. He would dress like a preppie one day, a punk the next, a glam rocker out of Duran Duran the week following. Inside, he felt incredibly restless, as if he needed to be somewhere else. He would try to do three or more things at once, such as finishing his homework while talking on the phone with his best friend, Paige, while changing tapes to find his favorite song, and ordering around his little brother, Jimmy.

The only structure in his life came from his stepfather's fanatical need to be in charge. Jimmy and Randy were responsible for cleaning the house. Once, after Randy had cleaned the bathroom thoroughly, scrubbing the tile with cleanser, his stepfather found a hair in one corner and made Randy scrub the entire bathroom again. A second inspection found another flaw, and his father ordered a third scrubbing. Randy didn't argue much because his stepfather dished out spankings that became beatings, which eventually turned into brawling.

The first time Randy stood up to his stepdad, the man put him in a headlock and repeatedly punched his temple, giving Randy a concussion. His mother escaped with the boys to an apartment where she promised their abusive stepdad couldn't find them. Within days, however, the man had found them, and his mother blamed Randy for the trouble, saying that if he hadn't been so disobedient, his stepfather never would have treated him that way. She screamed at Randy until he agreed to return to his stepfather's home.

In high school Randy began to lead a double life. At age sixteen he had a first sexual encounter with a male coworker at the fast-food restaurant where they both worked. About the same time, Randy attracted a girlfriend. He liked her as a friend, and he liked her being attracted to him—she made the first move. Their status as a couple allowed Randy to appear normal, relieving the harassment of his peers. Randy and his girlfriend even did their share of backseat groping, but Randy felt little excitement during these encounters, even as he gave his girlfriend pleasure. He knew he was using her.

Another job in a fast-food restaurant landed him in the midst of a gay subculture. The managers of the restaurant were lesbians, and they hired, as it turned out, exclusively gay men, which Randy didn't realize until later. One day as the staff prepped for the evening's customers, the managers and the other employees gathered around Randy and asked him a mysterious question. "Are you family?"

"What?" Randy asked. "What do you mean?"

"Are you family? You know, *family*. Are you gay?"

Everyone wanted to know if he had ever been to a gay bar. He hadn't. "You have to go!" they said. Terry, a thirtysomething man who wore mascara, volunteered to take him after their shift. The others promised to join them later.

Terry had no trouble shepherding Randy through the front door. The minute it opened and the thump of the loud music hit him, Randy thought he was in heaven. He expected a room full of gay stereotypes—effeminate men with boas. He found all types, though, an amazing diversity whose only common denominator seemed to be their sexual orientation. Randy, with his dark hair and boyish, almost cherubic looks, quickly attracted many admirers. Terry and other older men brought him free drinks all night long. Randy was welcomed as he never had been anywhere before. He felt a new sense of identity and community. That night, very drunk, Randy went home with Terry and had sex.

During Randy's junior and senior years of high school, his double life became a fixed pattern. He kept his gay identity hidden from his family and his high school peers, worked after school and on the weekends for spending money, and hit the gay bars nearly every night. In addition to supplying alcohol, the gay bars were full of marijuana, ecstasy, and cocaine. Randy began smoking a lot of dope and frequently taking X. The cocaine was usually too expensive, although sometimes the older men he attracted were generous.

As Randy became accustomed to the gay life, he began discerning patterns that partially accounted for the community's joyous reception of a newbie. The older men craved the glory of youth that they found fading in themselves, while teenage boys longed for older, authority figures. Old and young alike were attracted to extensions of themselves; they sought their own idealized images. Randy was smart enough to see the narcissism that pervades gay culture.

Still, Randy harbored the dream of finding a true love—a man with whom he could grow old. Soon after high school, Randy thought he had found the real thing in a tall, powerfully built man named Ron.

They actually went out on a date together before having sex. Randy dreamed of living with Ron in a ranch-style house, with twin Honda Accords in the driveway, Pomeranian and husky dogs as pets, and a porch where they could sit in their rocking chairs, hold hands, and watch the sun go down. Ron was the first man with whom Randy formed a strong emotional as well as physical attachment; he was the first person with whom Randy shared his hopes and dreams—a first love. The relationship lasted only three months, however.

The first year after high school, Randy was still living at home while attending classes at Middle Tennessee State University. He also worked at least two jobs in order to party in the gay bars harder than ever. As a checkout clerk at a grocery store, he became almost a local celebrity, performing impressions and keeping up a gay comedy routine as he totaled people's purchases. His line of mostly gay customers would often stretch back deep into the store, while the lines for other checkers were hardly full.

Randy's alcohol and drug use continued to intensify. He could find no cure for the restlessness and boredom that afflicted him, other than trying to find the next love, or at least the next sexual partner. One acute hangover led to carelessness, and he left an invitation to a gay and lesbian Valentine's Day party in his jeans, where his mother found it while doing the laundry.

Randy's mother asked him into her bedroom for a talk. The minute he walked into the room, he saw the invitation at the foot of her bed. "I found this in your jeans," she said. "Are you gay?"

He admitted he was.

"You can't be," she said, instantly angry. "That's ridiculous. I mean, do you really know what it means?"

He laughed nervously. "I suppose so."

"Young men go through transitions and have an experience or two," she said, waving at the air. "It doesn't necessarily mean anything. Are you telling me it does? Are you telling me that you have had sex with a man?"

"Yes, Mom."

"With more than one?"

He didn't answer.

"You've already had sex with a lot of men? Older men or people your own age?" His mother became more and more agitated, pacing up and down in front of him. She described different sexual acts and quizzed him about whether and where and when he had engaged in such acts. Her questions fueled her building rage.

"You *can't* be gay!" she screamed. "My son's not a fag!"

"I'm me, Mom."

"Does your brother know?" Her tone turned desperate and imploring for a moment. "You haven't told Jimmy, have you?"

"He guessed, when a friend started calling here. So I told him."

"Jimmy knows? He knew before I did? How could you have done that to him? How can you do that to the family?"

"I'm not doing anything to the family. It's my business."

"And God's. Do you know what God thinks of fags? Do you? Fags end up in hell. God hates fags."

"It's my life, whether I'm here or in hell, I suppose."

"What does that mean? You're not going to stop?"

"I don't see how I would, Mom. I should have the right to live my own life, don't you think?"

"You can have all the rights you want. Sure. But this is the end . . . this is the end of my being made a fool of . . . while you go off and do what-I-can't-even-bring-myself-to-imagine. And putting it out there for *Jimmy!* I don't want you even talking to your brother. Good, merciful, blessed . . . What were you thinking?" She put her hand to her forehead and massaged her temples. Then she glared at him. "Pack up all your stuff. Pack it up. You've got one hour. *One hour!* You have to be out of this house in one hour!" She picked up the invitation and tore it in half. "I don't want this filth in here. I don't want to see it. This is . . . so bad . . . even *God* can't look at it. So just get out! Live your own life! Go right ahead! Just so long as you are out of this house for good! You can never come back here. Never!"

For the next three weeks, Randy lived out of his car. His friends at one place or another would let him sleep on a couch. Their own lives were far from tidy, and one night Randy found himself on a couch that stunk from cat pee and was infested with roaches. He decided not to stay the night there and slept in his car instead. As the weeks of his homelessness wore on, Randy became so desperate that he began thinking about suicide.

A friend of a friend finally took pity on Randy and invited him to stay for a while at his condo. The condo owner, known mostly by his stage name, Carmella Marcella Garcia, was a drag queen. When Carmella met Randy at the door, the man was wearing a muumuu, a stocking skullcap over his hair, and lots of eye makeup. Carmella was about to don a wig and race off to his next show. He had prepared for Randy's arrival, however, making the young vagabond a home-cooked meal of cornbread, ham, and peas. When Randy entered the house, his host said, "I want to welcome you into my house in Jesus' name. The Lord told me that he wanted me to help you get back on your feet."

As Randy ate the much-appreciated dinner, he cried and cried. So much had happened to him. He felt as if Carmella's welcome had solidified forever his identification with the gay community. Where else did he have to go? By this time, his mother had somewhat repented, presenting him with a two-page list of conditions he would need to satisfy in order to return home. He had some pride, though. He felt that only his gay friends understood and cared for him.

Yet, Carmella had spoken of Jesus. That was strange. A contrast to his mother's rant about gays' going to hell. Besides, when had she ever been interested in God? She had taught her family next to nothing about spiritual things. He knew so little about the Bible that until he was in high school, he'd thought Moses and Jesus were cousins. The family had attended church for only a few weeks when his mother and his stepfather first married and wanted Jimmy and him to be baptized. Not that they believed baptism was all that significant; it was just his parents' way of trying to be respectable.

It was funny, though. Randy understood almost nothing about the significance of baptism, but he'd never forgotten how he felt when he came up out of that water. He felt lighter and happier than he ever had before in his life, and somehow he knew that God was pleased. But that was a long time ago, and he was only a little kid then.

As Randy ate the food Carmella had prepared, he realized that the only baptism he was looking forward to at that moment was his first shower in three weeks. He knew he stunk.

Randy's stay at the transvestite's house did not last long. His drug-fueled party life produced chaos for everyone around him. He repaid

Carmella's kindness with behavior so bad that he left the condo ashamed of himself.

At that point Randy took off for Long Island, where his biological father was living. Randy had not seen his father since the fifth grade, when his dad, who had been an infrequent presence throughout his childhood years, deserted the family for good.

Randy had two dominant memories of his father. When Randy was five years old, his mother and dad were arguing one night. They shut him in his baby brother's room, away from their fighting. He stood by Jimmy's crib and listened to his parents' screaming. Their voices kept rising. Then he heard a shattering, almost musical crash against the closed door. After another screaming exchange, Randy heard a ripping sound and then a final clunking *thunk*.

Cautiously, Randy opened the door and found his favorite three-legged red stool scattered in pieces at his feet. That was what had hit the door. The other sound must have come from his father's striking his mother. She was crumpled in the middle of the floor, with her head in her hands, moaning and crying. Randy went over to her. "Daddy's a bad man," he told his mother. "Don't worry. I'll take care of you."

Randy's other memory of his dad came from the last time he'd seen his father. He was ten years old, and his mother and the man who would soon become his stepdad were already living together. His father was supposed to take care of Randy and Jimmy at least once a month. What his father actually did was pick up the boys and drop them at Randy's grandmother's house. Most often, Jimmy and Randy wouldn't see their dad until it was time for him to take them back to their mom's house. When their dad did show up, he most often was high on drugs and alcohol—not in the mood to play.

The last Sunday night Randy's father had taken the boys home, Randy told his mom how the weekend had gone. This prompted a fight between his mom and dad, and then between his dad and his soon-to-be stepdad. Once the three adults exhausted their quarreling, Randy's father left. As Randy stood at the screen door, watching him drive away, his dad rolled down the car window and growled, "I'll call you tomorrow." Randy didn't hear from his dad again—not until Randy reached manhood himself.

When Randy arrived at his dad's place, things didn't go well.

Using "rage therapy" techniques, his father tried to provoke Randy to express his anger in one boozy confrontation after another. Randy took off to avoid killing his dad.

Randy landed back in Tennessee and rented a couch in a home occupied by four other homosexual men. For eighteen months, Randy had only the couch and the front hall closet to himself.

In the midst of Randy's careening life, a former coworker, Bruce, invited him to a home Bible study. Randy thought Bruce was handsome—handsome enough for him to endure an hour of piety for the sake of a possible score. At the time Randy sported a hoop earring and wore his streaked-blond hair spiky in the front and long against his neck. He anticipated the study members' dirty looks, which would only underscore his belief that all Christians were hypocrites.

As it happened, the Bible study participants took his flamboyant looks in stride and immediately made him part of the group. Much to his surprise, they handed the Bible to him and asked him to take a turn reading verses from a long chapter. At the end of the night, when a woman led the final prayer, she addressed God as "Abba." Randy had never heard this term before. The only "Abba" he knew was the seventies rock group from Sweden. After the study he asked the woman about the name, and she explained that *Abba* was an Aramaic word for "father," the form of address Jesus used in teaching his disciples the Lord's Prayer. She said that the English equivalent to the word *Abba* was "Daddy." Randy had never before thought of God with such affection.

Randy attended this Bible study sporadically while continuing the cycle of waiting tables and partying. He closely observed the married couples at the Bible study. Previously, he had known very few people who had successful marriages, certainly no one within his immediate family. He saw that the Bible study couples were more well-rounded, more outwardly directed than the gay couples he knew. Their prayers addressed the lives of their children, what was happening at work, the charitable organizations in which they were interested.

Randy saw in these couples a contentment he had never seen before—one that was in glaring contrast to the desperation that characterized the lives of gay couples. His gay friends were always fearful and pensive, and their whole identity was wrapped up in their homosexuality. Gay couples involved in long-term relationships were still on the hunt for the next high, whether that meant alcohol and drugs or affairs or finding ways to idealize their relationship. The restlessness and isolation and fits of boredom that were part of the gay lifestyle never went away. The sexual encounters that allayed these feelings for a time only increased them in the long run. Randy's gay friends were like people who were trying to slake a thirst by drinking salt water.

The married couples at the Bible study completed one another in a way gay couples did not. By observing the heterosexual couples, Randy started down a path that eventually led to a number of surprising revelations. He came to believe that for a man to be fully a man—or a woman fully a woman—he or she must experience the ways in which the other sex is different. This doesn't necessarily involve sexual relations; it can happen in normal friendships.

Randy came to see that homosexual men are attracted to other men because they do not feel masculine enough. They see other men—rather than women—as essentially different from themselves, as "the other"—which is an illusion, and a powerful one. They look to other men to complete what they lack in themselves. While being attracted to the masculine in others, they fear it at the same time. This produces an ambivalence that tends to make homosexual partners hypercritical and deeply suspicious of each another.

In heterosexual relationships the differences between the sexes draw out the distinctiveness of each sex. Heterosexual relationships also balance the distinctive traits of each with complementary characteristics. The complement of male and female initiates a husband and wife into the true drama of sex: the creation of another human being. Every child is meant to be the literal incarnation of a husband's and wife's love.

Randy heard one of his friends remark that the birth of his children taught him what sex is truly all about. The curve of his wife's hip, his muscled shoulders that drew his wife's hands, the pleasures they found in one another's touch—these were nothing but costuming and scenery and lighting, the spectacle that accompanied the drama. The plot that gave the drama its essential meaning was the conception and birth of a child. Having a child together revealed the true creative power of sex, its profound mystery. Randy's friends' children directed the couple away from their own selfish desires and virtually forced them to concentrate on selfless giving—the key, as we have seen, to living the good life and creating a viable culture.

Randy realized that same-sex relationships can never fully realize this outward direction of affection; homosexuality does not lead either partner to love someone whose gender brings with it essential differences, someone who is truly "other" than himself or herself. Homosexuality does not naturally direct couples' affection toward their children, since this is a biological impossibility. Homosexual couples' desire to adopt children is a testimony to the simple human need to be outwardly directed. They know that part of their humanity can be satisfied only by experiences that their sexual orientation naturally precludes.

In many ways, those who suffer from same-sex attraction find their sexuality leads to an obsession with self. For example, homosexual couples often celebrate how they look, emphasizing everything visual, from fashion to haircuts to body sculpting. Because the visual never leads to the profundities of procreation, however, the visual becomes an end in itself, which makes homosexuals more attentive to the self. As homosexuals grow older, many become desperate to regain their youth symbolically through affairs with young men. Others find they cannot cope with their own idealized self-images. The sexual go-round wears itself out, and they suffer from depression, loneliness, and despair.

———•◦•———

In sum, the disordered nature of homosexuality feeds pride, and pride eventually renders its victims incapable of living with themselves. Many of these realizations came to Randy much later, of course, but when he compared the lives of the Bible study couples with those of his gay friends, he could see the truth: His life violated the natural order and left him in despair. One night after the Bible study, he prayed, simply, "Abba, help me."

Soon afterward, one of his aunts heard about the way he was living and sent him a Greyhound bus ticket to Dallas. Randy had job prospects at a telemarketing call center there, and the bus ticket was his aunt's way of encouraging him to start anew. Unfortunately, Dallas had an even more powerful, varied, and attractive gay community than

Nashville, and the drugs were better in quality and more plentiful. Randy's very life was soon in jeopardy.

On New Year's Day of 1992, Randy found himself alone in the first apartment he had ever been able to rent. He had gotten himself smashed the previous night on alcohol and a variety of drugs, burning through every cent he had, including the next month's rent. After going into the bathroom and getting sick, he looked at himself in the mirror. His hair was matted to his face, and his skin looked colorless, ashen. In his mind, he heard a voice that said, "This is what you'll look like when you die." Randy's heart began thumping wildly with fear. He collapsed on the ground and started screaming, "Why? Why? *Why?*" Eventually, he blacked out.

Through the invitation of a friend, Randy began attending a twelve-step meeting. At first he didn't think he was an addict, but after hearing people's stories in the meeting, which were so much like his own, he knew that he was. He began to "work the program," as twelve-steppers say, admitting he was powerless over drugs and alcohol, and making an inventory of all the people he had hurt and all the damage he had done during his years as a user. The third step of the program involved finding one's higher power. Anything could be one's higher power, people in the program would say. The clock on the wall can be your higher power. Just start praying and reaching out for guidance.

One day Randy was driving home from work on a central Dallas parkway when he saw the sun uncover from towering peaks of silver cloud, its rays splaying out. His heart filled with an unexpected joy. The witness of creation led him to accept the reality of God's presence in his life. He discovered the real Higher Power, and he began weeping with gratitude to the God who had made him. He chose to believe that God loved him, had a purpose for him, and wanted to direct him into a new life.

Over the next year, Randy became clean and sober. As he began acting on the truth he knew, his reason and imagination began grasping ever-greater realities. "Seek and you will find" is the way the good life works. Eventually, through the witness of friends who assured him that God would accept him just as he was, Randy became a Christian.

Soon he realized that the disordered nature of homosexuality is not what God intended. Randy was free enough in his thinking to see that God does not condemn homosexuals; God only points out that homosexual acts are contrary to His plan. When Randy saw this, he ceased to identify himself as a gay man.

Randy entered into counseling and began a course of what's called "reparative therapy"—a path toward reorienting his sexuality.[3] As part of his therapy, he developed nonsexual friendships with men. He did fitness workouts to feel more comfortable in his own skin, to claim his inherent masculinity. These measures helped him not only to see himself as a man among men but also to see women as the other sex. He cut the apron strings of the matriarchal household in which he grew up and claimed his rightful place as an adult man.

Three years after seeking a new way of being, Randy was watching television when a beautiful young woman danced across the screen. He looked at her more closely—the way her hair whipped about as she danced, her curvaceous body, the smallness of her waist. He found himself swallowing hard.

*So that's it!* he thought, shocked and delighted. He had a new accountability issue—heterosexuality!

Randy Thomas's sexual reorientation happened about nine years ago. As with any recovery from a deeply ingrained disorder, Randy still experiences an occasional troubling moment of same-sex attraction. His main concern with relationships these days, however, is finding a woman to love and marry. He's looking forward to being a father. Randy likes being "one of the guys," feeling normal. In his daily life he experiences a freedom that he thought he'd never know. The transformation has even extended to other relationships. Randy has experienced substantial healing with his mom and stepdad.

Talking with Randy makes it clear why those who suffer from same-sex attraction, whether men or women, find judgments of their condition as disordered so threatening. They have often been the victims of childhood abuse and maddeningly dysfunctional families, as well as the object of scorn by their childhood peers. The gay life holds the promise of the approval, affection, and attention that they never received as children. It seems to provide an identity they have lacked all their lives and a community whose solidarity is forged through pleasure. Anyone would be threatened by having all this taken away.

Those who recruited Randy into the gay bar scene asked, "Are you family?" Think about that for a moment. What a poignant and disturbing and ironic question. "Are you family?" The question witnesses to the desire for the created order even in the midst of the shadowland of homosexuality.

Most straight people, not understanding homosexuality very well, do not want to impose burdens that are too difficult to bear. They know how much their own sexual lives mean to them, and they are wary of taking stands that would seem to condemn people to lifelong chastity. So our culture now talks about homosexuality as a "lifestyle"—one among several equally acceptable options—rather than a violation of the created order.

This is an understandable response, but ultimately it's the response of pity, not true compassion. True compassion wants to give middle school students a booklet that explains the true genesis of feelings of attraction to the opposite sex. True compassion wants to keep husbands from beating up their wives and leaving them to the psychological care of a five-year-old like Randy Thomas. True compassion wants to show women their true identity as God's deeply loved children so that they don't fail to protect their children from the violence of abusive husbands. True compassion wants to uphold loving heterosexual families and the self-sacrificing love that sustains them. True compassion embraces the truth of the created order, just as Randy Thomas did when he looked at the married couples in his Bible study and realized his life violated the natural order. Pity toward homosexuality will only further institutionalize the emotional slavery that caught up Randy Thomas.

In addition to the move toward legalizing homosexual marriage, we are now seeing what's called "positive therapy" introduced nationwide in high schools. This teaches young people with same-sex attraction to embrace the gay life. In all these ways, we are enslaving young people for the sake of maintaining the gay lobby's false view of same-sex attraction. Young people are easily attracted to this big lie, falling for the placards "Sexual identity is a personal choice!" and "Homosexuality is natural!"

Ultimately, the compromises that pity wants to make won't work because pity does not search to the depths of the truth. Pity always turns cruel and then repressive. Today's political correctness demands that the media systematically ignore people like Randy Thomas and an entire movement—including organizations like Exodus International and the National Association for Research and Therapy of Homosexuality (NARTH)—devoted to helping men and women recover from same-sex attraction.[4] The culture has committed itself to a destructive illusion —to living a lie. As Havel taught us, we cannot live a lie and live the good life.

———•••———

Christians believe that the world works the way it does because God designed it that way. Not entirely as we know it now, but in its perfection, before evil afflicted creation, causing disease as well as personality disorders like same-sex attraction. (By calling same-sex attraction a "personality disorder," I do not mean to imply that free will doesn't enter into the practice of homosexuality. I believe it does, as with any sin.) God created gender, sexuality, and love. He created man for woman and woman for man. He created the state of marriage in which men and women realize the distinctiveness of their own gender while uniting in a greater, complementary humanity. What God intended is what is natural, what is beautiful.

*The good life cannot be found in living in opposition to the natural order, no matter how difficult its moral demands may be.*

Homosexuality is not what God intended, and the gay life becomes a sad and vain attempt to re-create heterosexual beauty and happiness. The good life cannot be found in living in opposition to the natural order, no matter how difficult its moral demands may be. In the end these demands are the only path to liberation—to the kind of new life Randy Thomas found.

# CHAPTER 22

# THE GIFT OF KNOWING RIGHT FROM WRONG

As RANDY THOMAS became a teenager, he found himself in a curious as well as terrifying fix. He could see the obvious—that men and women are made for each other. This biological reality was backed up by a host of cultural attitudes and religious teachings. On the other hand, he felt sexually attracted to men, and the majority of psychologists, as he found in the booklet about human sexuality, thought that was perfectly all right. He should just accept his sexual inclinations and act on them. How was he to know what to do? What was right? What was wrong?

The terrifying nature of his predicament makes it hard to focus on its curiosity—the way in which it participates in a central mystery of the human condition: how we know right from wrong. While receiving mixed messages from different sources, Randy had to decide whose version of reality he would accept. Someone had to be right, someone wrong, and his life hung in the balance. Think of Randy at thirteen years old. What should he do?

What a terrible question, but on the other hand, what a wonderful question as well. Knowing how to interpret the world and the directions it gives us—what we *should* do—makes life, comparatively speaking, a piece of cake. The truly terrifying thing is to be without direction—to be lost.

No one likes to be told what to do, of course. We don't like our mothers insisting that we "have to"; we don't appreciate preachers thundering, "Thou shalt not." *Says who?* we demand. Our rebellious natures stop short, however, when our lives are on the line and we have the sense that our destinies hang in the balance.

As Randy Thomas learned, we can know what is right and true. The created order gives us direction so that we can live rationally within the constraints of physical and biological reality. This is the liberating basis of true morality. Ethics do not derive from the haphazard commands of authority figures; morality is a matter of the sense the world makes by virtue of its design. Call it cosmic architecture, if you like. The scholar Neal Plantinga describes this recognition of the correct order of life as wisdom. It is finding out the truth about what life is, what makes the world work, and how we *ought* to live to fit into it.

In the beginning of his superb book *Not the Way It's Supposed to Be: A Breviary of Sin,* Plantinga illustrates his point with a scene from the movie *Grand Canyon.* (If you can get by the language and some offensive scenes, the movie has humorous and insightful moments.) The protagonist, an attorney (played by Kevin Kline), in his eagerness to get home after a basketball game, leaves the traffic jam of the highways and attempts the side roads. Quickly he realizes he's lost, and he soon discovers he's driven his luxury Lexus into one of the most desperate areas of the city. Then the nightmare begins. His car stalls.

The attorney phones for help, but before it arrives, a group of young, especially mean-looking kids surround his car and begin to threaten him. The attorney looks helpless, trapped in the car.

Then, like the cavalry coming over the hill in an old Western, a tow truck arrives. Its driver (played by Danny Glover) steps out to hook up the car. The teenagers protest. The truck driver is spoiling their sadistic fun.

The driver takes the leader of the group aside and announces firmly, "Man, the world ain't *supposed* to work like this. Maybe you don't know that, but this ain't the way it's supposed to be. I'm supposed to be able to do my job without askin' you if I can. And that dude"—referring to the lawyer—"is supposed to be able to wait with his car without you rippin' him off. Everything's supposed to be different than what it is here."[1]

Plantinga describes the tow-truck driver as "an heir of St. Augustine," whose analysis of "the way it's supposed to be but isn't" belongs in every book of theology.[2] In the Christian understanding, the world is designed a certain way, which imparts to each one of us a sense of the way things *ought* to be; but the Christian faith also teaches that the world isn't as it's supposed to be because of the impact of sin.

The great modern philosopher Etienne Gilson argues that this ability to know how the world works and how we should fit into it—that is, our capacity to make responsible choices, cooperating with the natural order—is what sets humans apart from other animals. Morality, Gilson argues, is "essentially normality; for a rational being to act and behave either without reason or contrary to its dictates is to act and behave, not exactly as a beast; but as a beastly man, which is worse."[3]

No one in modern times has more clearly articulated the case for our ability to know the natural moral order than C. S. Lewis. Just as all bodies are governed by the law of gravity and all organisms are governed by biological laws, Lewis wrote, so too we humans are governed by law—the moral law. The only difference, he notes, is that the individual has the right to obey or not to obey. Which is, of course, the very point the tow-truck driver made. According to Lewis, "People know the law of nature; they break it. These two facts are the foundation of all clear thinking about ourselves and the universe we live in."[4]

Lewis contends that humans throughout history have embraced a common moral teaching, observed by the Egyptians, the Babylonians, the Hindus, the Greeks, the Romans—by every civilization we know anything about. All the laws and customs, though they have some significant differences, basically agree on what could be called major principles. "Think of a country," Lewis suggests, "where people were admired for running away in battle, or where a man felt proud of double-crossing all the people who had been kindest to him."[5]

Lewis says even children understand and know the moral order. One school child will angrily say to another child, "You took my ruler." Today the child might say, "You took my Game Boy." The other child's response is never, "That's okay. If I want to take your Game Boy, it's mine." Rather, the other child says, "I *didn't* take it."[6] Both children accept the concept that it is wrong to take another child's things.

Although Lewis wrote before the postmodern era, he foresaw what it would mean. "Some people," he argues, say the "idea of a Law of Nature or decent behavior known to all men is unsound" because different civilizations have different moralities. But, he says, "this is not true."[7]

He argues, "The [moral] law was called the Law of Nature, because people thought that everyone *knew* it by nature and did not need to be taught it."[8] The moral law is, in short, self-evident. This doesn't mean that everybody gets the moral law straight all the time, any more, as he put it, than people get their multiplication tables correct every time. But, as with multiplication tables, there is a correct answer.

I've often equated natural law with common sense. Is it common sense that if you put your hand over the fire, it will burn you? Of course. Is it also common sense that it is wrong to put someone else's hand over the fire? Of course it is.

Children get this, as Lewis observed and as I have discovered. In speaking to young people, I invariably ask them whether there is any such thing as absolute moral truth. Generally only a few students raise their hands in argreement—with hesitation.[9]

Then I use an old illustration, one that the popular philosopher Francis Schaeffer, I believe, first offered. I ask the young people what they would do if they came to a busy street corner, traffic whizzing by in both directions, and saw an elderly woman standing there, holding a shopping bag and looking bewildered. They have three choices. The first is to help the woman across the street. The second is to ignore her. The third is to push her into the traffic.

I then ask the students if they know what is right. Amidst chuckles, all the hands go up. What they're saying, of course, is that they don't know if anyone in today's world should say there is absolute moral truth—it sounds so intolerant—but they believe that pushing the bewildered woman into the traffic is an absolute wrong. It's enjoyable to watch the lightbulbs going on when the kids get it.

Adults, even convinced postmodernist activists, know this as well. The experience of my friend George Weigel, eminent theologian and historian, illustrates this. Weigel appeared on *All Things Considered,* the National Public Radio flagship issues show. The hostess was a liberal feminist, as was the other guest. When a debate arose over the question of moral truth, both women took the adamant position that there was no such thing. One of the women then hurled a challenge at Weigel. "Can you give me one example of an absolute moral truth that everyone would agree on?"

In a moment of inspiration, Weigel answered, "Yes. Rape is wrong." An awkward silence followed and the hostess changeed the subject.[10]

We often discover the moral law viscerally, through our emotions. Contemporary scholar F. H. Buckley writes that we have an innate "distaste for liars." This is not the result of rational analysis. It's intuitive. He said that often "feelings of boredom and disgust provide us with useful stopping rules that short-circuit wasteful mental calculation."[11] What he's driving at is that we are offended by what is wrong and attracted to what is right. Whether these feelings always guide us correctly is another matter.

———•·•———

The most common of human experiences indicates that we all do, indeed, know right from wrong. The apologist Greg Koukl often tells his audience that he knows an indisputable truth about them. People look around, curious. Then he simply answers, "You all feel guilt."[12] No one to this day has ever challenged him. The human conscience affirms what Professor J. Budziszewski of the University of Texas at Austin calls the "truth that can't *not* be known."[13] Conscience, the knowledge that we have done wrong, often makes us uncomfortable—as it is intended to do—because we do know better.

That's exactly what the apostle Paul meant in his letter to the young church at Rome. Referring to the Gentiles, he said the law was "written on their hearts," their consciences alternately accusing and defending them.[14] Who of us has not had our conscience accuse or defend us? Only a sociopath, I suspect.

Would we feel guilty if we did not think we had done something wrong? Graham Greene's riveting novel *The Quiet American* follows the story of a British journalist in Vietnam. The man, a thoroughgoing reprobate, deceives himself into believing in his own moral superiority because he understands the political situation better than most. The man appears to be without conscience. Near the end of the story, the journalist arranges to kill the rival for his mistress's affection. At the end of the novel the journalist finally gets everything he wants—a large salary, alcohol, drugs, and the woman he has killed for. But he is unhappy.

In the closing lines of the novel, he confesses, "I wish there existed someone to whom I could say that I was sorry."[15]

Part of the big lie in our society is that guilt gives us no true guide to behavior. Freudian mental-health professionals tell us guilt is not a good thing but a dysfunction that requires therapy. We refuse to consider guilt as a normal consequence of wrongdoing because to do so would mean we have to accept the reality of a moral law and human sin, things that are never acknowledged in polite or politically correct company these days. So, our Oprahized culture says if you feel guilty, go see Dr. Phil. But therapy can only help us clarify our dilemmas. Therapy itself supplies no lasting answers. What people more often need today is not therapy but repentance and forgiveness.

The simple truth is that you cannot live the good life without a conscience, which convicts and guides us. I've known hundreds who have tried to suppress their consciences, but I've never known one who was successful in doing so. The very attempt, the dismissal of guilt as a Freudian dysfunction, leads inevitably to a dysfunctional and wretched life marked by a continuous state of denial. This is why the existentialist Albert Camus said that the "absurd is sin without God."[16] This is the very essence of liberalism: One denies sin, denies God; life is inevitably absurd.

Wisdom, remember, is conforming to the way the world is. To go against that reality, Neal Plantinga argues, is folly. It is like cutting against the grain of the wood or spitting into the wind—absurd.[17]

One place I've most dramatically encountered the reality of guilt and the working of the conscience is in the prisons. I have met literally thousands of inmates who are deeply stricken by their guilt; they find freedom when they realize they need to confess their sin and their crime.

*You cannot live the good life without a conscience.*

One remarkable story involves a middle-aged man who was happily married and had a family. He was employed, owned his own home, and was seemingly on top of the world. After this man became a Christian, however, he could no longer live with his guilt. He flew to Kansas City and turned himself in to the district attorney, confessing a murder he had committed twenty years earlier—a murder for which he was never charged. Today that man remains in prison in Kansas, stripped of his former successful life but at peace with his conscience.

Countless times I have had hardened convicts, tattoos all over their muscular bodies, the toughest guys on the block, break down and cry like babies when they realize that their sins could be forgiven. They know they have done wrong, as all of us do.

Right and wrong are not abstract concepts. They are human reality. The knowledge of right and wrong is in us, and we know in our heart of hearts when we have failed to measure up.

—◆—

I believe this inherent sense of right and wrong is so deeply ingrained in us that even when we deny it, we behave as if it exists. We may not like our consciences to dictate to us, but we all long for the goal that conscience prods us toward—justice. I remember driving one day with a man who is a convinced skeptic, a self-confessed atheist. As we approached an intersection, a car ran a red light and headed toward us. Only because I had very good brakes was I able to avoid what would have been a serious accident. My friend started shaking his fist at the other driver, exclaiming, "You'll get your due someday. You'll get yours."

I told him that he was asserting a very problematic proposition for an atheist. If an atheist really believes that there is no God and that the universe is simply cruel, unjust, and random, he has to explain how he gets the idea of just and unjust. If there is no sense of justice or right and wrong, no standard for behavior, no universal judge in the universe, why would you expect wrongdoers to "get their due"? How would you even know they were wrongdoers? My friend was asking a God he didn't believe in to administer what only God can finally supply: justice.

Our innate sense of justice, that people will one day face judgment and get their just deserts, totally undermines the atheist's position. We have an inborn sense of abiding standards. When someone cheats or when someone takes credit for our work, we get furious, just as my friend in the car did. When I was young, I enjoyed reading a newspaper cartoon "There Oughta Be a Law." The characters in the cartoon were constantly ranting against the abuses of others, and the punch line was that there *ought* to be a law against such things.

The idea that there *ought* to be a law tells us that there is a standard that ought to be followed, and if it is not followed, somebody, in the end, is going to pay for it. Each person is going to get his or her due and be punished. That's what justice means. Every religious system in the world believes in this.

This idea of justice and judgment, of right and wrong, is ingrained in us. It's not the result of some carryover superstition from an earlier, unenlightened era. It's real to us. Talk to victims of any serious crime, and you will see people who have a passion to see that crime avenged. They want to see the scales of justice, which have been tipped against them, righted. This innate sense is what accounts for the enormous popularity of movies like *Dirty Harry, Highlander,* and the Western classic *High Noon.* We hunger to see injustice confronted and punished.

Where does this sense of justice come from? It has to be from the God who created us; it could not come out of the nothingness of a random universe.

---

Let's sum up the ground we've covered so far in this section on finding the truth in order to live the good life. Saint Augustine said, "Deep within man there dwells the truth."[18] I believe this. We *can* know the truth. We can see clear evidence of design in the universe and a natural order whose laws are inviolable. The good life is found in figuring this out and accommodating our behavior to it. The natural order thus has a moral dimension, which is objective and marks our souls. Our consciences convict us to the point that even the most determined postmodernist knows that rape is wrong.

> *The natural order has a moral dimension, which is objective and marks our souls.*

Once you accept the idea of a created order, a world with intention and design, a world that comes from a Creator, then certain things come into focus, and you discover that the natural order gives us the key ingredients of the good life. Among these are justice and the liberation of morality, as we have seen. You can rebel against receiving these gifts from the Creator, but you absolutely cannot concoct them yourself, as we shall see in the following chapters. In contrast, those who open their eyes to their Creator receive the best things in life in full measure.

# CHAPTER 23

# BEAUTY: THE SIGN
# OF GOD'S CARE

THIS IS THE story of the premieres of two of the most celebrated musical compositions of the twentieth century. One took place late in the summer of 1952, in leafy Woodstock, New York, where the softly arcing Catskill Mountains fall down to narrow valleys that are watered by trout streams. The other was performed during a bitter, wartime winter, in the border area between Germany and Poland known as Silesia. The American concert was attended mainly by professional musicians on holiday from the New York Philharmonic. The Silesian concert was attended by French and Polish soldiers captured by German forces not long after the outbreak of World War II. Both new compositions came from musicians who were, in very different ways, deep thinkers. Both pieces owed their inspiration to religious quests. Neither piece spoke directly to the time and place of its composition, yet each has come to stand as the symbol of its world.

SILESIAN PRISON CAMP, FRIDAY, JANUARY 15, 1941

The wintry Silesian concert took place at six o'clock in the evening in Barracks 27B of Stalag VIIIA. The German prison camp held between 20,000 and 30,000 prisoners, most in outpost barracks near work sites. In these far-flung barracks the prisoners were forced into labor, timbering and making bricks. Those who were housed directly within the barbed wire confines of Stalag VIIIA performed the cooking, cleaning, washing, and other domestic chores for the German administrators. The Germans loved music, and they put any captured musicians by themselves in Barracks 27B, to which they allotted a better ration of coal.

The camp was a place of extreme privation. The Germans had not expected to capture so many so quickly at the outbreak of the war. Prisoners were given no bread. They survived on one portion of watery soup per day and two distributions of grease pretending to be cheese. Even those imprisoned for a short time lost their teeth as a result of the diet. Men were shot for stealing as few as three potatoes.

Barracks 27B, the camp's "concert hall," served as a haven from the stalag's brutal monotony. Every Friday night the musicians gave classical concerts, followed by the prisoners' theatrical productions and lighter musical revues. The audience enjoyed hearing Bach and Brahms and Beethoven from four outstanding musicians: pianist Olivier Messiaen, clarinetist Henri Akoka, cellist Etienne Pasquier, and violinist Jean Le Boulaire. All had attended France's premier musical institute, the Paris Conservatoire.

Olivier Messiaen was already known as his generation's star composer. So his fellow prisoners were understandably intrigued when they heard that a new Messiaen composition—most of which he had written while in camp—would be performed at the regular Friday evening concert. It was to be a piece of chamber music called *Quartet for the End of Time*.

The music was likely to be above their heads, but Messiaen's comrades were so excited about the performance that they asked permission for prisoners in the outlying barracks to attend. Furthermore, they insisted that quarantined prisoners awaiting repatriation—the Germans were sending thousands back into France every day—also be allowed to attend.[1] The German commandant, thinking to use the concert for propaganda purposes, allowed a printed program to be created for the occasion.

The audience assembled, walking through snowdrifts from the outlying barracks under armed guard, scrambling from kitchen duties, or breaking away from the huddles that ringed the barracks' coal stoves. Muffled in the heaviest possible clothes to ward off the freezing cold, they packed Barracks 27B. The German officials were there, too, sitting in front of the makeshift stage. The captured French priests came out in force as well. From former university professors to day laborers, across class, religious, and national boundaries, the crowd assembled to hear what music Messiaen might have dreamt in the midst of their desolation.

## WOODSTOCK, NEW YORK, AUGUST 29, 1952

At the American premiere, professional musicians and others on holiday stepped into the Maverick Concert Hall for an evening benefiting the Benefit Artist Welfare Fund. The men wore their fifties-style double-pocket, short-sleeved shirts, khakis, and boat shoes; the women had their hair up in kerchiefs and wore pedal pushers, their calves bright with sunburn and lotion. The Maverick Concert Hall, a "music chapel" built by Hervey White in 1916, was a barnlike wooden structure that opened up in the back to the surrounding woods. Over its four Gothic-arched doorways rose a pointed tympanum of six painted windows. Ivory-tinted walls were ribbed with logs that arched upward along broken angles to the pine roof. This music chapel smelled of rain, sun, dust, and the resinous metals of the many percussion instruments on the stage.

The audience knew that they would be hearing mainly atonal or nonharmonic works dominated by rhythms no conventional score could accommodate. This was what the featured composers Morton Feldman, Earle Brown, and John Cage were famous for. The audience was game because they understood all the conventions that were to be broken, they thought. The press had already given these composers a lot of notice, particularly Cage. He was famous for inventing the "prepared piano"—a regular piano turned into a percussion instrument through applying mechanical restraints to the strings. Cage's prepared piano *plunked* and *tonked* and *whapped* and *ticked* unpredictably, even when the same keys were pressed. What would Cage have up his sleeve?

——————

Before the concert at Stalag VIIIA, the composer Olivier Messiaen stood in front of his barracks-busting audience of four hundred in his bottle-green prison uniform. Although his hair was beginning to recede and thin on top, it fluffed out in ringlets on the side. He wore round glasses with thick black rims his eyes focused keenly. His cheeks had lost their usual cherubic fullness, but his nose remained fleshy, his lips full, if blue from the cold. He looked the Harlequin—a disturbing clown. The minute he spoke, however, he assumed a new authority. He told his audience that his composition *Quartet for the End of Time* took its inspiration from the New Testament book of Revelation. He read aloud the relevant passage:

> And I saw another mighty angel coming down from heaven, wrapped in a cloud, with a rainbow on his head; his face was like the sun, and his legs like pillars of fire. . . . Setting his right foot on the sea and his left foot on the land . . . and, standing on the sea and the land [he] raised his right hand to heaven and swore by him who lives forever and ever . . . saying, "There will be no more Time; but in the days when the seventh angel is to blow his trumpet, the mystery of God will be fulfilled."[2]

Messiaen said his music was spiritual, that it expressed his Catholic faith. He hoped that his *Quartet for the End of Time* would bring the listener closer to the presence of eternity in their midst.[3]

The quartet's first movement, "Liturgy of Crystal," tried to capture that time between three and four o'clock in the morning, when the birds first awaken. His audience would hear a blackbird or a nightingale improvising in praise of the rising sun. "For me," Messiaen said, "the bird's call transposes the harmonious silence of heaven."[4]

With that, Messiaen sat down at the old, out-of-tune upright piano and looked to Henri Akoka, the clarinetist, who was an Algerian and, unbeknownst to the Germans, a Jew. Henri's narrow, shadowed eyes set atop a long, flaring nose gave him a badgered look. Yet he was so full of optimism, charm, and life that women thought of him as dashing. He smiled at the audience and immediately drew them in. He took up his clarinet and began to play. The blackbird sang.

What the audience heard was like nothing they had ever encountered. Messiaen's *Quartet* was structured more like a poem than conventional chamber music. There was no dominant melody. Each movement had a "signature," or typical progression of harmonizing chords. The music proceeded like a prayerful meditation, like windows opening to an eternal music that was always present and yet otherwise unheard.

The imitations of birdcalls that Messiaen used in the piece's first movement came from one of the profound and repeated experiences of his life. For the brief time he was a soldier, he arranged to have his guard duty during the hours when dark turns to dawn. He loved how the birds began calling; first one, a tentative peep in the night, then after a few more moments, another, more quickly another, until the birds' voices pooled with first light. The birds sang to herald the sun, report their plans, and agree on awaiting tasks. Then they flew away into the early morning quiet as the sun mounted higher, gaining strength. Messiaen rejoiced in how the orchestra of the world tuned up each morning.

In the second movement the angel from the Apocalypse announced the end of time with strange harmonies. The music seemed to remind the prisoners of a place they had never been and yet could not forget—perhaps heaven.

A long, dragging clarinet solo followed, suggesting what it was like to be subject to monotony—the "abyss" of time the prisoners knew so well.

Then came "Praise to the Eternity of Jesus," a complex Christmas carol. The cello announced that something great had happened, something wonderful, something close and dear—the coming of eternity into history through Jesus.

Then, cataclysmic events were at hand. There was terror—the kind one might feel in the presence of angels. That signature theme of the second movement returned. The angelic hosts were going into battle. The speed of the music increased until, like the spokes of a spinning wheel, the music seemed to stand still. The cataclysm—the end of time—was accomplished, and all four instruments joined in a closely harmonized final chord.

The last movement, indescribably beautiful, was Messiaen's praise to the immortality of Jesus. Here the violin led the other players in a poignant song. The earthly—the birdsong at morning greeting the dawn—and the heavenly—the terror-invoking angel—merged, as the Babe of the carol ascended to the Father and humanity received divinity through turning toward God. The violin climbed higher and higher into a final reconciling note.

Despite few having ever heard anything remotely like *Quartet for the End of Time,* the Barracks 27B audience kept absolutely silent through the nearly hour-long performance. When it ended, the silence continued for a moment or two before hesitant applause broke out and grew into unrestrained celebration, wild applause, and cheers. The Poles, the French, the Germans, enemies and friends alike, made that cold barracks shake the chill off with their fervent approval. The word most frequently mentioned in reference to the performance is *miraculous*.

The depth of the audience's reaction might be judged by its aftershocks years later. When Aleksander Lyczewski, one of the Polish prisoners in attendance, heard the music played unexpectedly years later at a friend's house, he began to weep. It took some time for him to regain his composure. He explained to his host, the British musicologist Charles Bodman Rae, that he had been present at the *Quartet's* premiere—its miraculous birth.

After reading numerous accounts of the event, I like to imagine the conversations that must have ensued among the prisoners. Imagine three Frenchmen, their teeth already rotting, being marched under guard back to their outlying barracks that night.

"So that was all very well done," Jean says, "but what was it?"

"Didn't you read the notes about the Scripture? The use of birdsong?" says Gilbert.

"I couldn't tell what was what with all that squiggling on the clarinet," Jean says. "What about you, Emile? You had your eyes closed. Were you praying?"

Emile says nothing at first.

"Transported to heaven with the angel, were you?"

Emile gives Jean a sidelong glance. "I haven't been able to pray. Who can pray in a place like this? I was thinking."

"What about?" Gilbert asks.

"At the end there, I was thinking about waking up beside my wife on a Sunday morning. The sun coming through the window. Being warm. Being with her."

"That would be heaven, or pretty close," Jean says.

"For myself," Gilbert says, "it made me feel free. It was like an act of revenge against our captivity."[5]

"Yes," Jean says, "at moments, I have to admit, I caught myself believing in a better world."

Messiaen profoundly influenced the worldview of the cellist, Etienne Pasquier. He ceased to be an avowed agnostic and opened his mind to

God. He wrote the following dedication to the composer on the back of his copy of the program notes: "The camp at Gorlitz . . . Barracks 27B, our theater. . . . Outside, night, snow, misery. . . . Here, a miracle. . . . The quartet 'for the end of time' transports us to a wonderful Paradise, lifts us from this abominable earth. Thank you immensely, dear Olivier Messiaen, poet of Eternal Purity."[6]

———•·•———

In Woodstock, the program notes announced the premiere of John Cage's *4'33"* (four minutes thirty-three seconds) after the works of Brown and Feldman. When the time arrived, a young pianist, David Tudor, took his place at the Maverick's grand piano. Critics said that Tudor was so adept at playing the difficult scores of experimental composers that he could play the raisins in a fruitcake. As Tudor prepared to begin, John Cage's mother whispered to her friend that what was to follow could be thought of as being "like a prayer."[7]

For the first movement, Tudor opened the lid on the keyboard and waited with his hands poised above the keys. He waited for the exact period of time called for by the score. Then, without ever having struck a key, he closed the piano's lid on the first movement. He waited a moment. For the second movement he opened the lid once more. Then again, after the specified period, he closed it, never having played a note. The third movement saw the same opening, the same closing, and silence throughout. The performance had taken exactly four minutes and thirty-three seconds—the inspiration for the title.

At the end of the concert, the featured composers, Earle Brown, Morton Feldman, and John Cage, went onstage to take the audience's questions. Cage's *4'33"* made a lot of the professional musicians and others in the audience angry. "There was a lot of discussion," Earle Brown recalled. "A lot of uproar. . . . It infuriated most of the audience." Another attendee, Peter Yates, remarked, "The audience had come prepared to be shocked but not to be dismayed."[8]

From all I have read of the incident, the question-and-answer session with Cage must have gone something like this.

"What was that, Cage? That four-minute-thirty-three-second thing? Was that supposed to be some kind of a joke?"

"Not at all."

"But the pianist didn't play anything. Silence isn't music!"

"Was it silent?" Cage asked.

"It's not even pianissimo if the player never touches the keys!"

"What did you hear?"

"Nothing!"

"That's not what I heard," Cage might have said, becoming bold. "What I heard was the sound of the wind in the trees in the first movement. The delightful rain on the roof in the second. And for the finale, some very interesting muttering among the crowd."

"Those are sounds, Cage, not music."

"Is there a difference?"

---

Born in 1912, John Cage was the son of an inventor with a background in electrical engineering. A gifted child, Cage began playing the piano at the age of nine and immediately began studying the original, classical scores in the Los Angeles Public Library's collection. His early ambition had been to follow his grandfather into the Methodist Episcopal Church ministry, but he abandoned this goal soon after reaching Pomona College at age sixteen.

After two years of college, Cage left formal studies and spent a year in France, where he studied painting, architecture, and music, taking piano lessons with Lazare Levy, the leading teacher at the Paris Conservatoire.

Back in Los Angeles in 1931, living at his parents' home in Pacific Palisades, Cage tried to support himself by giving lectures on writing, painting, and composing. When the time came for him to lecture on twentieth-century composers, he realized he knew nothing about one of its masters, Arnold Schoenberg. So he found a Schoenberg expert, Richard Buhlig, and asked him to explain Schoenberg to him. After Buhlig gave him lessons in composition, Cage resolved to devote his life to music.

In 1934, Cage studied with Schoenberg himself, and in the process Cage confronted his great musical disability—he had no feeling for harmony. For that reason Schoenberg was less than encouraging to his devoted pupil. He did understand the young man's gifts, however. Later, he told the critic Peter Yates that Cage was "not a composer, but an inventor—of genius."[9]

Because Cage had no feel for harmonics, he turned to composing percussion music. He made up his own instruments out of things such as automobile brake drums and hubcaps. His "prepared piano" followed in 1938. Cage's early pieces were all about dismantling the distinction between the music of instruments and the sounds of everyday life.

The breakup of Cage's marriage motivated a religious search. He began attending lectures by D. T. Suzuki, one of the outstanding spokesmen for Zen Buddhism. Cage soon became convinced that the goal of music is to prompt audiences to reconcile themselves to life just as it is. He took inspiration from the Indian philosopher Ananda Coomaraswamy's statement that art should "imitate nature *in her manner of operation.*"[10] Cage's music had to forsake self-expression—which he wasn't good at, anyway—and cause people "to wake up to the very life" they were living. Cage believed that the artist was to imitate nature in what he believed to be its random character.

From that time on, Cage's activity involved inventing ways to defeat anything he might bring to composing—any thoughts, any feelings, anything. As critic Calvin Tomkins, music and religion editor for *Newsweek,* writes, "All of his efforts are directed to the difficult process of getting rid of his own tastes, imagination, memory, and ideas, so that he will then be able to 'let sounds be sounds.'"[11] The sculptor Richard Lippold similarly noted, "John has the most brilliant intellect of any man I've ever met, and for years he's been trying to do away with it. Once he said to me, 'Richard, you have a beautiful mind, but it's time you threw it away.'"[12]

Cage thought he had found the perfect method for accomplishing his purposes when he discovered the *I Ching*—the ancient Chinese "book of changes." Throwing yarrow sticks according to the *I Ching's* charts and hexagrams seemingly provided a method of composing without being in control of the result. Cage's *Music of Changes* and other such chance compositions followed.[13]

Cage found that composing music in imitation of what he conceived of as nature's random manner was a greater problem than he had imagined. He could find no way to do it, in fact, except not to compose at all, which led, of course, to *4'33"*—to silence. In *4'33"* the music became whatever background noises occurred.

As music, Cage's work is worthless. As philosophic invention, it's interesting, if profoundly wrong. It is the sudden gesture of a Zen master ("What is the sound of one hand clapping?") meant to teach the disciple Zen's point of view. Cage's adopted view of life, Zen Buddhism, is an invitation to reconcile ourselves to the world just as it is—to discard our habits of hoping and wishing, to give up our illusion of freedom and our desire for justice. It is an attempt to perceive the world as entirely alien to the longings of the human heart. Cage became, in his own words, like a "fundamentalist Protestant preacher" in proclaiming these Buddhist teachings.[14]

The question is, Are the longings of the heart mere illusions? Are the constructs of the imagination and the use of reason illusions as well? Must we reconcile ourselves to a random world?

Psychoanalyst Adam Phillips tells the following story about Cage. The musician attended the concert of another composer, who said in the program notes that he hoped his music would diminish the suffering in the world. Afterward, Cage told his friend that he loved the music but hated the notes. He didn't think there was too much suffering in the world. He believed there was just the "right amount."[15]

However much Cage's remarks may sound cruel and insensitive, they are consistent with Cage's Buddhist and postmodernist position. If the world comes out of and returns to an inexplicable chaos, then there is not too much or too little suffering: Suffering simply *is*.

Imagine, though, if Cage were to have said this to the prisoners of war in Stalag VIIIA. Was there the "right amount" of suffering in Messiaen's Stalag?

What made Messiaen's work so different from Cage's? Olivier Messiaen claimed that he had practically been born a Christian believer. From the time he was a young boy, his mother, a poet, and his father, a teacher of English and a translator of Shakespeare, read him the fairy tales of Hans Christian Andersen and the plays of Shakespeare. Gradually Messiaen began to find how the hopes and dreams that all fairy tales express—their longing for justice and freedom—were taken up and made real by faith. While Shakespeare offered him "super fairy tales," Messiaen found Christianity far more mysterious and wonderful.[16] Later in his life, he told interviewers that he found one simple difference between the stories he loved as a child and the Christian faith: Christianity is true.

Messiaen said, "The first idea that I wanted to express . . . is the existence of the truths of the Catholic faith. . . . That is the first aspect of my work, the most noble, doubtless the most useful, the most valuable, the only one, perhaps, that I will not regret at the hour of my death."[17]

We can see in *Quartet for the End of Time* so many of the themes that we've discovered in our own search for truth. The first is the presence of the natural order. The blackbird that sings in Messiaen's music and the sun that rises are intimately connected—in tune, one might say—with one another. It's nature's design that produces a universe in which the lives of small creatures are made possible by the astronomical relationship of the earth to the sun. Behind this natural order lies God Himself, who does not dwell in time but is time's master. The eternal and time ultimately meet in God's "emptying of Himself" to come among us as a child—the man who dies to live again.

What Messiaen captures so wonderfully is the interdependence of time and eternity, which is the secret of beauty—for beauty is God's glory shining in creation. Can we not see and experience this?

———•◦•———

I've told the stories of these two world premieres, Messiaen's *Quartet for the End of Time* and Cage's *4'33"*, because they so perfectly reflect the opposing belief systems of the world we live in today. For Cage, enlightenment consists in reconciling ourselves to a random universe. In stark contrast, Olivier Messiaen's music reflects a profound understanding of the natural order and how this order ultimately derives from its Creator. He embraced the world's beauty. Even in a Nazi prison camp, he could see how God's glory shines in creation.

Very few people today understand beauty as an extension of the creation. Many people say that "beauty is in the eye of the beholder" or "beauty is a matter of taste." To declare something is beautiful means only that it pleases them. Such value judgments are always merely one person's opinion.

To the Christian and the classical mind, however, beauty is not a subjective value judgment, and art is not merely the expression of an artist's inner world. Beauty, like goodness and truth, is part of reality; beauty is essential to the created order, part and parcel of the world in which we live.

The reason one person judges one thing to be beautiful while another disagrees is that different people are more or less able to perceive beauty. Some people's judgments about beauty are more accurate. This may be an idea that many people in our culture find intolerable; nevertheless, it's true.

*Beauty is not a subjective value judgment.*

The Christian view of beauty has its basis in its theory of origins—how the world came to be. God made a world that reflects His identity, not only His unimaginable genius but also His majesty—His beauty. The ancient Greeks understood from the order and beauty of creation alone that truth, beauty, and goodness were interconnected absolutely. This understanding was captured powerfully by theologian Hans Urs von Balthasar: "Beauty demands for itself at least as much courage and decision as do truth and goodness, and she will not allow herself to be separated . . . from her two sisters."[18]

*God made a world that reflects His identity, not only His unimaginable genius but also His majesty—His beauty.*

The beauty of the world communicates God's love for us. He designed a universe in which the sun's rising and setting, the pale moon hanging in the sky, and the power of rushing clouds would inspire us each day. He made a world in which we can delight in a field of daffodils, be haunted by a loon's call, and find amazement in the chameleon's powers of camouflage. In his poem "The Tiger," poet William Blake recognized God's hand behind the beauty of His creation:

> Tiger! Tiger! burning bright,
> In the forest of the night
> What immortal hand or eye
> Could frame thy fearful symmetry?[19]

God's ways are far beyond ours, yet the beauty of His creation shows us His love.[20]

Because Olivier Messiaen believed that beauty is a sign of God's care, he paid tribute in his music to a loving Creator. Messiaen's audience was far less tutored than Cage's in musical theory, and yet Messiaen's music communicated to his fellow prisoners that the world was ultimately God's, not the Nazis', and that every human hope has a legitimate basis in God's rule. He wasn't selling cheap comfort or "expressing himself." Who among his fellow prisoners could possibly have cared about that? He was translating truth that they needed to hear—truth essential to the good life—into music.

———•—•———

All of us intuitively understand the connection between beauty and truth. Ask teenagers and even younger children whether they can tell the difference between good art and bad art. Most groups, as I noted before, are not sure whether they believe in absolute truths. Often I'll ask them to imagine a painting that catches their eye, that they can't stop looking at—perhaps J. M. W. Turner's famous marine painting showing a sailboat, keeling under the wind, plowing through the seas. It's so lifelike that you can almost feel the boat's driving motion. The colors are at once watery yet startling.

I ask my young audience, "If you saw a painting like that, wouldn't you say it's cool?" They all nod approvingly.

I then ask them, "If you went to Germany today and saw an exhibit of body parts, a huge mural on a wall with pieces of flesh hanging from it, would you say that's cool?"

Most of them instantly look revolted. I confirm what they are thinking: "No, you would say it's yuck, right?" They all nod.

> *The beauty of the world communicates God's love for us.*

They get it. There is a difference between cool and yuck. And there are absolutes.

Something in us resonates with beauty. It inspires us. It lifts us, exactly as Messiaen's music lifted the prisoners of war in Stalag VIIIA during World War II.

The arts are so powerful because they communicate directly to our emotions as well as our intellect—to the heart and its superior reasons.

The students I've talked with would immediately understand the difference between Cage and Messiaen—Cage, the emperor without clothes, and Messiaen, the maestro of creation, whose work captures a history of time from the perspective of eternity.

While the arts capture our thoughts and penetrate our imaginations, they awaken us to the world's wonder and touch our emotions. At their best, the arts reflect the truth of the human experience in its heartfelt wholeness.

The arts point to what lies beyond the merely human because the source of beauty, I believe, is beyond the merely human, as we shall see in the next chapter.

# CHAPTER 24

# WRITTEN ON THE HEART

MY PATERNAL GRANDFATHER, son of Swedish immigrants, was orphaned as a young child and raised in a Boston orphanage. Astonishingly, he taught himself to play musical instruments, and as an adult he became a renowned musician—cornet soloist for the Boston Symphony Orchestra. Unfortunately for both my father and me, we missed out when those musical genes were passed on. I don't even sing in church for fear of throwing others off-key.

If you are similarly musically challenged, you might wonder why I've included all this discussion of Messiaen and Cage. This is a book about seeking truth and discovering the good life, after all. Doesn't this discussion about highbrow music take us off track?

The arts aren't merely a diversion, though—that's the very point I'm making. The arts confront us with the truth and make it real, in a heartfelt way.

In fact, our appreciation of beauty is very much a part of what makes us human. No archaeologist has discovered an animal's cave that has primitive stick drawings of ancient humans. Animals simply don't have this capacity. Only humans continuously strive to express beauty in varying forms and ways. Although animals and insects may create beauty, as in the case of Nien Cheng's spider, they do not *intend* to do so.

The human person alone both creates and reflects on the significance of creating. This is true not only of artists. Almost every type of work imaginable involves an element of creativity, whether what we create is a service—like selling insurance or fixing computers—or whether we build houses or cars or design business systems. As discussed earlier, a great deal of the satisfaction of work comes from using our imagination, invention, and skill to do our work well. Through the exercise of our own creativity and witnessing the creativity of others, we come to appreciate God's creativity and care in making our beautiful world. We begin to suspect what the Bible declares, that we human beings are made in God's image, that our own powers of reason and imagination and the ability to love selflessly have been conferred on us by a God who possesses these attributes in their complete and absolute perfection. God, the Creator, made us to be creators as well.

Because creativity and the arts spring from our essential humanity and from how that humanity reflects who God is, the arts have an incredible power to awaken us to life's greatest questions and the answers to these questions lodged within us. When we reflect on the creativity of humans or the great Designer, we are moved powerfully in the very core of our being.

When I need inspiration, I sometimes take a walk on a beach near my neighborhood in Naples, Florida. I've always been moved by the majesty of the oceans. The nearby Gulf of Mexico, year-round, storm or no storm, is an absolutely beautiful sight. It is particularly striking during the summer. As the sun sets over the gulf in the west, pink, gray, and blue hues color the puffy cumulus clouds floating by. Even on days when I am burdened, I experience awe and wonder and gain perspective from my walks; the problems always seem less daunting. Standing on the beach, I identify with the feeling of the Scottish mountaineer W. H. Murray, who described his unspeakable joy at witnessing a great mountain peak as one of those "fleeting glimpses of that beauty which all men who have known it have been compelled to call truth."[1]

> *God, the Creator, made us to be creators as well.*

The great philosopher Jacques Maritain described beauty as metaphysical "bait."[2] Beauty leads us to reflect on its source. Where did it come from? Why does the sight of the oceans move us? Why does it make us *long* for something beyond our own experience, for something . . . something *more* than what we know in this life alone? The writer and scholar C. S. Lewis said that if we feel a desire for something that no experience in this world can satisfy, the most probable explanation is that we were made for another world.

We are spurred by the beauty of the world to ask whether the "immortal hand or eye" that made the tiger made us as well. We wonder whether this Creator has a purpose for us in this life—and even beyond this life. The beauty of God's design speaks of promise. Such wonderings may seem strange to some, but any survey of history and literature tells us that these questions are universal. This is why we cannot go through life without divine restlessness, as Emmanuel Mournier called it. In commenting on Mournier's perspective, Lorenzo Albacete wrote, "Indeed, what makes our lives truly human is the ceaseless questioning before Mystery, before 'something greater,' whether we are three or ninety years old. This questioning allows us to see even every-day sights with the same amazement and wonder we felt the first time we saw them and to keep our hearts awake to the world around us."[3]

Blaise Pascal, the French mathematician and philosopher, said, "The heart has reasons reason knows not."[4] He meant that the wholeness of our humanity possesses the power to grasp truths far beyond what reason alone can understand. Our humanity includes our emotions as well as our intellect, our intuition and imagination as well as our powers of calculation.

With all I've said against basing our lives on emotions, I don't mean to say that our emotions are not an important guide to truth. If we make pleasant emotions the be-all and end-all, they will, of course, mislead us; but if we reflect carefully on our intuitive reactions, we sometimes find that we know much more than we can reason out.

Our very wonderings about the source of all things, including beauty, increase the probability that there is indeed something greater—that is, God. Nothing else could account for that wonder.

In the eleventh century, Bishop Anselm of Canterbury expressed it this way in a prayer: "O Lord, you are not only that than which none greater can be conceived, but you are greater than all that can be conceived. . . . If you were not such, something greater than you could be thought, but this is impossible."[5]

At first this sounds like circular reasoning, only proving the necessity that such an idea exists. But Jonathan Edwards, the colonial theologian, looked at the other side: Nothingness, he said, is "what sleeping rocks dream of."[6] Because we cannot conceive of our own nonexistence, we can be certain both of our existence and of that Being who is greater than all that can be conceived. This is called the *ontological argument,* and the more you think about it, the more you'll appreciate its wisdom.

---

I discovered this at a point in my life when I was distinctly irreligious, at best a Christian in name only. I was on a lake in New Hampshire where I had taken a fourteen-foot Day Sailer to teach my two sons to sail. On one of our ventures across the lake, Christian, who was then ten, grabbed the sheet and was so excited over actually being able to sail the boat that his eyes sparkled. I was in the stern holding the tiller. I saw in my son's expression the joy of a new discovery as he felt the wind's power in his hands. In that unguarded moment, I found myself saying, "Thank you, God, for giving me this son—for giving us this one wonderful moment." I went on to tell God that if I were to die tomorrow, I would feel my life had been fulfilled.

When I realized what I had done, I was startled. I had no intention of trying to talk to God, whoever He was—if He did exist and was even knowable. I was certainly not intellectually convinced that God existed. But I had to admit that I was simply overcome with gratitude for that unforgettably rich experience with my son Chris, and I needed to thank someone—God.

At one level, it seemed, I couldn't conceive of His not existing. But I shook this experience off. I reasoned that I had been under a lot of stress in my life. Strange things happen.

What moved me that day to talk to God was an overwhelming sense of gratitude for that incredibly joyous experience. Gratitude, I have discovered, is built into every one of us, as much a universal human characteristic as guilt. When you wake up in the morning, lift the window, feel the fresh spring breezes, and see the sun rising in the east, aren't you filled with gratitude? I am grateful every day that I'm alive, grateful that I have a wonderful family, grateful that I have a purpose in life. Can you imagine believing that you didn't? If there's nothing out there except a great vacuum, why should you feel grateful for anything?

I have a friend who had been talking to one of his business colleagues about his Christian faith. The colleague, a top executive in a multinational corporation, was extremely well read, with deep interests in economics and philosophy. My friend was trying to explain his belief in the existence of God and was probing his colleague on what he thought about life. His colleague volunteered that he felt a deep sense of gratitude about life. When my friend asked him whom he thanked, he was taken aback. He didn't believe there was anyone to express it to, he acknowledged. "But why do you feel grateful?" my friend persisted. "You can be grateful only if there is a person to whom you are grateful."

*Gratitude is built into every one of us, as much a universal human characteristic as guilt.*

At this point, the colleague said, "That's why people make up God. They have to have a mythological being to whom they can express gratitude."

On its face, this is a preposterous argument. James Ryan did not return to the grave marker in Normandy to express gratitude to someone he had made up in his own mind. Captain Miller did indeed save his life. Gratitude without someone to be grateful to is a meaningless concept, and no one's going to make up God just so he can thank Him. If there is no Creator, why do we feel gratitude?

The gratitude James Ryan felt, the gratitude I felt that day on the lake, the gratitude all of us feel at so many times in our lives, including my friend's business partner, presupposes that there is someone to be grateful to. Just as the universal characteristic of guilt tells us there is a moral law, so too the universal experience of gratitude leads us to know—in a way that perhaps only the heart can know—that there is a source of our being—God. My experience

*The universal experience of gratitude leads us to know that there is a source of our being—God.*

with my son in New Hampshire was the perfect expression of this knowledge written on the heart.

If we know the reality of beauty and gratitude deep within us, why is it so hard to live in the light of this knowledge?

Because everything around us keeps hammering away at the

opposite proposition. The placards tell us "There is no truth." "God is a myth." And our culture has bought into the big lie.

Once again, this is the great dysfunction of contemporary life. This dysfunction becomes ever more apparent when we examine how postmodernist thinking plays out in everyday life in its self-contradictory and, indeed, irrational nature. Postmodernists do the darnedest things.

# CHAPTER 25

# POSTMODERNISTS IN RECOVERY

"BIRDS DO IT, BEES DO IT / Even educated fleas do it," goes the old Cole Porter song. "Let's do it, let's fall in love."[1] Alas, giant pandas have a very difficult time falling in love, which is one of the main reasons they are near extinction. Environmental groups and zoos around the world have participated in a massive effort to bring this most lovable—if sexually indifferent—bear back from the brink.

The Wolong Giant Panda Protection Center in China's southwestern Sichuan province has taken the lead role in this effort. Scientists at Wolong have found that the threat to pandas comes almost as much from themselves as from their shrinking habitat. They feed on bamboo stems and leaves, whose poor nutritional value is further compromised by the panda's naturally carnivorous digestive system. Groups of giant pandas live far from one another, and the males are notoriously awkward with their come-hithers. Female pandas, who give birth to twins half the time, pick one cub to nurture, often allowing the other to die of neglect. So, although "Cold Cape Cod clams, 'gainst their wish, do it / Even lazy jellyfish do it," pandas don't.[2] Or they raise only a few healthy cubs when they do.

The scientists at the China Conservation and Research Center for the Giant Panda, Wolong Nature Reserve, have found ingenious ways to encourage pandas toward what should come naturally. When the San Diego Zoo shipped a four-year-old female panda, Hua Mei, back to China, her caretakers at Wolong prepared for a series of "blind dates" in hopes that Hua Mei might increase the panda population. Hua Mei had lived all of her life in captivity, however, so the Wolong scientists worried that she wouldn't know how to act. To help her along, they resorted to what might be called panda porn. They showed Hua Mei videos of mating pandas, which a late-night comedian might have dubbed *Panda-monium!* or *Behind the Green Bamboo Shoots.*

In June of 2004, the Wolong scientists proudly announced that Hua Mei was with panda child.[3] If she had twins, they could save both through switching the cubs until they could survive Hua Mei's singular focus.

I tell this amusing story for two reasons, both of which expose the fallacy of postmodern thought. First, naturalists—those who believe a random universe is all we have—are unable or unwilling to behave consistently with their own beliefs. If they did, they'd let the giant panda become extinct since that's the way natural selection works, right? The giant panda means nothing to biodiversity or any other notion that naturalists use to justify their embarrassing altruism.

The story also shows that Peter Singer is wrong when he says that humans are no different from animals. Our love and care distinguish the human species from all others. In fact, they are the very things that make us *human.* We do not act on the basis of Singer's cold utilitarian calculus; we act far more generously on behalf of the earth and its creatures. It's almost as if they were entrusted to our care. Actually, it's exactly as if that were the case, which proves that in regard to the giant panda's future, the book of Genesis is far more relevant than Darwin's *The Origin of Species.* While preaching that there's really no difference between humanity and the rest of creation, naturalists behave as if there is a world of difference. This is one of many examples of how postmodernism on its face contradicts itself.

———•◦•———

Postmodernism, in fact, could have been invented by Yogi Berra. It's filled with propositions like Yogi's, "No one goes to that restaurant anymore because it's too crowded." The obvious self-refuting nature of many postmodernist positions leads people to spout similar absurdities. Later in this chapter we'll read how a prominent architect of postmodernism repudiated his own self-contradictory teaching.

But most people live in the big lie of postmodernism without ever realizing how it undercuts their own reasoning. Once a reporter asked the colorful and sometimes boisterous California congresswoman Maxine Waters why she was marching in an abortion-rights demonstration. She answered it was because, "my mother didn't have the right to an abortion."[4] And she said it with a straight face.

So why don't we see through this? We seem to have lost our capacity for critical thinking. The greatest difficulty with accepting our common reality may simply be our culture's all-pervasive prejudice against this idea. "Everyone knows there is no such thing as *the* truth." This proposition has become an evil enchantment that has intimidated us into believing that everything is relative.

This relativity has affected all of us. We are all, to one degree or another, postmodernists in recovery. Postmodernism profoundly skews our thinking about who we are as humans. Take the current obsession with self. Carry this to its logical extreme, and you end up with army recruiting slogans such as "An Army of One."

When I first heard that "An Army of One" was the army's new recruiting slogan, I expected so many cartoons and articles and late-night cracks about the slogan that the army would be laughed out of town. The military had done its research well, though. They had focus groups and review boards study the slogan's potential. Amazingly, the recruiting effort succeeded. The former slogan, "Be All You Can Be," was directed at self-gratification, but "Army of One" made the ultimate corporate activity sound like volunteering to become a superhero.

The military doesn't work that way, as I learned during my time in the marines. I loved being out in the field with the men, loved the physical challenges, the training, the discipline. But most of all I loved the esprit de corps, the sense of unit cohesion. No matter what ragtag bunch of recruits might be assembled, once they are molded into a fighting force, each person experiences a solidarity that's unparalleled in civilian life.

There's a simple reason for this. The military isn't in the business of producing widgets; it's in the life-and-death business of fighting wars. That involves teamwork.

As a platoon commander, I learned that my life depended on obeying the command I received from the company commander—and being sure that my men down the line obeyed that same order. Military discipline went only so far toward ensuring the order was carried out.

As an officer, I had to earn the men's respect. The military is ultimately about the bonds of officers and their people staying strong under extreme conditions—it's relational.

And fighting tactics demand cooperation. The way in which a platoon advances on an enemy position is all teamwork: One squad of thirteen people stays prone, providing covering fire for another squad, which advances. And within each squad are fire teams, groups of four, which the squad leader deploys in the same way: one advancing, one covering the advance with firepower. An army moves across a field in a highly coordinated way.

In a firefight, the soldier you share a foxhole with takes responsibility for 180 degrees, and you take the other 180 degrees. Your buddy and you fight literally back-to-back. Before serving in Vietnam, Allen Chambers, who is African-American, was a militant who hated white men. But Vietnam ended his racism because his foxhole buddy was white; they bonded as one person. Otherwise, Allen would have died.

An army of one? That's a joke. That our society doesn't get it proves how seriously we have been sucked into the big lie about the supreme, self-sufficient individual.

It is one thing to join the army on the grounds that you can be an army of one and then discover, of course, that you are part of a community that has to function in a very specific way. That simply comes under the heading of false advertising. But it is quite another thing to build your life on self-refuting propositions that can lead to wrong decisions about life-and-death issues. This is why it's so important not only to understand the basic ideas behind the things we hear and witness in our society—but also to see through them.

———•◦•———

Pressed hard enough, people can be forced to see the irrationality of postmodernism and the fact that it creates an impasse that in time makes life untenable. We've already seen in the story of Dennis Kozlowski what happens when a person abandons all ethics in the pursuit of personal gain. And his story is tragically common. Cases like these raise the question of how a society that has rejected all truth claims can maintain ethics. The word *ethics* derives from a Greek word meaning "stable." Ethics do not change. But how can you have ethics when there is no truth?

Fifteen years ago, a friend gave $20 million to Harvard Business School to establish a course on ethics. I told him he was wasting his money, that Harvard, committed as it is to philosophical relativism, would never be able to teach ethics. Later I wrote an article to this effect, which caused consternation among friends on the Harvard board. To satisfy their objections, I suggested they send me the curriculum. When I read it, it confirmed my worst suspicions, and I wrote an even stronger article. This led to Harvard's inviting me in 1991 to give a lecture, which I entitled "Why Harvard Can't Teach Ethics."

I don't think I've ever worked so hard on a speech. I studied everything I could get my hands on because I knew I would be assaulted by the best and the brightest. My heart was pounding the day I stood in "the well" and spoke to a packed semicircular lecture hall, rows of students ascending before me.

The speech turned out to be a disappointment because no one challenged what I had said; no one asked a good question. The students, I concluded, didn't have enough grounding in moral philosophy to dispute me, which is the saddest commentary of all.

The Harvard invitation led to others over the years, including several at other Ivy League schools. Over the past decade, I've consistently asserted that no prominent American institution, except a handful of "Great Books schools" or explicitly religious institutions, can teach ethics. Time and again I've had friends challenge me; *their* alma mater or the school on whose board they serve is teaching outstanding ethics. I will invariably ask them to send me the course curriculum, which I soon discover has less to do with ethics than with diversity or the environment. The only standard is pragmatism. Getting in trouble is bad for business.

So why should we be surprised when people are ripping off major corporations? They've been taught that they can do anything they want. Choose their own values. They just can't do anything that will get into the newspapers. (Many of them miss that part of it.) No one in these academic halls acknowledges the postmodern impasse: We let students make their own decisions about truth, and then we are surprised when they cheat.

No one, that is, except a lone professor I found at my own alma mater, Brown University. I returned for my fiftieth reunion at Brown, partly because I was invited to give one of the lectures during commencement weekend. To my great surprise, Brown, a bastion of politically correct liberalism, told me that I could pick the topic, which I did: "Why the Ivy League Can't Teach Ethics."

As I was introduced to an overflow crowd in a large lecture hall, the professor welcomed me to the campus and said he was interested in my subject. He said that he *used* to teach ethics at Brown, but then he told the crowd: "Perhaps after you've heard Mr. Colson speak, you'll understand why I had to give up the course." Then he sat down. I had found an honest man.

---

One of the most celebrated proponents of postmodernism's main idea—that we create our own reality—discovered that the notion made his life unlivable and miserable. This giant of the literary world was a rebel without a cause. For the past fifty years his work has been used to inculcate the postmodernist mentality in university students. Yet, in midcareer he had to turn around from the many dead ends into which his ideas had led. He found himself rejecting the illusions that had made him famous.

Wallace Stevens was born on October 2, 1879, into a Pennsylvania Dutch home in Reading, Pennsylvania. He grew up wearing "patent leather pumps with silver buckles on 'em" to go to Sunday school at the Presbyterian church.[5] His mother's family, the Zellers, were German Pietists.

Wallace's father, Garrett, was a successful lawyer who used his legal fees to invest in farms, rental properties, and new businesses. The family prospered until the turn of the century, when market downturns and a fire at one of Garrett Stevens's businesses, a bicycle plant, undermined their stability. From the turn of the century onward Garrett struggled to maintain his family's position in Reading society, of which he was extremely jealous.

Wallace, the second of five children, enrolled at Harvard in 1897. He had already cultivated a love of literature, and while in college, Stevens contributed his first poems, stories, and sketches to the *Harvard Advocate* and *Harvard Monthly*. His professors found him gifted. Stevens was influenced by French poetry, particularly Paul Verlaine's work, which explores how the mind creates a private world. Stevens became a lifelong Francophile, reading extensively about Paris and eventually ordering books and paintings from shops there. He could describe, in minute detail, cafés on the Champs Elysées. He never actually took a trip to France, though. He wanted only the Paris of his imagination. He preferred that his own private world not be compromised by reality.

Wallace's family immediately noticed that Harvard changed him. His parents' own social ambitions quickly became in their son an enduring intellectual snobbery. "Wallace went off to college and came back with a Harvard accent!" his siblings declared.[6]

His father advised Wallace to follow him into law, but Wallace thought he'd try writing. He moved to New York in 1900 and worked as a stringer for the *New York Tribune* and as an editorial assistant for the monthly magazine *World's Work*. This proved a tough way to make a living, and after a short while he took his father's advice. He attended New York Law School and was admitted to the bar in 1904.

That summer while on a visit to Reading, he met Elsie Moll. Her mother, who came from a once-prominent family, had a troubled history, marrying spendthrifts who plunged the family into debt and then died. Elsie's father passed away while she was still a child, and her mother's next husband couldn't afford to keep Elsie in school. She left high school at the age of fourteen to work in a shop.

Wallace Stevens was soon smitten with Elsie Moll simply because she was the most beautiful girl he had ever seen. She became his "muse," as he began writing poetry in her honor. Elsie was such a good-looking young blonde that she won a beauty pageant and would one day be the model for the Liberty Head dime.

Wallace and Elsie courted for five years as Stevens struggled to establish himself as a lawyer in New York. During that time the two young people saw relatively little of each other, but they kept up an intense correspondence. The time they spent together occurred during Stevens's summer and holiday visits home—stays when Wallace was so preoccupied with Elsie that his father protested that Wallace was using his family as a laundry service.

Initially, Stevens's career as a lawyer did not go well. He had neither the temperament for trial work nor the entrepreneurial spirit necessary to establish a successful practice. Finally, though, he secured a good position on the legal staff of the American Bonding Company, where he became an expert on surety bonds—a form of insurance.

In 1909, Stevens felt secure enough to marry Elsie Moll. One summer evening he presented the beautiful young woman to his family at dinner. They had known Elsie for years, first as a classmate of Wallace's younger brother and sisters and then during the years of courtship. It was soon obvious that Stevens's parents disapproved of the match.

After Wallace had taken Elsie back to her home, he and his father quarreled. Stevens took his parents' objections against Elsie as rank prejudice against her social background. Yet his sisters, who had less reason to prefer a more socially acceptable future sister-in-law, wondered at how Wallace could be interested in Elsie. They found her dull and conventional. Stevens's father undoubtedly understood that lust had vanquished all other considerations. He tried to put a stop to the wedding.

At the culmination of the argument between father and son, Wallace shouted that if Elsie was not welcome, then he would never visit his father's house again.

Elsie and Wallace married soon thereafter, holding a small ceremony, which none of Wallace's family attended. Unlike most shouting-match threats, Wallace's came true. His father died two years later in 1911, without ever having had Wallace visit him again.

In New York, Wallace became part of an avant-garde group of artists. At Harvard he had become friends with Walter Conrad Arensberg, a wealthy young man with poetic aspirations. Arensberg gathered experimental painters and other artists around him in New York. Stevens met the soon-to-be-famous painters Man Ray, Francis Picabia, and Marcel Duchamp. The young poet became aware of the emerging artistic movements whose strands gathered in what came to be known as modernism.

Modernism was essentially the attempt to establish the arts on a purely human basis, to create works that did not imitate life (because life was random) but were worlds unto themselves. Modernism relied on what were considered the unassailable materialistic assumptions of science. Stevens commented that "one must live in the world of Darwin and not of Plato."[7]

Stevens began writing his first mature poems during the years of World War I. These were published in magazines like *Trend* and Harriet Monroe's journal, *Poetry*. Stevens's free verse had a tremendous musical quality, a sensuous delight, and an ironic, witty intelligence that began to attract attention.

In 1916, Stevens joined the Hartford Accident and Indemnity Company, heading up its new surety bond department. He and Elsie moved to Hartford, Connecticut.

From this time until his death in 1955, Stevens's life settled into dual tracks. On the one track he was a highly paid insurance executive, who spent his days dictating memoranda on bond claims and parceling out the company's legal work to regional law firms. Stevens became a vice president of the Hartford Company in 1934. He made $17,000 a year in the midst of the depression—an enormous sum. Well-to-do doctors and lawyers in those years were earning $2,000 a year.

On the other track, Stevens the poet rose at six o'clock every morning to read for two hours, stoking his meditations for his daily forty-minute walk from his home to his office. (Stevens never learned to drive a car.) He composed much of his poetry on these walks, then dictated to his secretary the lines he had just conceived. Occasionally, he stole time from his work to finish a poem, frequenting the firm's library, where he was an assiduous user of its massive dictionary.

In 1923, when Stevens was forty-three years old, A. A. Knopf published his first major collection of poems, *Harmonium,* which includes many of the poems universities currently teach their students. "A High-Toned Old Christian Woman" flatly denounces traditional faith, and "Sunday Morning" celebrates neo-paganism. The latter poem praises lusty bodily life as a far finer thing than heaven. The poet asks, "Shall our blood fail? Or shall it come to be / The blood of paradise?"[8]

Critics recognized that a major poetic talent had debuted with *Harmonium.* A few found Stevens's belief in art as life's ultimate value facile and empty, however. Latter-day critics have been defending Stevens against these charges ever since, but Stevens himself seems to have taken the criticism to heart. For very personal reasons he was coming to recognize that our blood carries the seeds of our own destruction as well as the possibility of erotic bliss.

Not long after Stevens was married, he must have begun to reconsider his family's objections to Elsie Moll. He found that the youthful beauty he had married was also a person with her own likes and dislikes, many of which were contrary to his. Even though Elsie was happier in Hartford, which was more like their hometown, Wallace lamented the loss of his New York life.

In Hartford, Elsie quickly restricted the family's social life. She didn't like Stevens's fashionable friends and was glad not to have them around. Indeed, because she felt unable to share in Stevens's literary life, she came to despise it. No doubt Stevens played his unwitting part in encouraging her to feel this way. He was often a pompous fool.

Elsie became dismissive of her husband's poetry, calling it "affected"—as indeed some of it is. When Stevens set her up in a big home on Westerly Terrace in one of Hartford's best neighborhoods, Elsie became a recluse. The neighborhood children called her "the witch." She countered Wallace's mastery in many things with her perfectionism in a few. She became an obsessive gardener, turning her spacious backyard into a flower show. She also became a gourmet cook, stuffing her tall husband until, by some accounts, he weighed more than three hundred pounds. She might have been trying to kill him with culinary kindness.

In 1924, when Wallace and Elsie had a baby, Holly Bright Stevens, Elsie mothered her child in a manner that excluded Wallace from his daughter's life. Both Wallace and his daughter longed for each other's affection, but until Holly grew into a young woman, she saw little of her father in a house of three people. Elsie, the young beauty queen, grew old just as quickly as she could. She dressed like a spinster and became as dowdy as possible. Photographs of the family in the Huntington Library's collection show the perverse speed of this transformation.[9] She seems to have been saying to Wallace, "You married me, and I'm yours to keep. But you'll not have the young, beautiful girl of your fantasies because you never knew the real me."

Stevens's life, far from being a neo-pagan riot on a Greek isle, quickly became wintry, grave, and cold. Elsie and Wallace set up separate suites for themselves in the house on Westerly Terrace. At night they ate dinner together in stony silence before retreating to their separate bedrooms.

The grimness of Stevens's life was partly relieved by the winter trips he took south every year from the mid-1920s to 1940. His sojourns to the South, where he drank a lot and went hunting and fishing with friends, breathed into him some life and new inspiration for his poetry.

A favorite Stevens poem, "The Idea of Order at Key West," came out of such a trip. This poem typifies much of Stevens's work, particularly in its attention to how the mind shapes our experience. He imagines a woman singing by the sea, contrasting the sophisticated design of her song—the imaginative world it brings into being—with the monotonous and unmindful sound of the sea itself.

> She was the single artificer of the world
> In which she sang. And when she sang, the sea,
> Whatever self it had, became the self
> That was her song, for she was the maker.[10]

The trouble with being the singer—the maker—of one's own world becomes apparent as soon as one tries to live there. What makes Stevens truly great, in my opinion, is that he thought through answers that were too easy and discarded them.

Stevens's own dissatisfaction with the point of view of *Harmonium* virtually put a stop to his poetry writing for seven years. He would eventually make fun of his own affectations. In "The Motive for Metaphor," Stevens writes how he used poetry to evade seeing himself clearly. His poetry was the place "Where you yourself were never quite yourself / And did not want nor have to be."[11]

Gradually, several developments in his life began to call Stevens out of his despair. He remained faithful to Elsie, despite their alienation, and as a result his relationship with his daughter slowly developed and became increasingly important. As the father began to think deeply about what he wanted for his daughter, he came to recognize that life had a meaning beyond the two tracks of his own life: materialism and aestheticism. He hoped that Holly would study history and languages—two carriers of tradition.

Sadly, Stevens also came to understand the heartbreak of his own parents, as Holly left Vassar College after little more than a year to marry a man who repaired business machines. The marriage quickly broke up after the birth of a grandson, Peter. The new grandfather and his daughter became closer than ever, though, and the poet delighted in his grandson.

Stevens's relationship with Holly finally directed his attention back to his family in Reading. When his youngest brother, John Bergen Stevens, died in 1940, Wallace attended the funeral. Only one of his four siblings, Elizabeth, remained alive. At the funeral, Stevens met most of his nieces and nephews for the first time. He began sending them gifts and doing small favors to advance their careers. His nieces and nephews grew so fond of him that they wrote him a collective letter full of enthusiasm for his presence in their lives.

To this, he responded, "I am a little hepped on family ties. It is one of the sources of strength in life."[12] (Alone with his thoughts, Stevens must have rued his break with his father.)

By this time, Stevens, in his sixties, had performed a complete about-face on the importance of relationship and community. He began a quest to trace his genealogy. Stevens wanted to come to terms with the people who had made him what he was—particularly his mother's line, the Zellers, whose religious faith Stevens found it impossible to forget. Every time he went to New York, he visited St. Patrick's Cathedral, becoming so knowledgeable about the cathedral's history that he took friends on guided tours.

In Stevens's final poems, several among his greatest, he began to glimpse an imagination at work in the world, an imagination that was far greater than his own. Stevens had always written as if the poet's art imposed order on an otherwise dead and meaningless world. He finally saw that the poet's imagination only touched the far greater imagination of his Maker.[13]

In the poem "Not Ideas about the Thing but the Thing Itself," the poet hears a bird's call before sunrise—the same way Messiaen's *Quartet for the End of Time* begins. At first the poet thinks this birdcall may have been produced by his imagination, but then he realizes that this "scrawny cry" has come from outside himself and speaks of the whole created order—the bird's cry is part and parcel of the sun's rising. The "rising of the sun" has been used repeatedly in English poetry as an image for Christ's resurrection. The poet says of this cry, "It was like / A new knowledge of reality."[14]

———•◦•———

On April 26, 1955, Stevens underwent exploratory surgery that revealed inoperable stomach cancer. He was not told of his terminal condition, as was then the practice. Those close to him guessed that he knew how sick he was, though.

He began to talk with the chaplain of St. Francis Hospital, Father Arthur Hanley, about becoming a Catholic and being baptized. Father Hanley counseled with Stevens more than ten times over a period of months before baptizing him and receiving him into the Catholic church.

The questions that the ultrasophisticated poet Stevens and Father Hanley discussed turn out to be the questions that everyone asks: Stevens wanted to know whether hell truly exists and why the world is full of suffering. Father Hanley explained the necessity of free will and Jesus' own insistence on the reality of hell.[15] In the end Stevens found Father Hanley's answers liberating.

After his baptism, Stevens, according to Father Hanley, seemed very much at peace. Hanley quotes Stevens as saying, "Now I'm in the fold."[16] No doubt he said this with a touch of irony, acknowledging his past rebelliousness and the improbability that he could ever be mistaken for a lamb, but also with the greater understanding that his ultimate fate and happiness lay in the recognition of a common truth. Stevens finally realized that life is not about inventing ourselves but about finding "the center," the place in God's world where we are kept secure.[17]

———•◦•———

I've chosen to tell the Stevens story because it's not one that many people know or, if they do, will even admit to. *The Norton Anthology of World Literature,* a standard textbook in many universities, describes Stevens's poetry this way: "Stevens finds the ultimate human value in the artist's freedom to imagine the world anew in a 'supreme fiction' . . . [an] artistic transformation whose creation is enough to give meaning to an otherwise meaningless universe."[18] That's an accurate statement about Stevens's early work, but it's the only part of Stevens's story most people know, leaving an impression that Stevens himself found this point of view satisfying. Instead, the whole of Stevens's life and work reveals the unlivable and self-refuting nature of postmodernism.

Stevens thought he could live life purely on his own terms, and he was heralded as the one who would usher out the Christian era, at least in literature. And he used his truly amazing intellectual talents to try to do just that.

What he discovered is what all of us will find, that the worldview he followed, the one contrary to the Christian view of reality, simply isn't workable. It can't be true because it fails to conform to reality. Toward the end of his life, Wallace Stevens realized that humankind was God's idea, not God humankind's—and he reconciled himself with reality's Author.

Stevens must have had doubts about the worldview he was following as he pursued his own two-track professional career. During his morning meditations and as he wrote poetry while walking to work, he believed that the only order in life came from the human mind. There was no overarching truth, no natural order. It was whatever humans construct it to be.

At nine o'clock in the morning, when people were in their offices, at their desks, he shed his poet's notions and helped administer an insurance company, whose business was predicated on the ironically contrary notion that human behavior is highly predictable—a sure sign of a *common* reality. Not one that we make up but one that we share. So from the start of the business day until he left his office at night, he followed a worldview contrary to his poems' celebration of humanity's triumph in making the only order we supposedly possess. How powerful fashionable intellectual currents can be. How blinding the big lie is.

It's clear from Stevens's story that his life was compartmentalized in yet another way. He was one person professionally, the distinguished man, the revered poet with his face turned to the world. How could one want more? But at night, he and his wife dined in stony silence and then went to their separate rooms. The love of his life deteriorated before his eyes, and he could do nothing about it. His relationship with his daughter was in peril from the start.

As Stevens grew older, he recognized that rather than being his own self-invention, his identity was forged by his lineage, his family, and his community. What became important was not the acclaim of literary critics but the love he would find in relationships, a point we have made repeatedly in this book. This became for Wallace Stevens the richest thing in his life.

And then, of course, he found the ultimate relationship.

> *How blinding the big lie is.*

Stevens's poetry shows that he was moving for years toward a Christian view of reality. His decision to be baptized may well have been hastened by his impending death, but this deathbed conversion was the logical culmination of the hard lessons experience had taught Stevens. The great poet was finally smart enough and honest enough to cast off his celebrated illusions and live the truth. Repenting of his rebellious nature, he gave himself to his immediate family, to the broader community of his nieces and nephews, and finally to God. He found the good life, at last.

# CHAPTER 26

# HOPE, FREEDOM, AND HAPPINESS

WALLACE STEVENS DISCOVERED the hopeless and dysfunctional life of postmodernism, but before he died, he also discovered where hope can be found. People all over the world have this same experience, as I saw personally on a visit to India.

In the mid-1980s, Prison Fellowship International president, Ron Nikkel, and I traveled to India to visit prisons. We crisscrossed the country, ending up in Trivandrum, which is the capital of Kerala, India's southernmost province.

Trivandrum is a city of paradoxes. When we were there, Kerala was the only freely elected Communist state in India. The airport a hub for Russian planes; red flags hung everywhere in the city. But it also was the most Christian province in India, with a strong church thriving under an oppressive Communist system.

We felt the opposing magnetic fields as we walked through the city's crowded and dangerous streets. The humid air smelled sour from the open fires on which people cooked food with pungent spices—paprika, mace, red pepper, cumin, and cinnamon.

We were escorted to the prison by the head of the prison system, a high-caste Brahmin Hindu. The facility where a thousand inmates were confined had been built by the British a century earlier, an old-style fortress, surrounded by high brick walls that made it look forbidding and invulnerable.

At the gates we were met by the Indian guards, handsomely dressed in their khaki shorts, shirts with red epaulets on the shoulders, swagger sticks at their sides. We were marched to the center of the prison, which is like the hub of a wheel, with different cell blocks extending out like spokes. There we found a control building fronted by a large platform, a welcoming banner waving above it. Many local officials dressed in suits and ties were already gathered, as were the inmates, who sat on their haunches in a great muddy yard. The prisoners wore white loincloths and very little else on their dark bodies, which glistened with perspiration in the midmorning heat.

The inmates stared blankly as we walked up onto the platform. I was greeted as a visiting dignitary; people embraced me and threw leis around my neck. I wondered what the inmates could be making of this. How many had heard of Richard Nixon, much less me? Suddenly I began to sweat as I wondered how I could connect with the people I was really there for—the prisoners.

The program began with tedious preliminaries, the introductions and acknowledgments that always try an audience's patience. Eventually the head of the prison system introduced me.

As I stood at the lectern, one of our Prison Fellowship men stood alongside to translate into Hindi. It's always difficult speaking through a translator because you have to speak mostly in staccato bursts and then pause to give the translator time to catch up. As my speech began, I could tell I wasn't connecting. The audience was staring at me suspiciously.

When I began to tell my own story, however, and began talking about Jesus—a man with brown skin like theirs, a man who was thrown into prison—the inmates leaned forward, straining to catch every word. Their eyes soon grew big, their expressions full of wonder. I told them that Christ had gone to the cross and died for their sins, and that they could be forgiven and have a new life. Christ gave them hope—real hope, even for those who had committed the worst of crimes.

I have never seen any crowd anywhere suddenly become so responsive to my message.

Hope is a rare commodity in those prisons. In India, criminals become outcasts, occupying the lowest stratum in the Indian caste system, lower even than "untouchables." One reason the Brahmin head of the prison system did not mind my preaching was that these men had no way back into Indian society—no one would care about anything they heard or experienced. Most inmates would have to live on the streets after prison; their families would have nothing to do with them.

The inmates' hopelessness also extended beyond this life. In the Hindu belief system, what people do in this life will be done to them in the next. Because of their crimes, the inmates believed they were pinned to an endless Wheel of Suffering and would be reincarnated as criminals or untouchables or as lower life forms.

Here were men who truly had nothing to live for. And here I was saying that God had created them and sent His Son not only to die on a cross but also to rise again, conquering sin and death. Jesus loved them so much that He took their crimes on Himself so that they could have hope and a new life. This was absolutely mind-boggling news.

I then led them in a prayer. The men bowed their heads. I did not ask those who wanted to become Christians to come forward or stand, because I didn't know what they were allowed to do. But I sensed from people's expressions and the audience's reverent silence that they were responding powerfully.

When I finished speaking, the guard started to walk me back to my seat, but I stopped. I had not thought in advance about what I did next. I just felt I needed to touch those men. So I jumped down off the platform, which startled the inmates and startled the guards even more. I walked straight toward the nearest man to shake his hand. I knew that few people who visited that prison would ever do that. I thought that if I shook hands with a few men, they'd know I'd come to help them.

Almost instantaneously, a thousand men rose up like a flock of birds and winged toward me. All the while I had talked, they had remained on their haunches, not applauding, not making any visible move. But as I grabbed the first man's hand, the entire crowd encircled me. I looked back toward the platform and saw Ron Nikkel trying to get to me. The guards looked horrified. The head of the prison system was pale.

No harm came to me. Far from it. The most orderly process imaginable took over: I was ringed with people, but no man came closer than two feet. I kept shaking hands with as many inmates as possible, while those at my sides and behind me reached out and touched my shoulders, back, and upper arms. The men kept trading places at the front of the circle, as politely as they could, no pushing or shoving. One man would touch, back away, and somebody else would take his place. They just wanted another person's touch.

I'm not exaggerating when I say that a significant number of the men were in tears. The few that could speak English would say things such as, "Thank you for bringing us God." We were all very emotional, very caught up in this unusual collective blessing. None of the officials could get to me until those men and I were finished. I was there a good twenty minutes.

The men were not reaching out to me because I was a celebrity or because I had been welcomed by the officials. They didn't know who I was. They were touching me to make a connection, to see if this love I spoke of was real.

I came away renewed. What I saw in the faces of the Trivandrum prisoners—their eyes widening as I talked about Jesus, their tears flowing as we greeted one another in that circle—was *hope*. It was the one thing Hinduism could never offer them. Probably for the first time in their lives those men realized that somebody cared about them, somebody wanted their lives to work out, somebody wanted *them*. God wanted them. It was a life-changing discovery a thousand men made that day.

———•◦•———

My experience at the Trivandrum prison illustrates the enormous importance of our worldview, the way we understand the world and how we fit into it. When the Trivandrum inmates looked at the world from a Hindu worldview, their futures were bleak indeed: life on the streets followed by a similar, if not worse, fate in the next reincarnation. When these same inmates looked at the world from a Christian worldview, they discovered real hope. They understood the deep implications of that often-ridiculed phrase *born again*. They could start life anew as God's friend, for now and through eternity.

When you compare worldviews, you realize that hope is a unique characteristic of the Christian understanding of the world. None of the great religions, as laudable as they are in many respects, offers the kind of hope Christianity offers: the assurance of reconciliation with God for those who have failed. And we *all* have failed. The other great religions include ways to work toward reconciliation. Jews and Muslims, for example, believe in a theology that depends on good works: Do good things, keep the law, and maybe God will be satisfied on Judgment Day. Muslims have one sure way of getting past judgment into heaven, and that's to participate in a jihad and die a martyr. Some very misguided people have created huge suffering and sadness in the world by believing this.

Buddhism, in some forms, seeks to remove devotees from evil and suffering by extinguishing every desire, including hope. Other forms of Buddhism are much like Hinduism—and Judaism and Islam as well, for that matter—in seeing the key as good behavior. Scholars of Eastern religions sometimes recognize the inadequacy of their belief system. I once met a Buddhist professor who was teaching comparative religion in Japan. I asked him how he dealt with prisoners, since Buddhism has little to offer someone who has failed. "Oh," he said, half chuckling, "we have created 'Pure Land Buddhism,' a form that provides forgiveness." He frankly acknowledged that the idea of forgiveness had been borrowed from Christianity, simply because forgiveness and the hope it brings are such deep human needs. But who would want to believe in a religion that some professor can adjust to meet some need?

The humanism practiced by most Western elites has its own theology of good works, when you think about it. Humanists believe in serving others, and their hope lies in reforming the world through humanitarian endeavors and politics. This is utopianism. It's one reason politics becomes the humanists' religion. I know all about this; it's precisely what motivated me earlier in life.

But humanism, like the other faiths, offers nothing to people who have failed except to pick themselves up and try again. Humanists often have a tremendous sense of the moral law—the need for justice and peace and the necessity of righting wrongs. But a moral law without any belief in God brings with it a sense of utter hopelessness and futility. Remember Camus's statement: "The absurd is sin without God."[1]

That's one reason many secularists baptize their utopianism in New Age beliefs. New Age philosophy presents a picture of a benign world—"the universe gives you what you need"—while promising a new and better life through "insight" into the divine self. Would any of the Trivandrum inmates have believed that?

The fact is, only the Christian worldview provides true hope, without which life becomes dark and unbearable. I know this from my days in prison—and from the thousands of inmates I've met and worked with. As we saw in the Ernest Gordon story, even under the most desperate circumstances, hope keeps us alive. It is essential to the good life.

———•◦•———

We have compared how different religions and worldviews provide hope. Making such comparisons is not meant to put down other belief systems; it is the way we test what is true, which is the question we are exploring in these chapters. It is possible by such comparisons to empirically compare which views "fit" reality, which ones enable us to live in conformity with the natural, physical, and moral order—the way the world is *supposed* to function.

It is an exhaustive undertaking, of course, to study worldview thoroughly, which Nancy Pearcey and I did in our book *How Now Shall We Live?*\* In this chapter we are simply singling out a few of the most critical categories for comparison—those so clearly involved in the good life.

The first category is *hope.* But whether the promise of that hope rests on truth can be fully verified only when we go to God or God comes to us at the end of time. Nonetheless, we can look at evidence for its truth in the effects hope has on people and on life.

What happened at Trivandrum produced evidence of cultural transformation that I should have expected but didn't. In 2000, I spoke to a gathering of ten thousand Third World evangelists in Amsterdam. During my talk, I told the Trivandrum story. The next morning I conducted a seminar for people involved in prison work around the world. During the question-and-answer period, a dark-skinned man with a mustache and a bright smile rose to share his story.

---

\*This book provides a thorough means to test whether Christianity, or any other way of thinking, is true. It offers a basis for comparing worldviews, testing them as to how well they answer four of life's great questions. The question of origins: Where do we come from? The question of evil and suffering: What's wrong with this world (and possibly with us)? The question of remedy, or redemption: Can we right ourselves and fix what is wrong? The question of purpose: What are we here for?

I was awestruck as this man, Reny George, told how he had been one of the outcasts in Trivandrum's prison that day. He said he was staggered by what he had heard and experienced at the time. The inmates talked about the event for weeks; many came to Christ. Reny did not become a Christian that day, but he did later as the result of Prison Fellowship's ongoing ministry.

Reny spent fourteen years in prison. When he was released, he was indeed an outcast to Indian society, as were his children. He stayed close to the people involved in Prison Fellowship, and eventually he and his wife, Teena, began running the Precious Children's home in Bangalore.

The home was part of a larger network of five Prison Fellowship Precious Children's homes begun in 1985 by the head of Prison Fellowship India, Dr. Kunjumon Chacko. Because of India's caste system, parents won't let their children go to school with prisoners' children, who are relegated to the streets. The Prison Fellowship homes provide elementary education, Bible instruction, and vocational training for the children of inmates. The Precious Children's homes literally rescue children from being discarded.

In 2003, Reny George told his story at the Prison Fellowship International World Convocation in Toronto. He spoke of how he remains ostracized from Indian society, making his job of running the children's home a difficult one since government officials and businesspeople sometimes refuse to deal with him. But he still manages to care for the forty-seven children entrusted to him, as well as to raise the necessary funds to support the work.

Not long after the Toronto conference, George assumed more responsibilities developing and overseeing the Precious Children's Home in Bangalore. He lives what I spoke of at Trivandrum: the hope that a new life gives us. And he helps others experience it as well.

Wherever Christianity has spread, it has done so in this same way: One person finds hope and passes it on, and communities in turn are eventually changed. Just ask the thousands of children who have been cared for in Reny George's homes. Visit their communities.

Hope, forgiveness, and reconciliation go to the very heart of the good life. They heal relationships. They enable us to live at peace with others and be restored. Jesus calls us to love God with all our heart, mind, and soul, *and our neighbor as ourselves.*[2] He asks us to return the love with which God loves us. This transforms not only individuals but also the culture—just as we saw in the Ernest Gordon story. British soldiers during World War II who were willing to give their lives for each other transformed their prison camp along the Railroad of Death into a haven of life and culture.

Stories like Reny George's or Ernest Gordon's have been repeated thousands of times throughout the course of Western civilization. Rodney Stark, whose work *For the Glory of God* was cited earlier, argues that we cannot understand Western civilization without reference to Christian theology. Stark shows that a belief in God who makes moral demands and exercises judgment in the afterlife is an essential component in Western developments such as science and the abolition of slavery. "Western civilization really was God-given," Stark concludes.[3] The transforming power of Christianity testifies to its truth.

—————•◦•—————

The second critical category for comparing worldviews is securing *human liberty.* The Christian worldview provides the most certain grounding of liberty because it holds that every human being is created in the image of God and thus has an inherent dignity. This bedrock belief moved our Founders to write in the Declaration of Independence: "We hold these truths to be self-evident, that all men are created equal, that they are endowed by their Creator with certain unalienable Rights."[4]

Remember, too, that men and women created in God's image have a free will, the exercise of which demands civil liberty. God has provided a guide to the exercise of this free will through conscience and the moral order, as we discussed earlier. This helps assure the maintenance of civil liberty, which demands both free choice and voluntary restraint. The way in which the Christian worldview assures liberty was expressed well by the historian Lord Acton, who wrote: "Liberty . . . is itself the highest political end."[5] He later said, "No country can be free without religion. It creates and strengthens the notion of duty. If men are not kept straight by duty, they must be by fear. The more they are kept by fear, the less they are free. The greater the strength of duty, the greater the liberty."[6]

This is why democratic freedoms have taken strongest root in cultures influenced by Christianity. The success of Great Britain and the United States, in particular, as enduring beacons of freedom suggests that the Christian understanding of freedom corresponds with reality. No system of governance that flouts reality, as we saw with the Nazis and the Red Chinese Cultural Revolution, can long endure.

———•••———

The third critical category for testing a worldview is how it provides for *happiness.* Besides providing a hope that transforms individuals and cultures, and assuring individual liberty and dignity, Christianity offers the surest foundation for happiness, when that word is correctly understood. You'll remember earlier we discussed the ancients' understanding of happiness. The Greek word *eudaimonia* refers to a life well lived, a life of virtue, and it implies a life rooted in the truth. The American Founders were referring to this conception of happiness, of the good life, when they declared liberty and the *pursuit of happiness* as inalienable rights. They were not thinking of happiness as a life of hedonistic pleasure; they understood that hedonism—the party life—is destructive of humans and freedom. The pursuit of pleasure for its own sake results finally in misery.

The classical understanding of happiness, which is also the Christian view, is in direct conflict with the way people think in today's society. We are still living under the spell cast by Sigmund Freud, the most influential psychiatrist of the twentieth century.

Armand Nicholi, professor of psychiatry at Harvard University, has written *The Question of God,* a brilliant book (now an award-winning PBS documentary) comparing the views of Freud and C. S. Lewis. These two men represent polar opposite views on the nature of human happiness: Freud embraced the "pleasure principle"; Lewis taught virtue and dignity rooted in the love of God.

Freud believed that the main goal in life is "to become happy and remain so," and he made a direct correlation between happiness and pleasure, particularly the pleasure that comes from sexual experience. The "pleasure principle," he said, "dominates the operation of the mental apparatus from the very beginning."[7] He argued that people live in psychological dysfunction and are unhappy because social conventions limit our doing what we really find pleasure in.

Freud suggested that we would find happiness if we could simply break all of these social conventions. The fact that we don't do so creates guilt (which he, too, believed is universal). In his sober reflections he realized the dilemma his view creates. He wondered what would happen if men were to take any woman they chose. Asking the question made him draw back, recognizing that the individual's desires had to be balanced with society's interest. This gave life its inevitably tragic element.

Pleasure, Freud acknowledged, was fleeting, so it could not, in the end, provide real happiness. This is why Freud's worldview was so despairing and why in many respects he lived such an unhappy life.

Freud dismissed religion as contrary to science and reason, merely "fulfilling wishes," a desire "to obtain assurance of happiness . . . by a delusional transformation of reality."[8] Nicholi points out, however, that Freud admitted that religious people do find happiness in this "delusion" and that they feel good when they're able to obey the moral law, which Freud believed was a myth.

In contrast, C. S. Lewis argued that the tragic element in life does not come from the conflicts of the individual's desire for pleasure with society's need for conformity; rather, it results primarily from immoral or wrong choices. It's the unhappy corollary of our free will.

Would we give up our free will to avoid this? Of course not. Free will is the only thing that makes love possible, and in turn, the only thing that makes life possible, if indeed our primary purpose in life, as Lewis argues, is to find a love relationship with the One who put us here.[9]

Lewis says happiness is found in relationships, not in merely gratifying our own desires. That has certainly been true in my life. I find the most lasting fulfillment and joy in love relationships, with God, with my wife, with my children and grandchildren, with my colleagues and friends.

A singular moment that illustrates how relationships lead to true happiness came in my own spiritual journey when I was in prison. I was particularly depressed over the death of my father and the fact that my younger, college-age son had gotten in trouble over marijuana. At the time, January 1975, the other Watergate inmates, who had all been sentenced by Judge John Sirica, had been released early and had left prison.

I was the only one sentenced by another judge, Gerhard Gesell, who seemed immovable. I felt abandoned.

Al Quie, at the time a senior member of Congress and later governor of Minnesota, was a member of a small prayer group that surrounded me immediately after I became a Christian. One day Al phoned me in prison to tell me that he wanted to see the president; he proposed asking him if he could serve the rest of my prison sentence so I could be sent home to my family. As I described in *Born Again,* Al Quie did not have to make that visit to the president. Five days later, Judge Gesell cut my sentence to time served, and I was set free. However, I had been set free inside the prison after Quie's call. No greater love than this, that a man will lay his life down for his brother. True happiness is found in such relationships.

C. S. Lewis disputes Freud on almost every count. While saying that our greatest happiness will be found in our relationship to God, Lewis cautions that we are never intended to be completely happy. We are always yearning for something more, something beyond this life, which he argues presupposes the existence of something more we're created for—heaven. This Lewis describes as joy.

———•◦•———

What do these two worldviews look like in the lives of two men—one who lived as Freud taught, the other following C. S. Lewis's beliefs? Their lives provide a good empirical test of the truth of the two worldviews. Which one produces what it promises?

The first man is Hugh Hefner—the paragon of the pleasure principle. In 1953, Hefner founded *Playboy* magazine, which now has 4.5 million readers. Hefner was a marketing genius, and he took pornography from the underworld into the mainstream. He cast himself as a Victorian gentleman in a smoking jacket, enjoying all the best things in life, especially the company of many beautiful women. He turned sex into a commodity—one of the many things sophisticated people know how to enjoy. With Hefner, promiscuity became a lifestyle, one of the many choices a man could make if he were smart enough to make it. In the magazine, centerfolds portray glamorous, nearly naked women alongside glossy ads for stereo equipment, new cars, and aftershave. "The brilliance of *Playboy*," as one critic put it, "was that it combined the commodification of sex with the sexualization of commodities."[10]

For many people Hugh Hefner appears to be proof that the pleasure principle works. Who wouldn't want his life? He's rich, can do anything he pleases, and even in his seventies has the sexiest young women imaginable throwing themselves at him. Maybe Freud was both right and wrong. Maybe pleasure does last—at least until death.

Recently, though, Hugh Hefner's desperation has come to light. In the June 2001 issue of *Philadelphia Magazine*, Ben Wallace interviewed Sandy Bentley, who, with her twin sister, Mandy, served as Hefner's dual girlfriends. Sandy Bentley talked about the lengths to which Hefner must go to find satisfaction—or something like it. "The heterosexual icon [Hugh Hefner] . . . had trouble finding satisfaction through intercourse; instead, he liked [us] to pleasure each other while he masturbated and watched gay porn."[11]

About this statement, Read Mercer Schuchardt, another commentator, remarks, "Hugh Hefner embodies what his detractors have been saying for years. . . . All pornography stifles the development of genuine human relationships. All pornography is a manifestation of arrested development. . . . All pornography, indulged long enough, hollows out sex to the point where even the horniest old Viagra-stoked goat is unable to physically enjoy the bodies of nubile young females."[12]

Hugh Hefner turns out to be not a paragon of pleasure but a pathetic old man, a real human tragedy.

Now consider the life of a man whom I knew as a close friend, Jack Eckerd, who lived out the truths of C. S. Lewis's teaching. Eckerd also embodied many people's dreams of success. He had been administrator of the General Services Administration in Washington and had run for governor of Florida. When I first met Jack, he was in his late sixties and had turned two small drugstores into a chain of 1700 stores across the Southeast, making a considerable fortune in the process.

Jack Eckerd wanted to live life to the fullest every minute—and did. As a kid, he learned to fly. When he went into the U.S. Army Air Corps during World War II, he flew the most dangerous routes over the Himalayas. He kept on flying through much of his life—and sailing, and helping kids, all the while building a giant business empire. When I visited Jack on his eightieth birthday in his office in Clearwater, Florida, he had just been out rappelling down a wall and going on an overhead hand-to-hand line that had been suspended for kids to play on. Remarkable.

When I first met Jack, he was still very much a driven man, but he was beginning to wonder what his life was about. He became interested in my work in criminal justice reform—and it quickly became his passion. One day Jack and I got into his airplane and went from city to city in Florida, giving speeches and meeting with key leaders. The results were some very constructive changes in Florida's justice system.

From the beginning of our friendship, Jack Eckerd and I talked a lot about my faith. He heard about my journey the first night we ever met. He began reading my books and became interested in the big questions of life. Somewhere along the way—I'm not sure exactly how it happened—Jack Eckerd went through a spiritual transformation. Like C. S. Lewis, Jack Eckerd became a Christian.

One day he called me and just announced, "Now that I'm a Christian. . . ." He described an awakening, a moment in which he fully realized what being a Christian meant. He didn't experience wracking guilt, it seemed, or go through a time of tear-filled remorse. His transition to faith was a quiet one, but it had absolutely dramatic effects. As in every other area of his life, whether stunt flying, becoming a world-class sailor, or starting businesses, Jack Eckerd threw himself into his faith completely. One thing he did immediately after becoming a Christian was to remove *Playboy* and *Penthouse* from all of his stores, even though that decision cost him lots of money in lost revenue. Once he had made his decision, Eckerd never looked back. He was sold out for God.

I watched a remarkable change come over that man's life. He and I visited prisons all over the world. When we arrived one day at La Modelo prison in Colombia, we discovered there had been a sewer backup and no running water for two weeks. The place was filled with kids swept up off the streets of Bogota. As Jack, our group, and I walked through the prison, most of us held our noses. Jack never seemed to notice the stench. He walked through the place wearing a radiant smile. He'd stop kids and talk to them. One of my favorite pictures is a photograph of Jack embracing a young man who was in his late teens. Only I can truly appreciate how bad that kid smelled and how happy Jack was.

Even before Jack's conversion, he had a real passion for helping troubled kids get a break in life. He set up a chain of camps to take care of juveniles. These camps all across the Southeast have had a tremendous effect on thousands upon thousands of kids. After Jack became a Christian, his personal interest in helping people only deepened.

We traveled together to the Muntinlupa prison in the Philippines, where killings among the seven thousand inmates were routine. The guards didn't try to control the place, exactly, just kept everyone inside the perimeter, which was not that tough because the prison was located in the midst of the jungle. The prison was really a desperate place, with many inmates lying on their bunks in various states of illness. In the makeshift prison hospital, Eckerd stopped at every single bunk and talked to every man. He embraced many, including those dying of AIDS, about which little was known at the time. He was St. Francis embracing the leper and doing it with his characteristic smile. He always encouraged the inmates he met.

As always, Jack asked the prison officials what kinds of medicines they had. We discovered the prison hospital had almost nothing; the shelves were bare. That broke Jack's heart, and he returned to the States and intensified his efforts to get drugs shipped overseas. He was responsible for sending medical supplies to the Philippines, to Russia, and many other places around the world.

When we walked outside, Jack turned back to look at the prison and said to me, "Someday we're going to find a time and place where we don't treat human beings like this." He had a vision, one that was not merely utopian but grounded in his own willingness to give himself away.

In fact, in his later years Jack Eckerd began giving away his life, his time, and his money with increasing abandon. He had discovered what true happiness is. Not the self-centered, hedonistic life but the life that's directed to others.

---

Jack Eckerd or Hugh Hefner? Who would you rather be like? Which worldview do you embrace for your life?

# CHAPTER 27

# THE BAD NEWS

THE REALITY OF Christian hope, freedom, and happiness—and their effects in the world—makes the truth of Christianity credible. The evidence is, I believe, convincing: Christianity is the worldview that best enables people to live in harmony with the natural order, the way they are meant to live. You can best test which worldview is true by living out your beliefs to see where they lead. Sadly, most people discover the truth too late.

Look again at the life of Wallace Stevens, a man who propagated the most radical beliefs of postmodernism. A determined secularist, Stevens discovered truth when he encountered the realities of life—not the way he imagined them to be but the way they really are.

Wallace Stevens's life shows us not only that the postmodern view of life is false but also that there is in us a divine restlessness that demands to know the truth, a spur to keep us searching. Even one of the great critics of Christianity, Bertrand Russell, acknowledged this in his own life when he wrote: "One is a ghost, floating through the world without any real contact. Even when one feels nearest to other people, something in one seems obstinately to belong to God and to refuse to enter into any earthly communion—at least that is how I should express it if I thought there was a God. It is odd, isn't it? I care passionately for this world and many things and people in it, and yet what is it all? There must be something more important, one feels, though I don't believe there is."[1] Unlike Stevens, Bertrand Russell stopped seeking, and that's what makes his life so tragic.

Don't be like Bertrand Russell. Keep seeking. Pascal argued that those who seek truth will eventually find it, and in finding truth, they will find God.

When you seek, what do you discover? The apostle Paul claims that we can know God exists through the witness of nature. In his letter to the church in Rome, Paul wrote, "Since the creation of the world God's invisible qualities—his eternal power and divine nature—have been clearly seen, being understood from what has been made, so that men are without excuse."[2]

In creation we clearly see the order of a Designer, exposing the "grand evolutionary myth," as the philosopher Alvin Plantinga calls it.[3] We see as well a natural moral order—how human behavior has to be shaped to conform to physical and biological reality; this is what the apostle Paul describes as the law written on our hearts. We also discover that truth penetrates our very being when it is conveyed to us by beauty. There is a truth that can't be denied, a truth we can't *not* know.

This brings us back to the great human dilemma, which is the bad news of this chapter: We know what is true and right, but we can't or won't do it. This is one of the great paradoxes, and it's the most crucial for seekers to understand. It's the one that fools us because it's in our very nature to be blind to it. This paradox, as discussed earlier, is known in theological terms as *sin*.

It is in our nature to rebel. The human race was given free will, and our first parents, Adam and Eve, did not choose the good. They chose what St. Augustine called the non-good. (Even if you take the Genesis creation narrative as mythological, which I don't, its point that human-kind—not God—is responsible for sin remains.) This original sin, or the Fall, as Christians know it, has distorted our nature. Our fallen nature causes us to do wrong even when we know what is right, and it can distort our vision to the point that we can no longer see the truth. We become vulnerable to pervasive cultural lies. We can even flee from the truth, which, as the Bible frequently says, hardens our hearts. In that state we can deliberately choose alienation from God for its own sake and become evil within ourselves.

---

I saw this up close when, in the early 1980s, I was invited to New York for the filming of David Frost's short-lived variety program on NBC television. It was produced on one of the most spectacular sets in broadcasting at the time. The audience was seated in bleachers, much as they would be at a football game. Frost sat on a grand stage in front of the audience, with his guests seated on either side against a dramatic backdrop. The show interspersed interviews with musical performances and brief dramas. At the time, Frost was among the most prestigious interviewers in the world, having just released his much publicized in-depth interviews with the disgraced former president, Richard Nixon.

Frost invited me for what he billed as an "open debate" with Madalyn Murray O'Hair, the famous atheist who in 1963 brought the court case that eliminated official public school prayers. Some of my friends told me not to do it, that Frost would not give me an even break and that Madalyn Murray O'Hair was a vicious debater. She had made even more of a name for herself by a series of well-publicized, well-attended, and very lucrative debates with the Chaplain of Bourbon Street, Bob Harrington.

When I arrived for the filming at NBC headquarters in Rockefeller Plaza, I was ushered by two attendants into the makeup room and then whisked to the greenroom, where guests were plied with canapés and vintage wines. (The wines were not the best thing for keeping your wits about you on television.)

When it was time for filming the interview portion of the show, two aides dressed in blazers and ties escorted me to the studio. As I walked in, the directors were demonstrating the cue cards and signals for the audience. The crowd was instructed when to applaud, when to laugh, when to respond. (It takes a lot of work to make these shows spontaneous.) Seated to Frost's left on the almost throne-like stage was Madalyn Murray O'Hair. Frost greeted me warmly in his courtly British manner. O'Hair said nothing. I reached over to shake her hand, and she refused. She wore a very unhappy expression.

*Our fallen nature causes us to do wrong even when we know what is right, and it can distort our vision to the point that we can no longer see the truth.*

I had read all of the O'Hair-Harrington debates and had discovered that invariably Madalyn Murray O'Hair scored debating points by referring to passages in the Bible. She had graduated from an evangelical college, had a close knowledge of the Scriptures. It's my opinion, based on accounts of her early life, that at one point she had even been intellectually convinced of the truth of Christianity. I noticed in the Harrington debates that she would make vague, sweeping generalizations about what the Bible said, often to Harrington's embarrassment, so I decided to tuck my black leather Bible under my arm, keeping it out of sight as much as possible.

By the time the show got under way, the handlers had the crowd heated to a noisy, enthusiastic boil. The cameras swiveled and trained on us.

Frost began the questioning with me, reciting some of my Watergate misdeeds to oohs and aahs and occasional boos. I began explaining how my new faith had opened my eyes to the true nature of my actions. Frost countered, "But you're a convicted felon, Mr. Colson. Why should we be listening to you about these kinds of issues?" At that, the boobirds really erupted.

Frost then asked me to give my testimony, to explain how Nixon's "hatchet man" had turned to God.

I had only a few minutes to tell the involved story, but I started talking, looking straight at Frost. As I was speaking, Mrs. O'Hair leaned forward in her seat and turned her head to the right, glaring at me just over Frost's shoulder.

That was disconcerting enough, but then she started making grotesque faces. I couldn't believe she was actually doing this. She turned down her bottom lip and bared her teeth. Her eyes became ice picks.

I averted my gaze slightly from Frost to the red-lighted camera, only to find Mrs. O'Hair back in my peripheral vision, becoming ever more extreme in her antics. She even moved her chair for this purpose. She began gesturing aggressively with both hands and mouthing words I didn't want to guess at.

I've spoken in a lot of noisy and hostile places, from baseball locker rooms to prisons on the verge of riot. I've been heckled at political rallies. I should have taken Mrs. O'Hair's bizarre behavior in stride. But I didn't. I found it hard to keep my concentration, and I'm not sure how well my message came through. At first I dismissed her behavior as just adolescent razzing, like yelling to throw off the other team's signals. I concluded that this woman was genuinely trying to destroy my ability to tell my story.

During the discussion, Frost skillfully took us across a wide range of subjects. Most of the time the audience, perhaps on cue, gave by far the more supportive response to Mrs. O'Hair's answers. Then Frost gave her an opening with a reference to the Bible. "The Bible," she thundered, "is full of murder and hate, the killing of little children. It is a brutal, horrible book."

That was the moment that I had been waiting for, and I quickly reached across Frost and thrust my Bible at her. "Mrs. O'Hair, if you're going to characterize the Bible, you'd better quote it. You're a Bible student. Read to us what you are talking about," I said.

She backed away from me as if I had a weapon in my hands.

I pressed her again.

David Frost chimed in, "That's fair enough, Mrs. O'Hair. Mr. Colson's right. If you're going to talk about the Bible, why don't you quote it?"

"No, no!" she said, as she backed away farther, refusing to take the Bible from my hands. "It's full of hate and murder!" She would not touch the book.

That immediately swung the debate. From then on the crowd was on my side, as was David Frost, who pressed Mrs. O'Hair several times on her failure to answer my questions.

The debate ran for a full twenty minutes, and when the cameras were turned off, I felt exhausted. David Frost shook hands and thanked me for my candor.

As I was talking to some of the people from the audience, I glanced to the side and noticed that Mrs. O'Hair had gone off to a stool in a corner and was sitting by herself. I walked over to her, leaned forward, and said, "Mrs. O'Hair, I want you to know that I, like millions of Christians, am praying for you, praying that you will find the truth."

She looked up angrily and snarled, "Well, I don't pray, but if I did, I'd pray that you will lose. You will lose, Mr. Colson. You will fail."

I responded as calmly as I could that I might fail, but the cause in which I believed could not.

Why the furious response? If Mrs. O'Hair believed there was no God, why fight so hard against people like me? If she thought I was pursuing superstition, why not leave me alone, or even laugh at me? That's what I would do.

I concluded that the only reason Mrs. O'Hair could not leave people to their faith was that she really *knew* the truth. As I said earlier, I suspect Mrs. O'Hair must have once embraced the truth before turning utterly against it. Perhaps, then, succumbing to sin, she became evil within herself and had to try to destroy the belief system she knew was true.[4]

That was my best guess, at least, and later, when I learned how Madalyn Murray O'Hair died, I realized I had met a woman truly given to destruction. The story of Mrs. O'Hair's death is like something straight out of Marlowe's *Doctor Faustus*. In this classic play, Faustus sells his soul to the devil to acquire knowledge and power. By the end of the play, as the demons gather, Faustus's will is so corrupt that he finds it impossible to repent. He can only scream in unimaginable horror as he's dragged into hell. In a similar way, Mrs. O'Hair's death reveals our fate when we deliberately turn against the good. The following is where the practice of evil leads.

———— • ◦ • ————

Madalyn Murray O'Hair, after bringing the lawsuit that removed prayer from public schools, founded the American Atheists organization. She crusaded for the banishment of references to God in public life.

In the spring of 1995, some fifteen years after I met her, Mrs. O'Hair was in San Diego, defending herself against a lawsuit brought by the atheist organization Truth Seeker, which claimed that she had attempted a forced takeover of their organization. Her methods, they claimed, included issuing phony stock certificates.

Several sources documented the astonishing events that followed. *Crime* magazine, Ted Dracos's book *Ungodly*, and reports from Madalyn Murray O'Hair's son Bill Murray allow us to piece together the events as they happened.

Mrs. O'Hair had left the Austin, Texas, home office of American Atheists in the charge of an employee, David Waters, who had a long criminal record, including a conviction for murder. Nevertheless, he had risen to the position of office manager and had access to the organization's bank accounts. It appears that Mrs. O'Hair did not hire David Waters in spite of his past, as a compassionate gesture; she may have hired him because of it. Mrs. O'Hair, it turns out, ran American Atheists in a crooked manner, taking contributions whose uses were never fully divulged. She probably hoped that ex-convicts like Waters could be counted on to turn a blind eye to her tax evasion.

While Mrs. O'Hair was in San Diego with the two other American Atheists chief staff members—her forty-year-old son, Jon Garth Murray, and her granddaughter, Robin Murray—Waters laid off the rest of the staff, closed the office, and emptied the working bank accounts, stealing more than $50,000.[5]

Waters claimed to police that Jon Garth had called from San Diego to say that the lawsuit was going against them. According to the affidavit, Jon Garth instructed Waters to steal as much as $100,000 by cashing the organization's contributions in hand. Waters was to keep $15,000 for his services and leave $40,000 in the office safe for Jon Garth to retrieve upon his return.[6]

Waters's betrayal made Madalyn Murray O'Hair furious. The foot-dragging of the local authorities in bringing Waters to trial angered her further. His lenient sentence—restitution and probation—sent her into a scorched-earth rage. She decided to let everyone know the exact nature of the man who had betrayed her. According to the American Atheists' newsletter the teenage David Waters helped beat another boy to death with a post. When Waters was released, he apparently assaulted his own mother, knocking her senseless with a broom handle and then urinating on her. He had gone on to forge checks, commit burglaries, and be arrested for a number of assaults. Mrs. O'Hair claimed that the judiciary's leniency with such a ruthless animal could be explained only by its prejudice against her. If David Waters had stolen the same amount of money from a church, he would have been sent away for life.[7]

David Waters was not one to forget or forgive—or suffer any pangs of conscience in taking his revenge. When he finally acted, he counted on Mrs. O'Hair's history of hiding assets. People around her knew that the suit by Truth Seeker prompted preparations to conceal more assets—especially her multimillion-dollar library—in anticipation of going into hiding.

When Madalyn Murray O'Hair, Jon Garth Murray, and Robin Murray disappeared from their Texas home on August 28, 1995, nearly everyone believed that they had fled from public view to live off illegally funded foreign accounts.

That was the conclusion American Atheist employee David Travis drew when he came to work on August 28 and found a note posted on the door: "The Murray-O'Hair family has been called out of town on an emergency basis. We do not know how long we will be gone at the time of the writing of this memo."[8] Several months earlier Travis had opened a letter from New Zealand and found a bank statement from a secret account worth over a million dollars. He was naturally suspicious.

Police could find no signs of violence at the house the Murray-O'Hairs shared. But a few things didn't add up. Breakfast dishes had been left out. Mrs. O'Hair's diabetes medication sat on a kitchen counter. Most disturbing, the family's two cocker spaniels, Shannon and Gannon, had been left unattended. People knew that Robin loved her dogs far more than she did people.

The police did nothing. The lead investigator said that it wasn't a crime in Texas to disappear.

Two board members of American Atheists rapidly assumed control. Ellen Johnson and Spike Tyson reopened the headquarters and began processing back orders for books, all the while denying in public that anything was wrong. Tyson moved into the vacant Murray-O'Hair house. Johnson, the organization's newly proclaimed president, told reporters, "We just don't suspect foul play. . . . And I cannot tell you all the reasons why. We just—we just don't."[9] Johnson assured everyone that no organizational funds were missing.

Spike Tyson had apparently made cell-phone contact with Jon Garth Murray, who repeated that the family had been called away for reasons he didn't want to discuss. Sporadic phone contact with the Murray-O'Hairs continued for several weeks. Jon Garth and Robin continued to claim that nothing was wrong, although their tone indicated the opposite. Robin Murray's last words to Ellen Johnson were: "I know you will do the right thing."[10]

What was the right thing, though? For the new officials at American Atheists, the right thing turned out to be protecting the organization's reputation at all costs—not the lives of the Murray-O'Hairs. As Ellen Johnson and Spike Tyson delved into the records of the American Atheists, they found reason to believe that the trio had gone on the lam. The books showed that the Murray-O'Hairs had treated American Atheists as their own piggy bank.

Despite this, Johnson and Tyson continued to deny anything was wrong. Tyson specifically defended the Murray-O'Hairs against the rumor that they had stolen money. "We know where every bank account is," he said. "Every penny is accounted for."[11]

The only person who seemed to believe that the Murray-O'Hair trio might have been the victims of a crime, apparently, was William J. Murray III, Madalyn Murray O'Hair's estranged son. In 1980, Bill Murray publicly announced his conversion to Christianity, after which his mother would have nothing to do with him. She publicly repudiated her son. "One could call this a postnatal abortion on the part of a mother, I guess; I repudiate him entirely and completely for now and all times. . . . He is beyond human forgiveness."[12]

A year after the Murray-O'Hairs disappeared, Bill Murray filed a missing-persons report with the Austin police. This aroused protests from American Atheists. Spike Tyson accused Bill Murray of filing the report in order to gain publicity for his Christian ministry.[13]

About this same time, the summer of 1996, San Antonio reporter John MacCormack became interested in the case. MacCormack and private investigator Tim Young began tracking the movements of the Murray-O'Hairs during September of the previous year, using Jon Garth Murray's cell-phone records. MacCormack's stories spurred anonymous tips, which led to new leads, on which the police finally acted. The story of the last days of Madalyn Murray O'Hair, Jon Garth Murray, and Robin Murray proved gruesome.

It appears that the exposed employee, David Waters, recruited two of his jailhouse friends, Danny Fry and Gary Karr, into his scheme to kidnap the three Murray-O'Hairs and extort them. The men took the trio from Austin to San Antonio, sequestering them in a run-down hotel, the Warren Inn. While they kept Madalyn and her granddaughter under lock and key, Waters and his accomplices demanded that Jon Garth facilitate their theft of more than $600,000.

Karr allegedly flew with Jon Garth to New Jersey to arrange for an electronic transfer of funds to a San Antonio jeweler. Jon Garth was then forced to request that San Antonio jeweler Cory Ticknor convert $600,000 into gold coins. While this scheme was being worked out, the criminals were making huge cash withdrawals on the credit cards belonging to the Murray-O'Hairs.[14]

Although Jon Garth had ample opportunity to flee his kidnapper or contact the authorities, he apparently never attempted to do so. It seems that Bill Murray reasoned that his brother, who had always been derided by his mother as a nincompoop, thought he might finally prove his worth to his mother by being her rescuer. There's also the possibility, in my mind, that as much as the Murray-O'Hairs believed their lives were in danger, they were even more convinced that their lives as America's leading atheists would be over if they came under too much scrutiny. They were hoping to pay their way out of the mess and then truly go underground—using additional hidden assets that the murderous thieves never discovered.[15]

Once the money had been laundered through the purchase of gold coins, David Waters, Gary Karr, and Danny Fry evidently had no more use for the Murray-O'Hairs, however. After Robin was sexually molested, all three were murdered, probably by strangulation at the hands of David Waters. The bodies were then transported to a storage locker rented by another associate of Waters, "Chico" Osborne. In this confined space the bodies were dismembered with a bow saw and then stuffed into oil barrels. At some point, the bodies were partially burned. Afterward, the criminals transported their victims 120 miles to a desolate ranch and buried them, unbeknownst to the property's owner, in shallow graves.[16]

A day or two later, Danny Fry's services were apparently no longer needed by his criminal associates, and he was murdered. His naked, headless corpse was left along a lonesome Texas highway.

After the crimes, Waters cleaned out the storage locker with water and bleach. Waters, Karr, and their girlfriends then set to partying with $80,000 worth of the gold coins. They stashed the remainder of the loot in another storage locker rented by Waters's girlfriend.

Once the cash and the hangovers demanded refreshment, Waters returned to the storage locker to find that the remainder of the gold was missing. In a suitable twist of fate, another thieving party, who possessed a master key to the type of lock Waters's girlfriend used, happened on the treasure trove. In the end, the police recovered only one gold coin; the rest went to dissipation and disaster.

"I know you'll do the right thing," Robin Murray had said, pleading for her life. David Waters counted on the fact that grandmother Madalyn Murray O'Hair had long ago ruled out "the right thing."

———•◦•———

Madalyn Murray O'Hair's sad and sordid life becomes a contemporary parable of what happens when you know the truth and give yourself to a lie. You become evil yourself, neither able to live a good life nor die a good death.

Mrs. O'Hair may seem an extreme and uncommon example, but in fact, we are all more like her than we would care to think. We all are guilty of denying the truth and living in defiance of the good.

Try a little experiment. When you get up in the morning, pick one of your favorite sins—not the visible ones, but the ones you dream about—whether that's lust or gluttony or materialism (covetousness). Whatever you find most tempting. Then will yourself not to commit that sin in your thoughts, knowing that a sin in the mind leads eventually to sinful action. Start out the day absolutely determined, for example, that you will not covet, not want more things—no matter what happens.

Now I suppose you can avoid coveting or committing whatever your favorite sin happens to be by not turning on the television, not reading a magazine, not walking out of your home. Perhaps you can keep repeating to yourself for the entire day, "I will not covet." But in the normal course of life, you will not get through a single day without thinking the very thing that you have vowed not to. You can train your mind to think a certain way; you can even discipline your emotions, although that's much harder. But the will cannot be reformed by your best efforts. Your will has always, from birth, been bent out of shape. It takes a Higher Power—the infinite, personal God through Jesus Christ, I believe—to straighten it back out.

Happily, people can hear the truth, come to it, and reach for it. Or unhappily, they can fall short of the mark, their sin preventing them from accepting what they suspect to be the truth. These are the people to be most pitied. They can see God in the design of the universe, and they can recognize ethical certainties because the moral law has been written on their hearts. But they cannot get by their rebellious will, even when they know they should. People in that state are doomed at the very least to dysfunctional lives. Knowing one thing to be true and doing something else is the very definition of *dysfunction*.

It's easy to see Madalyn Murray O'Hair's dysfunction, but we all are dysfunctional in the same sense. We all sin. We know the truth but live in denial of it. We pursue the good life but consistently choose the opposite.

Some of us go further—we stop resisting the power of sin in our lives and give ourselves over to it. This happens when people who know the truth to the point of conviction willingly and perversely rebel against it. Sin has so worked in their hearts as to sear and harden their consciences. These are the most tragic cases because these individuals become evil in themselves and live the most wretched of lives.

You see the progression: The consistent denial of the truth leads to the willful defiance of the good. A horrifying prospect, which is why we have told the Madalyn Murray O'Hair story here as a cautionary tale.

---

But as stubborn as the human will can be, there is never any cause for despair. One of the questions most frequently thrown at Christians is, Why don't we see God acting in human history? The fact is, we do. We are not alone in the world with our destructive choices.

Years ago, I was speaking at the College of William and Mary. There was a question-and-answer period following my talk, and a man identifying himself as chair of the philosophy department walked to the microphone and engaged in an extended monologue about logical positivism. At some point he said, "And so, Mr. Colson, you can't prove God exists. But I'll give you the chance to do so right now. Ask your God to do a miracle. Let us see it right here." There was a good bit of laughter in the crowd and some applause at the gauntlet he threw down before me.

The audience may have thought for a moment he had me. I don't recall now all of what was going through my mind, but I suppose I was thinking through a number of logical rebuttals. But then something far more direct came to mind.

I told the man that if he wanted to see a miracle, he simply had to look at me. If he knew how totally God had transformed my heart and my will, he wouldn't need to look any further for miracles.

As we will see in the next chapter, God does act in history and in our lives. Christians call this Providence.

# LIVING

*the*

# GOOD LIFE

# CHAPTER 28

# PROVIDENCE

ONE SUNDAY MY church showed a video of random interviews with people at an upscale shopping center. The cameraman asked whether people felt their lives were directed by a power beyond themselves.

Apparently the cameraman encountered no Darwinists because, to my amazement, no one said no. Instead, the interviewees almost unanimously expressed their confidence that some force was guiding their lives. One person mentioned God, the others fate or destiny. One of the men interviewed said he used to think he was in control of his life, but he now understands he isn't. He often waits for signs, he said, before making important decisions. He added that as he looks back, he realizes that many signs were placed in his path, but he just didn't see them. He didn't speculate who might have put them there.

As humans, we have an innate sense that our lives are governed by something beyond us. I believe that sense is implanted within each of us by the purposeful Designer. That's why all religions and most philosophic systems seek to explain the connection between the individual and the universal will. Christianity's explanation is that God has not only created us but also sustains us and guides us. Ultimately, God shapes all of history, and our part in it, toward His own ends. That's Providence.

Even people who speak as if they believe in something less than a personal God end up attributing some of the Christian God's characteristics to their own conceptions. Remember Heather Mills McCartney, whose life story and advocacy against land mines we discussed in chapter 3? When she lost her leg in the accident, she said, "It seems like fate's way of telling me there is something else in store."[1]

How can *fate* "tell us" anything? The ancient Stoics believed that every event is determined by fate. But the Stoics' fate, or destiny, didn't make suggestions; fate governed human life as surely as gravity. Yet Heather Mills McCartney's statement suggests that the power governing her life cares for her on some level. Fate cannot operate in this way; it's simply the way things turn out. Ms. McCartney's statement suggests she believes that a more personal force behind fate actually controls the course of events.

People's widespread belief that their lives are governed by greater purposes than their own self-will contradicts the belief in a random universe. If the world is governed by chance, then life is a matter of luck, and concepts like fate and destiny are worthless. Life is truly "sound and fury, signifying nothing."[2] But something in us protests, suggesting that the shape of our lives does have its reason.

Film critic Brian Godawa uses the movie *Cast Away* to illustrate how our culture tries to substitute fate for a God who is in control. Tom Hanks plays the part of a FedEx employee whose plane crashes in the Pacific and who is then washed up on a deserted island. We watch Hanks build a shelter, create tools, and seek companionship by painting a face (from his blood) on a volleyball. He eventually builds a sail-fitted boat, sets out to sea, and is rescued one morning by a ship whose bellowing horn rouses him from near unconsciousness.

When Hanks returns to civilization, he discovers he has lost his fiancée. But that's okay, because the one FedEx package he's safeguarded through his entire ordeal leads him to another lovely woman. The movie ends hopefully, with Hanks at a crossroads, contemplating signs that are pointing in two different directions. He looks both ways, stares, studies, thinks, shrugs his shoulders, and walks in one direction, looking forward to where fate will take him next.[3] (Or perhaps hopelessly, if one road is as good as another and our choices have no consequences.)

We cannot live with randomness and nothingness, as Puritan theologian Jonathan Edwards argued. The thought that we are alive on this spinning planet with no purpose, no plan, no future is simply untenable. So those who reject God as their guide in life often fall for just about any substitute to fill the void. That's why one-quarter of the

American people read and believe astrology columns. Nancy Reagan, when she was in the White House, believed in astrology so much she advised the president to order his schedule according to the alignment of the stars.

Do intelligent people really believe that the stars affect us? What they do believe is that individual will and the universal will must be connected, and they would like the connection to come without any moral strings attached. C. S. Lewis remarked, "It is nice to be able to think of this great, mysterious Force rolling on through the centuries and carrying you on its crest . . . [provided it is] only a blind force with no morals and no mind, [and] will never interfere with you like that troublesome God we learned about when we were children."[4]

People run away from God because, unlike a mysterious force, the God of the Bible imposes moral demands they are unwilling to face. But they never cease to hunger for the assurance that only God can provide, even as they check out the astrology column. That assurance is there if we open our eyes. Over and over we see the evidence of God's hand that guides both individuals and nations.

The feisty Berkeley law professor Phillip Johnson, whom we met ealier, experienced Providence in an unmistakable way. Johnson and I have worked closely together for more than a decade. I've watched him masterfully take over as commanding general of the great movement of scientists and intellectuals who are bringing forward the evidence of Intelligent Design, as we discussed in chapter 20. What an incredibly important and strategic job Johnson has had.

Then in his early sixties, at the peak of his game, Johnson was suddenly struck down with a serious stroke that left him paralyzed and confined to bed. I remember how depressed the news left me. All the reports I heard from Johnson's close friends and family were grim; he would likely not recover his faculties. How could God allow such a thing to happen? Surely God must know that Johnson's role was indispensable.

With great medical care and devoted attention from his family, Johnson slowly managed to recover most of his physical capacities. Fortunately, his mind was not impaired. An earnest, determined man, he worked hard with his speech and physical therapists until he could once again function—at least with the aid of others.

Johnson wrote a poignant memoir about his illness.[5] The one thing he feared most in life, he confessed, was damage to his brain; death was far less frightening than the "shame of helplessness." There were times as he lay in the hospital bed, confused and depressed, the left side of his body paralyzed, when he wished he would just die. Self-pity gripped him, along with, as he puts it, "the dragons of the mind," exaggerated terrors.

Johnson writes about his experience in the hospital room, which was often filled with loving friends praying for him. On one visit, a friend from his church sang a simple hymn: "On Christ the solid rock I stand, all other ground is sinking sand."[6] The words of that song pierced the depth of Johnson's soul. He realized that he had built his life on shifting sand, not on solid rock. Oh, he was a Christian—at least he saw himself that way. He had become a believer, though, because he was "a skeptic about everything else." A "recovering rationalist" who had found all the flaws in the world's logic, he had never come to trust his life fully to Jesus Christ. Such an intimately personal faith "seemed too sentimental a thing to bear the full weight of a life at its most desperate moment."[7] But as he lay helpless in the hospital, the words of the hymn filling his thoughts, he realized that only Jesus could be his solid rock. In that moment, he went from being an intellectual Christian, one who could argue for the truth, to a Christian genuinely filled with God's Spirit.

Although Johnson still has health problems and experiences aftereffects of the stroke, he has become a far more effective advocate, fiercely determined. He is also a much, much different person, both calmer and gentler.

Did God give Johnson the stroke to get this proud professor's attention? I do not believe that for a moment. Illness affects every mortal body. We're all headed toward decay. Dust to dust. No, I don't think God delivers these nearly fatal blows to punish or teach us, but He does allow them to happen, and He uses them for His purposes.

---

Providence is often something that we understand only in retrospect. I look back on my life and see clearly the evidence of its invisible hand guiding my life at critical points—even before I was a believer. I took so much of what happened in my life to be my own design—my time in the U.S. Marines, law school, government. But I now see it instead as preparation for something much greater.

If you were to design a prototypical prison-ministry leader, someone who could relate to inmates and evangelize them, you might design someone just like me. First of all, I've been in prison. When I was visiting a very tough prison one day, surrounded by inmates, one of them taunted me, "Colson, you were in one of those country clubs. What are you doing coming to talk to us in here?" It was one of the rare occasions when a prisoner has challenged me. There were probably a hundred inmates in the room at the time, and before I could respond, the other inmates shouted down the heckler, saying, "No! He's been just where we are. He knows what prison is like. He's one of us."

Second, I have a reputation for being tough. Sadly, too many prisons operate on the law of the jungle; the tough survive. Today I may arrive at a prison dressed like a business executive in a coat and tie, but the inmates know I was also a marine officer, and there is no more respected profession in a prison than the marines. On top of that, I was known as Nixon's tough guy, a description I didn't like at the time, but one that has served me well over the years in prisons.

Finally, I was a lawyer and a high government official. Prison inmates are in a nearly constant tangle with the legal system, and they have to deal with the problems caused by government policies and decisions.

I'm always a little bit surprised by the attention the inmates give me when I preach in prisons—and I've been in hundreds and hundreds of prisons and preached thousands of times. The younger inmates have no memory of Watergate or President Nixon, but still they're keenly interested in what I have to say. Why? Because of how God prepared me—and, of course, because I've kept coming back over the years.

Did God declare His purpose for me during those first months after I was released from prison and was questioning what to do with my life? I had some very tempting offers in business and in law. I wanted to do something that was far less public. I wanted to be with my kids and spend some time getting my life together. Yet I kept feeling a persistent urge that I should be doing something for prisoners. That was not what I wanted to do. It's not a very glamorous way to spend your life. A Washington acquaintance who befriended me during this period and organized a small prayer group for my support wanted me to work with political leaders through Bible studies. That certainly would have been logical.

Still, I couldn't shake off the conviction that I was being called into prisons. Like Jacob of the Old Testament, I wrestled with God until the break of day. Jacob ended up with a bad hip; I ended up with a conviction that I should be in the prisons.

Was it Providence? It certainly wasn't my self-will.

———•◦•———

A number of years ago, I experienced how God shapes events for His own purposes when I suffered the most serious illness of my life, one that gave me a taste of what it's like to die. I was in the Philippines, scheduled to give a speech, when my stomach started acting up. I was experiencing a great deal more discomfort than accompanies the usual digestive travel woes. Then I discovered I was bleeding internally and assumed I had a hemorrhaging stomach ulcer. I went ahead and gave the speech, which was a big mistake; the pain began hitting me harder than ever.

Back in my hotel room, I considered my options. Becoming seriously ill in a Third World country always carries an added element of panic. Would I get adequate medical treatment? Would I survive?

A friend persuaded a local urologist to look at me (not the right specialty, but the only one available). He prescribed Zantac and some other medication. I decided to sleep through the night and make my decision about entering the hospital in the morning. When I awoke, I decided I'd fly home. The doctor advised against the flight—he couldn't tell whether my internal hemorrhaging had stopped—but I went anyway.

The flight took fourteen hours, and I was later told that if the bleeding hadn't stopped on its own accord, I would have died in flight.

When I went in for tests at home, the radiologist looked at the X-rays and diagnosed an ulcer. He said it wasn't bleeding any longer, and he thought if I took the right medicines, I'd be okay. My regular doctor, Joe Spano, didn't trust the X-ray, however. It didn't seem right to him that the ulcer had bled and then stopped on its own. He performed an endoscopy and—just as he suspected—discovered a tumor. I didn't actually have an ulcer at all. The tumor had simply irritated the stomach lining, which caused the bleeding and made it appear on the X-ray as if an ulcer existed. Additional tests indicated the tumor was benign.

I had my schedule booked for the next year, so I thought I'd wait to have the tumor operated on. But Joe Bailey, a stomach surgeon and supporter of the ministry, advised against waiting. "Get it out now," he said. He knew that if a benign gastric tumor turned cancerous and began to penetrate the stomach lining, it could be deadly.

My friends in Washington recommended Georgetown University Hospital. When I met with the surgeon there, I told him that my doctor in Florida had advised me that because the tumor was benign, the surgeon should simply take it out and not do a stomach resection.

"Do you want to compromise the surgery?" the surgeon asked me. "I won't know what the state of this tumor is until I get a good look at it. For all I know, you do have cancer, Mr. Colson."

I detected a good bit of arrogance in his attitude, and I should have walked out the door right then. But I decided to go ahead with the surgery.

I was on the operating table for four hours, during which time the surgeon extracted the tumor and surrounding lymph nodes. He did a major stomach resection, in which all of his interns took part as a learning exercise.

When I came out of the anesthesia, I saw Patty and Emily looking down at me.

"Was it cancer?" I asked.

"Yes," they said.

"Did they get it all?"

"Yes."

I said, "Great!" and that truly expressed my feeling, which I put down to God's grace. I really wasn't afraid.[8]

During the next five days my condition worsened and became hellish. The tube draining my stomach wasn't inserted properly, and my stomach began to bloat, tearing at the incisions. I developed a serious infection and a fever so high that I became delusional.

The surgeon came to my room to solve the infection problem. I couldn't take painkillers in adequate dosages because with my fever, they were making me delirious. For this or whatever reason, the surgeon dispensed with any anesthesia to solve the problem. He simply took his scalpel, leaned across my body on the bed—I remember the smell of cigars on him—punched a hole in the stitched-up incision and inserted a drainage tube. I've never before or since screamed that loud.

On the following Saturday night, my fever was raging, and I was clearly out of my head. The nurse thought I was dying, and she called Patty and Emily. I remember surfacing from the delusions for a moment or two here and there. I remember thinking this really could be the end. I knew that my body was struggling to stay alive and that it wasn't winning the battle. I felt at peace, though, because I knew I was in God's hands.

I lost thirty pounds during the course of a twenty-eight-day recovery in the hospital. My wounds had to remain open in order to heal from the outside in. Every four hours the wounds had to be dressed, which meant taking off the bandages, swabbing the wounds, and putting the bandages back on. I survived the pain of this procedure by hanging on to the bedposts and clenching all of my muscles. The pain continued to be unbearable and couldn't be treated with morphine because the drug slows down all bodily functions, including the stomach. If I wanted to recover, I simply had to tough it out.

When I had been in the hospital for three and a half weeks, I was still connected to a host of IVs, but I was mobile. I could walk around the hospital, which was a great relief.

The hospital administrator came in one day to ask how I was doing. He mentioned that he had just been fending off reporter Bob Woodward from trying to sneak into former Director of Central Intelligence Bill Casey's room. Casey had recently had extensive brain surgery. Apparently, Woodward had been as aggressive as always because the administrator said, "I never realized what you went through in Watergate until now."

"Where is Bill?" I asked. Casey was a good friend of mine, and I was concerned about him.

"He's on the floor right above you. When you hear all those chairs being moved around, that's Casey's security people."

I told the administrator that I'd like to see my friend. He said that Casey's security detail was keeping everyone out—only Vice President Bush, the general counsel of the CIA, and Casey's family had been allowed in. But he told me he would inquire.

Twenty minutes later, Bill Casey's wife, Sophia, called. If I wanted to see Bill, I could come up. So, with Patty providing invaluable assistance with my IV hanger and its multiple lines, we took the elevator upstairs.

Two security guards stood outside Casey's room. When Bill saw me coming through the door, he smiled. He was leaning against a bank of pillows, propped on his side. His expression was like that of a stroke victim, with one side of his face frozen and his mouth curling down. The right side of his head, where the surgery had been performed, was caved in, creating a grotesque effect. He became a little weepy at seeing me.

I told him my story to explain how I had come to see him in my pajama-and-IV finery. He couldn't reply, only smile and grunt. Not one intelligible word—a detail that's important for a reason I'll mention later.

I asked if he would like me to pray with him. He quickly nodded to this suggestion. I asked him, "Do you know the Lord? Are you at peace with Jesus?"

He looked at me quizzically—as if to say, why would you ask me such a question? I knew that he was a devout Catholic, and I wasn't presuming to judge his faith; I simply wanted to make sure that he had the personal assurance I knew in facing death. "See that crucifix on the wall?" I asked. "You know what that means, that Jesus died for your sins. That's what it's all about. Nothing else matters. Would you like to pray?"

He nodded enthusiastically. Sophia, Bill, and I joined hands. We prayed together, and when we finished praying, there were tears running down Bill Casey's cheeks. I don't know what went on inside Bill's mind that day. I do believe at the least that his faith was deepened and strengthened. All I know for sure is that I was in that hospital at that time in order to pray with him. God used my illness, my treatment decisions, and my own brush with death to bring me into that room and make me sensitive to what my friend was thinking and feeling—the questions he needed to be reminded of and the assurance he needed to hear. Sophia told me later that my visit was the most meaningful thing that happened to Bill while he was in the hospital. He died two months later.

Two years after my hospital stay, Bob Woodward released a book in which he claimed that Casey had "confessed" to approving the illegal

Iran-Contra weapons-for-money exchange. Woodward's book depicts Casey as having made this admission, in his own words, while sitting in his hospital room, looking normal. I knew from my visit with Bill Casey, within hours of Woodward's supposed visit, that such a confession could never have happened. First, the security guards would never have allowed Woodward in, and, second, Casey simply couldn't speak even if they had. When Casey's purported confession made headlines, I was able to rebut the charges. That was another good thing that came out of my illness. I was in a position to keep that part of history straight and defend a fine man's honor.

On a subsequent thorough biopsy, my tumor proved to be benign. If they'd known that during the operation, they would have simply removed the tumor without taking much of my stomach. But then, of course, I wouldn't have been in the hospital for a month and wouldn't have seen Bill Casey. So sometimes Providence can cost us.

You can choose to see all of the above as happenstance, of course. Or you can see the hand of God. The workings of Providence require eyes of faith because experience can always be read in different ways. The experience of grace I saw in Bill Casey's tear-filled eyes assured me that God had brought a great good out of a most difficult time.

———•◦•———

As I look back over my life, I realize I have had many experiences like my visit with Bill Casey: highlights of God's guidance. God's presence has been evident in small things as well. I've written more than twenty books, and repeatedly I've had the extraordinary experience of being deeply immersed in a difficult, serious subject, wrestling with how best to present it, only to pick up a book or article that directly addresses the issue. In writing this book, while I was concentrating on the story of Nien Cheng's experience of seeing the spider in her cell, I happened during a lunch break to rummage through a box of books that had been sent to me six months earlier by a member of my staff. The first book I picked up was published in Germany and translated into English. I had never heard of it. I cracked the book open to the very page where it described the intricacies of the spider and its web. Now, of course, that could have been a coincidence, except in my writing career the same type of "coincidence" has happened on dozens of occasions. Aleksandr Solzhenitsyn, the great Soviet dissident writer, had the same experience, which he describes in his memoirs, *The Oak and the Calf.* He tells about how he would often sit down to write and feel an invisible hand take his and guide it across the page as the words flowed.

———·•·———

I've also seen evidence of Providence in big decisions. On a trip to Europe in 1996, I felt particularly exhausted and drained. At the time, I was chairman not only of Prison Fellowship in the United States but also of Prison Fellowship International, which is a separate ministry that reaches more than one hundred countries throughout the world. On this particular trip I was to visit prisons and volunteers in Russia, Romania, Bulgaria, and the Czech Republic. It was an exhilarating experience, particularly walking through the Russian prisons and seeing the great work that was being done ministering to people in the most hopeless circumstances. Sitting alone in a Moscow hotel room, however, I came to the conclusion that it was time for me to turn over the chairmanship of Prison Fellowship International to someone else. The president of that organization, Ron Nikkel, is an extraordinarily gifted man with great cross-cultural sensitivities. Surely we could find a chairman who could spend more time helping Ron. I was simply stretched too thin. I prayed, asking God what I should do.

At Prison Fellowship International's next board meeting, in Paris, I announced to the startled directors that I would be stepping down as chairman and would ask Tom Pratt, then president of Prison Fellowship in the U.S., to take the seat *pro tem* while the board conducted a search for a new chairman. Despite the shocked reaction of the board, I sensed it was the right thing to do. If I had procrastinated, the board might never have acted.

After the meeting, a few of the board members gathered, and we all agreed that the perfect candidate would be Mike Timmis, an American businessman and member of the board of Prison Fellowship in the United States. Mike had extensive interests abroad and was a deeply devoted Christian. I suspected he wasn't looking for volunteer work that might demand up to half of his time. Nevertheless, we placed a call from the hotel room in Paris, tracked him down, and asked him if he would take the job. He wondered if we had been spending too much time in the legendary French vineyards.

For the next six months, Mike and his wife, Nancy, thought about the offer, prayed about it, and visited with Patty and me on many evenings. It was a huge commitment, and Mike needed to think and pray it through carefully.

One day I received an excited call from Mike. He said, "Chuck, my wife, Nancy, is not one to see visions or detect signs from God. She's a very reserved, down-to-earth Christian. But she had an incredible experience while I was away on a trip. She believes that God told her—in an audible voice—that I should take this position. I'm going to accept."

Mike Timmis turned out to be a far better leader of the international movement than I was, and the overseas ministry has almost doubled in size since he became chairman.

The providential experience we had in finding my successor in the domestic ministry of Prison Fellowship may have been even more dramatic. When I turned sixty-two, Prison Fellowship decided to find the person we could bring in and train as my successor. Board member Ken Wessner said, "You know, the time has come. A good leader always plans for his succession."

So we formed a committee. We decided what the ministry should look like and the kind of person who could bring about our vision. We hired a recruiter—a high-profile headhunter. He sat at the conference table one night and asked the board, "Tell me who would be the perfect person to fill your position. If you could pick one person who was suited in every respect to take the job, who would that be?"

I said, "Mark Earley."

I barely knew Mark, having met him only once, but I had read a lot about this young, dynamic politician. He had served in the Virginia State Senate and had recently been elected attorney general by the largest margin in the state's history. He was highly respected. I had already written about him as a praiseworthy example of a Christian in politics.

"He won't do it," I told the headhunter, "because he's the newly elected attorney general in Virginia, but he would be perfect. He has a missionary background, and he's incredibly bright—a young man in his forties. But, as I say, he probably won't take the job."

The headhunter and several members of the committee went to see Mark Earley. When the recruiter reported to me, he said, "You are absolutely right. He would be perfect. He has all the qualifications, the personality, everything. As you said, though, he intends to fill out his term as attorney general. He'd be interested were it not for his present commitment."

We might have chosen to wait out Mark's term, but I suspected he'd be running for governor in four years, which is the usual career path for an attorney general in Virginia. Because Virginia was a Republican state and Mark Earley was an extraordinarily popular Republican, I thought he was a cinch to win. So he appeared to be out of the picture.

We continued to search for four years, from 1997 to 2001. During that time, we brought in twenty-five candidates, and we came close to offering the position to several.

One time we had almost settled on a man who had a terrific and highly successful background in business and finance. He'd left his position in midlife to work in fund-raising for another ministry. Some of the board members questioned his spiritual maturity, but I was sold; by this time, I was willing to overlook some things. The board was close to making this man an offer; the train was out of the station and rolling down the track. Then, on a bus ride in California with Prison Fellowship volunteers, I happened to be discussing the candidate with another ministry leader. One of the volunteers overhead the conversation and suggested we do a bit more checking. I called the leader of the ministry where the candidate had been working, and he raised several red flags.

I nearly threw up my hands. Would we *ever* find the right person?

That was in October 2001, two weeks before Election Day, when the governorship of Virginia would be decided. As I had expected, Mark Earley had won the Republican nomination and was running as a heavy favorite. His opponent, however, had a deep war chest. Democrat Mark Warner was a venture capitalist who had made a substantial fortune in the high-tech boom of the 1990s. According to published accounts, he spent millions of his own money on his campaign.[9] He absolutely blitzed Mark Earley with ads.

The Earley campaign had trouble gaining traction—everything that could go wrong, did go wrong. President Bush was supposed to campaign for him, but because of the terrorist attacks, the president never made it. The Republican National Committee figured Earley was going to win and took little interest.

Against every prediction, including my own, Mark Earley lost the election.

Within a week I called him. "Are you interested?" I asked.

"Yes," he responded. After the campaign, Mark sensed that God was calling him to something else. In his morning devotional time he kept reading about justice and prisoners.

He came and had lunch with me, and I immediately knew he was the right person for the job. A few weeks later, after we had conducted due diligence reports and Mark had met with the board, he was hired.

Mark Earley has turned out to be a tremendous leader. Our ministry has performed better in his hands than it did in mine by any measure—contributions, budget, ministry achieved, and morale. That is Providence.

---

Providence is the Christian's answer to fate, destiny, or chance. Christians believe that God has a purpose for history and that He works this purpose out through people's lives.

In the colonial era of Jonathan Edwards, Enlightenment thinkers challenged the historical basis of biblical teaching, saying that history was an unreliable guide to any truth that might claim universality. In their view, history was too particular and idiosyncratic.

> *Christians believe that God has a purpose for history and that He works this purpose out through people's lives.*

Edwards and others responded by saying that history has been guided by God's invisible hand, and it reveals a providential order in which God is the primary actor.[10] If history were the result of accidental processes, we would have no way of gleaning universal truth because no one—apart from Christ Himself—has ever stood outside of history. This is why theology and history have been so closely related.

Scripture also tells us that God determines the times set for nations and individuals as well as the places they shall live.[11] That is, Providence applies not only to individual lives but also to the affairs of state.

Our Founders certainly understood this. In the closing words of the Declaration of Independence, the authors expressed their "firm reliance on the protection of divine Providence." The Founders referred to this concept repeatedly in the Federalist Papers.

No American figure dealt more eloquently and meaningfully with the concept of Providence than Abraham Lincoln. Books have been written about Lincoln's spiritual life, none of which has fully answered the question about whether he was a theist or a Christian believer. One thing, however, is absolutely clear: Lincoln understood and relied on Providence. "I hold myself in my present position and with the authority vested in me as an instrument of Providence," he wrote to a friend.[12] His famous "Proclamation Appointing a National Fast Day" is replete with references to God's firm hand directing the affairs of the nation.

Lincoln's private thoughts ran along exactly the same lines; his invocation of Providence was not merely political rhetoric. In a conversation with a minister working with soldiers during the Civil War, Lincoln said, "If it were not for my firm belief in an overruling Providence, it would be difficult for me, in the midst of such complications of affairs, to keep my reason on its seat. But I am confident that the Almighty has His plans, and will work them out; and, whether we see it or not, they will be best for us."[13] In 1862, he told Quaker confidantes that God "permits [the war] for some wise purpose of His own, mysterious and unknown to us. . . . We cannot but believe that He who made the world still governs it."[14]

———•◦•———

If God is with us, if the steps of our lives are indeed ordered not by fate or luck but by divine Providence, then so, too, are the events of our deaths. A truly good life looks forward to a final mercy, a good death. Is there such a thing? What does death reveal about the way we have lived?

# CHAPTER 29

# A GOOD DEATH

ONE OF THE most remarkable men I've known was Bill Bright. As a young businessman he heard God's call to abandon his thriving business—Bright's California Confections—and give his life to evangelism. In 1951, he and his wife, Vonette, started the ministry of Campus Crusade for Christ. It began with a handful of friends gathered together for a meeting. Today the Orlando-based ministry employs more than 26,000 full-time staff and more than 550,000 trained volunteers working in more than 190 countries. It is a well-run, vibrant Christian ministry.

For more than fifty years Bill and Vonette gave themselves totally to the ministry, never once looking back. Bill had boundless energy, even into his later years, keeping a travel schedule that would have withered most men half his age. He was an amazingly humble man, simple in his ways but completely focused on one goal: to evangelize the world.

When Bill was in his late seventies, he was diagnosed with pulmonary fibrosis, a disease that almost always results in a slow, agonizing death. As the lung tissue hardens, the lungs lose their capacity to process oxygen. If something like a heart attack doesn't intervene, the person slowly suffocates. I've known a number of people who found pulmonary fibrosis so debilitating that they simply wanted to give up. It saps energy, leaving the person in an ever-deteriorating state of exhaustion.

When Bill told me about his prognosis, he did so without self-pity. He was his usual buoyant self over the telephone, filled with excitement and enthusiasm about the various projects he was undertaking,

even as he knew he would go through a two- or three-year process leading to death.

Bill's doctor found his attitude inexplicable. After the doctor told
Bill that pulmonary fibrosis was worse than a heart attack or cancer, he
bluntly told Bill, "You will choke to death."

Bill replied, "Thank you, Lord."

The doctor countered, "You don't understand," and he reiterated
how awful Bill Bright's death was going to be. He worried that Bill was
in denial about his condition.

Bill explained he was only affirming his faith. "I believe the Bible,
and it says Christians are to give thanks in *all* things and to rejoice whatever the news."[1]

I visited Bill many times in the three years between the diagnosis
and his death. At times, he had difficulty walking as he had to lug
around an oxygen tank and keep its tubes in his nostrils. He was always
upbeat, though. In one of those meetings he spent over an hour giving
me suggestions for how Prison Fellowship could be made more effective, many of which we have followed, to our great advantage.

Throughout this period Bill would send me manuscripts of books,
articles, and radio transcripts he had written while virtually bedridden.
During 2001 and 2002, he worked on more than eighty projects, according to one aide's count.[2] He organized conferences, arranged speakers,
and made videotapes as part of his teaching legacy.

Two weeks before his death, Bill and I had a last phone conversation. I wanted to let him know what I would be saying at his funeral. It
wasn't a morbid conversation in the slightest. I said, "Bill, I want you to
hear the things that I'm going to say about you when you're gone, but I
want you to hear them while you're alive, not just when you're watching us from heaven." I told him, as I said at the memorial service later,
that I would never forget sitting at a table one day with him and other
Christian leaders. We were debating deep theological issues. Bill interrupted the contentious discussion and said, "I'm not as concerned
about theology as I am about standing before the Lord someday and not
having to confess that I failed to lead every single person I could to
Christ." What a courageous, direct spirit he had!

In our conversations during those last years, I never detected a hint
of self-pity or discouragement. He must have had those moments, but

only Vonette, who was constantly at his side, would have known. Bill was born a leader and would never show discouragement or disappointment to those charged with following him. To the end of his life, he was always looking for ways to help other people.

In his final days Bill Bright gave his staff a charge, which ended with these words: "By faith, walk in His light, enjoy His presence, love with His love, and rejoice that you are never alone; He is with you, always to bless!"[3] Bill Bright understood that the good life means accepting that our lives ultimately belong to God. He resisted taking sedatives that would have hastened his death. He also talked with Vonette about the importance of yielding to God's final call. Perhaps as a result of his attitude (and, I have to think, his godliness), his last moments were not the unmitigated horror his doctor had predicted. Right before Bill died, Vonette leaned close and said, "I want you to go to be with Jesus, and Jesus wants you to come to him. Why don't you let him carry you to heaven?" She looked away, and when she looked back, her husband was no longer breathing. She saw the last pulse in his neck, and with that he was gone. She thought of the psalm "Precious in the sight of the Lord is the death of his saints," and the prayer of St. Francis of Assisi: "For it is in dying, we are born to eternal life."[4]

Living the good life means not only living it to the fullest every moment we're alive but also facing death with equanimity and then dying well. A lot of people have this wrong. They think that you live life to the fullest and enjoy every moment you can, and then when death comes, you simply accept the hard fact. The good time is over. Life is ended.

*The good life means accepting that our lives ultimately belong to God.*

That's not the way to see it.

I've discovered that some of the people who are best adjusted to the reality of life and the question of death are those on death row, particularly Christians. Over the years, I have visited literally thousands of condemned men and women in many countries of the world. You would think that someone given a death sentence, confined to a cold cell, maybe getting an hour of exercise in a barbed-wire-enclosed yard outside would despair and give up on life. Many inmates do not. Earlier I mentioned Sam, the death-row inmate who was studying to be a minister and didn't want to waste his time by watching television.

Something about the certainty of death forces us to focus our lives. Samuel Johnson once said, "When a man knows he is to be hanged in a fortnight, it concentrates his mind wonderfully."[5] I have found this to be more than a facetious quip. In one sense it is a very healthy thing to live knowing we are going to die. The old saints used to keep skulls on their desks for this very reason. If we believe that our lives belong to God, as Bill Bright did, then we can say with the apostle Paul, "to live is Christ and to die is gain"—and mean it.[6] We can *enjoy* every stage of life, including old age and final illness, entrusting our lives to God's care. We need to accept the seasons of life and learn what God has to teach us through each.

———•◦•———

This is hardly the secular attitude. Western culture has become obsessed with forestalling aging and death. People fight it, beginning at an amazingly early age in life, with Botox, tummy tucks, hair dyes and implants, and massive consumption of vitamins and nutritional supplements. In today's biotech era, we are tantalized by the possibility of extending life, both in length and quality. Gene implants may allow us to conceive and bear children until we're a hundred years old. With the possibility of organ transplants, people ask why we should ever have to die. They are so fascinated by this that they are unwilling to contemplate any ethical restraints on biotech research. We seem to be on the verge of truly discovering the proverbial Fountain of Youth.

> *Something about the certainty of death forces us to focus our lives.*

To think this way mocks our humanity and God's wisdom, however. The Christian has a stereoscopic vision of death—one understanding from two slightly different angles. First, death is always the great enemy, God's judgment on humankind for sin. But we also believe Jesus, by His death, has conquered sin and death.[7] Christ's bodily resurrection is the Christian's guarantee that "if we died with Christ, we believe that we will also live with him."[8]

Yet from another perspective God's judgment is also his mercy, in death as in everything else. Here's what I mean. It's often said that aging isn't for sissies. I used to leap out of bed in the morning. I still leap, but now I hear the loud cracks in my joints, and pain sometimes grips my back. As I've aged, I've noticed other changes as well, some of which are for me even more regrettable. I've always prided myself on having a photographic memory. If I still do, it's a little harder getting the lens to focus. So there's a price to pay as our bodies slow down. Dying goes on in the midst of life.

> *Living the good life means not only living it to the fullest every moment we're alive but also facing death with equanimity and then dying well.*

These reminders of mortality help us focus, though, on the things that really matter. A healthy awareness of death spurs us to enjoy our relationships with family and friends more. Why do you think men are often so much more patient as grandfathers than they were as fathers? Contemplating death is healthy, not unhealthy.

For me, aging has brought a deep appreciation of natural beauty. It was there all along, but now this appreciation has greatly intensified in the autumn of my life. The world has become dearer.

The aches and pains of old age make the prospect of death far less frightening. We are being led, as French essayist Montaigne put it, "by nature's hand, down a gentle and virtually imperceptible slope, bit by bit, one step at a time she rolls us into this wretched state and makes us familiar with it; so that we find no shock when youth dies within us, which in essence and in truth is a harder death than the complete death of a languishing life or death of old age."[9]

Because we are fallen creatures, the idea that we could live forever is an invitation to total irresponsibility. If we lived forever, we would no longer care about our children because we could live beyond them. We would feel no responsibility to pass on the wisdom we have acquired in life. We would become insufferable in our presumed invincibility. We see from history what happens to people when they believe they have unlimited power—and how much more power could we have to believe that we could live forever? That's why God's judgment on humanity was also a mercy; death delivers us from enduring a never-ending life of pride and isolation.

The sentence of death is also felt in our lack of satisfaction with this life. Limitations drive us to seek and find whatever speaks of eternity. The poet Wallace Stevens wisely said, "Not to have is the beginning of desire."[10] What he meant, of course, is that fulfillment paradoxically begins with need. Leon Kass, chairman of the President's Council on Bioethics, believes that the shortness of our lives urges us to fulfill our capacities. Genuine human happiness, according to Kass, comes with the satisfaction one realizes as "the bloom that graces unimpeded soul-exercising activity."[11]

The reality that we will face death spurs our aspiration, the desire to accomplish much with our lives while we can. When we act on our ambitions and exercise our God-given powers, we feel God's pleasure in His creation and His creatures. Great fulfillment has come in my life from the aspirations for greater things, particularly after these goals were driven less by my ego and more by addressing the needs God showed me. Working against the deadline of mortality forces us to come to a reckoning, an accounting with our lives: What have we done right, and what have we done wrong? This had to be one of James Ryan's principal motivations when he went back at age seventy to the grave marker of the man who saved his life at age twenty. In a sense, we're preparing for what we all suspect will be an accounting, and this in turn may lead us to find the God who alone can deliver us from mortality.

In the latter stages of life, we can also feel great fulfillment as we reflect on a life well lived, which requires submission to the number of years God has allotted us. This applies to all of us when we think about our families, our friends, and the good things we have done. When we reflect on the sun's rising to the call of the birds, as the composer Messiaen did. When we enjoy all the gifts God gives us in His creation. When we have worked hard and well. In the end, may we be able to have inscribed on our tombstones, as Bill Bright did, "Slave of Christ."

Death calls us to consider what this life is for, even as our longings for eternity suggest that mortal life is but a preparation for immortality. That's why a Christian's natural fear of death is mitigated; death is merely a transition point from the world in which we have been privileged to live into the promised world to come. This is why Christians face death with equanimity and in some cases even joy.

A man who mentored me in my ministry and was one of my closest friends, Ken Wessner, was stricken with kidney cancer when he was seventy-one. He bore up with great resolution through the painful and difficult period of operations, radiation, and chemotherapy. Just like Bill Bright, Ken never seemed dismayed.

When I visited with Ken in the hospital, he was alert and vibrant. He had been the successful CEO of ServiceMaster, then spent his retirement years committed to the ministries for which he had such a passion. The day I visited, I had no idea that he was near death. One couldn't tell by looking at him. He obviously knew it, though, and was making preparations carefully and deliberately, as he dictated detailed instructions to his wife, Norma, on a wide range of matters.

Norma told me that two days after my visit, Ken Wessner spoke with his friend Ken Hansen, the man whom Wessner had succeeded as head of ServiceMaster. Hansen, also a devout Christian, was in another hospital, dying as well. Norma said the conversation between the two friends was extraordinary; both men were almost jubilant, talking about how they looked forward to their reunion in heaven. There were no tears, no remorse, only pure joy. Both men started talking about Jesus' promises of the coming resurrection and having new bodies. Since both had suffered so much in their last illnesses, the thought of having new bodies led them to break out laughing. What a relief that was going to be!

Isn't this the way every one of us wants to die, celebrating life in the expectation of what God has for us, not angry, bitter, dejected, and certainly not fearful? In stark contrast, think of what my one-time debating partner, Madalyn Murray O'Hair, said: "I hope I live my life in such a manner that when I die, someone cares—even if it is only my dogs. I think I want some human being somewhere to weep for me."[12] When you consider the tragic and lonely way she died, you wonder if anyone did weep.

One of the boldest assertions of faith in the face of death came from one of the great lawyers and Washington power brokers of our age, Edward Bennett Williams. Anyone who ever witnessed Williams in court realized what an extraordinarily gifted man he was. For one full generation he was the man to go to if your life was on the line. His client list reads like a who's who of American celebrities over a thirty- or forty-year period, starting with Joe McCarthy and Jimmy Hoffa, through Frank Sinatra, and a series of senators and high government officials.

Although Williams was quiet about it, he was a deeply religious man, a daily communicant in the Roman Catholic Church. He fought a long and valiant fight against cancer. As he struggled on his deathbed and as it became clear that he was losing the battle, his son showed him an article that named him one of the most powerful men in Washington. The *Washington Post,* for whom Williams was counsel, wrote that he "waved the magazine away." He then said, "They don't realize what power really is. . . . I'm about to see true power. Fighting death is selfish. It's time to let go and see what real power is."[13] Williams died peacefully, as unshakable in his conviction about the resurrection as he had ever been in the cases he argued so brilliantly in court.

---

These are illustrations, of course, of people who lived what we think of as full and productive and successful lives. It's relatively easy to be sanguine in those circumstances. What about when death takes a person in the very prime of life?

Obviously, no one has an answer to why someone's life should end, from our perspective, prematurely. We do not understand the how or why of what seems to us, on the surface, to be terribly unfair. For the Christian believer, at least, there is the assurance that this life is not the end—except in the sense that it is our last earthly witness. Sometimes our deaths can be more powerful than anything else we've ever done in our lives.

Take, for example, the story of David Bloom, the enormously popular young NBC journalist. I first met David when he was a rising star in NBC circles. Some said he might be the next host of the *Today* show or even anchor the nightly news. One day David and I both attended a small breakfast meeting convened by Christian businessman Jim Lane. David had been growing in his faith, something very few of his colleagues or friends in the media knew about. I felt close to David immediately, partly because *Born Again,* my spiritual autobiography, had a profound effect on him, he told me, and David reached out to me as a mentor and friend.

When the second war with Iraq started, David volunteered to cover it. It was a risky decision. He and his wife were more than aware of the dangers he would face as a journalist embedded with the troops during the invasion of Iraq. This was his profession, though, the way he served people.

Some months before David left for Iraq, he got into the habit of calling Jim Lane every morning. Together they studied Oswald Chambers's *My Utmost for His Highest,* a classic Christian devotional book. According to Jim, David repeatedly talked about his complete joy as a Christian. He was free and forgiven: free to be the man, the father, the husband, and the journalist God created him to be.

David and Jim stayed in close touch during the time Bloom was in Kuwait City, preparing to move into Iraq. In his last telephone conversation with Jim, David said in a matter-of-fact way that if he didn't make it back, he wanted a message given to his wife, Melanie, and his three daughters. He wanted them to know how much he loved them, more than life itself.

Listen to David's sentiments in his own words, through one of his last e-mails to Melanie.

> You can't begin to fathom—cannot begin to even glimpse the enormity—of the changes I have and am continuing to undergo. God takes you to the depths of your being—until you are at rock bottom—and then, if you turn to him with utter and blind faith, and resolve in your heart and mind to walk only with him and toward him, he picks you up by your bootstraps and leads you home. I hope and pray that all my guys get out of this in one piece. But I tell you, Mel, I am at peace. Deeply saddened by the glimpses of death and destruction I have seen, but at peace with my God and with you. I know only that my whole way of looking at life has turned upside down—here I am, supposedly at the peak of professional success, and I could frankly care less. Yes, I'm proud of the good job we've all been doing, but—in the scheme of things—it matters little compared to my relationship with you, and the girls, and Jesus. There is something far beyond my level of human understanding or

comprehension going on here, some forging of metal through fire.[14]

During the Iraq invasion, I stayed glued to NBC because I wanted to catch as many glimpses as I could of David. He was everywhere, broadcasting from inside tanks, in bunkers and foxholes, walking among the troops.

Then came the tragic news. David Bloom, thirty-nine years old, had died of a pulmonary embolism, possibly caused by sitting too long in one of the tanks.

Bloom's funeral at St. Patrick's Cathedral in New York City was attended by the entire executive leadership of NBC, by the hundreds of reporters who knew him, by the mayor, public officials, and by executives from across New York. St. Patrick's was packed, and the crowd sat in stunned, tearful silence as Jim Lane gave the eulogy, telling the story of his relationship with David and of David's relationship with Jesus. Jim read David's e-mails and quoted from David's favorite songs and devotionals. He concluded his eulogy by quoting Jesus from the Gospel of John: "Now is your time of grief, but I will see you again and you will rejoice, and no one will take away your joy."[15] People who attended the service that day were deeply affected. It was a time of high emotion and powerful witness. In his death David Bloom had a greater impact on people than he might have if he had lived another fifty years.

Of course, that doesn't take away his wife and children's grief, his friends' loss. His great contributions in broadcasting are at an end, consigned to our memories. Death yields to no easy formulas.

David Bloom's death certainly did verify his life as a good one, though. He lived a magnificently good life. And in death he inspired, encouraged, and raised the hopes of thousands, perhaps millions, because of that truly good life. How many people have that kind of opportunity? Death came as an enemy, as it always does, but death's sting proved a paradoxical witness to the life David had found.

———— • • • ————

The insight of a man who came very close to dying gives us precisely the right prescription for facing death. Ten years ago my friend Father

Richard Neuhaus was stricken by an intestinal blockage and was taken to a New York hospital, where he underwent emergency surgery. Com-plications set in, and his friends were sum-moned to his bedside. The doctors feared that he might have been too long getting to the hospital. His vital signs were dropping.

*Death came as an enemy, as it always does, but death's sting proved a paradoxical witness to the life David had found.*

He survived that initial crisis, but sev-eral more followed. The doctors performed a second operation, a colostomy, which brought on a renewed battle with infection. Many times his closest friends felt that he was on the brink of death.

Richard Neuhaus's recovery took more than a year, as he re-ceived chemotherapy and radiation treatment, then yet another oper-ation to reverse the colostomy. He endured a long period of weakness, but his wonderfully vibrant, fertile mind hardly slowed. He began to contemplate what he had learned from that near-death experience and wrote a short but profound book entitled *As I Lay Dying: Meditations upon Returning.*

After chapters of deep philosophical ruminations, Neuhaus comes to a very simple conclusion in the book's final pages. He refers to Des-cartes's famous formulation *cogito, ergo sum:* "I think, therefore I am." As Neuhaus lay near death, he came to believe that phrase should be cor-rected to *cogitor, ergo sum:* "I am thought, therefore I am."[16] This echoes Wallace Stevens's final insight that he was the product of God's imagina-tion rather than God the product of his. We exist not in our own thoughts, Richard Neuhaus saw, but each of us has been spoken into existence and sus-tained by the One who knew us before the be-ginning of the world.

*Each of us has been spoken into existence and sustained by the One who knew us before the beginning of the world.*

Neuhaus writes, "In the destiny of Christ is my destiny; and so it had been all along, and so it would be forever. This, too, broke through: That, when I die, in his Body, the Church, of which I am a part, and in his body in the Eucha-rist, which this body has received times beyond numbering, body and soul are already reunited, however imperfectly. What is now imper-fect will one day be perfected in resurrection. The maggots should enjoy me while they can; they will not have the last word. Mortal dust already stirs with its longing for that great reunion."

Neuhaus concludes, "So he promised, and so I came to believe more surely than I had ever believed before."[17]

The good life? A life worth living? Indeed. But the good life is possible only if we live in expectation that life will end as richly as we lived it, if we can laugh off the maggots and affirm that these bones shall live in the resurrection. Live each day as if it were the best of days and the last of days. And when the last of days comes, live it as the best of days.

# CHAPTER 30

# INFINITE TRUTH AND LOVE

TOGETHER WE HAVE searched for the meaning and purpose of life. I trust that in the process we have touched on the questions and yearnings that you have about the mysteries of the universe and of the human heart.

What is the good life? What does it mean to live well? We saw that living for ourselves brings only misery. The way to live successfully is to live for others. But in doing so, you must find the truth and live it, lest you bring destruction to yourself and those you are serving. Only a life lived in service to the truth can be a good life.

We've talked together about the truth and exposed the big lie that says there is no truth, that this is a purposeless, random universe. The truth can be known; we see it in an intelligently designed universe, one that has a purpose. In fact, nature everywhere suggests her purposes, so much so that the moral order is simply complementary to the natural, physical order. And truth is knowable from observing how these laws work, testing them, and living accordingly. Our appreciation of beauty, our emotions, and our reason powerfully suggest the existence of God and His care for us.

Everything we have discovered points to the Christian worldview as the only one that "fits" the way the world works and that fills the needs of the human heart. Everything else, as I hope I've made clear, turns out to fail in some key respect. Clearly, the postmodern generation is in the grip of a philosophical framework that makes life unlivable. The intelligent seeker has good reason to reject the big lie of the postmodern world and to find the sources of renewal offered by Christianity.

I've spent more than twenty-five years seriously studying these propositions. If I were arguing this case in court, I would feel I had presented an
unassailable argument. After all, haven't I demonstrated that reason, the
deepest human intuitions, and even the empirical evidence are on my
side?

But we have to confront one last, stunning, paradoxical truth. You
cannot find the good life through searching alone. You have to be found by
God. In the end, all seekers discover that while they thought they were
searching for God, God was searching for them. He longs for us and pur-
sues us.

That's why reason alone falls short. The sin that is in our nature
corrupts our will—as well as every other faculty, including reason—and
blocks us. Only God transforms the will. We first encountered this
problem in the chapter on the great paradoxes and explored it in greater
depth through the life and death of Madalyn Murray O'Hair.

So, has all our searching been in vain? Has this book been based on a
false premise and finally revealed itself as an exercise in futility? Not at all.
The search prepares the heart to accept the true object of its longing—the
God whose love the human heart desires. The
search also reveals our inner rebellion; it shows
us our need to surrender to God's consuming
embrace. We must offer ourselves to God
through His gift to us—faith.

> *You cannot find the*
> *good life through*
> *searching alone.*
> *You have to be*
> *found by God.*

Some people get seriously hung up at
this point. A few years ago I encountered a
keen lawyer who had his life together about
as well as anyone I have met. He had a beautiful wife and family, a good
home, an established law practice, an excellent reputation. He was attractive, articulate, and very bright. On the occasions we had been together, we had discussed theology, philosophy, and history. This man
had obviously read widely and thought deeply. We could talk about the
natural order, Aristotle, Anselm's proof of God, and the medieval syn-
thesis of Aquinas. My friend had also read the great Reformation scholars, including Calvin, and had a good grasp of theology.

During a retreat we were sitting on a hotel porch when my friend told me that he was glad his wife had brought him to the conference. He explained that she was the believer in the family; he wasn't.

I very nearly fell off my chair. How could someone know so much about the Christian faith and all the apologetic arguments for it and yet describe himself as a nonbeliever? I thought he must be joking.

He wasn't. This man had gone forward at an evangelistic rally early in life, then become disillusioned with the church. Seeking answers no one in church could give him, he began an exhaustive study. Was theology a trustworthy guide to God? Could he really find evidence and arguments to prove that God exists?

I asked him how his search had come out. "Oh, I don't think there's any doubt it's true," he said. "But I can't get to that final step. I don't have personal belief."

---

I understood his experience better than he may have suspected. Almost twenty-five years ago I became enamored of the writings of serious theologians and apologists. I began studying writers like Francis Schaeffer and R. C. Sproul, and then the heavyweights like Abraham Kuyper, Calvin, Augustine. A clear worldview began taking shape in my head. Amazingly, the more I studied, the more my faith was confirmed.

Then in 1996, I signed a contract to write a major work on worldview. The result was *How Now Shall We Live?* That book, written with Nancy Pearcey, is an exhaustive examination of the arguments in defense of the biblical worldview. I had arrived at the point where I believed everything about the biblical worldview to be true and the evidence for its truth to be overwhelming. Indeed, provable.

Then one morning during my prayer time, I began to wonder. *I know it's all true,* I told myself. I had proven to my own satisfaction that nothing other than a Christian worldview made sense. I believed I could prove it rationally, but I couldn't get to the final step. How could I know for sure I'd be in God's presence someday?

This difficulty led to what could only be described as spiritual malaise. I went through months of wondering—not really doubting my faith; that was too securely rooted—but wondering why I couldn't complete the connection through rational thinking. Why couldn't I reason my way all the way through? I realize now that my real problem was what has always been the great hang-up of my life, the great sin, really: pride. I was so puffed up by what I could accomplish with my own mind that I couldn't imagine there would be something I couldn't figure out. I realized also it's precisely what was hanging up my lawyer friend.

Then one day the answer hit me like a thunderbolt. I remembered Pascal arguing that God has given us just enough light so that we can understand and just enough darkness or obscurity to deny the truth, if we wish. That was it. Of course, God cannot reveal Himself in a rationally irrefutable manner. If God were as plain to us as the tree outside our window, as one great theologian once wrote, we would have no need for faith. If we saw God in His true character, in His glory, in anything like the way we see the world around us, our free will would be meaningless. We could not help but believe in God. It would be impossible to deny Him. This would destroy the possibility of *choosing* to believe—of faith—and with it the possibility of love, because love cannot be compelled. We cannot love God if we are not given the option of rejecting Him. Remember, God has given us just enough light to see by, but not enough to eliminate the need to see with eyes of faith. Our pride has to get out of the way, and we have to recognize that faith is not faith unless it

*The search prepares the heart to accept the true object of its longing— the God whose love the human heart desires.*

is accompanied by doubt—or at least, as Catholic piety would say, difficulties. Doubt is what gives faith its meaning, hard as that is for tough-minded, analytical thinkers to recognize. This was precisely the problem my lawyer friend had. He didn't think he could believe until he had proven his case. But if he had proven his case, he wouldn't be able to believe, he wouldn't be able to have faith. He was in a catch-22. (Later my friend resolved the question and is today secure in his faith.)

And remember what happened to Phillip Johnson in the hospital. By his great mind he had reasoned so carefully about the Christian gospel. It all made perfect sense. He could put all the pieces in place. But only when he was lying on his back in a hospital and heard the lyrics "On Christ the solid rock I stand" did he fully accept God's gift of faith. Until that time, his Christian experience had been too much an intellectual exercise. He needed it to become a deep personal commitment.

He needed to embrace the gift of Jesus, whose atonement on the cross reconciled us to God. There's a big difference between the two.

The proud person has a hard time coming to God. We want God on our terms, in our understanding. It's simply impossible. He wants us, as He tells us in the Bible, on His terms. He wants our childlike faith. The Good Shepherd goes out to find those who finally come to understand they are lost without Him. I experienced precisely this.

----•·•----

When I left the White House in the spring of 1973, I thought I was smarter than the other guys caught up in Watergate. After all, I hadn't been in the meetings that later became the basis for all the criminal indictments. I had refused to get involved in discussions that could lead to obstruction of justice. The first set of prosecutors told me that I wasn't a target of the investigation. Early on I was, in fact, given a clean slate.

Yet something was desperately wrong in my life. I had no sense of joy or fulfillment. I was worried about all the negative headlines and the attacks on my friend President Nixon, of course, but Watergate was not at the root of my discomfort. I was forty-one years old, in the prime of life, with three and a half years in the While House under my belt, returning to a law firm that would make me rich. And I was miserable. *What's the meaning of all this?* I wondered. *Is this all life can be? Is this as good as it gets? What do I do for a follow-up?*

I thought my depression was due in part to the incredibly high-pressure job I'd had for so long. But no amount of rest cured it. I know now that I was close to despair.

Later that summer, the Watergate scandal deepened. I still wasn't a target, but I was dragged before hearings and grand juries, and was under a daily and withering assault from the press. It is a peculiar form of torture to wake up in the morning and see your name splashed across the headlines of the *Washington Post* or the *New York Times,* when more than half of the charges were utterly false.

Patty and I were heading for a vacation on the Maine coast, and we decided to spend a couple of days with my parents just outside of Boston. While there, I called Tom Phillips, the president of Raytheon, the largest corporation in New England. I asked if I might visit him. I had met with

Tom four months earlier to talk about my becoming counsel once again for Raytheon. I had been impressed that day with how much he had changed from the man I had known before I went to the White House. Tom had seemed very much at peace with himself. I had asked him what happened to him. I can remember to this day his exact words: "Chuck, I have accepted Jesus Christ and committed my life to Him." I nervously changed the subject. I'd never before heard anyone talk that way. In my mind, Jesus was merely an ancient historical figure. But in the months that followed, I couldn't get Tom's words out of my mind.

So, while visiting with my parents in Boston, I met with Tom at his home. I wanted him to explain what had happened in his life. *Maybe, just maybe,* I thought, *he might help me.*

We spent a hot, sultry August evening sitting on his porch. He described to me what had happened to him. Some years earlier he had gone to a Billy Graham crusade in New York and found himself strangely moved by the message. He was so moved that at the end, when Graham gave an invitation to accept Christ as one's personal Lord and Savior, Tom Phillips walked forward with hundreds of others and surrendered his life to Christ. He then described how his life had been dramatically transformed.

As he told me his story, he pulled a paperback book off the table next to him and asked if he might read a chapter to me. The book was *Mere Christianity,* C. S. Lewis's classic work, and the chapter that Phillips read from was titled "The Great Sin." Pride.

Tom's reading of that chapter was for me a totally devastating moment. I saw myself and my life captured in Lewis's incredible words about that great sin that we quickly see in others but rarely recognize in ourselves: the haughty, arrogant attitude that comes from building our life around ourselves.

As Phillips was reading, I could feel the perspiration under my shirt and on my brow, and it wasn't just the warm night. My life experiences were flashing across my mind, just like the movie scenes where people see their lives lived out in the instant before they die. I now realize that I was, in a sense, about to die.

I thought about my insufferable arrogance. Oh, sure, I had done good deeds for people and took care of the underdog. I did *pro bono* work when I was practicing law. I gave gifts to charity. I was a pretty decent guy, so I thought. In truth, my smug sense of self-righteousness hid my total self-obsession.

Through the years in which I rose quickly in law and politics at the cost of my first marriage, I justified everything. I told myself I was doing it all for my family and my country, for national security. I was convinced that it was all a selfless endeavor. I realized that night at Tom's house that it had all been about me.

As Tom read Lewis's words, some of them hit me with particular force, shattering the defense mechanism I'd built up over all of those years—the tough-guy exterior. The truth suddenly made sense. As C. S. Lewis wrote, someone who is so proud and so wrapped up in himself and so capable of rationalizing anything could not possibly see something immeasurably greater than himself—God.

I was so uncomfortable that I couldn't wait to get out of Tom's home that night. He asked me if he could pray for me, and he did, a prayer like I'd never heard in church. Like I'd never heard anywhere. It was warm, moving, and caring. And what struck me as much as anything else was that Tom Phillips, one of the busiest, most successful businessmen in America, really, genuinely cared for me, Chuck Colson. Not the big-time Washington operator, but Chuck Colson the human being.

I said good-bye to Tom and headed for my car, but as I walked toward it that night, I felt a sudden desperate desire to go back and pray again with Tom Phillips. I turned around and looked at the house, but the lights downstairs were already going out. Too late, I realized. So I got in the car, started the ignition, and drove out of the driveway. I could get no farther than a hundred yards from his house, however, because I was crying too hard to drive the car. The former marine captain, the tough White House "hatchet man" who thought he was as good as or better than anybody else, felt wretched.

For the first time in my life I had looked inside of my own heart and detested what I saw. It was corrupt. I thought of the people I had hurt, the wrong I had done to others, how cold, hard, and self-centered I was. For the very first time in my life, I was deeply convicted of my own sin. I felt unclean, ashamed, horribly alone and horribly lost. Tom's words kept flowing over me about turning to God and making that simple surrender. I found myself in those moments almost involuntarily crying out: "God, I don't know the right words, and I'm not much, but please take me. Take me just the way I am." I sat there for half an hour, perhaps an hour, alone with my thoughts, tears flowing freely as they had never done before in my life. I experienced a feeling of total surrender and total release. I knew at that moment God was real, personal, and had heard my prayers.

I expected to wake up the next morning feeling embarrassed. I was not one who ever cried, or at least let anyone know if I did. I was hard, tough, seasoned, independent, and proud. But not that morning. For the first time in my life I felt free. Nothing had changed about my circumstances. I still saw my name in the headlines that August morning. But nothing was the same that day. And it would never be the same again.

In the week that followed I devoured my own copy of *Mere Christianity*. Everything I read confirmed the experience I'd had, and everything I'd experienced confirmed Pascal's saying: "The heart has reasons, reason knows not of."[1] I knew with assurance that I had a new relationship with God. I prayed that week, asking Jesus Christ to take over my life. That began the greatest journey of my life—the greatest journey anyone can have. I experienced the fullness of one of the great paradoxes: We find ourselves only when we lose ourselves, in God.

———•———

How about you? Are you persuaded by the rational arguments and the evidence that we've presented in this book? What hinders you from giving yourself to God in Jesus Christ?

Put yourself back into the beginning of this book. Go back to Private Ryan as he walks with faltering steps toward the grave marker of the man who saved his life. The scene is one of the most amazing I've ever seen on film. There is Ryan, lip quivering, tears running down his face, looking at the grave marker, wondering if he's worthy of the sacrifice of Captain Miller and the others who died so that he might live. As the seventy-year-old Ryan talks to his wife at the grave, he is plagued by the questions that plague us all: Am I worthy? Have I been a good person? Have I lived a good life?

The grave marker is a simple white cross, so what we see is a man on his knees, trembling and crying in front of the cross. He is Everyman, for in truth, we are all in front of the cross. At some time in every hu-

man being's life, he or she has to look at that cross and what it represents
and ask that question: Am I worthy?

Remember the gospel as we've explained it. It is maddeningly simple. Too good to be true, as we suggested. God loved us so much that
He created us and gave us a free will. We've sinned, and we know it
when we look in our own hearts. And there's a price to pay for our sin.
But God, in His love for us, sent His Son, Jesus, to die on the cross to
pay for our sin so that we can be forgiven. Christ's sacrifice allows us to
be reconciled to God as it incorporates us into God's own life. No wonder John Newton called it amazing grace.

Perhaps in your heart you feel a last moment of rebellion. You refuse to be convinced by the light you've been given that God exists and
that He loves you. In fact, many of you look at the evil in the world and
conclude that God cannot exist, or if God does, then He is a monster.

The cross answers this final objection too. The existence of evil
might cause everything we've been arguing here to fall apart—if it were
not for Jesus Christ, stretched out on the cross. He opens His arms to our
objection against God's love. He invites us to hurl whatever scathing indictment we care to at His heavenly Father. Such hatred of God is the
very force that drove the nails through Christ's hands. He submitted to
our hatred of God in order to demonstrate God's innocence. Looking at
Christ crucified, we understand who is at fault for the evil in the world.
We are the guilty ones, not God, who is willing to see His only Son executed
as a criminal in order to show us the nature of our own hearts and His love.

What does God want from every one of us? That we look at that
cross and ask exactly the question that Ryan asked: Have I been worthy?
The answer, of course, is that no human being can possibly be worthy
of that kind of sacrifice. No, we can never do enough good works to balance the scales of justice in God's eyes. All God wants from us is the
simple faith to come to that cross and surrender ourselves. Say no to the
lies. Embrace the truth. Accept God's magnificent invitation to come as
a little child by faith. End the search by being found.

What motivated Ryan to come to that grave marker was his overwhelming gratitude for Captain Miller. But how do we express gratitude
for the far more extraordinary sacrifice of Christ—the most momentous
event in all of human history? We do it by surrendering ourselves and turning to Christ. We confess our guilt and ask to be received by God's love.

At the cross our search ends. The truth we've struggled to know is made incarnate in Christ. I am *The Truth,* Jesus tells us.[2] *The Truth* means ultimate reality. Jesus is identified in the Bible by the Greek word *Logos*—meaning the reason, or plan, of creation. Scripture further tells us that all things were created by Him and for Him, and in Him are all things held together.[3] I can be more certain of Christ's reality than my own because my reality depends on Him. Ultimate meaning and purpose and reality can be found in the paradox of the Cross, where humanity's evil and death—are converted into life and eternal hope.

------·•·------

Even as I pen these words, the moment that I broke down outside Tom Phillips's house thirty-two years ago is as plain and clear, powerful and vivid, as it was that night. My hope in Christ is the central reality of my life. If I did not know for sure that Jesus died for my sin, I would not be alive today. I'd have suffocated in the stench of my own sin. Jesus is life. The brief faith crisis I experienced after I'd studied so much about Christianity passed like a vapor when I faced my pride and remembered that first moment of childlike surrender.

> *Ultimate meaning and purpose and reality can be found in the ultimate paradox of the Cross, where humanity's evil is converted into life and eternal hope.*

Living a life in gratitude to God opens a whole new world, one in which life continues to have a deeper and richer meaning with each passing day. In describing this new life, Jesus used the term *born again,* which was the title I gave to my spiritual autobiography.[4] The phrase isn't, as some think, a tired cliché. It's the reality that there is, on the other side of the Cross, a new life.

I found this new life in my relationships with my family. They'd always been dear to me, even in those years when I was too engrossed in my work. But suddenly they became the most important thing in the world next to my relationship with God. My marriage strengthened, and I saw it as a covenant made before God, not as a contract, not as something I would enter into and leave when I felt like leaving.

I began to have a different understanding of other people, a deeper identification with people less fortunate. In prison I would realize that I was no different from the other prisoners.

Eventually, my whole life changed. I had new friends that came from my first Bible study group, and then God gave me a wonderful ministry through the experience of prison.

God also renewed my mind.[5] I'd been a good student, graduating near the top of my class in law school. But that was just preparation, just a foretaste of what it was like to open my mind to the things of God. Ever since my conversion I've had an unquenchable appetite for learning about history and theology and almost everything else in the world. Every day something new and fresh excites me about God's world.

As I studied the Bible and the way the world works, I made what was for me an important discovery: There is no disparity between faith, on the one hand, and reason, or what we can discover about the natural order, on the other. Nothing in the one contradicts the other. What God reveals about Himself in the Bible enlarges the capacities of both reason and the imagination. Revelation enables our human faculties to understand truths that they cannot comprehend without the additional information that God alone can supply.

This helped me to answer a question I'd pondered for some time. Is something true because the Bible says it is (Christians believe on faith that the Bible is the inspired, authoritative word of God), or does the Bible say something is true because it *is* true? I came to see that both statements are accurate. The source of both the Scripture and truth is the same: Christ. All truth, as the much-repeated saying has it, is God's truth.

I then began to study the historicity of the Scripture and the accumulated archaeological record, which attests overwhelmingly to the Bible's truthfulness. My most abiding hunger today is to better understand God's Word.

---

I said at the outset of this book that I have been a seeker all my life, as all human beings are, and I continue to seek today. The wonderful thing about the Christian life is that we never exhaust the Bible's riches. Every time we read it, we can find something profound to teach us about God's world, His character, and His purposes for us.

All believers seek an ever-deeper love relationship with Jesus, our Lord. This is really what's on the other side of the Cross, the divide that God's grace brings us across. Once you accept God's offer of salvation, you discover that God begins transforming you more and more into the likeness of Christ.

Who is God? In the Christian understanding, He is infinite love. This is His very nature and character. Many religions in the world get this wrong because they believe that God is simply His own overpowering presence as one person. But Christian theology teaches us about the Trinity: one God, who exists in three persons, Father, Son, and Holy Spirit. This is hard to understand—a mystery. Yet the mystery helps us understand God's character as love. Within the Godhead is a love relationship among three persons—Father, Son, and Holy Spirit. When we surrender to God, He enfolds us into the love relationship of the Godhead itself. We participate in the communion of the Father, Son, and Holy Spirit. In our feeble, stumbling ways we become part of the infinite love of God, something even greater than the universe itself. This is why basic Christian teaching frequently affirms that the object of life is to love God and enjoy Him forever.

What hinders you from opening yourself to God's love through the simplest of prayers? "Jesus, forgive me and save me." The greatest story ever told has given us the greatest news ever—that through Jesus' death and resurrection we can have what we were made for—a relationship with God. The work of Christ makes possible what reason and the imagination and conscience anticipate, and what our hearts long for. The good life turns out to be life fulfilled in Christ, for now and eternity. It's everything we most want: purpose, meaning, relationship, truth, and love.

*The good life turns out to be life fulfilled in Christ, for now and eternity.*

———•◦•———

If my experience is any guide, life in Christ also entails great adventure. It takes us to unimaginable places—to a world that is both the same and utterly transformed. Let me say one more word about how a man who despaired of ever living a significant life again found himself doing something that really counted at last.

# BACK TO THE BEGINNING

THE ROOSEVELT ROOM, JUNE 18, 2003

The first thing I thought was, *Nothing has changed.* The paneled doors on either side of the fireplace, the one on the right closest to the Oval Office; the painting of Teddy Roosevelt as a Rough Rider; the Chippendale table and its buttoned leather chairs. Although thirty years had passed, the only difference I noticed was the patina the furniture had acquired through long use and polishing.

I was back at the White House, standing in the Roosevelt Room, where it had all started that Monday after the first Pentagon Papers story appeared in the *New York Times,* with Kissinger exploding about the catastrophic implications and the rest of President Nixon's senior staff, including me, calling for vengeance against our enemies. This was where my own crusade against Daniel Ellsberg had begun—a crusade that saw me fall from the heights of power to the depths of a jail cell. Nothing had changed.

Yet everything was different.

In the spring of 2003, I led a small party to the White House at President George W. Bush's invitation. At the previous year's White House Christmas party, I had mentioned to the president that Prison Fellowship was having a study done on the InnerChange Freedom Initiative at the Carol Vance Unit of the Texas state prison system near Houston, Texas. The president had expressed interest. His connection with the program had produced an unforgettable photograph. Of the thousands upon thousands of pictures taken of him, only one, I'm guessing, shows him with his arm around a convicted murderer and singing "Amazing Grace." He was governor of Texas at the time, and the photograph appeared on the front page of the *Houston Chronicle* on Friday, October 17, 1997.[1]

— • ◦ • —

After a trip I led to South America in 1996 to see two successful Prison Fellowship programs in Brazil and Ecuador, Carol Vance, a corrections official, recommended to then-Texas Governor George W. Bush that he authorize a faith-based program in a Texas prison. Vance, in his sixties, was a tall, athletically built man who wore horn-rim glasses that gave him a bookish look. He had been district attorney of Harris County—which comprises the greater Houston area—before Bush's predecessor in the governor's office, Ann Richards, appointed him to the Texas Department of Criminal Justice. Vance was someone Governor Bush trusted.

Still, I doubted I'd ever see the day-to-day operations of a Texas prison given over to Prison Fellowship, as the prisons had been in Brazil and Ecuador. We had tried to start similar programs at several locations in the United States, but church-and-state objections scuttled our proposals every time.

Vance carried the idea to Governor Bush, who had been thinking about faith-based solutions. Within a short time, the governor called to say he wanted to go forward. Prison Fellowship quickly negotiated a contract with the state of Texas for the ministry to take over the day-to-day programming of approximately half of what was then known as the Jester II prison facility.

The InnerChange Freedom Initiative, as we called it, at Jester II (later renamed in honor of Carol Vance) began working with more than fifty prisoners who would be released within a year to eighteen months. (The number of prisoners involved in that program today is close to three hundred.) During that time, the prisoners went through a "Bible boot camp," which included courses on personal responsibility, anger management, parenting, and personal finance. No televisions were allowed in the unit. The InnerChange program demands intensive Bible study. In order to keep up with their study assignments, many prisoners find it necessary to rise as early as four o'clock in the morning and work until lights-out at ten o'clock at night.

The InnerChange program takes prisoners on a spiritual journey that has striking affinities to the themes discussed in this book. Inmates are forced to confront their responsibility for the decisions they have made in life. "Free-world people"—as prisoners call those in the outside world—might assume that incarcerated men and women are all too aware of their guilt. But I've found that most blame their circumstances on their background, on people who have wronged them, and on the failure of society to deliver on its promises. The devastating spiritual milieu of prisons—the "prison code"—encourages this denial of responsibility. No one speaks of regret for fear of showing weakness. Prisoners who let down their guard may suffer violence and can expect to be betrayed by those they trust. To admit their responsibility for being incarcerated is a huge step—it's at least as difficult as it is for free-world people to do the same.

An amazing transformation begins, however, once the participants in the InnerChange program look squarely at their past deeds. They begin to see the staff of the program and its volunteers with different eyes. Instead of questioning everyone's motives, the inmates become grateful for the contribution these people are making to their lives. For the first time, they are able to accept the love of others as real. Their attitudes toward themselves change as well, and once they acknowledge their guilt, they cease to be preoccupied with it. They begin to see themselves as people who could be loved. They have a real and deep experience of Christian grace.

When we opened the prison, Governor Bush attended the dedication. We set up a makeshift platform in the prison yard for the governor to hold a press conference. One of our men had the idea to assemble the inmates in squad formation and march them out to the courtyard for the ceremony. The inmates started singing "Amazing Grace" as they stepped smartly out to the assembled crowd. I was surprised when Governor Bush walked over to the inmates lined up singing, stepped into their midst, and put his arms around men on both sides of him. The governor was singing along with the men. The *Houston Chronicle* reported, "Gov. George W. Bush put his arm around convicted murderer George Mason, 46, and joined him and 55 other Texas prison inmates in a most unusual blending of church and state."[2]

This was not perhaps the best politics for a governor who would soon run for reelection. But it was "amazing grace, how sweet the sound."

————•◦•————

That was the story behind my return to the Roosevelt Room. President Bush was naturally interested in how well the faith-based initiative InnerChange was faring. The president's staff asked me to bring an assortment of people with me, including the principal researcher of the study, Dr. Byron Johnson of the University of Pennsylvania; a few staff members who knew the ministry at ground level; and three InnerChange graduates. The request for graduates surprised me. Once, when I was working for President Nixon, I had wanted to bring some labor leaders to meet with him. But because they had criminal records, the Secret Service wouldn't let them in. Now I was being asked to bring hardened criminals into the White House! In my wildest dreams I could never have envisioned this—not thirty years before, not even long after the ministry had started, not ever.

When we entered the room, Attorney General John Ashcroft and Secretary of Labor Elaine Chao were already there. I introduced them to my group, which included several additional key people. The original idea for the study had come from the brilliant psychiatrist-researcher David Larson. He had died before the report was completed, but his wife, Susan, was with me. I was also proud to have brought along Mark Earley, the new president of Prison Fellowship in the United States and former attorney general of Virginia. Our graduates of InnerChange included James Peterson, who had given up parole to finish the program; Bernard Veal, an African-American businessman; and George Mason, also African-American—the same man then-Governor Bush had put his arm around while singing "Amazing Grace" at the prison in Texas.

A tall, handsome man, with a crew cut and the build of a linebacker, George Mason took a good picture, but his story was not a nice one. He was far from a one-time offender who'd made a mistake, paid his debt to society, and then gone back, neatly, to the life from which he'd never truly departed. George Mason represented something else entirely.

The circumstances surrounding the 1985 murder of Mason's

common-law wife, Francine Jackson, were hazy. The couple had a history of domestic disturbances that required police intervention. On this particular occasion when the two were arguing, George started playing around with his shotgun. He pointed it at Francine. The gun went off.

Mason claimed that he hadn't meant to shoot her, and the police half-believed him. The reason he received a thirty-five-year sentence had as much to do with his past life of crime as it did with the shooting itself. He was known in his Houston neighborhood for the sawed-off shotgun he carried. It broke down into two pieces, which he stuffed into his boots for rapid assembly when he needed to shoot someone. George Mason was the type of hardened criminal that our society would just as soon lock away for the rest of his life. If true spiritual transformation weren't possible, I'd think the same thing.

Mason was so notorious that when he left prison, he changed his name to Robert Sutton so that everything, including his name, would be new about his life. And everything is. Today, Robert Sutton works as a janitor at his church, conducts a men's Bible study, and serves as a mentor for other men coming out of the InnerChange program. Robert Sutton is a new man.

When the president walked through the doorway to the right of the Roosevelt Room fireplace, everyone stood and applauded. He gave me that little wave all Texans seem to favor. Then he marched right over to Robert Sutton, embraced him, and announced, "I'm sure glad you're here in this place." Then he added, "I knew someday you'd be here with me. You're a good man." The president shook Robert Sutton's shoulders in confirmation, gave him a slap on the back, and then took his place at the center of the table. Sutton was so stunned, he didn't know where he was the rest of the day!

The president convened the meeting and asked Byron Johnson to summarize the study's findings. Dr. Johnson explained that 171 participants in the InnerChange program were compared to a matched group of 1,754 inmates from the prison's general population. The study found that only 8 percent of InnerChange graduates, as opposed to 20.3 percent of inmates in the matched comparison group, became offenders again in a two-year period.[3]

"So the program cuts the recidivism rate by almost two-thirds?" the president asked.

364 The Good Life

"Yes, it does," Dr. Johnson said. "But only for those who complete the program. Those who are dismissed for disciplinary reasons or who drop out voluntarily, or those who are paroled before completion, have a comparable rate of rearrest and incarceration."

"It's vital to complete the program then."

"Yes. If you look deeper into the subcategories of control groups—"

"I'd like to hear all the details, Dr. Johnson," the president said, "but I've got President Putin waiting on a callback." The president turned from Dr. Johnson and looked at me. "The staff has both the executive summary and the full study?"

"Yes, Mr. President," I said.

"What do you say about all this?"

I told him how grateful we were that he had cut through the red tape and made the program happen. The president talked at length about his commitment to faith-based programs. He inquired of others in our group and was fascinated with what had been happening inside the prisons. Then the phone call began to weigh on his mind again, I could tell.

"Mr. President," I said, "before we leave, could we pray together?"

"Absolutely," he said. "But at this table, we hold hands when we pray. You lead us, Chuck."

I watched as the president joined hands with Dr. Johnson on one side and Susan Larson on the other. They grasped the hands of two former inmates, James Peterson and Robert Sutton, who were linked to the attorney general and the secretary of labor, and so on until the chain reached me across the table.

After I finished praying, I thought about the different spirit that existed in this room compared to the spirit following the Pentagon Papers' release. I was deeply affected by the paradox of my life—how God had brought good out of disaster.

I had sought vengeance against Daniel Ellsberg and never noticed when my self-righteousness betrayed me. Many others around me did the same, and a presidency crumbled. I thought of words from the New Testament: "But God chose the foolish things of the world to shame the wise; God chose the weak things of the world to shame the strong."[4] God used my own foolishness to shame the worldly wisdom right out of me.

When I was sent to prison, my greatest fear was that I would never be able to do something significant in life again. Now I saw that I would never have been able to do anything truly significant *without* prison. My fall enabled my life and my work to rise. As the Lord told the apostle Paul, "My grace is sufficient for you, for my power is made perfect in weakness."[5] Nothing had changed in the Roosevelt Room; yet everything was different because I had changed. Utterly. Just like Robert Sutton. Robert Sutton and I are exactly the same. Our spiritual journeys are similar. The most powerful man in the world might have been praying with us, but we were *all* alike because we all stand on level ground at the foot of the cross.

That's why I can say to you, based on my life and what it has taught me, that the good life is near at hand. It's both God's will for you and His free gift to you. It doesn't matter whether you are young or old, rich or poor, at the height of your abilities or in decline, because the good life is God's life in Christ. The Lord takes us from just where we are into a future that's limitless.

AFTER *How Now Shall We Live?* was published in 1999, and thereafter became a best seller, I encountered many friends who told me that while they found it a great classic work, it was densely written; some found it difficult to apply all that it taught to their lives. In the course of many conversations, however, I discovered that people were hungry, searching, looking for purpose and meaning, trying to make sense out of life. I realized there was a need for something more. A dear friend, Wally Zellmer, confronted me one day in my office. "Chuck," he said, "you've got to write a simple, direct book. Just talk to the reader about what matters most in life." I have always appreciated Wally, a man of rare insights and wise counsel. His advice pushed me over the edge, from thinking about a book to writing it.

Writing this book has been an enriching experience in many ways. I've worked with some very able writers over the years on the more than twenty books I've published, but none more congenial or more intellectually compatible than Harold Fickett. I asked Harold to join me in this particular work because he's such an outstanding storyteller (he drafted many of the story chapters of *How Now Shall We Live?*) and because he's a very keen thinker. We soon found that not only were our hearts knit together but our minds were as well.

No matter how successful the end product turns out to be, we both profited greatly from some long and stimulating discussions. I think I understand the world a lot better as a result of our work. If working sometimes twelve hours a day, scribbling notes on airplanes, dictating memos from thoughts in the night, and grinding over draft after draft of chapters can be considered pleasurable, writing this book certainly was.

As good a relationship as Harold and I have, we couldn't have completed this book without the incredible assistance of my team at Prison Fellowship. First, there was Nancy Niemeyer, who worked for me for twenty-five years and was a most valued assistant through this and other books. When Nancy moved on to another position, in God's providence, Sherrie Irvin replaced her. Sherrie has worked patiently through draft after draft during the past twelve months. I hope that both Nancy and Sherrie feel a great sense of satisfaction, a partial reward, at least, for long hours spent at the computer screens.

I'm grateful, as well, to my assistant Val Merrill, who has attended to my schedule and kept everything in my office functioning smoothly, allowing me the time to work on the book. I thank Kim Robbins Moreland, who for the past fifteen years has helped me with research, tirelessly tracking down information in libraries and on the Internet. Kim did much of the critical digging for *The Good Life*. Thanks are due as well to my longtime friend and colleague Ellen Vaughn, a distinguished author who contributed some stimulating suggestions for this book.

Every writer has a love-hate relationship with his editor. You love your editors because you can't live without them, but you hate to see your deathless prose on the cutting-room floor. I have been genuinely blessed in this undertaking, having as my editor Ken Petersen, who has shepherded this book from its conceptual state through the final product. He has seen the big picture and has cared about the little details. He's become a great friend and colleague in the process. Although I miss the assistance of Judith Markham, who edited for me for twenty years, she was able to read an early draft as well as the final proofs, offering suggestions in the process. She knew all along I couldn't finish this book without her.

Ken was ably assisted by Lynn Vanderzalm, who did much of the heavy-lifting editing of this manuscript. I'm grateful to Lynn for her precision, her insistence on checking and rechecking facts, and her critique of the overall flow of the manuscript.

I'm deeply indebted as well to T. M. Moore, who is teaching pastor at Cedar Springs Presbyterian Church in Knoxville, Tennessee, and a fellow of the Wilberforce Forum. He gave me his theological expertise, keeping us from running the cart into the ditch on one side of the road or the other.

Neal Plantinga, the president of Calvin Theological Seminary, assisted by reading some of these chapters and by inspiring others. He is, in my mind, one of the keenest intellectuals in the Christian world today and truly has a broad grasp of so many of the worldview questions raised in *The Good Life*.

I am most grateful as well to my longtime mentor, Jim Packer, for reading and critiquing the manuscript. Similarly Joni Eareckson Tada and Richard John Neuhaus read the manuscript and gave helpful directions. Finally, Rick Warren, author of *The Purpose-Driven Life,* one of the most remarkable publishing and spiritual phenomena of our time, inspired me in many ways and read the manuscript.

Last, but certainly not least, both Harold and I are profoundly grateful to our faithful wives. Patty has lived through twenty of these books, which is quite a feat. I'm not sure there are rewards for such service here on earth, but there certainly will be in heaven. Karen Fickett, who is an able writer herself, has given moral and intellectual support to Harold throughout the process.

The book, as you have seen, is dedicated to my children. I've done that because, of course, they are chief among my legacies. When making that decision, I also thought of the wonderful legacies, the living monuments I've described in this book, men and women whose lives have been transformed, who are now living the truth. All of them, I hope, know what an encouragement they are to me.

Finally, I give thanks to the One who makes all this possible, the Author of all Truth, who time and again through this writing project would drop in my lap a particular piece of research or inspire in my mind an idea or bring across my desk or the screen of my mind a reference vital to this work. In these pages I've written of Providence, and in the process of writing this manuscript, I have experienced it. To God be the glory.

Harold would also like to thank his administrative assistant, Meredith Patterson, for keeping him organized and on track. Meredith somehow kept four file boxes, more than a thousand e-mails, and numerous drafts of each chapter straight. Harold extends our appreciation to the authorities and scholars who helped him with various stories, particularly Dr. Janet McCann of Texas A&M University, Dr. Alan Filreis of the University of Pennsylvania, Dr. Michael R. Linton of Middle Tennessee State University, Dr. Joseph Nicolosi of NARTH, Dr. Philip Mango of St. Michael's Institute, Alan Chambers of Exodus International, Richard Cohen of the International Healing Foundation, and Melissa Fryear of Focus on the Family. Dr. Mark Simmons and Dr. Dillard Tinsley were invaluable intellectual companions to Harold during the course of this journey.

## Introduction: The Good Life

1. T. S. Eliot, "The Four Quartets: East Coker," *The Complete Poems and Plays 1909–1950* (New York: Harcourt, Brace & World, 1962), 129.

## Chapter 1: The Unavoidable Question

1. This and other quotations in this story are taken from *Saving Private Ryan,* written by Robert Rodat, directed by Steven Spielberg, and produced by DreamWorks SKG, Paramount Pictures Corporation, and Amblin Entertainment, Inc., 1998.
2. *Planned Parenthood v. Casey,* 112 S. Ct. 2791 (1992).
3. *Planned Parenthood v. Casey* affirmed the *Roe v. Wade* decision, legalizing abortion on demand. It shifted the grounds for legalization, to a degree, from the "right of privacy" to the nature of individual liberty. While each of us is "condemned to freedom," in the sense of making our own decisions about the great questions, our democracy should rely, I believe, on natural law theory and the Judeo-Christian tradition that informs the Declaration of Independence, the Constitution, and the Bill of Rights when interpreting the law. Governments and their courts must have some unified understanding of life's meaning in order to enforce the most basic provisions of the law—against theft, murder, etc. If people were allowed to determine absolutely what meaning they wished to ascribe to the universe, then, theoretically, the Nazi who believes that a Jew's life has only a negative meaning, if any, would be enabled to carry out his own personal "final solution" against any Jew he could lay his hands on. In practice the courts today rely either on natural law theory or their intuition (or personal preference) about what the community consensus is or should be on a given issue. The change from natural law theory to the court's best approximation of the community's consensus as a guide to legal interpretation is one of the great cultural watersheds of our time.
4. Emmanuel Mounier, quoted in Lorenzo Albacete, "The Cry of Suffering," *God at the Ritz: Attraction to Infinity* (New York: Crossroad, 2002), http://www.godspy.com/faith/The-Cry-of-Suffering.cfm.
5. John Paul II, *Fides et Ratio* (the encyclical letter of John Paul II to the bishops on the relationship between faith and reason), chapter 3, section 28, http://www.vatican.va/edocs/ENG0216/_P8.HTM.

## Chapter 2: A Shattered Life

1. In the end, 60,000 would lose their lives; more than 300,000 would be wounded.

## Chapter 3: The Great Paradoxes

1. G. K. Chesterton, "When Doctors Disagree," in *The Paradoxes of Mr. Pond* (New York: Dover, 1990).
2. The halted execution was part of the mind game Czar Nicholas often played with the prisoners. He wanted them to believe that they would be executed, even though

he had already instructed the guards not to kill the prisoners. The czar wanted people to feel both his power and his mercy. See Joseph Frank, *Dostoyevsky: Years of Ordeal (1850–1859)* (Princeton, N.J.: Princeton University Press, 1983), 50.

3. Fyodor Dostoyevsky, quoted in Frank, *Dostoyevsky: Years of Ordeal,* 62.

4. This story is based on Francis Hartigan, *Bill W: A Biography of Alcoholics Anonymous Cofounder Bill Wilson* (New York: St. Martin's, 2000), 38.

5. Ibid., 61.

6. See *Adopt-A-Minefield* Web site at http://www.landmines.org.

7. Hebrews 2:11

8. Dostoyevsky in *Diary of a Writer,* quoted in Frank, *Dostoyevsky: Years of Ordeal,* 123.

9. Ibid., 88.

10. This quotation by Pierre Bezukhov is taken from *War and Peace,* adapted by Bridget Boland and Mario Camerini, directed by King Vidor, and produced by Paramount Pictures, 1956.

11. "Egil Krogh: A Nixon White House 'Plumber' Crusades for Integrity," *Christian Science Sentinel,* 103, no. 19 (May 7, 2001): 12.

## Chapter 4: A Nice Party with a Lot of Nice People

1. For details about the party video, we are indebted to Dan Ackman, "L. Dennis Kozlowski Is Not Fabulous," *Forbes,* October 29, 2003, http://www.forbes.com/2003/10/29/cx_da_1029topnews_print.html.

2. John L. Fort III, quoted in Anthony Bianco et al., "The Rise and Fall of Dennis Kozlowski," *BusinessWeek Online,* December 23, 2002, http://www.businessweek.com/magazine/content/02_51/b3813001.htm.

3. R. Jerry Conklin, quoted in Bianco et al., "The Rise and Fall of Dennis Kozlowski."

4. Melanie Warner, "Exorcism at Tyco," *Fortune,* April 14, 2003, 106.

5. *Tyco International Ltd. and Tyco International (US) Inc. v. L. Dennis Kozlowsi,* par. 23b and par. 23d (S.D. N.Y. 2002). Tyco apparently did carry the apartment on its books as an asset.

6. *BusinessWeek* ranked Kozlowski second only to Computer Associates' Charles Wang, whose 1999 compensation package totaled a whopping $655.4 million. See Michael Hennigan, "U.S. Corporate Scandals and the Laws of Unintended Consequences," http://www.finfacts.com/usscandals.htm.

7. Laura Italiano, "Defense Fights to Bar Tyco Tell-All," *New York Post,* February 5, 2004, 29.

8. L. Dennis Kozlowski, quoted in "The Most Aggressive CEO," *BusinessWeek Online,* May 28, 2001, http://www.businessweek.com/magazine/content/01_22/b3734001.htm.

9. The following account of Irwin Nack's role relies on Nanette Byrnes, "The Hunch That Led to Tyco's Tumble," *BusinessWeek Online,* December 23, 2002, http://www.businessweek.com/magazine/content/02_51/b3813013.htm.

10. Kozlowski and Swartz's first prosecution ended in a mistrial. Their defense consisted chiefly in arguing that Tyco's board knew about and approved their compensation. It's not so much the facts that were questioned. Under question was the men's authority to receive and grant such compensation.

11. Even now (February 23, 2004) Tyco disputes how destructive these effects were, claiming in its lawsuit against Kozlowski that even given the enormous unauthorized sums Kozlowski extracted for himself and others, these losses had no "material effect" on the company. Whether or not this is true, it's an indication of just how big and lucrative the Tyco operation was.

12. Tyco would sell the CIT Group in 2002 at a loss of $7 billion.

13. L. Dennis Kozlowski, quoted in Bianco et al., "The Rise and Fall of Dennis Kozlowski."

14. Quotation taken from *Groundhog Day,* written by Danny Rubin, directed by Harold Ramis, and produced by Columbia/Tristar Studios, 1993.

## Chapter 5: Shopping for the Holy Grail

1. Kate Berry, "Home Prices May Expose Economy to Credit Peril," *Los Angeles Business Journal* 26, no. 25 (June 21, 2004): 1.

2. April Witt, "Acquiring Minds: Inside America's All-Consuming Passion," *Washington Post,* December 14, 2003, W14, http://www.washingtonpost.com/wp-dyn/articles/A53732-2003Dec10.html.

3. Ibid.

4. Ibid.

5. Ibid.

6. Ibid.

7. Laura Berman Fortgang, *Living Your Best Life,* quoted in Stephanie Armour, "After 9/11 Some Workers Turn Their Lives Upside Down," *USA Today,* May 8, 2002.

8. George Barna study, quoted in Douglas Groothuis, *Truth Decay* (Downers Grove, Ill.: InterVarsity, 2000), 22.

9. Philip Kennicott, "Rich with Irony: When Golden CEO Jack Welch Stepped Down, It Was into the Mud," *Washington Post,* October 14, 2002, C1.

10. See 1 Timothy 6:10.

11. George Will discusses Easterbrook's conclusions in "Afflicted by Comfort," *Washington Post,* January 11, 2004, http://www.washingtonpost.com/ac2/wp-dyn?pagename=article&contentId=A4928-2004Jan9&notFound=true.

12. "Go Figure" feature in *Christianity Today* 48, no. 3, March 2004, 22.

13. John Gertner, "The Futile Pursuit of Happiness," *New York Times Magazine,* September 7, 2003.

14. Ibid., emphasis added.

## Chapter 6: Laughing at Death

1. The story of Nien Cheng's heroic life during the Cultural Revolution is drawn from her outstanding and important book *Life and Death in Shanghai,* which remains a key primary document for understanding China under Mao's rule and the nature of totalitarianism itself.
2. Nien Cheng, *Life and Death in Shanghai* (New York: Grove Press, 1986), 71.
3. Ibid., 76.
4. Ibid., 76–77.
5. Ibid., 86.
6. Ibid., 120.
7. Ibid., 122.
8. Ibid., 132.
9. Ibid., 136.
10. Ibid., 130.
11. Ibid., 146.
12. Ibid., 147–48.
13. Ibid., 149–50.
14. Ibid., 235.
15. Ibid., 256.
16. Ibid., 307.
17. Ibid., 308.
18. Ibid., 308–9.
19. Ibid., 314.
20. Ibid., 324.
21. Ibid., 347.
22. It is likely that the infamous Gang of Four—Jiang Qing (Mao's fourth wife), Zhang Chunqiao, Yao Wenyuan, and Wang Hongwen—or an official allied with this group, was reponsible for Nien Cheng's arrest.
23. Cheng, *Life and Death in Shanghai,* 353–54.

## Chapter 7: More Important Than Life Itself

1. Dorothy L. Sayers, *Creed or Chaos?* (Manchester, N.H.: Sophia Institute Press, 1974), 44.
2. Quoted in Joe Loconte, "Human Rights and Wrongs" *Weekly Standard* 9, no. 27 (March 22, 2004): 27.
3. Joseph Biden, quoted in Michael Potemra, "Shelf Life: Defending the Human," *National Review,* May 19, 2003.

## Chapter 8: A Life of Significance

1. Richard Bernstein, "Modern German Duty: The Obligation to Play," *New York Times,* July 2, 2003.

2. The details and quotations from these stories are found in "The Age Wave," *60 Minutes,* CBS News, August 10, 2003, http://www.cbsnews.com/stories/2003/08/08/60minutes/main567331.shtml.

3. Howard Butt Jr., quoted in Matt Curry, "Texas Businessman Wants Christians to Carry Faith from Church to Workplace," *Abilene Reporter-News,* November 15, 2002; see http://www.texnews.com/1998/2002/texas/texas_Texas_bus1115.html.

4. Dorothy L. Sayers, *Creed or Chaos?* (Manchester, N.H.: Sophia Institute Press, 1974), 72.

5. Ibid., 73.

## Chapter 9: A Silent Good-bye

1. John Ehrlichman, "Live from the Oval Office," *Newsweek,* December 2, 1996, 37.

2. John Ehrlichman, "Nixon's 'It,'" *New York Times,* June 17, 1982, 27.

## Chapter 10: My Happiness, Right or Wrong

1. This and other quotations in this story are taken from *The Hours,* written by David Hare, directed by Stephen Daldry, and produced by Miramax Films, 2002.

2. Gloria Steinem, "Self-discovery: A Noble Journey," *Los Angeles Times,* January 12, 2003.

## Chapter 11: Whose Life Is It?

1. *Hardwired to Connect: The New Scientific Case for Authoritative Communities,* sponsored by the YMCA of the USA, Dartmouth Medical School, the Institute for American Values (2003). See a companion summary of the report at http://www.ymca.net/hardwired_report/HW_companion.summ.pdf.

2. Kenneth Boa, "Forming an Authentic Self in an Inauthentic World: Part 2," a Reflections teaching letter, August 2004, http://reflections.gospelcom.net/newsletters.php?id=1&newsletter_id=305&year=2004.

3. Russell Kirk, *The Conservative Mind: From Burke to Eliot* (Washington, D.C.: Regnery, 1995), 23.

4. Ibid., 17.

5. Alexis de Tocqueville, *Democracy in America* (New York: Washington Square, 1964), bk. 1, chap. 2.

6. The story about Staff Sergeant Dustin Tuller was aired on *Scarborough Country* on May 24, 2004. Writers for the show were Kerry Sanders, Wayne Downing, Peggy Noonan, and Joe Scarborough.

## Chapter 12: A Very Rich Man

1. The story of Warren Schmidt and the quotations used in this chapter are based on the movie *About Schmidt,* written and directed by Alexander Payne, and produced by New Line Home Entertainment, 2002.

## Chapter 13: Living Legacies

1. To read the full account of this amazing love story, see Robertson McQuilkin, *A Promise Kept* (Wheaton, Ill.: Tyndale, 1998).
2. For more information about Angel Tree, see the Web site at http://www.pfm.org/AM/Template.cfm?Section=Angel_Tree1.

## Chapter 14: Greater Love Hath No Man Than This

1. Facts about the Japanese campaigns at the beginning of World War II are taken primarily from *TheBritannica.com*.
2. Ernest Gordon, *To End All Wars* (Grand Rapids: Zondervan, 2002), 48.
3. John 15:13, quoted in Gordon, *To End All Wars*, 100–101.
4. Gordon, *To End All Wars*, 126.
5. Ibid., 118–19.
6. Ibid., 110, emphasis added.

## Chapter 16: Journey into Illusion

1. Albert Speer, quoted in Joachim Fest, *Speer: The Final Verdict*, trans. Ewald Osers and Alexandra Dring (New York: Harcourt, 2001), 319.
2. Ibid., 320.
3. Ibid., 22.
4. John Milton, "Lycidas," *The Complete Poetical Works of John Milton*, ed. Douglas Bush (Boston: Houghton Mifflin, 1965), 144.
5. Fest, *Speer: The Final Verdict*, 9–10.
6. Ibid.
7. Ibid., 51.
8. Ibid., 116.
9. Hermann Friedrich Grabe, *IMT*, vol. xxxi, 433ff, quoted in ibid., 304.
10. Ibid., 347–48.

## Chapter 17: Living within the Truth

1. The episode described here is one that led to a later charge that I had ordered the bombing of the Brookings Institution. The charge was untrue, but I was never able to establish it. As much as anything in Watergate, that charge stuck with me. On the thirtieth anniversary of Watergate, John Dean chaired a seminar at the Kennedy School at Harvard, and he went on at great length about my "insane" plan to bomb Brookings. In 2003, I received a phone call from Jack Caulfield, who had been one of the chief investigators John Ehrlichman and John Dean employed. Jack apologized to me, saying that before he died, he wanted to make things right with those he had hurt. It turns out, as he told my biographer later, that perjury had been committed with respect to the charge that I ordered the bombing of Brookings. By

whom I did not ask. A small thing, perhaps, but all part of history. It was some comfort, at least.

2. Some of the hush money was on her person at the time.

3. Albert Speer, quoted in Joachim Fest, *Speer: The Final Verdict,* trans. Ewald Osers and Alexandra Dring (New York: Harcourt, 2001), 287.

4. Ibid., 18.

5. Albert Speer, quoted in Charles W. Colson, *Who Speaks for God?* (Westchester, Ill.: Crossway, 1985), 75.

6. One fascination of Speer's great book *Inside the Third Reich* is its exposé of Hitler's utterly destructive management style. Hitler had many strategic advantages during World War II. He encountered little effective resistance until his war machine reached the Russian front, and even the resistance there came more as a result of weather and supply-line problems than from an army that could match Germany's. The Allies had to mount what was essentially a counteroffensive and do it by air and sea. Their transport problems alone were huge. Hitler's self-worship led him to contrive a bureaucratic structure whose main purpose was to secure his power through setting his subordinates against each other. Their competing responsibilities and the vicious way he spurred their personal animosities made effective administration impossible. If Speer had not been an ingenious technocrat and brought some rational analysis to the Nazi war machine, the war might have lasted only half as long. Views that are out of conformity with reality simply don't work—not in the long run. Hitler's were so erroneous that the Third Reich could have survived as long as it did only through the unbounded violence it practiced. Its eventual doom was sure and certain.

7. The charter's title came from the date of its publication: January 7, 1977.

8. Václav Havel, "The Power of the Powerless," in Václav Havel et al., *The Power of the Powerless: Citizens against the State in Central-Eastern Europe*, ed. John Keane (Armonk, N.Y.: M. E. Sharpe, 1985), 41.

9. Ibid., 43.

10. Jerzy Popieluszko, quoted in Grazyna Sikorska, *Jerzy Popieluszko: A Martyr for the Truth* (Grand Rapids: Eerdmans, 1985), 56.

## Chapter 18: Can We Know the Truth?

1. The phrase "prison house of language" was used by Fredric Jameson, *The Prison-House of Language* (Princeton, N.J.: Princeton University Press, 1972).

2. Rod Dreher, "Losing Lutherans," *National Review,* February 21, 2002, and George Barna, "How America's Faith Has Changed Since 9-11," November 26, 2001, http://www.barna.org/FlexPage.aspx?Page=BarnaUpdate&Barna UpdateID=102.

3. The story is told in Phillip E. Johnson, *The Right Questions: Truth, Meaning, and Public Debate* (Downers Grove, Ill.: InterVarsity Press, 2002), 128.

4. George W. Bush, address given at the 9/11 memorial service held at Washington's National Cathedral, September 14, 2001.

5. Stanley Fish, *New York Times,* October 15, 2001, quoted in Henry F. Schaefer III, *Science and Christianity: Conflict or Coherence?* (Watkinsville, Ga.: The Apollos Trust, 2004), 109.

6. Paul Marshall, "Fundamentalists and Other Fun People: To Know Them Is Not to Despise Them," *Weekly Standard* 10, no. 10, November 22, 2004.

7. Kofi Annan, address at Trinity Institute's thirty-fifth national conference, "Naming Evil," May 2, 2001, http://www.un.org/News/Press/docs/2004/sgsm9286.doc.htm.

8. Dorothy L. Sayers, *Creed or Chaos?* (Manchester, N.H.: Sophia Institute Press, 1974), 108.

9. *Lee v. Weisman,* 505 U.S. 577 (1992).

10. Ibid. Is postmodernism written into the law? Tolerance no longer means freedom; it means repression.

11. See John 14:6.

## CHAPTER 19: WHAT IS LIFE WORTH?

1. Melmark New England School Services Motivation Survey Results (January 2004).

2. Michael Specter, "The Dangerous Philosopher," *New Yorker,* September 6, 1999, http://www.michaelspecter.com/ny/1999/1999_09_06_philosopher.html.

3. Johann Hari, "Some People Are More Equal Than Others," *Independent* July 1, 2004, 2–3, http://news.independent.co.uk/people/profiles/story.jsp?story=536906.

4. But what is a defect? It's a notoriously slippery word. Is it a defect to get a baby girl when you wanted a baby boy? Certainly people believe that in China, where infanticide is practiced to get rid of the less desirable babies—girls—and obey the government's policy of no more than two children. People believe that in India, where abortion is openly practiced for the purpose of sex selection.

5. Singer, quoted in Hari, "Some People Are More Equal Than Others."

6. Leo Alexander, "Medical Science under Dictatorship," *New England Journal of Medicine* 241, no. 2 (July 14, 1949): 39.

7. Ibid.

8. Ibid.

9. Ibid.

10. Tanis Doe, "The New Reproductive Technologies: Discriminating Misconceptions of Choice," *Herizons* 8, no.1 (Spring 1994): 44.

11. Amy Richards, quoted in Amy Barrett, "Lives: When One Is Enough," *New York Times,* Magazine Desk, July 18, 2004, 58.

12. Rebecca Allison, "Does a Cleft Palate Justify an Abortion? Curate Wins Right to Challenge Doctors," *Guardian,* December 2, 2003, 3.

13. In a recent *New York Times* article Barbara Ehrenreich asks, "What makes it morally more congenial to kill a particular 'defective' fetus than to kill whatever fetus happens to come along, on an equal opportunity basis?" She confesses, "I had two abortions during my all-too-fertile years. You can call me a bad woman, but not a bad mother. I was a dollar-a-word freelancer and my husband a warehouse worker, so it was all we could do to support the existing children at a grubby lower-middle-class level." Ehrenreich sees no reason to differentiate between abortion for the sake of maintaining one's standard of living and abortion for health reasons. (See Barbara Ehrenreich, "Owning Up to Abortion," *New York Times*, July 22, 2004.)

    What is the difference? There's certainly a difference in terms of the potential sacrifice required of the parents—and of society in general. But is the moral standing of an unborn child with health problems different from the standing of a normal child?

14. "Annual Report of Medicare and Social Security Transfers," reported in *Congressional Quarterly*, March 23, 2001.

15. Hari, "Some People Are More Equal Than Others," emphasis added.

16. The quotations in this story are taken from Harriet McBryde Johnson, "Should I Have Been Killed at Birth? The Case for My Life," *New York Times Magazine*, February 16, 2003.

17. Ibid.

## CHAPTER 20: GOD'S ID

1. All quotations in this illustration about the spider are taken from Nien Cheng, *Life and Death in Shanghai* (New York: Grove Press, 1986), 143.

2. Werner Gitt, *In the Beginning Was Information* (Neuhausen-Stuttgart, Germany: Hanssler, 1994), 12.

3. "NABT Unveils New Statement on Teaching Evolution," *The American Biological Teacher* 68, no. 1 (January 1996): 61. The original NABT statement created such an uproar that the organization subsequently dropped the words *unsupervised* and *impersonal*. The change was largely cosmetic, however, since the remaining words *unpredictable* and *natural* were understood to mean essentially the same thing.

4. People who call themselves theistic evolutionists suggest that God used evolution but guided its results, in order to produce creation. The problem with this is that the Darwinian theory rules out the premise of theistic evolution. By its very nature Darwinism demands that evolution be unguided—that its results have no end purpose in view. Otherwise the theory falls apart; the combination of mutation and natural selection becomes something other than "natural" if the course of evolution is governed by anything other than chance. The explanatory power of Darwinian theory absolutely demands that time plus chance alone were sufficient to produce everything around us. Any "theistic" overlay is regarded by people who truly understand the theory as worse than beside the

point; it's antithetical to the system itself. A lot of Christians believe that theistic evolution will spare them the abuse of rigid Darwinians and will allow them not to appear intellectually inferior. It's a marriage of sorts. The problem with it is, however, that while the Christian believing in God feels married to the evolutionist, the evolutionist doesn't share the same affections—and can't. It's a one-sided marriage.

5. The movement has spilled across the disciplines and fractured traditional alliances. David Berlinski, a distinguished mathematician and popular writer, for example, published in the respected Jewish intellectual magazine *Commentary* an article entitled "The Deniable Darwin."

6. Unless otherwise noted, all quotes from Michael Behe are from a personal telephone interview conducted August 10, 2004.

7. Percival Davis and Dean H. Kenyon, *Of Pandas and People: The Central Question of Biological Origins* (Dallas: Haughton, 1993).

8. Behe uses cilia—whiplike hairs on the surface of cells—as another example of irreducible complexity. The cilia, as many as two hundred to a single cell, flow in a fluid motion across a cell's surface, waving back and forth in coordination with each other. For example, the cilia on the cells in the back of the throat clear away mucus; the cilia keep us from drowning in our own secretions. Each individual cilium is a biological micromachine made up of about two hundred protein parts that form three basic components: rods, linkers, and motors. Take away one of these components, and the cilia cease to function. It's not that they are less efficient; they don't work at all. These cilia could not have come together through a gradual process.

9. Michael J. Behe, "Rube Goldberg in the Blood," *Darwin's Black Box: The Biochemical Challenge of Evolution* (New York: Free Press, 1996), 74–97.

10. Ibid.

11. T. H. Bugge et al., "Loss of Fibrinogen Rescues Mice from the Pleiotropic Effects of Plasminogen Deficiency," *Cell* 87 (November 15, 1996): 709–19.

12. Russell F. Doolittle, "A Delicate Balance," *Boston Review* (February/March 1997), http://www.bostonreview.net/BR22.1/doolittle.html.

13. Richard Dawkins, quoted in Mary Wakefield, "The Mystery of the Missing Links," *The Spectator,* October 25, 2003, http://www.spectator.co.uk/article.php?table=old&section=current&issue=2004-08-21&id=4051&searchText=Mary%20Wakefield.

14. Behe's work is only one example of the growing body of evidence supporting Intelligent Design. For a more detailed discussion of the subject, see the book I wrote with Nancy Pearcey, *How Now Shall We Live?*

15. Rodney Stark, *For the Glory of God: How Monotheism Led to Reformations, Science, Witch-Hunts, and the End of Slavery* (Princeton, N.J.: Princeton University Press, 2003), 176.

16. Julian Huxley, *The Evolution of Life,* vol. 1, of *Evolution after Darwin* (Chicago: University of Chicago, 1960), 2.

17. Stark, *For the Glory of God,* 185.

18. Richard Dawkins, *The Blind Watchmaker: Why the Evidence of Evolution Reveals a Universe without Design* (New York: W. W. Norton, 1986), 287, quoted in Stark, *For the Glory of God,* 176.

19. Charles Darwin, *The Origin of Species* (New York: Modern Library, 1993), 316, quoted in Stark, *For the Glory of God,* 179.

20. Stark, *For the Glory of God,* 184.

21. Ibid., 191.

22. Richard Dawkins, *The Blind Watchmaker,* 6, quoted in ibid.,185.

23. Annie Besant, quoted in Stark, *For the Glory of God,* 186.

24. Stark, *For the Glory of God,* 186.

25. Ibid.

26. *Scientist,* May 19, 2003, quoted in Henry F. Schaefer, *Science and Christianity: Conflict or Coherence?* (Watkinsville, Ga.: Apollos Trust, 2003), 12.

27. Charles Townes, quoted in Schaefer, *Science and Christianity,* 102.

28. Associated Press, "Famous Atheist Now Believes in God," December 9, 2004, http://abcnews.go.com/US/wireStory?id=315976.

29. This quotation is from Flew's video "Has Science Discovered God?" quoted in ibid.

## CHAPTER 21: MORALITY AND THE NATURAL ORDER

1. This story is told in Cornelius Plantinga Jr., *Not the Way It's Supposed to Be* (Grand Rapids: Eerdmans, 1995), 118–19.

2. Stephen R. Covey, "Ethical Vertigo," *Executive Excellence* 14, no. 6 (June 1997): 3–4.

3. If you are interested in finding out more about the nature of same-sex attraction or reparative therapy, contact Exodus International, http://www.exodus.to; The National Association for Research and Therapy of Homosexuality (NARTH), http://www.narth.com/; or James Dobson's Focus on the Family, http://www.family.org/cforum/fosi/homosexuality/. Focus on the Family runs helpful conferences—Love Won Out—on the causes and cures for same-sex attraction; see http://www.lovewonout.com/.

4. Serving as the membership director of Exodus International, Randy Thomas now helps others find the same freedom he has found.

## CHAPTER 22: THE GIFT OF KNOWING RIGHT FROM WRONG

1. Quoted in Cornelius Plantinga Jr., *Not the Way It's Supposed to Be: A Breviary of Sin* (Grand Rapids: Eerdmans, 1995), 7.

2. Ibid., 8.

3. Etienne Gilson, *The Unity of Philosophical Experience* (San Francisco: St. Ignatius, 1999), 274.

4. C. S. Lewis, *Mere Christianity* (New York: Touchstone, 1996), 21.

5. Ibid., 19.

6. Illustration based on one Lewis used in ibid., 17.

7. Ibid., 19.

8. Ibid., 18, emphasis added.

9. Polls indicate that only 6 percent of teenagers believe there is absolute moral truth; 73 percent of college graduates, when asked what they had learned about ethics, chose the following answer: "What is right and wrong depends on differences of individual values and cultural diversity." (And the students thought they were getting ethics.) Cited in John Leo, "Professors Who See No Evil," *U.S. News & World Report,* July 22, 2002, 14.

10. This incident was verified by George Weigel in an e-mail message on August 3, 2004.

11. F. H. Buckley, "Are Emotions Moral?" *The New Criterion* 22, no. 5 (January 2004), http://www.newcriterion.com/archive/22/jan04/emotion.htm.

12. Greg Koukl, "A Ten-Minute Witness," http://www.lifeway.com/lwc/article_main_page/0,1703,A%253D153981%2526M%253D200165,00.html.

13. J. Budziszewski explores conscience and the natural order in his book *What We Can't Not Know* (Dallas: Spence, 2003), emphasis added.

14. See Romans 2:14-15.

15. Graham Greene, *The Quiet American* (New York: Viking, 1956), 249.

16. See Albert Camus, *L'étranger* and *The Myth of Sisyphus.*

17. Neal Plantinga Jr., "Fashions and Folly: Sin and Character in the 90s" (presented at the January Lecture Series, Calvin Theological Seminary, Grand Rapids, Michigan, January 15, 1993), 14–15.

18. Saint Augustine, quoted in John Paul II, *Fides et Ratio* (the encyclical letter of John Paul II to the bishops on the relationship between faith and reason), chapter 1, section 15, http://www.vatican.va/edocs/ENG0216/__P4.HTM.

## CHAPTER 23: BEAUTY: THE SIGN OF GOD'S CARE

1. The collaborationist Vichy government and the Germans had already signed an armistice agreement that made the care and feeding of so many prisoners of war unnecessary.

2. Revelation 10:1-7, quoted in Rebecca Rischin, *For the End of Time: The Story of the Messiaen Quartet* (Ithaca, N.Y.: Cornell University Press, 2003), 129.

3. The language of this introduction is taken indirectly from Messiaen's "Composers Preface," in Rischin, *For the End of Time,* 129.

4. Rischin, *For the End of Time,* 130.

5. This statement is based on the conclusions of Marcel Haedrich, one of the pris-

oners, who published an account of the premiere of *Quartet for the End of Time* in *Le Figaro* in 1942. The full quotation is found in ibid., 70.

6. Rischin, *For the End of Time,* 70.

7. Calvin Tomkins, *The Bride and the Bachelors: The Heretical Courtship in Modern Art* (New York: Viking, 1965), 119.

8. Quoted in David Revill, *The Roaring Silence: John Cage: A Life* (New York: Arcade, 1992), 165–66.

9. Peter Yates, quoted in Tomkins, *The Bride and the Bachelors,* 85.

10. Ananda K. Coomaraswamy, emphasis added, quoted in Tomkins, *The Bride and the Bachelors,* 100.

11. Tomkins, *The Bride and the Bachelors,* 74.

12. Richard Lippold, quoted in ibid.

13. The I Ching is not, in itself, about chance. It's a method of divination—of being in touch with larger and perhaps darker forces than the individual's judgment.

14. Revill, *The Roaring Silence,* 167.

15. Lorenzo Albacete, "The Cry of Suffering," *God at the Ritz: Attraction to Infinity* (New York: Crossroad, 2002), http://www.godspy.com/faith/The-Cry-of-Suffering.cfm.

16. Paul Griffiths, *Olivier Messiaen and the Music of Time* (Ithaca, N.Y.: Cornell University Press, 1985), 21–22.

17. Ibid., 50.

18. Hans Urs von Balthasar, *The Glory of the Lord: A Theological Aesthetics,* trans. Erasmo Leiva-Merikakis, ed. Joseph Fessio and John Riches (San Francisco: St. Ignatius, 1983), 18.

19. William Blake, "The Tiger," *Eighteenth Century Poetry and Prose,* ed. Louis I. Bredvold et al. (New York: Ronald Press, 1956), 1060.

20. Jesus tells us that the beauties of creation are a sign of the heavenly Father's care: "Consider how the lilies grow. They do not labor or spin. Yet I tell you, not even Solomon in all his splendor was dressed like one of these. If that is how God clothes the grass of the field, which is here today, and tomorrow is thrown into the fire, how much more will he clothe you, O you of little faith!" (Luke 12:27-28).

## CHAPTER 24: WRITTEN ON THE HEART

1. Frank Gaebelein, *The Christian, the Arts, and Truth: Regaining the Vision of Greatness* (Portland, Ore.: Multnomah, 1985), 95.

2. Jacques Maritain, *The Degrees of Knowledge,* trans. Gerald B. Phelan (Notre Dame, Ind.: Notre Dame Press, 1995), 264.

3. Lorenzo Albacete, "The Cry of Suffering," *God at the Ritz: Attraction to Infinity* (New York: Crossroad, 2002), http://www.godspy.com/faith/The-Cry-of-Suffering.cfm.

4. Blaise Pascal, *Pensées,* section IV, paragraph 277, http://www.classicallibrary.org/pascal/pensees/index.htm.

5. Bishop Anselm, quoted in John Paul II, *Fides et Ratio* (the encyclical letter of John Paul II to the bishops on the relationship between faith and reason), chapter 1, section 14, http://www.vatican.va/edocs/ENG0216/__P4.HTM.

6. Jonathan Edwards, *Of Being* (1721), http://www.jonathanedwards.com/text/Of%20Being.htm.

## Chapter 25: Postmodernists in Recovery

1. Cole Porter, "Let's Do It (Let's Fall in Love)," Warner Bros., Inc., (1995).

2. Ibid.

3. The story of Hua Mei's pregnancy is based on "Sexy Videos Help Panda Get Pregnant," *Orlando Sentinel,* June 17, 2004. Further background information on the Wolong Giant Panda Protection Center and pandas themselves comes from Roberto Rivera, "Panda Man: Do They Want to Be Extinct?" *BreakPoint Worldview* (June 2004): 6–8.

4. M. D. Harmond, "March for Women's Lives Leaves Some Women on the Sidelines: Those Would Be the Women There to Support Life and the Women Who Could Never Attend," *Portland (Maine) Press Herald,* May 3, 2004, 9.

5. Joan Richardson, *Wallace Stevens: The Early Years 1879–1923* (New York: William Morris, 1986), 56.

6. Holly Stevens, *Souvenirs and Prophecies: The Young Wallace Stevens* (New York: Knopf, 1977), 16. This is the source of the sentiment; the quote itself is a fictional representation of the sentiment.

7. Charles M. Murphy, *Wallace Stevens: A Spiritual Poet in a Secular Age* (New York: Paulist, 1997), 10.

8. Wallace Stevens, *The Collected Poems of Wallace Stevens* (New York: Knopf, 1974), 68.

9. Janet McCann, *Wallace Stevens Revisited: "The Celestial Possible"* (New York: Twayne, 1995), 25.

10. Stevens, *Collected Poems,* 129.

11. Ibid., 288.

12. McCann, *Wallace Stevens Revisited,* 77.

13. This idea is presented tentatively but unmistakably.

14. Stevens, *Collected Poems,* 534.

15. Peter Brazeau, *Parts of a World: Wallace Stevens Remembered* (New York: Random House, 1977), 294.

16. Ibid., 295.

17. Despite the peace that Stevens found in the weeks before his death, his conversion made everyone around him nervous, even the clergy. Stevens asked Father Hanley, Sister Bernetta Quinn, and others who knew about his conversion to